HAROLD NORSE

in the
hub
OF THE
fiery force

COLLECTED POEMS
OF HAROLD NORSE
1934-2003

▼

thunder's mouth press
new york

IN THE HUB OF THE FIERY FORCE

© 2003 by Harold Norse

Published by
Thunder's Mouth Press
An Imprint of Avalon Publishing Group Incorporated
245 West 17th Street, 11th Floor
New York, NY 10011

Library of Congress Cataloging-in-Publication Data:

Norse, Harold.
In the hub of the fiery force :
collected poems of Harold Norse, 1934–2003.
p. cm.
ISBN 1-56025-548-X — ISBN 1-56025-520-X (pbk.)
I. Title.
PS3527.O56 A6 2003
811'.54—dc21   2003055964

ISBN: 1-56025-520-X

9 8 7 6 5 4 3 2 1

Designed by Pauline Neuwirth, Neuwirth & Associates, Inc.

Printed in the United States of America
Distributed by Publishers Group West

acknowledgments

Over the many years of my life I have had friends, both poets and non-poets, who have offered assistance such as typing out my manuscripts and/or offering suggestions. In the computer age I've been doing it mostly myself via word processor. Thus, for this collection of my selected poems over many decades, I wish to thank my friends, living or not, for our past and current friendships, for their moral support and belief in my poetry. I hereby dedicate these poems to many friends, some of whom are legal advisers. I thank them all for their professional advice and unique intelligence and talents. Thus, I hereby dedicate these poems to all those friends, living or deceased, from the beginning of my career: Sir Harold Acton, W. H. Auden, James Baldwin, Linda and Charles Bukowski, William S. Burroughs, Julian Beck, Judith Malina Beck, Barry Benjamin, Betty Best, Bayla Bower, Paul and Jane Bowles, Marlon Brando, Ronnie Burk, James van Buskirk, Edward Camp, Marc Chagall, Ronald Chase, Neeli Cherkovski, Jean Cocteau, Andrei Codrescu, Ira Cohen, Leonard Cohen, Gregory Corso, e. e. cummings, Robert De Niro, Lawrence Ferlinghetti, Charles Henri Ford, Allen Ginsberg, Matthew Gonzalez, James Grauerholz, Robert Graves, Brion Gysin, Erika Horn, Chester Kallman and his father Edward Kallman, Kevin Killian, Julia Chanler Laurin, Jeffrey Lilly, Gerard Malanga, Tom Maschler, Frances McCann, Michael McClure, James Nawrocki, Gerald Nicosia, Anais Nin, Frank O'Hara, Don Parks, Pamela Pasti, Kenneth Patchen, Pauline Petchy, Nancy Peters, Ned Rorem, Howard Schrager, Arnold Schwarzenegger, Ann Smart, Todd Swindell, Dylan Thomas, James Thorp, Nanos Valaoritis, Mark Vermeulen, Gore Vidal, Eric Wilcox, Tennessee Williams, William Carlos Williams. Any omissions of friends or helpers are unintentional. I regret the oversights.

H.N.

▼

to my many friends

▼

contents

previously unpublished

▼

preface

While living in Naples, Italy, on December 12, 1958 I wrote to my great friend William Carlos Williams: "I've got a wonderful title for this new book I'm working on: *Classic Frieze in a Garage*. The old world and the new! In Naples I actually saw an incredible juxtaposition in a garage. Mechanics were welding, greasing and blow-torching autos under a vast marble classic frieze. It stood majestically over the Fiats, mechanics and puddles of gasoline on the floor." Williams' response (Dec. 17, 1958) was enthusiastic: "A damn good title."

The American Idiom, our correspondence together, was published in 1990. I sent him a batch of new poems and he replied (Jan. 30, 1959): "*Piccolo Paradiso* will stand up anywhere among the best poems of our time. . . . We have also marked *Masaccio* and. . . ." He mentioned eight more and ended his letter saying: "You have breached a new lead, shown a new power over the language . . . unchecked by academic rules. Your freedom in the measure is worth all the rest to me." I responded: "I don't think I'll ever go back to the traditional measure."

When I relapsed now and then I earned his disapproval. The old doctor treated me with strong medicine (verbally) and I was cured of my conventional use of fixed meters. In his final letter before his death he wrote: ". . . these poems headed by 'Classic Frieze in a Garage' are the best I have seen of yours. . . . I counted on you as being the one guy who would carry the battle without flagging deep into enemy territory . . . the onslaught of the iambic pentameter, blank verse . . . the academy. . . . The American idiom won out in the end . . . this poem ["Classic Frieze in a Garage"] is the sign of it. . . ." (June 13, 1960)

Despite his insistence on the "variable foot" he never defined it. It is simply free verse played by ear as it is spoken. Free verse is not new. It began with Walt Whitman in the 19th century and was continued early in the 20th century in America. Based on phrasal breath units of speech and spaced on the page as a notation of speech, it liberated poetry from conventional rules, primarily from iambic pentameter and emphasized colloquial American speech as never before.

Many of my collected poems appeared in magazines, anthologies and my books. Then one night, as I lay in the dark thinking of something else, I had the title that I conceived over 40 years ago!

"I look to see more poems, a bookful, exploiting what you have begun of the interrelationship of the renaissance and the modern," wrote Williams (Feb. 14, 1957). This was indeed the motif of *Classic Frieze in a Garage*—the life of the past still protruding into the present with similar myths and symbols, the same unchanging human nature from antiquity to the present with the new modern speech. It was "the bookful" he wanted to see. Many of these poems appeared in *Hotel Nirvana*, my book published by City Lights in the Pocket Poet Series, 1974.

I thank the great spirit of William Carlos Williams who fought so hard to make me aware of my own voice and style. He was the teacher and father I had wanted. He fulfilled the adage, "When the student is ready the master appears." Williams returned poetry to its roots of everyday common speech as Whitman had done before him. Remarkably enough, Williams turned the tide single-handed against the dominant academic school of Ezra Pound, T. S. Eliot and the "New Critics" and poets they spawned in the universities. I was one of them until, half-way to my Ph.D. I dropped out, thanks to Williams.

Poetry finally reached large audiences, foreseen by Whitman and Williams. In the first half of the 20th century, poetry audiences were whittled down to a privileged few dominated by the formal academic tradition. Poetry was predominantly the domain of scholars and students. Of course the academy produced major poets such as T. S. Eliot, Ezra Pound, Wallace Stevens, Sylvia Plath and others, dominating the first half of the twentieth century. But it shut its doors on all except the elite.

However, with the breakthrough of poetry to large audiences by the Beat Generation in the second half of the century, thanks to Allen Ginsberg, Jack Kerouac and William S. Burroughs, poetry of common speech prevails in the twenty-first century and reaches vast audiences. I was welcomed by Kerouac, Ginsberg and Burroughs as a friend, fellow-poet and Beat Generation brother. How did it all begin? I quote from my autobiography, *Memoirs of a Bastard Angel*: "One night in 1944 I met eighteen-year old Allen Ginsberg, a student at Columbia University. It was his first trip to Greenwich Village and I was the first writer he met." Allen came to my room in the Village and we corresponded for years.

In his letter of August 4, 1966, he wrote: "The poems of '65-'66 in *Olé* [an avant-garde magazine] are open & clear or utter lifelike, I thought, reading them tonite, you really made it to recognizable communicable self thru all the rawness, & in medium of the 'american language' very naked real exclamation—certainly justifies Williams' [William Carlos] sympathy-prophetic care—*Showdown* in hospital got my attention most as being solitary reality scene like everyone else & the *morning vision* traces of everyone's mood, so, commonly encouraging. Poem to Williams bouncy & *gone gone gone* right mortal dream sense. I'm glimpsing age 40 now. *words you can taste* near that too. *Kali Yug* nice desperate, & one of those mornings

& between 2 fires both get back to life—sense of reality I guess is the thing I kept amazed at in your awareness in these poems. Anyway the whole set of writings turned me on to your life for the first time clearly—I didn't like that rawness before as much because the self-survey or person was not yet so definite as you seem now. . . . Love, Allen." I passed the Ginsberg test.

The Beat Generation poets finally established a firm foothold in the halls of academe. I chose *Classic Frieze in a Garage* as a symbolic title for bringing together classical and common speech as I heard it while growing up in my birthplace, New York City. I grew up with opera on the radio on Sundays and wanted my poems to have a powerful effect like opera. The spoken voice haunted me. In Italy, where opera began, visual, dramatic and ecstatic, it was an art that reached the upper, middle and lower classes. I wanted my poetry to do the same.

This is what the Beat Generation achieved in poetry and prose, reaching readers and audiences around the world. The unknown Charles Bukowski wrote to me with high praise that began a mutual admiration society between us. My old friend Allen Ginsberg, who was eighteen when we first met in the New York subway, had a common goal like mine, to reach the masses through feeling and plain talk. Unknown at that time, he wrote to me while I was living in Europe and North Africa. When I repatriated we finally met again. By then he had become famous.

The reader may wonder why the title of this book is *I Am in the Hub of the Fiery Force* instead of *Classic Frieze in a Garage*. As time passed I began to see the difference between the two poems. Both had one thing in common—they were singled out by friends and people I met at readings. Other poems of mine were also mentioned but finally I decided that *I Am In The Hub Of The Fiery Force* was the most striking title for my Selected or Collected Poems, mainly because it is a chant, a poem that grasps the visceral level, the most powerful level of all.

Chanting has the power of reaching beyond the conscious mind, This is what religion and the arts have in common and why chanting is basic for both. They reach levels "tending to inspire awe usually because of elevated quality as of beauty, nobility or grandeur," says Webster's *New Collegiate Dictionary*. The difference between *I Am in the Hub of the Fiery Force* and *Classic Frieze in a Garage* is, I believe, rather subtle. *Classic Frieze* is indicative of everyday reality and its bizarre contrasts and contradictions. *I Am in the Hub* is emblematic of life and its mysteries. But nothing is cut and dried in these poems. Mostly they reveal my lifetime experiences. It is a kind of autobiography in verse.

The fiery force is nothing more than the life force as we know it. It is the flame of desire and love, of sex and beauty, of pleasure and joy as we consume and are consumed, as we burn with pleasure and burn out in time. It's about living and dying, about heaven and hell on earth. In short, it is one poet's autobiography in a long life in many countries from hometown New York City to Italy, France, Germany, Greece, Morocco, England and finally California. In the end it is a tour halfway around the world recorded in poetry.

Harold Norse,
2003

PREVIOUSLY
published

▼

▼

god bless america—and lorca

Reading of Lorca in the public room—
His reasoned revolt against reason as social bias,
Refusing the unionization of poetry:
Rejecting the surrealist *décolletage* and the
Stamp of group approval: seeking the organic

In an era of inorganic emotion
:I pity the man at my right, myopic eyes two inches from *Life*:
And the one with the steel mustache
And *Outdoor Guide*: and the glandular adolescent
With the uncertain movements and wall-eyed erotic stare

Of confusion: who suddenly: from their divergent worlds
And obsessions that clash: like swimmers all lift
For a moment: undersea heads: they have caught
Sound waves from the street of commerce and waving flags

:Kate Smith singing "God Bless America".

the year is water

O love, you attract me . . . there is reason
To live . . . though the year is water
In the broken cities. And speeches wander
Through the worms of skulls. O love,
You do excite the memory of flesh
Whose stars still shine.

First I would call you occult,
Before the mirroring touch. And after confess,
O love, O love, your mouth is a sewer
With many rats of words. Your eyes
Two dunes of dung where ever dwell

The myriad maggots of lies.
And then would I make bold to praise
The infinite commerce of your teats;
You got it good, don't tell me no;
Who put it in two nights ago?
O love, the interest itself . . .
Is hardly worth it.

the photograph

1

This little square of time, this black and white
emblem—all other things are shaded, only
this square is not. Only this rude rectangle
argues the absolute. Here
in the fantoccini stare, the waxen child
looks out forever at the man who looks back
knowing he never will outlast the child,
knowing himself the child, but the child not he—
it is a rectangle of black and white.

2

This little square of time, this rectangle
whose right angles measure not space but time,
holding the tender face, the podex bare
and entertaining in the serpent's grip—
the serpent folds around, involves
in all the terrible nisus of its bowels.
The serpent and the baby wrestling
startle the man who, perched as a bird
on a crag of light, sees himself toppling.

3

(Not even the flower, not even the flower
naked and soft upon its midnight bed
escapes the forked mouth that devours the day,
the oxygen-destroying mouth, the light-
eating bowel that bores through our birth.
Not even the flower, the rich birth
of blossom in the dark night of the earth,
not even the flower, not even the flower
escapes the forked mouth that devours the night.)

How it reduces—this little square of time!—
all to its sepia haze: another half-
century, and the selfsame eye
stares back at the ageing selfsame eye; to reach
each other in that line of vision is
impossible, and yet they duel, the man
and child, only to touch, to meet! But
now between them, impervious as the past,
lies the blindworm, chumbling at the eye.

volutes

All day, its guns saluting in our ears,
the turquoise water pounded purple rocks,
beaten like tall drums. Fasten the years,
ah, batten them down fast, the pounding years
that like these waves attack us, make us roar
within the hollows of our brain, she said.

She sat, a figurehead—fixed in gold the light
fingered (so piracy will fondle spoil)—
that time's wormholes will groove. Yes, you are right,
quite right to talk of voyaging out of sight
beyond the close inflections of the shore,
the idolatry of almanacs, she said.

And took within a hand of gold seashells
that rambled whispering along the strand
and held them up, laughing. See, such farewells
as these, these white indelicacies of shells,
time treats pink bodies to—this talc, before
disintegrations on the shore, she said.

Then flung them in an arc upon the wind.
They whistled: one might have imagined them
in pain, but that they were mere rattling rind
—skeletons of the sea. In those volutes, mind
does not roar, but the naive, hollow air
which never pleads nor prays, held to the ear.

the voyage home

My first home was of water made and seed,
    a nest of fluid, kin to brine;
through cells like streaming light I burst
into a second home, an ocean glaze.
(The walls were dark, and that house was deep down
beneath a glaucous sea I breathed and drank.)

My third home was all white and clean; I cried
    to leave my undersea abode
where I was tadpole, scotched a tail;
until I felt warm flesh and I could sleep.
(Then walls were light, and brightness stung the eyes
and color flew like parrots in my sight.)

My fourth home was of plaster made and paint,
    a square of mice and argument;
there I could kick and scrabble to no end
but the blue bruise, the cuff upon the ear.
(And there learnt all the terrors fear could teach
and wept to feel the sea sting with keen waves.)

My fifth home was of glass and steel and speed,
    a plunging engine of the road;
it bore me to all distant coasts,
but there I found I had not sped from seed.
(I had not left nor sea nor seed behind,
but was more static than the roadside tree.)

My sixth home, oval made of bone and hair,
    I now inhabit like a hermit,
round and round the subtle halls
both in and outside at the selfsame time.
(I pace a deadmarch, touch no lock that gives
where no sea stings, no seed flows there like light.)

street scene

By guidance unconserved or
growth, those adolescents
necking in shadows on the steps
of the power plant are dead.

Their streaky laughter twisted
from what they misunderstand
saddens the look of the street
abandoned as their future.

And all the civic plans
and fronded parks and playgrounds
are an insulting suicide
to those already guilty faces.

Which (signaled by my heels)
like cunning elves of evil
lift from their crude embraces
dripping with lewd rebukes.

children and swan

See with what incandescence the swan goes
who lately in leaf darkness paddling
was but a bird! No bird now, nor emblem he,
nor flame of snow: but sensual mystery, —
the park's involvement with a vibrato string.

The bowing hands of players reach to press
(beyond what blossoms of incontinence,
what fronds of error, undergrowth snake green?)
his balanced bloom of motion, his white poise.
But strain back, fumbling: the children scream

about the feeding station, and the gazelle
locked in the enclosure with his thirst for softness
starts gently, rolling his eyes: over the trees
a skywriter draws a veil of messages
which enclose us in corruption . . . Will the swan

with his throaty stature, his cloud-music
sail those children higher than that smoke
of advertising—? The ribboned afternoon
vaulted with tunnels, blaring with balloons,
stretches to them like a circus. And they sing.

of memory, the strong box

Of memory, the strong box
where slides of action filed away
layers of chagrin collect
the heart could never dust, gainsay

—we still prefer no projection
where the slide bleeds like a mouth
beaten and purple; the voices rise
from childhood like whips; remember the street

where your friends, jibing, mocked

those lewd duets that broadcast from
your shameless, wounded parents' strife;
and you had bled and fled; that scene
is ice, is frozen hard within the box

whose key you sought to lose, but you it lost
where fiercely you would hurl it
down some boiling vortex of negation;
and you were hurled instead—the abyss

is deepest where memory would forget.

the railroad yard

1

Roll of the hills, seaward in paved waves:
In winter, sledding down dead slopes,
And the sudden accident, crying
From puffed lips—blood
Freaking the snow. Do you remember
(Mountains weft the years)
Lean miners—mariners of the sod!—
Blue-eyes charred, dug
From the pit,—Saturday evening
Revenants with blacker pittance?
Lamplit caps hung
In the dark shacks on the hillsides
—Scranton, down the years.

2

That day it rained
On one side of the street—
You watched from the porchrail
Sunlight across the road rolling,
Wonder lifted looks
Still innocent. The Erie track
Gave hoboes, coal and ice,—O run
Again, shouting to black-face friends!
Will the day ever die (in memory)
—More memorable deaths
Already forgotten?

3

You stood upon a mound with charcoal glass
Burned for the eclipse: the moon
Moved full across the sun . . .
Wonder of wonders—'twenty six
Or earlier? Too much
For childhood to take in—that darkness
In the heart of noon—stars sharp
In midday sky and memory
Stuck at this moment out of compulsion.
One day you'll understand.

4

She brought in chunks of ice
From the railroad yard. The shack
Had flowers, blue and yellow, like flywheels.
She grinned hello with teeth like a fork—
In the air coffee and smoke
Of locomotives, sweeter than cream—
Stretched dry limbs upon the cot, slyly
Beckoning—two wishbone fingers!
Panic trailed you home.

5

An old man with a sack
Bent over, called your name. How
Did he know your name? His chin
Spread withered splinters of gray stubble.
Train whistles screamed. He said
"Here's candy for you" and bent down
Suddenly. Your mouth
Contracted acid's kiss!
All afternoon the backyard hose
Couldn't wash out the sting.

6

School, I have not forgotten
In the room where I learned to spell,
Bright as a bird reciting poems—
His lips are cold and still—
And Mrs. Carpenter of the sheepwool hair
—Windows stapled wreaths of green!
Not forgotten—though memory
Ride back on roads torn up.

7

Two stories high were violets
In a window-box. Soft coal ash
Blew gently, wafted
Into the room. Downstairs
The fat landlady in a calico dress
Hung washing on the line. Heat
Punched and pounded her dress
As it pounded the walls.
In the room with the violets
I listened to *Waltz Bluette!*

O room with the whirl of *Waltz Bluette!*
—The phonograph winding winding—
That summer madness of the poor:
Over the dirty violets
My father flung the machine.

8

By the mine shaft standing I looked down
Into the dark hole where a circus clown
With crazy lamplit hat and weird streaked face
Had just descended. Down is another race.
There night, in long black passages, is glaring
Rock, black rock and slate. Skinny canaries
Pipe—drab semaphores of death. I peered
Down beneath the rubble and glass through time.
Querulous crypts, tunnels—some hell I feared
Had gulped him up, earth growling with high-geared
Hidden inner brakings. But the bells
Are caroling, are signaling as he sinks . . .
In The Church of Our Lady there will be litanies
And liturgies.—Wind blew around the mouth
Of that cave, I fell upon my knees
And heard, as I imagined, devils hooting
Out of the mud when he was raised in blood,—
The elevator groaning. On a cliff
They wait for him in an old frame shack that hangs
As if it would fall. Engines are throbbing—
Now the pile-driver heart
Beats in my temple choirs, waves and prayers.

9

Grey woofs of smoke muffle the clouds—soft
Fabric of cinder and dense fire
In the engine's larynx—coughed
Out, spewed from the funnel in a bolt of wool
Floating; unspooled, on rooftops and windowsills,
—Geraniums wrapped in wool
As the cloud wrapped. Something else—
It is wool on the memory,
Hooding the approach—is happening, a
Scene, two figures, in the dawn, dare
Under cover of wool, mysteries
Of motion, undulant—*pain* . . . ? Or
Possibly, as the window cools to pearl

Panes, clearing, it is—shuttling
There, in the lump of shadows
Parents weave—a bobbin in
My eyeballs, till they purl hot flame!
—Pulling the warp down over shame.

10

And then recall . . . factories, knitting mills—
Where sewing children's bathing suits
My mother sat behind the frosted glass:
And I, upon the curb, watched autos pass.
And peddlers with forget-me-nots
And ice-cream vendors by the gate
Joked with the girls who laughed but wouldn't wait
When the factory-whistle blew. The dusk came late
In summer, bringing assorted smells
Of locomotives, beer, gardenias . . .
We walked home, knitting hands, through traffic, noise
Of vendors crying, crying of newsboys.
And Peter Rabbit, somewhere in the din
Hopped chicken-wire to the cabbage patch.
—Jump, Peter, Brother Fang is hiding
There, behind that briar,—he will catch
You if you don't watch out!
                    But where
Could Peter go? The woods are dangerous.

i remember papa

I remember Papa—El
Producto—fistful of pinochle—
beer on Sunday—and baseball . . . He
had a way about him—took you

by surprise! Unlucky at cards
—of course—but my! how he could
talk: "That girl of yours, now,
how old did you say . . . ?"

—jovial and not-too-proud . . . The day
he came home, late—and fell

like a baby, crying, "Oh!
I didn't mean to go
that far—!" and all
the lights were out, the beer,

the loaded bases, decks of cards—
they didn't help him staunch the tears . . .

Oh, I remember Papa (on the floor)
rolling as if it wasn't Pennsylvania
but somewhere in Hell, where Papa turned
forked on the terrible spit of fear.

revelation

In a dream of innocence, he travels
a foreign world of faces, sober
glass and stone; dreams (in a hard light
hostility has drained of understanding)
banks of purring grass and sibilant sun,
sunlight labial on the singeing skin.

Picks up the Holy Bible on the table,
lumbers through *Revelation*, fingers doom
as the thump thump rhythm, in the adjacent cell,
warns: Emptiness to come, the senseless blood.
His senses laid out in the lap of gloom,
the bible trapping disbelief,

his need he cannot spell: the page
rings out, clanging John and faith,
that second death more terrible than the first
—the two-sword word from the holy mouth
will slay with everlasting thirst
the lukewarm traveler, nor hot nor cold.

But angels are far away; voices from heaven
farther than stars: what's near is not vision
of hell, a lake of fire, a great sign
—the woman clad with the sun; but dashing boys
in afternoon, the common ball in their hands,

and tedium of halls and slippered feet.

And trains and burr of drawls in dialects,
stations sour in the dawn,
the porter dragging his baggage like a limp:
the rest-room cubicles reveal Pompeiis
of carved graffiti, the fornicator's dream.
And dirty newsprint on the floor is another

kind of despair, telling of organized ruin
stepped up to scare.—Nonsense! There is no travel
but the one described in the *Apocalypse*.
The ways lead down and up, not home despite
the whizzing trees and cornfields. John was right
to hate the lukewarm, as The Spirit said.

god is a circle

                    whose centre is everywhere
—who sees the poet's home within
the Serpent's mouth. There also lies
the tail, where evil eats itself. I bear
recurring cycles, repetition of
passion and decay; and so like him
dwell not in the centre where all's still,
the saint's home, but upon the outer ring
where each living thing
buds, flowers, and returns to shriveling.

The nun I see before the black-bound book
sits in a circle of her devotion;
skirting the periphery of change
and motion, telling her still rosary,
she forms a circle of her spotless clothes
—the whole vast world between
the range of black and white. The white folds drape
below the table in the library,
the black hood bent on
contemplation of her highest One;

but I regard the passion of the book

toward which I lean: the way the dying light
falls on the mahogany, the lamps,
from winter's day; how readers look
out of their studies, boredom, lust or fear
in dumbshow,—frozen in these attitudes;
and how the old sit cramped as a cross-legged tailor
(stitch understanding slowly through the sleep
that warps the woof of sense).
I feel the pulse of the circumference.

Then when my eye wanders, falling upon
some likely-leaving form that snaps it up,
an emblem of delight (the body caught
in splendor of limbs, the ranting sexual heat
hoarse with its rabble-rousing in the vein),
I feel all the fangs sink in my bones,
the venom of that home wherein I dwell
eat through me—and I gaze at such calm nuns,
fixed as in a frieze,
and loathe and envy them their central ease.

magnificat

Et esultavit . . . no, Johann Sebastian,
not in the weak magnificat
we (sickly) weave, a minor
banner of our praise. That
is not for us. *Suscepit Israel* . . .
He hath received us O with cruel mercy
in the night like thieves like fallen lions.
Our exultation is not free.

But bound as Prometheus to the rock,
our liver eaten away by the vulture of God,
we have seen him put down the humble, exalt the mighty
—Abraham chained to the rock, covered with mud.

O Father Abraham the Holy Spirit your praise
your glory, look! look at the seed
of the father, the parched loins
and the wormwood creed!

colloquy of time and place

Dispersals, in that summer, of our group
took them away, the intricate, the naive —
to cool, white islands, wounds of scorpions
or the sudden liaison. Postcards like birds
flew back — "My dear — the Earthly Paradise
is here! Denmark's the place!" And the long ships
went steaming down the continents
mumbling neutral comment of tall flags.

"Whatever did they go for?" asked the one
who knew something of life. Something I stammered
back, in anger for causes, for the cause of place
— about the hunger of the eyes. He said,
"The eyes, when hungry, have the green of peace
to contemplate. Failing that, what leagues,
what fathoms, runes of coral, what jokulls
or wrecks of old mystiques in stone or wood

can heal warped diapasons of desire?"
Still stammering, but with a heat of fear,
I clung to wonder: "Tell me, is not place
the outer glory of the sense? Seeing
is active, surely, — how else can we learn
except through color, form — abstract from space?
How else? What gem so rare that is the peer
of bright waves flashing in the light of stars?"

He knew — or seemed to know — "Why do they speed
about, in vague pretense of vision? One
squats in a foreign cave, interminably plays
a game of double-crostics with his ego.
Another howls through Africa who weeps
alone in cities — and a third, his heart
an anchor of his guilt, sinks to the floor
beneath a Chinese sea, a worm of sores!"

"Where shall they go, then?" But a sign
of patience, with two fingers, like a saint,
motioned me still —
"All will return," he said: "will come with tales:
how this one found a pearl big as a head,
and that one, in a small Moroccan hut,

found easy lust to settle a deep greed:
they will return with wonder—but will return."

"And what if they do? You sound like a Great Boyg
who reads the fever chart of our wandering,
and, in a voice like Emptiness, incites
our simple wonder to a fear of place!"
"Not fear but wisdom brings you face to face
with a geography that is not place
but time—whose clefts and hachures you must read
and travel, calmly, from the wit's pretense."

graduate school:
the lives of the poets

All truth, and situation, is planed smooth
With tools of criticism, sharp but slow
In execution: here mutters the buzz-saw
Of research—that lops away like a harsh tooth
The soft, fat flesh of old biographies:
The legend's tissue and the myth's disease
But one half-truth the scholar files away.
This is the shop of fact, concrete as day—

'Though this is night school: the apprentice nods
Under the weight of notes and gimlet comments:
All the facts of suffering are intoned
In the mild air of learning. Is it the task
Of carving furniture of poets' lives
That so congests them? No,—for hardly their wives
Are quite so comfortable and familiar:
This is their shop, their resident milieu.

And yet surrounded by the mise-en-scene
Of suffering (the lives they study), they
Accept the miserable childhoods like a grade
—A thesis rests within each Magdalen.
And gargoyle Sin, inclemencies of Pain
Loom outside—in the winter's swollen rain—
This room's warm dozing: there the dangerous night
holds the unmeasurable and ungraded plight.

So these apprentices, the evening scholars,
Must move in fact to rituals of sense
Bounded by gongs, by loose-leaf memoranda,
And cooled by tragic ecstasy's events.
Then they break ranks, deploy like pigeons homeward
Into the weather of the suburbs, toward
Children and wives, and long, clean hours of study
In which exists no laudanum—nothing bloody.

new year poem

Dawn on the new year—and time slow
under the streeling blue, the cave of light.
Gyring, sunk like a past beneath the blur
of horns and kisses, the tinfoil, the smoke
and the liquor that makes it able to pretend
years are not time, not legal, the urban life
rolls in the fog and snow to its damp seed.

Where evergreen and baubles keep their watch
above the greeting cards and messages
(love in red ribbon, hope in cotton white)
the logs are going out, the embered flare
trembles, is snuffed away. So it is merely
another year, another holiday
within the cycle of boredom and decay.

Where the paper crown has fallen
from the gay baldness of a clerk, the wheels
of angry taxis turn, crushing the gold
in grey slush. Bells of holly
no longer gleam nor shine
in evergreen and lonely
bachelor eyes. Behind the eyes
(perennials of lingering, longing
over some gentleness
in which they have no part) the bright
balloons burst. The party, at last,
is over: the couples have paired away.

—O sing hosanna, swing the censer, with candle bless

each private king, and every kitten! Bring
love to time moving in a law of steel
and death. Save we the saviors who have been slain—
the saints whose blood perpetually we drain!

—Hosanna sing for laurel, bay and holly:
sing in the year time moves in time less jolly!

five voices

One way outward from all terror is to drink:

and after the curaçao and the gin
the task of morning, incumbent to begin;
the zinc-white fact, the gyroscopic day
requires level eyes. This is no way.

One way outward from dilemma is to think:

waking at night, who have drowned in self,
estuary of decisions and fauna of contradiction,
at the flaring brink of thinking your thoughts
like heat bubbles float out of sleep, hissing as they wake.

One way outward from an endless cycle is to compromise:

your hair grows sparse and still you stare
at early photographs with a helpless care;
what do they say: adjust yourself: be sure
to shift towards comfort; keep from being poor.

One way outward from impending failure is to grow wise:

what more egregious comfort to the weak
than power of encompassing the shadow of death?
And this is wisdom: for not only the sanctified
but you, who take the coldness of no flesh at your side.

There is no way outward for the broken self but dying:

and all the rest is lying, lying

I know that these killed sophistries persist
like razor returning to the coward wrist
too bare for the flashing edge, the turbid twist.

natura naturans

Winter, with its giant suggestions
to be definite, to thrust,
boldly with new meanings comes
on schedule: as the unprepared

in cities huddle with their doubt,
and even the friendly odor of carbon
in the grate will not aid the cynic,
and the alien moments are too real

for the depressed in their tiny rooms.
Where the omens are saddest, among
spirals of planes that whine death-
wards, horror is sharpened, a stone

of ice shaped to an arrow of death.
This points, uncritical, at the heart of all:
at the cold plaza, at the toyland lake
with the children, the photographers,

at the circle under the ignored statue,
and even in the dead center, the hub
where life seems most centrifugal:
the bristling nerve-waves of commerce.

And the season's repeated query, unsaid,
expressed as by a paralytic
in the huge, slow eyes, the gangling lips
slow, quavering, of a stricken continent:

do I dare recover?

the statue in the snow

The year of snow. The ode to disaster. The song
  written in ice; magnificent vowels cut in frost, glit-
  tering like icicles hanging from the wych-elm's
  glassy bough.

The year of cold. Drops, milky as pearls, frozen on
  tips of eyelids, tears on the statue's lids by the
  sanctuary; the lyricist of stone, set above frenzied
  squirrels, chin

poised above peacocks, grass. Is it the challenge of the
  bust we avoid, the tilt of the head, eyes piercing the cloud of snow?
  Because, in the pond, a rose frozen, redder than cannabis, glows

through the ice like a fever blazing towards death.
  Someone had thrown the rose from the flagstones,
  and now the bust and the rose, rigid as memories

of rage, wait for what touch, what force
  to thaw into the present sense.

the tankers

The gunmount flashes, flashing metal grey
also the opaque aft, as down the harbor
estuary under steam toward turquoise streams
she plies.
            And dagger-eyed the gull veers overhead

catching a splinter of sunlight on a glassy feather.

There in the danger-polluted currents
punctuated by periscopes in a grammar of death
another tanker bears another gift,

the gift of fuel, to light the faltering wick
that flutters in the pulse of Europe
whom monstrous maws of smoke consume.

Trade winds sweep through the crow's nest
bearing no whisper yet, no mutter
of peril but distance, fear but far

gulf heaven whose birds spangle with light.

And outward they travel, living center of power,
vortex of possibility a match could splay
smithereened, spate upon such clearness of coast:

yet the spirit of sailors dares the paths
in voyage of fire without fear: as the conscious prowler,
subaqueous and sly, waits under weather
camouflaged as creature, waits in the sea and rain
drawing a circumference of patience round the moving center.

But still the image of face without body
has no knack of daunting the will of boys
who, laughing, sprint along the direct catwalk

in the golden air, and consider only the laugh
and not the eventuality.
                                    And the earth
behind their monumental trip broadens
with the laugh, whose echo winds through pain,

in hills where their people dream of choice.

college town: princeton

Forsythia with butterfly yellow fingers
the well-kept streets. Late noon. Grackles flicker
from thick evergreens unnoticed and the neat
sprinkler-laundered lawns attest to visitors

more than a sense of order. A world of towers,
intricate as chess, stretches like tradition
backwards, to distil interpretations
reared in scorn, almost, against the softness

of the landscape, and the youth in uniform.

Chalk dust, axioms, syllogisms show
their comfortable character everywhere;
the rhythm is legato, the time slow,

vacant as stares that household servants wear.
There is no problem of security:
autos are plentiful; station wagons manage
the proper touch of relaxation: you
see no gorgons of conflict, almost believe

the logic of the status quo, are drawn
within the easy orbit of acceptance
and sangfroid: is terror actual
or dreamlike immaturity?

blue monday

My garden, bald and branchy, through the panes
presents an urban rubble, stiff and sterile —
behind the fence a sharp black dog keeps watch
planning a murder in his pointed eyes.

And these sick windows opposite, in brick
impossible to like, whose ledges wear
manila sacks with milk or cheese, the tree
of heaven in grace without murmur twines.

Beyond our grayness visible twin towers
stretch like nipples up, taut with life.
Their skyblown terraces are neat, and winds
may not ruffle the order of their form.

Which, to my eye below, as vision lifts
over opaque curtains and window-boxes
with beer and flowers, seems correct but wrong,
as choosing lesser evils to survive.

nightfall

When the hum stops and the desires are let out
like bears from narrowing cages,
and the busy hooks are pulled in,
wheeled on the pulleys, blood-stained metal
where humble lives are given up,

the tables are all lit, and the steel windows
show empty coldness to the passersby.

The blue cop on the corner,
his insolence all ruddy and raw,
stamps, and turns his pointed eyes
on children who tear to insoluble shreds
the silver gauze of evening
with the flukes of their screaming.

And the footpad like a sparrow
darts, dissembles, and the bars
beckon with their promissory glitter;
and on the gathering immobile hours
spreads the news, with its harpy messages.

Fan-like, events reticulate
with ever-increasing danger; the webbed knuckles of
this murder, that blaze of madness, the false cry
of peace (read doom) in the believer's ribs
smash, and the night folds black.

the news

Taking home the Sunday papers, late
    In the dawn under the stone
Looming of abandoned business structures,
Past the slumbering airport service, the all
        Night cafeteria where stray
Bits of dangerous trade, like gulls, hang out
Waiting, with eyes that fish,

You turn the lock, return, enter the known
　　Milieu of your feelings, bound
By the furniture, by books, two fireplaces
And that fur bunny someone dear at Easter
　　　Brought. It's Spring and the pages
Of *The New York Times* alternate
Between depressing and amusing

News. You hurry past wretched headlines
　　Of that bloody and interminable
Madness, war in the east, generals who bray
Their own particular neurosis into
　　　The radar of the nerves:
The gardening page presents
A nineteenth-century sentiment, pretends

Escape through the familiar yard,
　　Blaze and aloha and red volcano
Climbing roses, rose of forgetfulness —
Luring, perhaps, even the cold-flat
　　　Victim of colds and noises
To a vision of generation and response.
But swiftly riffled in impatience by

Columns of spring flowers, the Sports page
　　Holds your attention, holds it
With half-tones that pierce the heart, smiling
Collegiates in G-strings, athletes
　　　Poised at the edge of pools,
Or standing in rows, splendor of limbs blooming.
Remote as a Trappist, you stare

Speechless and pierced by those earnest poses,
　　Outspoken sinews, fresh
With sunny down. The papers are
Consumed as by fire, gossip and photos
　　　Charred and devoured
By the restless furnace where always glows
The intimate rose of desire.

But the news, always dangerous, enters
　　Without knocking, the doors
Of the body fling apart, the house is taken
Over, ransacked, rutted; the occupant,
　　　　No matter how calmly
Facing the intruder with his leveled gun,
Falls to the floor, undone, at the loud report.

and all the travelers return

Where the fire-escape puts forth
like a battered bowsprit
a sad geranium or nerveless daisy

that might be seaweed hung on a wrecked hull,

the huge arms of the brackish woman
grate on a flaked sill; she is the figurehead
of this dead ship. Lightly the winds
stir the pathetic weeds of her marine hair,

as waning lengthens the shadows of
Christopher Street; soon she will disappear
to unseen customary hells,
kitchen where a broth of dullness puffs

like a fat man ascending the walk-up of a friend.
And the quarter moon will slice
steeple, warehouse, crucifix,
and all the travelers return

who are drowned, and live in the sea.

serenade

What do you wait for in those provinces
under the fells of rumor, the round hills?
What do you hear on the porch so still

of a foaming whisper, as you rock and your hands
weave, and drum, drum, and weave on the air?

Along the ridge of the hills like a pale streamer
of gauze (winding in dusk) the freight's gray wail
twines up the wall of dark. The bells of leaves,
delicate and thin, tilt in the prod
of the wasp wind; and the coral

reefs of color in the shoals of the sky
in colonies travel down the undersea mountain.
Is the world buried, will this Atlantis mirror
of our provincial continent be washed away?
The cicadas are chirring in the purple wash of waters

that move on us, the brackish waters that browse
over the dozing bantams and grandmas;
the waters that you wait for who sit as the world
pops richly like a heartburst, or mildly like the last
purr of a continent tilting underseas.

elegy

What is it that they say
in rooms the music fills:
where the bright intellectual talk
shadow-boxes the night?
What is it that they say
(and unsay) as the heart
scrabbles and claws at dread;
and, vulnerable, the head
spirals from innocence?
What the quick senses fear,
involved as a fingerprint
through streets that lead
to twisted evenings: *Night
is arid for us all
within the maze: we fall
forward to doors that close
in labyrinths where pools
drown us . . . O the pale*

voices at Ste. Sulpice
—drinking the dark away. . . .

Here, as I walk beneath
the elms, the drying leaves
of shaking autumn saplings
in the cold, stone square, by the arch
where Washington's stone chin
is thrust at the speeding cars,
each midnight face betrays
its nympholeptic stare.
Concrete benches bear
the smokers, posed in shadows
with tense hands, trembling
toward the personal. But
the fountain, the oval pool
(where summer children rejoice)
yields journey's end. You
go half-hearted—there
is never the miracle
of tenderness: you flinch
from raw-fisted loneliness
pounding your penance home.
Is this the legend, the emphasis
of our consciousness—?
The lamps of Washington Square
glare coldly on the cold rails,
and the huge dogs savagely
lunge away, and tear
the leash from anonymous guides
who proudly ignore the night.
So into the burning crater
of night's fires that never go out
—the windy flame of lust—
the soul's bad habit thrusts!
Down the igneous gorge
of neon, chromium and glass
held by what cyclic disease
or compulsion of the nerves
they hardly know, the dolls
and intellectuals go.
So to the box-like rooms
and toward the ice-floes, I
direct my gaze; the East

River quietly flows
whether I gaze or no.

dream of the sidhe

Cuchulain, wake!

My midnight fight, my quarrel with the waves
Whose foam-flecked fingers hurl into night's coves
While the sword-points of my anger stab
Into the blind heart of the sea—*Wake!*
I hear echo down dull halls of the veins
—As if it were I those beautiful women seek,
The midnight hero caught in the sea's vines . . .
A burning tendril as I fall towards sleep
Hangs my deaf ghost between two worlds,
And from my groin dangles my limbs between
Warm hearth-fires and that country of wet weeds.
Algae I see, and sea-anemone
Float towards my bed; she of the glazed hair
Lean her marine breasts of chrysoprase—
That glaucous wife glozing my life, my fear.
But in that second when the ghost would rise
Into the enchantment, something knifes
All my senses, like twine in the flesh
Pulls back,—the waking and the shock of life!

What mad dream, morning, have I had, what flash
Of vision—hung by my tendril wish! I thought,
No, dreamed dark countries underseas poured gems
Out in a goddess' hands, all light held forth
—And I reached mine, but fell back into sense.

within this park

Within this park the branching night of lakes
rowboats and tunnels extends
its shadowy influence

which amorous throaty summer, weighted by trees,
to sensuous sailor offers
for him to seize.

Take all the paths, then, seeker, you who steer
with star and quadrant to discover
anchor, the unwandering lover.

cape's end

For R.S.

1. *Summer Seascape*

On this snake of land
crooked in the sea,
the whitecap coiling
lace in the sand, and
the west wind waltzing
on toes of shell,
the jetties quiver as
the spiles decay.

Seagulls like giant rats
in the wake of trawlers
scream at the sea-wrack
of silver gizzards;
a jazz dance laving
spars in the spray;
radio and mackerel
float in to shore.
At night the shells lisp
with tongues of glass,
and the damp snail whispers
like a thunderbolt in the room of time;

I shake the cold fingers
of the starfish like a pumice hand,
and watch the spoondrift glow
as the northern lights shine.

2. *The Beach at Night*

Anxiety like water combed the shore.
The phosphorescent dunes kept watch
crouching above the rocks and breakwater:
hunchback ghosts of the tide.

Facile enough, the rollercoaster dive
of gull on wind, the daring drop
to pluck the squirming life, or roost on poles
—mysterious to sense.

All the wrack in humid drench of moonlight:
mists, like melting webs—soaking the air.
A fishing scow, aglow with eerie masts,
will pass, and suck the questing eye.

What's this: the winding snail slow on a wreck
of wood entwined by weed: glass groomed to green
marble. A tiny cry . . . Southwest, the wind
drags inward; fish-bones howl.

And still we stride the crumbling beach
kicking at spines, at rustling teeth,
rattling bones with feet of fear.
World ebbing: low tide.

3. *Harbor*

But then there is one joy: your face
and the thoughts looking out of the shadows
—the still face . . . like a flower's look . . .
rose and white, and the dark heart of the eyes.

All night, with fear and tenderness I felt
and looked, and touched again and looked;
all night the broken window rattled and
the copper catch kept knocking. No one spoke.

Oh, how the fit of altercation passed!
We warmed against cold tides of doubt
our bodies, wedlocked as twin epitaphs!
The town lay, small and quiet, in the lull.

   4. Seascape with Figures

Their bodies nude and glistening
with water, golden in gold light,
their hair bronze-helmeted—a coppery crown
of workmanship set right
upon the burning eager head—
they clasped like statues, silhouettes
that would not part as the waves crept
silver leagues—about their feet
all day, birds flying as the sands flashed white!

There was a tapping as of beaks: a bird
would rub its beak upon a rock
and fly away five hundred years;
when it returned to wear away the rock
by rubbing of its beak, they stood
together—joined in the seminal mood!
The tide could never shift them with its shock
of change, incessant silver clamoring
—nor moon nor winter interrupt their spring.

Their spring in summer clung upon the shore
as seaweed rose, and fauna flooded
reefs in the wind, green scattered everywhere:
and coral, shaped like well-groomed gems
decked the island with magnificence.
For if these figures from the sea's deep dream
had risen like the seaweed, now they kept
the real within the dream—
and passionately woke where they had slept.

most often in the night

Most often in the night, when you lie sleeping
close beside me, and the air is harsh
with all the damp, cold sighs of a city's weeping
and the sharp, drunken cries stinging like blows,

I go to the window, which in the dark seems distant,
and heavy-limbed and -lidded peer through space
parceled with concrete structures, tall and vacant,
and there perhaps lean further than mere distance

—deep as this wakefulness will shuttle me.
Is it, then, something deeper than night's sleep
that owes me rest, moving in caves of want
like rank raw hollows, iced with memory?

The window cools; the light begins to creep
out of the sky, returning to the scene
of crime with outlawed stealth. Is it too far
we reach when leaning back to what-has-been?

hebrides

Easy as light love comes and fills the eyes,
    easy as light and light as lemonade.
Set all the sails, a fair wind in the skies
    blows love, blows love and light beyond the wave.

This is our voyage, friend, into the deep-
    sea levels of the heart, the unfathomed vein;
easy as light love plunges, and must keep
    the prow above the Hebrides of pain.

the mountain and the eye

Heaped against the vagueness of space it swells
the shape of earth like breasts; or is the temple
whose arching dome contains the mumble of bells
in the loam belfry, over the apse of marble.

It is a force: cathedral of seed and furrow,
the perfect and blue piety it utters
stirs the maculate eye scanted with shame
for its pipkin faith, veiled in the afterglow.

What may the mountain tell the eye
to implement the impatience of its journey?
O, that the trees are sad, and the winter dreary
and the dark crows on her shoulders shout and cry.

Not wed to piety the eye disdains
what is not wonder or color or swiftness;
change it devours, its iris spread with joy,
but shame and permanence glaze it with dulness.

On fiery roads, macadam by shadblow,
and rockpools dazzling under whistling pine
it dwells, speeding in coarse delight
to the affluent décors of theatricals.

Yet, having gorged, the satyr eye possesses
a domed, silent interior proper to
and not unlike the mountain's; there, too, bells
whisper in cadences of stillness;

as deep under purple shoulders the mountain
mourns, blind (with no head, the mole of space),
so, too, beneath the eye's convex riot is
blindness, bubbling from a sourceless fountain.

vultures

When we came to a place in the road
that moved—or seemed to move—
we slowed down till, like ropes
of smoke, languid and limp,
in long, uncertain coils
the vultures took the air.
In the comfort of the car
quick hair rose on my neck;
water flowed in my limbs.
In a bare tree like a stick
they took a peevish roost
—and I felt the brain grow sick—
as the car rolled heavily
on the spot they stooped to watch.

key west

1.

Spontaneous pearl, or bird-link caracara,
strange sport of nature neither here nor there:
last key, last bone of island vertebrae,
yet neither land nor sea
                    . . . but should you dig
in coral soil one fathom down,
a burst of liquid amethyst would geyser through

—I have seen water in the streets that is the sea . . .

2.

And so, at night, passing through white streets
spread out like sleeping beasts,
heavy with aimlessness,
my heels made no sound, by bougainvillea
of old houses with pitched roofs
I wandered, lush constellations sagging
low, bulging, almost, to touch the eaves.

Hot breezes swept the Spanish Main,
entering the reticule of palms and laughing bars,

juke box excitement of sailors in summer white
catching the brine's urge, sea swell in fierce loins—

O southern Key! where freedom is a lazy plant
by typhoon skies and pirate waters fed,
whose vital blossom has a tender lip
which all may kiss,—
                    upon the shore I knelt,
by pampas grass and thatched cabanas
mumbling, This is the staunch island
windswept as a mind with no location!
by skeletons of sea-change
haunted; set upon as subway-rushers leap
on dusk: elemental, dogged by ghosts,
embodiment of death
at life's center,—this is the island
naked before violence as the cultured heart:

Green monsters of the deep lie from my hand—
outstretched, dilated,—waves away—
                                        Yet
here I felt my childhood surging through
terror, and through the ice
of thought had thawed
the adult behavior of indifference. . . .

3.

Manhood raging with a need for love
grew when the wrecked childhood like debris
had gone aground
and slimed the future possibility
and left an ineffectual mind.

Toward shores potential, so our lives
have raged: whatever island we have sought
to ease the burden of our eyes
that inward turning find a hostile court
of errors, falsities, and poseur weaknesses
sitting in tacit judgment, patient, wise.

The meanings we have dared not face
at last, O island, come back with the tide—
we find, within eternal flux
and languid grace of such repose

as winds and oceans furl,
the answer to our speed and darkness
and our luxury of sin:
a world in flower and, in seed, a mind.

4.

But I remember times more angular—
the neurasthenic flora of the deep
recall those tentacles of hate the cities wave
and stretch, and clutching, suck your spirit
in: the stone of horror, terrible for life,
surrounded me.

                    Housefronts and schoolrooms,
others' worldly good I always saw from far
—and psychopathic cities breeding war. . . .
Half-lit, but more in shadows,
living showed a face that split,
and shared no secret, dwelt in fear,
and saved desire like a hobby.

Which, natural, sought a tunnel for escape,
and failing beauty's esprit de corps, read
maps, timetables and geography:
love of body shifted into love of lore.

But danger blossomed from the leaves
of travel; roads I saw
pour mile on mile
of sun and rail and stone
yet not the adjacent calm of earth.

5.

And there was talk of bombs when I arrived.
That day the bathers, luminous with sun,
fled the white beaches; loungers in hotels
forgot the poker and the rum;

hysteria and dusk together fell
violent, in riot-flashing hues
that shivered through the evening's spine:
leaving nor place nor time to choose—

And now the exile and the derelict

beneath a menace from vindictive blue
find, in their wasted gifts, an equal fate
with sheriff, politician,—hate

has equaled all, at last, huddled together
from the blundering of greed and will;
the modern climax, tragic, doctrinaire,
resolves with grace the wish to kill.

At midnight unseen dogs began to howl;
fenders with dimmers touched unwary thighs;
corners of streets showed uniforms like posts
dangerous, excited, scanning skies

for grief

      —the island had exploded now—

no bridges lead immunely from the nerves—

I saw fly outward into opal glow
my dream of safety, martyred, still unwon.

journey to the end

> *Being is better than not being . . .*
> —Aristotle

> *The dead are free from pain.*
> —King Oedipus, tr. by
> W. B. Yeats

At the end of this road always the wind screams
wildly. Here are no signposts. Nor blazing pharos
on sea-bitten rock beckons. The familiar numbers
blur. Features are missing. There is nothing warm.
Only the frozen darkness in which your hand
plunges like a fish—and disappears!

Imagine this action, walker, as unbegun.
These are the paths you had missed: delicate veins
that never flooded, filled you, warm with rushing

fire, the red-gold anger, the dilection. . . .
Listen! the pluck of the sea, the roar
of the breaking fjord boiling with its final

music! This is the whirlpool you had missed,
the darkness plunging after light; the sea
gathered sharp, to a helix foam, a spiral
surf. O air is a burning rod, an axle
on which the sea turns, the danger of the sea
turns! This you had missed. This ice . . . this darkness. . . .

—Lord, we were not prepared for the burning city,
death by memory, death by despair. Who wished
this flaming air, this force and fever? Now
all's fever, fear—and the axle of air
turns all the burning earth on its fiery rod
on which even the sea burns, dying!

And where the great cool birds
wheel overhead, the sky with cloud-wrack
like gray rock rolls—and you fare for the cliff,
where the cliff knows and expects you,
as you approach in a dream, like a feather, flying.

i ask the invisible ones

I ask the invisible Ones
Who guide our thoughts by theirs
Who ferry our lives across deathlands
—Angels & sages & heaven-agents—

I ask matrimony of sun & moon
In my double-cancerous horoscope
Courage to withdraw from the well
Wherein solar forces cannot enter

That Pan quit muddying my clear streams
—Old gods should be shut away—
And let the magnetic altar
With incense purify the air

And let there be no lunar beasts
Dancing around in my woods

florence

The City

Etruscan sky of frescoes, angelic witness
of clouds, flowers over Florence, lightens
gold hills, Raphael pines, rolls
a pale transparency about the city.

Venus born and the Spring of Botticelli:
conception's wave and branch, like that pagan Mary
in the center of seasons between the lady of leaves
and the lone indifferent youth, exquisite among branches.

From the goregushed *campagna* of Siena
and Florence, the red lily in its brash
thrust of dominion, plunging of horse and bone
where the knights rode the lance-tips of their pride —

Let them ride, let them; it is hard
to break into this light
from the fortress, the feudal law of the senses:
how should the senses flower but from such pride?

The city changes, but the light does not change,
O immutable behind those smiles
the masters fixed — those enigmatic smiles
worn by mild ladies in a mystery.

II
The Square

In the Piazza della Signoria
the old palace with its fountain
and rash statues tall as buildings
heavily tell of male dominion

crushing Hercules brushes the sun
over his shoulder, and David his neighbor
from his encounter with the slain
giant, in repose, marvel of promise

and Neptune, third colossus, crown

a home of pigeons, white above spray
and bronze goatmen with flapping phalli
pawky lips and fish-hook beaks

primed in the tilt of thigh and hoof
—the sexual cry in hoarse bronze
clanging over cobblestones
the loggia witnessing the silent

drama, from its chocolate gothic
barrel-vaults, Cellini's dream
Perseus, gorgeous with the gorgon
head, aloft, sinews rich

and limber over the female
demon, then the raped women
—what cinquecento madness led
the masters to such virile pride

in a bold access of the blood
carving all but the will aside?

III
The Gallery

In the Uffizi country
goldflake images
of scarecrow Christs to frighten us
up cross and crown to Paradise!

Past walls of flesh and haloed hair,
immolations, battles, hells,
we range our mythic dreams.
O murderous, all these slain!
The beast runs at the lance,
the hunter runs at the jaws.

Then out. Out! Then blue.
Infinite blue! Absolute white!

IV
The Prince

In October, in the Tuscan time
ripe as the persimmon when
burgeon the elements, the
journey from the north I made
    reaching its end

to Florence, without flowers, cool
fall of diamonds and chapels
where the lily was machines
lining the walk between the
    galleries, I

came: and there was sunlight and
broken bridges along the pillars
where the light leaked down to
mud; and along the Arno
    shuttled the cranes

patching them, the people watching
leaning on their elbows; and
(among garages) old prints, busts and
other remains; until on
    Giotto's campanile

the thin moon cut the dusk like a
file: in the morning woodsmoke
and bells, hammers and birds; the
mountains blue, distinct, Fiesole of
    wines and views.

Delays, delays; *gentilezza*
but hard, hard! in the piazzas,
under the porticoes, below the
faultless skies, the shadows of
    steeples and statues

fall, among the cameras, the stalls, the
deceit: O were it not for the
morning-of-the-world
smile . . . and

the beauty—in Taormina the rich
heiress from Tulsa, ten years of
villas and male whores, said: "Were
it not for the beauty, who'd
stay a minute?" waving
    emeralds in the

direction of Etna, but
when I looked, the foreground grinned
back, named Lucio in
jeans she had sent for
    from Tulsa

for him: the beauty—the light,
frescoes catching it out of the
air plentiful in the ripe
Tuscan gold and blue, with
    saints and trees

adorning creation; yet
Cosimo I, the Grand Duke, covered
them over at Santa Croce, with heavy
paint, eclipsing Giotto with a
    'palimpsest' of

Vasari, whose cleverness
had withered; still
the woman of shrunken
countenance, in one
hand a serpent and fish-
hook in the other, the
    lady of

Intellect, her shriveling dry
scorpion touch, by
Martianus Cappella
described: her
fingers stained with
    dust and

flaked the joyous coverings
of Tuscany; and blur the
face of Christ, and the
light crumbling. . . .

for voice and strings

Morning wide
to glance with light all colors of the town,
tall palms greeny and brown
    with wintry plumage like an old
        and shaggy pheasant's tail;
        pearl river rough on rocks
            rushing, and fishermen
with nets on poles lean down the bridge's sides.

O morning
I wake to, falling with a head of smoke,
as fingering mist fiddles on the sagging slum
    with cold allotments and woodfires
        and all the churchdomes touched
        and singing choirs of stone,
            hymns of pine
over the waters and the half-roused shore.

In the cool
of dawn's bright bells that carillon with birth
of sunday sun, I step from damp and death
    of being born, to spread my bones
        that move my flesh to feel
        the cold sheets round, the numb
            intransitives of self
wound round my chaos like a caul of wool.

Small birds tell
no airs of sorrow on the linden boughs,
nor worry in the eaves; fish flap the stream
    that glitters, and the eel
        slides in the mud
        and nothing cries that glides
            or flies, but forked in limb
and feeling only I am double hell.

I'll clang my way
braver than day to utter every vowel
of mood and move with words against the dark
    shift in the icy mouth
        of self that swallows time

like deadly bait, and pray
        the good ghost to grow
his holy blossoms in my blood of clay.

II

The pretense of the world,
youth's fallow candor spent,
breaks out of every bush,
from every rock and shell;
corruption in the eye
makes planet, moon and star
a villain in a mask
whose true face peels away
the more the glitter shows.
Who can utter *I*
not lying in his teeth?
who deceives? who knows?

III

I speak to you, my darling,
now, while the all hallowing
        toll of years
        claps
its christening eves
in my ears. You
whose face in a din of tears
wets the mistletoe! There
with the tree in the fire we
        embrace!
The grate howls back. The snow
piles on the pane. Where
        did the kiss go?
        Down
the funnel of years.

To you, to you, although
you will not have me, I
long since have sent
        no letter and
        no love,

I make these lines in
a city of bells and columns,
        pines and ice;

know
these words airmail my grief
and yours—the host
is borne across the waters where
          to eat
                    and bleed
our loves in separation
                    is our share.

evocazioni di roma

I

Heavy in the midnight damp
Where shadows (the klieg lights are off)
Spread about my room dim domes
Of churches, where eight pillars heave
Torn shoulders, Saturn's massive last
Stone breath, the Roman ambience
Bears down on me, phalanx of
Grandeur, criminality.
I'd crack upon the Mourning Steps
My own head if it did me good!
Let pour out the acid blood
Devouring my late youth—
As it ate Tiberius
Whom nobody understood.
I look out on the *Curia*,
Severely beautiful, and see
Ages of the acid eat
Senate, emperor and slave.
This maggot hunger, this blind tongue
That stains the peperino black
And snaps the rooftree, blunts the arch,
And turns each foul millenium back—
Praise it: it is love gone wrong.

II

Largesse, largesse . . . I'm glad I'm here!
I've seen the moonlight on the arch
Of Titus and of Severus
Spooky with silence whitely met.

When that dead Sacred Way was lit
I saw the columns standing bare
And bald as bones, and an ache
Prickled my skin and raised my hair.
I felt time at the base of my spine
Uncoil like the slide of a snake—
Caesar, your legions ride the rime
Of this white moonlight! I have grown
Monstrously simple . . . yes, I swear
I'm gliding as the chariots climb
Slow through the brain, and up the stair!

III

On Livingston I peered through a grate
That was our basement window—then
Through bearded Chinese curtains, toy
Fans, stuffed owls, my mother loomed
Larger than a trunk I dreamt
(Nightmares ago) upon my back.

Peering for paradisaic trees
And golden fruit through a dream wall
That opened sesame at my word
I bruised my knuckles and my knees,
Hearing rats scuttle along the hall.
Was it the sloth of my slack father
Whose gambling fancy kept us poor
Made paradise not worth the bother,
Damnation an open door?

Mother, the decades turn around:
The new-world gold you never found
I mined the old world for.
Rome is the world and the world's road
Paved with stone time turns to gold
That turns, when I touch it, back to stone.

IV

Spiritual exercise, prayer,
"Be ye transformed" by that—!
Menaced by the blind tug
Of lust's curiosity
Strained from fair to foul by chance,
I saw upon the *san pietrini*

Twisting, the bitchy female dance,
A white cat in heat, grimed
Maddened on the stones. Held off
By snarls, swift frenzied nails, the male,
Biding his moment—then he'll pounce
To seize with his teeth her teasing neck.
Spastic with venery, she spits,
Scrabbles the cobbles, screams.
Lambrettas baa like rams, fat
Thighs splayed by. . . . Behind the forum
By the same animal heat
Pulled, padding the same street
(My vows at war) I love and hate:
Spinning like Catullus through
The poles, admitting that he "knew
Not why"; fixed upon the wheel
That burns the senses to a shell
—O let us who the godhead shun
Till we struggle to the source,
Beg to conquer, if we can,
The shadowy passion running down
Our dark finite identities!

prayer for the new year (rome)

O gods, who weather mist and fiery darkness,
You Thrones and Powers moving as mind moves,
Subtler than symbol, more rarefied than logic,
More real than angels, more exact than angles,
O Thou to whom Idea weighs heavy as anchors,
More limber than lightning, more nimble than thunder,
Baffling reason with the breathing rhythm,
Take up this prayer, gather this notion,
Heed this dilemma:
May the years bring Thy presences still closer
When absence burns the blood that age wears cold,
Hermes, Apollo, Jesus.
Grant me this from the all-eye of Heaven.
Let not the fire of absence, let not that darkness
Void me, that bodiless and boneless darkness,
That evil flame of nothing, let it not lick

The wooden rectangle where I shall be borne
To porous earth, and the small mouths working my dust,
And the apple thudding, the ripe fruit overhead.
Grant me this, that all things in One compose,
Pleroma, Lord, Savior: grant
Me this, that time not end me, space not null me,
The sun crack and disperse me: Christ, hear me, hear me,
That Thou come closer, beyond the flesh that blocks me,
When the soul cries Mercy and the body is torn.

God of the world, O God . . . *numen* . . . *phalloi* . . . *charisma*. . . .

colosseum

The full moon on the Colosseum
Lights up the legends, shedding shadows
On the exhausted center, the arches
Where centuries played heartless games:
Earthquake, prince, barbarian
Brought tufa down and travertine,
Ate the arcades and raped the iron
And willed this gaping to the moon!

The Venerable Bede foretold it;
Jeremiah, John, Isaiah:
Hebrew apostles, visionaries,
Recorders of the future
Fall, all mysteries divined—
We are as the smoke and foam
Without the overflow of Love.
When falls the Colosseum Rome shall fall,
And when Rome falls with it shall fall the world.

Thus Bede; and thus the Kabbala
That vaulted language on the Word—
The corbel and the cornice of creation,
Keystone of *Zimzum*, holy love, light.
But here among Corinthian pilasters
And ruined cages, rackrent corridors,
Where, by one reflex, beasts and men
To nature's primal lust were moved,

I stand in moonlight and klieglight
Among the lonely watchers, lonely,
Scavenging for touch or *soldi*.
See where Rome falls, and Israel: tryst
Of pagan and prophecy, where boils
The fluid world in one arena, hurled
By error in the animal —
The broken word, the broken arch.

tiberius' villa at capri

Yes, it's really emerald, the water.
The air is really scented.
Magic's no cliché, survives
the boredom of uncertain lives.
Sweet pine, cyclamen, fragrances
giddy and powerful as the view.

From this height, amongst these smells,
who could not, would not be charmed
to vice, who'd want to stir again,
conquer an army or manipulate
an empire, a business?

Of course, it's all a jumble now,
brown rock, limestone, lizards, shards.

But pock-marked Tiberius had it soft
and easy, here indulged
and set the style for ages:
grandees, panders, vacationists.

It's hard to think of anything at all.

The great green water wraps
the senses up, and purple cliffs
forever at the vanishing point
have something, surely, to say —
but *what*? Perhaps that Prospero
will come and wave it all away.

color & sound (naples)

Across the bay
the volcano gathers
rusty scarves
around its neck.
One white ship
moves trance-like on the gray
spidery wake
of the white moon.
In the pines
on the cliff
leaning to the sea
over the yellow caves
warbling goldfinches
able to melt
the heart. Cactus
& date palm do
not stir. Breath
held—a roar
then (blow
torches by the
million?) bursts. The
U.S. carrier
propellers.

almonds like pink snow

I have never seen anything like this dense pink snow
Of almonds blossoming on the hillsides
And valleys in the province of Valencia
In January. The world is a promising place
Even for pessimists and spinsters
With head-colds along the Mediterranean.
Where oranges hang their gold and lemons their yellow
Under a sky starched almost like lace
Anything is possible, for all seasons are one,
Eternal summer and sun
Coaxing the trees to bloom four times a year.

What is wrong with this picture?
Do not expect me to distort the facts.
Much as I love mimosas clustering villas
And all the paraphernalia of the south,
When I focus my camera here and there
On some scene, say, with the *fico d'India*
Thrusting its swords, in the foreground, by a rolling coast,
And all the palms, almonds, persimmons imaginable,
There is always some face in a ragged cap,
Someone on a mule, indifferent or smiling,
Getting into the lens. He may not be as unhappy
As his clothing looks. He may live in a cave—
Every traveler knows
The hillsides and cliffsides are thick with them,
As much as with these dense pink snows—
But still he is smiling, and his photo
Comes on picturesque. This is the south,
And those rags and wrinkles of the peasantry,
What are they but part of the natural scenery
As far as anyone is concerned? It would be
Phoney were I or you
To confess that they have spoiled our fun.
We are as tough as anyone.
Now the picture's almost complete.
Anything missing? Listen; in the distance
Something like thunder in the sun.
I won't be boring and claim it's a gun,
Although that's been known to happen. The day
Is clear, so it can't be a storm.
But the peasants around here
Are whispering. They say
It's the end of the world—and they should know.
Still, they keep on working, and the almond trees
Look more than ever like pink snow.

on the steps of the castillo

El sueño de la razon produce monstruos

1

On the steps of the *castillo*,
Belvedere of balustrades
White and Moorish, out to the sea,
Percht on faulted honey slabs
Aslant like muskets at the sun,
And coalblack dories drunk on diamonds
Reeling, hauling studded squid
In weedy nets, I sat in Spain
At the dead end of the year
Gathering like catch in a seine
Focus from the multiple air.

2

The sun scattered those diamonds
Like coruscations of castanets
Over the sinewy blue belly
Of the sea; while one great rock rose,
The fat fin of a whaleshaped isle
Between the horizon, where a steamer dipt
Down, and the date palm lanes along
The shore. My hand smelled sweet when I
Rubbed my face, sweet with the sun.
I sat in meditation:
Ego, mutability.

3

Impermanence of world, O, see
Lives flitter, dazzling, in the eye:
Bare figures sunned on sand dunes, gulls
Coasting—smoke and foam. The days
Dwindle, darken and die out
Alarmingly, as I get on.
You say, "It's just the winter light."
Ah, but you're right. . . . My summers, too.
They're faster than a camera click.
The winter light is mental. That
Makes the sensual pace run quick

The winter light—but more than mental
Light is metaphysical.
Such light shines incombustible.
And Man is more than mineral.
That old man humming over flowerpots
As he waters them in the near-African blaze.
His light is a brief brittle tinkle
Over the big hibiscus blossoms,
Not like the noon with a roaring smash.
His dark Iberian fingers strum
The ivory rind of a calabash.

5

I see him hourly withering,
A sprig of Spain, the tortured tree.
Yet light is blossoming from his skull.
His *Adioses* fly like birds,
He hums farewell in diminished thirds.
Half his age, twice his desire,
I see what's tangible on fire,
What does not burn is the mystery.
If mind is light, then flesh is dark.
So from the two we shape to free
Combustible chaos of the heart.

Darkness of the flesh is rich
To trap the light enclosed in it,
As the vert velvet of a peach
Enclaves the intellectual pit
That, unfleshed in the fleshiest soil,
With unrehearsed response will turn,
Groping like an idea upwards,
Stone blind seed, into a tree,
When the sunlight encloses it.
But that tight seed breaks out free
When light of winter falls on it.

And now, this scene. The winter light
Fell on sand, on terraces, on hair,
On the white hair of a woman
In the doorway, on her horny nails.

And that old woman came out to us, singing,
'Ah, que c'est beau—' in the fine day
Standing among the tables, her only
Tooth saucily glistening;
And added then: 'de chier dans l'eau—'
In a voice like a loose string
On an antique cembalo.

<h2 style="text-align:center">8</h2>

She went on with the bawdy song, she spat
And took a seat in the glare. She sat
Knitting and spitting till the guests
Rose one by one. Then turned to me,
That ancient Spanish adventuress,
Grinned, 'Oiga!' and patted my knee.
'Obligaciones—' she cackled, 'tomarlas
y dejarlas!' Take 'em—and leave 'em. What she
Thought of responsibility.
The pension guests refused to stay.
But that old sorceress was free.

<h2 style="text-align:center">9</h2>

Or was she? When the letter came
All blatantly embossed in black,
Her horny hands, her fear-stained eyes
Hung for a moment in some near abyss
The sun could not cancel nor murmured lies.
'My son, my son!' her cacklings clacked
Like the knitting needles that grew slack
And dropped, as I tore, with pity's knife,
The envelope. Relief! relief!
It was her brother, turned ninety-nine.
But death had fingered the afternoon.

<h2 style="text-align:center">10</h2>

Death, the ego's blank—and change,
Incurable! mind's dim disease!
What motion but the withdrawing mind
Can halt the process of the dead
And hold it in eternal light?
I asked this question of the soul
Scratching for truth as in a hole
Back in the brain where secrets slept
And would, if secrets could be kept,

Send out a private husht response.
But no voice spoke, not even once.

11

Here now upon the Spanish coast
Where the sea's fist beats the shore
As children beat a waterlogged rat,
The foreigners down from the twisted North
Copulate and lie in the sun:
German exiles move and thrive,
Welcomed by palms and real estate,
Who slasht at the human soul, who splash
Contented in the winter waves.
The Spanish laborers dream of cash
And the nordic girls who blondely bathe.

12

Dead end of the year, in Spain:
And Spain is *spina*, spine, thorn,
Is pain—the hard and barren ground,
Tough land the harrow lacerates
To plough and furrow bloody tears.
Is bullrings and the broken horse
Who can't cry out his neighing fear:
The victim's vocal chords are cut
Before the sacrifice—who'll hear
The Virgin in the horse's heart
When the horn strikes and the crowds cheer?

13

Is lotteries, the blind, and lust;
Saints with severed breasts, lopped limbs;
Gaunt Christs hanging in museums
More limp and lessened and despaired
Than Goya's gutted stumps of flesh
Stuck on a tree; is black for dress,
For nuns and crones and nothingness;
Is *Nada* in the human dream
Of reason, from which monsters spring;
Is seven deadly sins that stream
With slippery faces and bat wings;

14

Murky monstrances, stone aisles
Where sunlight splinters like a knife
The clotted soul; is a cathedral
Close where clasped hands claw for life;
And is the innocence of the drowned,
The far gone whom no fire can touch,
Whose lot is labor like a sea
They breathe, over which they cannot rise;
Is death deep in the casual day
Buried in the bland delights
Of looking and touching time away.

15

On the steps of the *castillo*
I sat within the waning year,
The long pale light that starcht the blue
Rinsed every object, carved it clear,
Laid out the body of the world
Upon the yellow slabs of rock,
An old corpse flowering decay,
All senses stopt, no sound, no ear,
No song in the throat, no melody,
But a slow moaning in the air,
But an old rolling of the sea.

16

And this was beautiful, I saw,
Where belvedere and balcony
Gave each impoverished señor
Blue wave, blue air, blue seignory
Over his blood and thunder soil.
And he would have the long sad look
Of crucifixions carved in wood;
But when the flame has touched the stick
Of tinder where his body lies,
None to its rhythm leaps more quick.
Resurrection sprouts in his thighs.

an episode from procopius

(During the reign of the Emperor Justinian, whose general, Belisarius, besieged and captured Gelimer, the Vandal King of Africa, thereby restoring that continent to the Roman Empire after ninety-six years of Vandal domination)

I

I, Gelimer, on a hill in Africa,
Recently come to my senses, although it is late,
At the end of my kingdom and my years,
Have this to offer to the world: make peace.
A rough barbarian, I tell you this.
Make peace. The hunger in my guts is wild,
My gums clack like palm fronds cracking,
But I come from a strong race. I have learned,
In my extremity, to laugh at strength.
To you, Belisarius, who ask my head,
I reply: Thanks. Not yet. Give me leave,
Rather, for as long as I can hold out
Against your legions, lord of Byzantium,
To beg three things: a lyre, a sponge, a loaf of bread.
Bread, because it is our savage need.
A sponge, because one eye is swollen from dirt.
A lyre, to accompany an ode I made
Upon my sore affliction, to make men weep.
This is what I have learned, who have seized the world
From Rome, bent Italy to her knees, made Caesars
Stain with yellow all their purple front.
Make peace.

II

I saw this morning on Mount Papua
A sight that drove all kingdoms from my head.
It made me laugh so hard, weak as I was,
That painful laughter put an end to war.
A Moorish woman, black as pitch, had scratched
Some grains of corn from somewhere, and had baked
On the hot embers of a hearth, a cake
No bigger than a coin. Beside her watched
Her little son and my small nephew, parched
And shriveled with desire, with eyes like teeth.
My nephew seized it first, and though it still smoked
With flame and ash, he thrust it between his jaws.

He would have swallowed it, but the other, choked
With rage of famine beat him, tore his hair,
Until the prize disgorged from the burnt throat
Fell into the black boy's, and he swallowed quick.
And so, dear Belisarius, I came out
To you as you see me now, still laughing hard.
Take Africa. Such prizes make me sick.

roman ghetto

*Del Popolo d'Israele Sei Milioni le Innocenti Vittime in Europa del
Bieco Odio Razziale*

I

We are not loud. Our women dress in black,
Their hair tight and decorous, some beautiful.
We should be ugly or presumptuous,
          if it were true
What they say of us. But our dignity
Was not bought, we never connived
          like upstart princes
For an empire, whose guest we are.
They fenced us here, untitled, contraband.
What we are, we earned.
Our seven-branched candlestick lies in mud
Of the river by whose banks we pray.

In groups, embracing, at the iron gate
Of the synagogue, in the November dusk,
Here on the left bank of the Tiber,
By the date palms and plane trees,
Subdued, fresh from worship, we stand
In the old ghetto quarter, unpromised land.
We have come a long way.
If you ask, we could not tell
Where we have come from;
          we know only
That it is winter, that we light our candles
For the dead, we marry, cold and hunger
And exile divide, destroy.
          Where are we going?

To dinner, radios and children.
        Were we bitter,
Different and deformed, that caricature,
That lying nose scrawled on Europe's walls,
Should we, then, be so different, target
Of barbarian 'virtues'?
        Some recall
The journey in the desert, the rock that flowed,
The sea that spread an avenue hedged by waves
Suspended and trembling till we crossed
        the Red Sea bed.
        That was long ago; we do not pretend
Such importance now. There was no sea
That split, no mountain and no street
Of miracles, manna for memory
Here, by the busy shops
Where hanks of wool for mattresses
Hang like white hair
        and Octavia's Portico
With wounded pillars
Darkens by sides of beef
        and creaking palms.

Only the whispers in the kitchen,
The prayer in the closet.
Silence and defiance,
        and everyone confused.
Only the disaster
        without reason;
The fire and slander
        without an avenger;
Confusion without a prophet,
Squalor without a goal.
After the mourning, the freezing of hearts;
After the shame, the shred ends of decency.
        How long can a lie endure?
Two thousand years now we have crossed the river,
Over the Bridge of the Four Heads,
        Ponte de' Quattro Capi,
Worn smooth and faceless by wind,
Older than the emperors,
By wind, rain, touch;
And we going to market across the river,
Whose arms embrace the Island,

To market and to prayer. When
        will this end? When
Will the lie cease to devour
Our faith, older than most histories?

II

What are angels? We are not angels.
Our flesh, like bread, turns ash and coal
If we are baked, bones break in the ditch.
The wind howls through our ignorance.
If the essences
Of spirit speak to us, with staff and sword,
They speak to remind us: "You who are chosen
Cannot choose. You made the Lord,
The Lord of Hosts, and are the host
To Heaven, conscience of the Ghost.
(And we are cut to bits who wrestle most.)
Israel, striver with God, the devil
Will not give an inch, will sacrifice
Your seed and harvest till God rise
And spread his rainbow like a cloak
Of many-colored light upon your eyes."

III

We, I say we, I mean I: not race,
Nor nation, color, but sole self, dark
In cellar-hole hiding, cold
Where no light is; unloved, loved
One, open to glance and gesture,
Embrace and the struck face.
One, whirled out of Babylon
Beyond the waterclocks and stars,
Papyrus, camels and bulrushes,
Tablets of Sinai, knife of the cross.

From the Chaldean journey to the rock
Where Isaac knelt his head and the cleaver
Shook, from the beard of the patriarch,
And the slime-sown valleys of Noah,
The olive-dove and the salt-turned-wife,
I mean I, mouthing the bitter way,
Grape gone vinegar in the teeth,
And my Lebanon turned to gall.

When the tablets broke on the mountain,
After the lightning and holy anger,
Plague struck, the covenant cracked,
I could not pray. I have been praying.
I remember the fate of saints.
The circumcision stigmata
Running from the creative wound
Of God's finger, organ of birth.
The pain of my knowing wakes my death,
I make my death my life.

We, I mean One. I am that I am,
Of Jehovah and the prophet's loin,
Lean messiah and blood of the Lamb
Over the waters, world's egg,
Whale sperm and the field's clover.
I was there, bare, unfurled in prayer
As nude as light when light shone
Through chaos, and I was the only One.

ameana

(After Catullus)

Ameana, worn out like any other
Tart, has had the nerve to request one hundred
From me—that slob with the flat ugly nose,
The mistress of the tramps of Formia!
You, her relatives, in whose charge the girl is,
Call together doctors and friends: she is not
Sane, that girl, and never asks of the mirror
What she looks like—what an imagination!

beauty

(After G. G. Belli)

Come and have a look at my grandmother's beauty:
She has two feet of flesh under her throat;
It's dry and flaky like a Danish pastry;
It shakes and shivers more than a rowboat.

She has enough teeth left to munch soft crumbs;
Her eyes have got lost somewhere in a husk of skin;
And her nose, O the poor lady! ignoring her gums,
Holds deep converse with her bearded chin.

Arms and legs are delicate fan-sticks;
Her voice the broken croak of frog and fife:
Her breasts, flat water-bags where liquid drips.

Well, my grandmother was beautiful when young.
And you, in due time, if I am not wrong,
Will look much worse than even that, good wife!

reflections in the water

That love and hate are bred
In the same nest of worms
Mothered by muddy doubt in the head
Sired by blood storms,
I sat and cried by the river bank
Where the lacy lights were weaving
Rigmaroles on a black silk world
Of rippled palaces upside down,
Like the actual world, I said.

In this reflected state
Of pearl and ebony
Flood-lit, and bridges with bird-wing arcs
Where statues never sink but float
Like gondolas upon the dark
And motorcars are velvet swans
Misbegotten upon the rivery flood

Spread in anarchistic indolence,
In this calm nether state
Who would believe it if one wept
To find himself upon the brink
Of drowning in appearances,
The eye by tears sucked down
The electric liquid, swirling domes,
The tooled rococo pleasances.

And if this figure likewise runs
By imagination grained
As the mirror of the world
To a night-struck fanciful
Flowing through a city's streets,
Let each aching sense recall
How love made it once
Hate and weep upon a bridge's wall
For venomous veins had turned
Doubt to treachery
And innocence woke within a noose
To find too late the water close
Around its candid head,
Harangued by bubbles, mocked by moss,
Rejected by stones and bruised by fish.
Let the drowned senses bear
The toppling tale
Of how their trusting thrills
By deception hooked
Were pulled down to the swill
Beneath the showy skin,
The furor of blind worms
In river slime beneath the black
Silk rigmaroles of palaces.

meditation over snow

When we rode in chairs like yachts
Over snow-breakers, wakes and crests of pearl,
Sliding through whiteness in mountain passes,
Cypress and cedar furred like bears,
An ocean numbed in ermine, light-stunned, rolled
Away to cold horizons
By ski-trails tracked, wrinkling waves running,
And banked against the sky in a snow-swell
Its polar frost in hilly floes
That packed the world in a spell of ice.

When we sailed in a chair to the top of the light
On a powdery surf, we shed our weight,
Then time fell back
To the town clad in a cloud, in a valley
Vapored and misty, overhung
With veils of the bog and the stealthy moss
Of the gray-green fog that clung
To chimneystacks and smoke
Of the anxious engines in the discolored land—
Oh, did we sail upon icicles like cut gems,
Tread a live wire, hiss like a keel
On the keen straits of flakes,
Gliding on diamonds in noonday!

What is it, snows, we move through
When the high seas of the massif lift us
Into the white air? A sphere of absence,
Glissando realms of a glacier kingdom
Where no color is, no, nothing to break us
Out of the calm of the heart.
Here's drowning dumbness muffling matter
To sink within, steep fathoms, clean sweeps of bays
And glacial capes of feldspar silences,
Hushed oceans combing continents,
Stillness, absolute of elements,
Monosyllable of mass,
Holy ghostliness and doveness
Laying its wing's oneness over beastliness!

We move through sacramental fleece
Where struggling beasts burn red and black,

Where only snows congeal the flood and mire
Alone of all the raging elements
To pour wide signature of absolution
From azure embassies, some cloudwrapped hand
That signs assurances of peace.
The snow's white flag waves spiritual wands.

Thick fumaroles of the globe fissuring upwards
Summon our ghostly gaze with abstract look.
Are they propitiations, blood-sacrifices?
From such glittering gaiety who'd be torn?
Let the snowmastered universe abound!
Let there be light of snow only around us,
Let there be nothing but snow, and the sift of it,
The drifting parable of upper reaches,
The highest peak where the snowman hangs in the eaves
Hammered by his hands and feet to a cross of ice
Where thorns bleed crystal stars, and the earth
Falls from his eminence down paths of edelweiss
Pale as the lily, and the worm sings in the lily horn!

christmas in positano

I

Tomorrow will be Christmas.
The *cosmatesco* church
with its dome of checkered tiles
is being prepared for the holy birth
presepio and *parroco* are ready
everything follows the pattern
of prayer and propitiation—
the god born for the people's need
the virgin mother risen from antique mists
to give her son to the faithful that they may eat him and drink him
and thus assure a good harvest of lemons and babies
and in Spring a bumper crop of tourists.

So nature compensates: the head cut off
from the rest of her parts is forced to wander
all her dimensions for some final clue
to its real home, swinging in space

in a vicious orbit from which it can't break free
mirroring the restless planets novas nebulae
in broad or narrow movements without satisfaction
always on the make for its origin
always rolling against the mystery
like an eyeball blinded by light
and mistaking it for darkness.
Your fictions, Science, that come true
are not enough. The head seeks its body.
The body seeks its soul
—something vaster than space.
This is what these peasants are saying
who know the taste of superstition
but also the taste of intuition—*pazienza!*
Word filled with reincarnations
drenching body and soul like wafer and wine
on which these old women get tipsy
as they kiss the crucifix dribbling hopes
over the feet of holy images
aglitter with coins tapers brocades:
on withered bones whose incorruptible wounds
sweat miracles of manna to heal the dying
displayed in showcases of devotion
O Sant' Andrea, punisher of pirates,
who drowned the Saracens in blue tides of Amalfi!

> Cathedral of the south
> *your ceramic smile in the sun*
> *your fabulous ambo   your marble*
> *heraldic leviathan*
> *ingesting prophets and fluked seabeasts*
> *translucent mystiques*
> *paraded in a bazaar of relics*
> *I submit my imagination to your baroque*
> *altars and dense incense of chanting censers*
> *in return   o villages   for your grace*
> *of sunstruck stucco and mica mazes*
> *your infinite gold patience*
> *enlacing space*

Sunflower towns turning towards light!
Disasters wars poverty—you have known them all
but you do not sit hugging the darkness
believing it is the light.

You're not a city nursing your sick stone
great brain full of dope.
But you're Christmas-stars with scarlet petals
poinsettia burning by fat love-leaves
philodendrons, churchbells foliating
clusters of bronze
clapperclumps of tones
blooming in chimed air!
You're a green surprise!
Myths in odors and stems!
Races in rank roots! herbal
memorials! O quiet forms
that never doubt! mystic
fountains of verbs!

II

Torpedoes, campaniles, dogs.
Christmas *festa* of loud devotion.
Rain. Thunderclapped hills.
Grottoes stinking of ass-dung
perfect the scene for the supposed birth
although there are no stars.
A wet evening for the nativity.
But sparklers ease nature's distempers
which the children hurl into her tears.

> Salute the man who failed
> Unreason crying in the void
> to the All-father whose silence pressed
> the suffering sun-child
> underground to the guts of the worm
> to grow again in the carolling word

Failure is no loss—it's the flag of Good
humility's stemma on the wood of blood
where time must yield
whiteness of bones before the white light
of the painless infinite.

III

As I walked the beach at Positano
where keeled boats like stranded fish
lay blanched by bodiless lockers
and loverless sands drank down

the cool bright tides
parabolas rolled at my feet like dice
in dissolved numbers of foam!

Such threshed surfs, crashing cumuli, cloudsmash
of the sea, mistletoed moonlight! distillations-of-drift!
streaming veils, diaphanous
flailings of skullfloods the sea transposes
from pouring marble graves!
when the moon stood out of the clouds over the pale waves
well after midnight, and the still villas looked down from the hills.

Translucent darkness a lunar sun illuminates
where gold is dreaming green and soon about to wake!

—I think of churning ice and steam of snow. . . .

As I walked the beach at Positano
under the high mass of the silver
cathedral shining like coins
coves and shadows echoed
voices organs and spun pearl
the selves of the world flowed
into one dreamhole
for the space of a vision
when the cold rolling ciphers
summed like hairs of the head
Imagination was reality
to dance with the dead
in the trance of a ghost
until the Absolute come down
into the human form
to raise the mental up
and build another body there!

IV
Coda

What cosmic voyages are
yet in store for
the inward explorer
whereas to whiz
                    in space
        is an evasion

"the ultimate to which we must turn"
being within not in pursuit
of metals   machines   or the moon
        or the sun itself
but always within   the depth
        under the reason

not "an ass bearing
        a load of books"

but the power of seeing

Darkness & light together
        in one man as in many
as I stood by the luminous breakers
when the clouds parted over the great cliffs
& shed an uncanny glow
as if the waves were lit from below

the moment of birth   the god's
        moment come down
into the human darkness
to mix with it
                & make it shine
        in the heart
of matter
        light
in mineral
        dark

i heard evtushenko

"Today, in my country, it's the people who choose their poets and who, by their demand, determine the publication of their works. This certainly has an economic significance, but also political. . . . It's popular demand that counts." Evtushenko, interview in Les Lettres Françaises, 14.II.63.

I heard Evtushenko in Paris . . .

He looked so American —
over sixfoottall — sandyhaired
smiling casual rawboned gray sweater
golden boy from a tractor in Kansas
from a field of corn —
here on a stage in Paris . . .
five thousand people sobbing at the gates
police lines holding them back
making a chain of blue
to keep the mob from spilling
over parked cars . . .

Before he opens his mouth
the masses swallow him . . .
Before his words are out
the audience gulps him down
—for poetry? no . . . political vodka, rather . . .
He opens his mouth —
blast! flash! "barbaric splendor" kindles the blood —
wrong reasons burnt to cinders:
verbs exploding, flamethrowing nouns!
—old Boris Godunov
scooping the silver rubles
from a salver & scattering them
to the starving crowds
—surf-surge over sandcastled ears!
sdr-r-rrasvitya . . . kr-rrutitsya . . .
ver-rrtitsya . . . ochi-chor-rrnya . . .

Ah, American poets . . .
afraid to roar —
who reason who pray who mumble
who yak clack & hack
joke & croak
who doubt

                    who shout
                                who howl
to break thru
insect indifference . . .

Burn down your terrible desks!
your cold fortress of ivy!
The leaves of your brain are entangled
in lenses of horn & the wispy mists
of lank hair!
& your graveyard of words & your tomb of convictions
mourned by dull fingernails
too blunted to scratch!
The iceberg looms out of your eyes
which no flame can blast
& no mescaline suns can illumine!
Those eyes built on slabs
of streaked marble & death
those eyes of New England
those eyes of cold poles in the moss
of the liveoak
with icicle glint overhanging
our feelings like knives . . .

O American poets to whom nobody listens!
who don't sell 100,000 copies in one day!
who don't give the people what they want!
But you—smokers of the freedom weed
(not the opium pipe of the Kremlin
nor psychochemical cigars of the Pentagon)
Electromagnetic Poets of Nuclear Vision
asking unbearable questions: Is God a virus?
Am I the fourth dimension in the collage of World Mind?
With no mystical feelings about the workers or leaders;
you warn against leaders,
no government's good enough for you.
This is not a political poem.
This is a person-to-person poem
on fists & knees
—long distance . . .

Memoirs of Evtushenko on the sidewalks . . .
Evtushenko's in the decadent West!
Outside they sell *The Communist Manifesto*

& inside the chained bear growls . . .
Evtushenko I don't dig your speaking to this Century.
Besides they're making such noise I can't hear a word you're saying.
Oh, stop raving about bread & plowshares!
Stop nagging me
to quit sneering & get off my ass & shake things up
—that broad hint—that fiction from Hicksville . . .
And forget, please, your large expense account
forget the people who are behind you.
Tomorrow they'll be against you.

But remember if you're a poet
remember Mayakovsky soviet-suicide
& Essenin flipped on a bullet
& Pasternak JAILED in his dacha . . .
Can you forget the Writers Union? the plenum is wagging its finger!
How can you be so optimistic? are you really a Pavlov reflex?
Don't you get tired of Swan Lake? Ulanova's growing older . . .
It's Paris, where the *Rite of Spring* made a real Revolution!
Diaghilev gnashing his teeth in the grave . . .
& I danced the Polevetskian Dances in 1940
speaking high school French in the Yakovlev Russian Ballet
& mamma danced the kasatska in Coney Island with gold-braided hair
& said, "Don't trust duh Russians, doity rotten anti*semitts*!"
poor Brooklyn jews behind in the rent—

. . . I think of Antonin Artaud—
he made the French language spurt blood
raking arteries & veins
swept them clean of world shit
unleashing animal cries snarls grunts yelps
CACA   KRA   PEK   e
mangled tortured flips hurled at society

> *o reche modo*
> *poh ertsin*
> *ke tula*

HORROR!
THE SOUND BENEATH THE SOUND
SOUNDING MAD BLACK DEPTHS

of the sexual dance
of death

truth of the body
the thread winding from mouth to asshole
screaming
        GOD IS SHIT!
          GOD IS A VIRUS!
            GOD IS MICROBES!
    a dance
    of RAGE
      bona
      bouala
      bouraca
rage for the icicle tooth of Siberia
in caves & deserts of jackals
where a chemical moon of metallic silence
sees black sounds drift from poisoned bones

—timetable of future
             tectonic
                catastrophe—
in the brain's nightmare
of terminal need . . .
the "victim at the stake
signaling thru the flames"

language of hallucination
from the skull of Lorca & Rimbaud
—killed by truth!

Truth!
"what I'm fighting for . . ." Thou sayst—
agitprops, posters, slogans, feedback!
Meanwhile Pravda is screaming at you—
"High time for Evtushenko to face the truth!"
And the Writers Union is yelling: *Expel him! Expel him!*
For truth
is not political . . . o sad schizophrene
between art & the sickle guillotine . . .

Truth is water, running & changing.
Zen buddhist truth is satori
Aztec truth is death
for the junky truth is a fix
for Hollywood the Box-office is sublime truth!
Reason was truth once

God was truth
Beauty was truth
once.
I have seen truth fail.
War is the truth of our Century . . .

When I saw the mobs, loudspeakers & flash bulbs
& the beautiful filmstar Tierzieff reading
your poems in French—elegant hood—
I confess I envied you I began to pant a bit for glory . . .
Crushed in the crowd I studied the student faces
eyes of hammer-&-sickle
whispering or silently looking
or whistling fragments of Shostakovich

—I was a student in Brooklyn
hung up on Beauty, Marx & the Workers
with pockets blooming pamphlets of conditioned images
I almost signed up for Murmansk on a Liberty Ship for a thousand
        dollars
but Salome kept me at the Met with her ghostly glockenspiel
& a girl kept me out of imperialist war in her communist bed
& I took my B.A. & WPA—

All that pompous belief!
rhythmic chanting & applause!
uplift! public orgasm!
orgy of faith!
wanting the dangerous plunge beneath appearance
to flow out of oneself, to merge
into universal trance
in the ritual that expresses mystery—
& Hitler used this desperate urge
in his Nazi truth, the disease of history!

O great sounds! O triple-syllable rhyme!
But a truth that is not truth?
No! I won't have it! The sad lie
of the poet's naive faith—the anthill is not noble!
The State is not God!
Committees of insects to judge the poem!
Jump from the window! Blow out your brains!
The armored tank rolls over your words . . .

Listen—
I'm the individual
member of a party of One . . .
Fuck your social lie! the lie of the many
the many in which I panicked
feeling my bowels go soggy, my identity drowned in the herd
had to push my way to the end of the street to stand alone & get some air
Is this your truth Evtushenko? zombies at the wheel?
Generals covered with medals & murder?
I'm talking to you Evtushenko
not to Komsomolskaya Pravda.

There in the vast hall of the Mutualité
a Chinese boy
crippled in both legs
with sunglasses & inward-slanting eyes
lapped up your words from the loudspeaker
& limped to a table to applaud
& a tall ugly pimpled young woman with intense frown & white lips
compressed, head bent as you roared, she's got some dream of poetry
like religion like salvation like politics
like what she really needed was a lay
raising her desperate eyes to ogle handsome kids
in spite of poetry & salvation (perhaps she dreams of a gangbang)
& the peculiar parched neurotic face of a lone
man with gray beard & torn pants, crazy poet perhaps,
striding up & down looking in the mirror
measuring himself against all that mass hysteria
& a thin dark youth in rags with long hair & mad stare—
groping himself in the dark
keeps saying "Je suis malade" & coughs hoping it's blood—
some youthful cornball crap of glory mid psychosis—
This is your Twentieth Century . . .
just a few faces in the crowd
anxious & miserable
wanting to hear poetry
for poetry is
speaking self to self
over long-distance wires . . .

There in the vast hall of the Mutualité
where thousands grazed you in Paris
wanting it straight from the balls
(& for *Babi Yar*, shalom aleichem!

yourself later accused of "treacherous split" by the Party)
you missed the great goof boat
absurd irrational truth
like a tail hidden under your pants!
like the selves of a self
like coffee cups floating
& words floating
as astronauts float in space
the free-floating cut-up word that is YOU —
jumping from star to star
with kaleidoscope eyes of a fly —
trillions of Third Eyes! intergalactic subliminals!
all one Big I! & Who are YOU?
can you shatter in a flash the taped groove-think?
become someone else? *I is someone else!*
like the Indian who's the reincarnation
of Jesus Christ & Sir Isaac Newton
& wants the Nobel Prize for having discovered
"the sun is actually stone cold and not boiling hot"
& keeps writing each year to Sweden
asking for the money . . . stoned on bhang!
Wear a uniform? the tail sticks out — obscenely —
the tail of eyes . . .

& ourselves intersect in spacetime
in the garden of forking paths
where we are all One
& the Eternal Gardener is taking a little snooze
dreaming us up . . .

Yes, yes . . . a wiggy nap . . .
& the Dreamer's a cat called — Who?

Tonite in my drab gray room
smelling of kif & garlic
smelling of maté & nerves
& imagined lays
pulled off the streets & into the groaning bed
9 Rue Gît-le-Coeur where I'm cold & lonely
& getting no younger
among fantasies vegetables poverty & garbage
tonite I read of your strange country
in that Bible of modern insanity
the Paris Herald-Tribune February 18, 1963

"as a reprisal for smuggling manuscripts out to the West . . .
60-year-old Tarsis foresaw his own doom in 'The Bluebottle,'
a novel describing the fate of a non-conforming intellectual . . .
warning that he might be certified insane in accordance with
a well-known Russian custom . . . The spokesman for . . .
publishing house . . . information came . . . 'several reliable
sources' . . . declined to identify . . ."

I read this as I was writing my poem to you
with mourning fingernails
Evtushenko
This is history
so I'm recording this
that it be not forgotten
not murdered with musical phrases
—drugged Pasternak in his dacha dreaming of smorgasbord
a sad farewell I remember it well—
to you who say you're sometimes bugged
by the same things as
the hoods of the world
too hip to be conned,
hoods of America
teddy boys of England
teppisti of Italy
blousons noirs of France
halbstarke of Germany
raggare of Sweden
nozem of Holland
stilyagi of Russia
with their black hatred of lies
banks & cashiers
governments & politics
schools religions armies bombs . . .

But my irony cannot break the wall
they are building around your poem . . .
The bluebottle is buzzing you.

Paris: Feb.-April, 63

kick the dead! on which you're hooked with conditioned images—fedback obeah of sleep on the precipice—«voodoo by which zombies are con, son»—decayed syntax of ancient experience—Kick the habit of experience—grammar no longer viable for me—grooved cells in the brain, opening—Kick automatic timeforms, travel electromagnetmind—contact space to magic & telepathy—kick 2000 years of false egos—

Open the door—OUT! repeal the labyrinth—«mash the styles» as Lorca says, «painting with the dick.» painting with knees, ass—the sculpture as passport— «geometrical assurances» left behind, demon identity hidden beneath the spoken word the song borders of Death & Time—passport issued to Artist by the «path to word Awareness.» The Only Way. Identity hidden beneath wordblock.

Break thru the Singer—I is some one—The old fools—personality—a joke of the Ego only, that is the idea sung by skeletons who—since time immemorial—sing of brass—Wake you One-eyed Intellects! (those millions of zombies are controlled.)

Technical artists hip—meet at last the oldest key in the door—We are all the Key—can apply our total Know of metaphysics—turn key in the ass— Science Metaphysics Art meet Everyone—Walk thru this meetingpoint thru knowledge which will destroy U—cut thru word art at given habit point that is YOU—Pavlov-reflex pression point—built in structured nervous syst that is YOU terminably repeated & reflected Word-Image conditioned by greed—break reflex self inherited from a liminal could not work because it built repeated & reflected «your» ideas—see sound smell touch the SILENCE behind non-languge—See the Language of Ang—found to overlap subliminals who want to taste flow together—

Irate citizen from Hicksville: «Nuts! Bunch of crazies! These criminals wanna undermine our funeral! sacred institutions!»

«If ya wanna hang back with the apes—» I tell him coldly. «I've drawn you a map. But you'll have to read it your own archaic senile self! I will not pull your sloppy ass to western satori.»

Current language so impotent-thinking-habit-fixated on abuse—cut-words shatter groove-think—babel falls—emerge experiments in the rubble— writing on these ruins: New—riting have lagged half-century behind—no «accident»—even Voltaire at the end concluded: «CHANCE IS A WORD» TAKE A CHANCE IN THE VOID—LEAP! LET GO! no limit & no finite logic mind can reach—

KNOW THY SELF was writ over HAROLD HAROLD NORSE PARIS ORACLE!

calling all geniuses

FROM . . . reliable reports . . . received by psychedelic nervous commu-
nications . . . system . . . the usual supernatural broadcast wavicles . . .
from outer dimensional channels . . . EARTH . . . is scheduled for Apoc-
alyptic Holocaust . . . on September 13 . . . 1968 . . . this can result from
destruction of upper atmosphere . . . by roulette bomb . . . or giant aster-
oid . . . may take a bead . . . on us . . . immediate consequences thus far
to be considered among the Unknowables . . . magic circles everywhere
. . . keep busy at thought-transmitters . . . wiring instructions ritualistically
. . . just to stay in the act . . . prophets of every degree . . . from phoney to
adept . . . scurry antlike among pages of . . . I Ching . . . Kabbala . . .
Tibetan Book Of The Dead . . . Mayan Codices . . . The Secret Doctrine
. . . Subud . . . Tarot . . . Isis Unveiled . . . & other occult texts
. . . in quest of useful intelligence . . . trance is advised for all . . . who
would like to mutate . . . painlessly . . . it is advisable not to feel . . . or
think . . . most are in this respect prepared . . . at least sufficiently anaes-
thetised . . . by poisoned condition . . . of awareness mechanism . . . con-
ditioning factors . . . to confront reality . . . with disbelief . . .

CALLING ALL GENIUSES   CALLING ALL GENIUSES   CALL-
ING ALL GENIUSES

Scene: The Milky Way Academy

Prof. Vishnu (assuming the shape of benign genius): Science & clairvoy-
ance approach identical insight . . . intuition provides both with accurate
. . . information on miraculous nature of being . . . thus enlarged fotos . . .
of invisible micro-organisms . . . which I have produced . . . after years of
research . . . present a remarkable similarity to the work of the best non-
objective artists . . . logical training . . . as Dr. St George observed . . . blinds
scientists to powers latent . . . in mind's eye . . .

Precocious Student (scribbling hastily): what about Apocalypse huh . . . ?

Prof. V. (filling kif pipe with katami): awareness is attained . . . by making
the mind blank . . . this can be achieved by meditation . . . or repetition of
mantram . . . or fucking yourself silly . . . the latter method . . . in view of
imminent crisis . . . & prevailing conditions . . . is advisable to all . . . with
equipment still . . . unimpaired . . .

P.S. (scribbling hastily): would you repeat the last sentence please . . . ? OK
. . . what happens then? . . . after the mind is blank . . . what about Time
Death Reality . . . ?

Prof. V. (adjusting his laser beam fourth-dimension lenses): the dinosaurs . . . in the slime of the jurassic . . . are not without their counterparts today . . . if we are not fully aware . . . each second . . . by secret connection . . . with the flow of electrical energy . . . the life-force permeating . . . & permutating us . . . so that *we leave the body as in dream* . . . arriving . . . at a place . . . mapped out in dreams poems paintings . . . by hip cartographers . . . we are dissolved into wavicles . . . das ist alles . . . to put it another way . . . all knowledge is useless . . . that is not . . . self-knowledge . . .

P.S. (farting with excitement): herr professor . . . I mean . . . well . . . jesus christ . . . sir . . . when I'm stoned I think I know everything . . . some kinda universal telepathic language . . . clicks thru my head . . . I know what's in other people's minds . . . every word . . . every syllable & vowel . . . has tremendous significance . . . the walls slide . . . the floor heaves . . . I can see my own eyes . . . if ya get what I mean . . . my thoughts & images . . . if I catch them on paper . . . are pure connection with the Absolute . . . cosmic vibrations . . . next day it looks like shit . . . what's the good if you can't sustain it . . . I mean . . . trance . . . mescaline . . . mushrooms . . . pot . . . fourth dimension . . . LSD . . . ether . . . stroboscope . . . sutras . . . mudras . . . buddhi . . . slokas . . . mantras . . . meditation . . . masturbation . . . etc . . .

Prof. V. (metamorphosing progressively as he speaks . . . until at his last lines he fills the auditorium entirely with his thousand arms . . . his hundred eyes . . . his dongs . . . his heads . . .): you have 3 weeks before the final exam . . . this school is not called the Milky Way Academy for nothing . . . if you do not waken . . . gentlemen . . . by September 13 . . . you have never LIVED . . . this . . . then . . . is my last word . . . my hip manifesto . . . to you . . . I . . . professor Omar Vishnu . . . Scientific Poet Of The Superconscious . . . Magellan Of Metaphysics . . . Doctor Of Reality . . . Physicist Of Inner Space . . . Electroencephalographer In The Exploration Of Thought Phyla . . . Clairvoyant Radiologist . . . Medical Specialist In Functional Disturbances Of Faith In The Higher Primates After Puberty . . . Metempsychopathologist In Twentieth Century Diseases Of The Etheric Double . . . Alchemist Of The Word . . . Biochemist Of The Brain . . . First Degree Supersonic Mason . . . Adept In Mysteries . . . Cradled-In-Kundalini-With-The-Serpent-Fire-Up-My-Ass . . . Schooled-In-Shakti . . . Hierophant-In-Prana . . . Hip-In-Hereafter . . . On-The-Ball-In-Eternity . . . Master Mythoman . . . Medium-In-Ectoplasm . . . Table-Tapper-Doppelgänger . . . Catamite-In-Angel . . . Oracular Professor Of Visionary Mathematics . . . Demon-Dabbler-In-Divine-Abortion . . . Magus Of Is/Was/To Come . . . I say unto you . . . my last . . . word . . .

BLACKOUT

Beat Hotel, Paris 1961

restaurant

```
when
    in a restaurant
        ordering
    champignons à *la grècque*
            the waitress
        pushes it towards
me with a whiff
    of armpit
                    old
        goat pong
            i look at her
    & her peasant family
            talking in hoarse
    whispers
    a tribe     a clan     birthbound
        smug yet placed
                & personed


                        snow
        on the streets
        on the trottoirs
                    of this black
            french winter

i eat alone
```

paris

stood on the steel heart
of paris   gargoyles stuck out
    gray tongues
smiling an old man
came & kicked at the heart
saying *a fine night for secrets*!

    guitars unstrung the seine
students dived from le petit pont
     beer flowed under the bridges
gendarmes burned wax dolls
  o paris the eiffel tower sings
    of la gloire & peanuts!

      in the hotel
      you can smell
feet
      all the way
      to the top
floor

    outside the cafés of st. michel
hitch-hikers from cold countries
     draw in colored chalk
on the sidewalk
       neon crucifixions
      stone hair
       of girls

in the pinball air
  a rustle of levis
    a moisture of slacks
  like wheat in the wind
of western prairies

    bookshops & galleries
expose their wounds
    at cafe tables
  the artists dress them

arabs on the rive gauche
among parked trucks
  & stale piss

stare at the flux
dreaming of kif
      & soft fat fucks
paris city of cocksmen
striptease blondes with busy hips
city of night & ideas
false hair & paraffin tits
    nervous exhaustion
      a bout de souffle
boulevard of broken teeth
      & snarling flips
you've got cement in
      your cunt
           o bitter bitch!

in the 14th arrondissement
a mosque is weeping
& the santé
    grieves
the absence of genet

boys dance no more
with boys in boites
la reine blanche sob
    for blue jeans
  le fiacre
  is draped in black

    hang wreaths
  on the pissoirs

      (those
      that are left)

                            paris/ 1959

i arrive in malaga

i arrive in malaga

people are walking
  staring at shops

sitting in cafes
    movies
    ice cream
    movies
    coffee
    shoes

in tangier torremolinos athens

    marriage
    money
    movies
    children
    movies
    clothes

you've gotta hand it to them

they know how to tread
a tightrope
        between disasters

they sit at their meals & drinks
   gobbling
     gaping
       gossiping
giggling
      in boredom
but you've gotta hand it to them

they go on
   they go on
        sleepwalkers in deepfreeze
         on high tension wires

  never never
    never
     never

seeing the morning glory

                torremolinos/ 1961

greek customs

for Nanos Valaoritis

you could smell the salt over the fumes
& combustion as i wheeled
the old car into the square
near the white
ships
—rags of red eyes dripping doleful
unshakeable part of the landscape
lisping thru the booze
he sidles up for a handout
& we stand around in the big bare place
    waiting
        for the bored official
      who shifted his ass
    & smoked
        & sent out for coffee
          yakking
      with other bored officials
& after a long time
        noticed my presence
in a confusion of papers
        & passports
          & interruptions
    & sent me back
with forms
        to be signed

next day i drove
along the seafront road
old men on the beach
dragging nets
& wind from the sea
sunglint
on brown sand

& sure as death
& as full of useless information
    green gums clack a greeting
old kiss-of-death
      teary-eyed rattyhaired
& in we go to the slaughterhouse of the soul

and the form lies limp & lifeless on the counter ignored
by the great sea-elephant of a douanier who moves
in a wallow of piles & papers & looks blank over the
world of concrete metal & glass
                                    & time
                                                passes
i cease drumming my fingers
musing savagely

    if this isn't the perfect place in all the universe
    for practicing patience putting myself last holding
    to the center! what would Lao Tse do? speak
    o bearded ancient sage!
                                    he wouldn't own a car—

the sea-gorilla takes up the form
—no, it is no good—
something about 2 stamps
& the bastard ups & walks away
checks in a herd of krauts
    or swedes
        & i burn
            i burn with rage
                    & murder
                crushed by machinery
            by sly sadistic glee
    finito
        fini
                    purged on the path
                        to patience
                            & wisdom
            in the muddle of decay
        & concrete floor
                            & prisondrab walls
            red tape meaningless void
of soulless tyranny

                                            athens/ 1964

scenario for the anti-hero

kick him in the nuts again
the poor hurt bastard
        he doesn't know the score
because his smile is real
because he is broke
because he can feel

kick him in the nuts again
the poor decent slob
        he is looking for truth
because he is alone
because he shuts his eyes
because he will lose

kick him in the nuts
until he leaps wildly
among the dancing couples
until he falls
                unconscious
        out of the dream

                                athens/1964

the words you can taste a whole lifetime

voluptuous limpid golden gazelleschaft rumpelstiltskin
                                        fleece!
    hibiscus blossoms in the backyard
        my green aromatic boyhood
grass
moonlight
on the upright
piano on railroad ties
old negro gathers ice
chunks of sapphire gleam
soft coal locomotive tang
the lackawanna erie line
untranslatable wail of the train in the night
dripping on the wooden porch of the april rain

               fading doughboy
         snapshot &
                    victrola gloryhorn 1922
            red hot momma   hindustan
rasp in the furnished room
         sad green & blue
remember all alone & yesterdays
on the telephone
             seagreen tiles
      chlorine
               candybars
               wurlitzers
                             S
                             T
                             A
                             R

                             B
                             U
                             R
                             L
                             E
                             S
                             K

the poisoner of the dream poisons the dream
the words
            the words you can taste
            the words you can taste
                   a whole lifetime

                                   athens/1966

why i am a poet

snake eye
or rat eye
registering what bulges
whatever sticks out in front
or behind

wolf eye
or lynx eye
registering the head
severed from bloody trunk
and ripping of gut
total war nailing the brain
to newsprint cross

and you
return where poems
collect
and say

i have had enough
flywheels of insomnia
roar of thighbone trumpets
black gulfs rolling
smashed
under the eyelid's rivet
have explored
dicing human abysses
against the wall
of nine million dreams
steered
among the drowned
my laughable little death
on the pale spume
of thought

let the world pronounce
its rotting sentence
i have seen
the red snout of madness
pushing in a void

now is enough
let me know the moment

hydra/1965

fire over silence

suicide treeswirl
        moondark
           vortex
              deflected firegleam
             menace
              can't defend
her life
      blur
         in wild suns
         no meaning
can't cope   *with stupid*   *laws of* HATE
rule of law & reason   *suspended*   asylums/hospitals
          no meaning

insects scuttle over silence   pin her with uncertainty
clicking   black   eyes   scurry   on
    the mind   *can't cope*   her life a string   of
insects   armored   against   thrusts   born in
polluted waters   her mother's face wan
suicide   from winter   from a window   her father   taken
her picture   of   him   working   under
whip
      lash   of   pride

NO!   YOU'RE   NOT   BETTER   THAN   ME !!

stench   of   generations   of garbage
palette   of armored   inching   self   her
    colors   swerved
        amber-snarled

the girl
    ate her moondark
        heart

    shook
      in amber terror
coughing
  a sunflower
    moontree

pain & terror overshadowvoice
　　　　　friendship/trust?
　　　　　　　in these asylums/deserts?
lotte salom wrote　*can't cope*　*stupidsmugsmiles*
diary of
　　　　　fire over silence

　　　FL . . A S H . . .
ugly　brown　nasty　steelfaces　frenzied
　　　　　snarled
　　　　　　　　Sachsenhausen
fled
the scene
her paintings　absent otherworld
　　impenetrable
　　　　　　　she fled to what
hopeless desert　　　long white sands
　painted silence　　　sun-sea lonely
　　　　　　　　in Provence

but as she turned in upon herself attracting stares
　　acid stares that eat the flesh
　　　she painted a world that straggled
　　　　to a scream

　　　　　i wish everyone
　　　　　silence
　　　　　　to find
　　　　　　　their depths

　graygreen
　　　luminous
　　　　　DEATH
　　　　　　　did
　　　　　　　　not
　　　　　　　　　laugh
scream
　authorities
　　beat up
　　　torn hair
　　　　screamed
　　　　　confessed
　　　　　　forged card
　　　　　　verboten

                    framed
                  truck
                drew up
              beat up
            black torn hair
          screamed
        vortex
      swirl

                                              paris/ 1961

arrested in new york

          for looking at the moon
    for sitting in washington square
              for wearing long hair
          for walking the dog
        for answering a policeman
    & saying "this is a free country"
            for eating bonita
        for chewing morning glories
          for sniffing paradise cottons
    for sitting on a subway bench in the lotus position
        for looking intelligent
            & writing this poem

                                        madouri/ 1965

crab cycle dooms distinguished bathrooms

observation city
                                you get very starving
in the bathrooms   the dismal worrying
about FOOD in some of the BETTER bathrooms
in french public places
    ended up in emotional tile work

    now the landlord installing
a wing
        with tiny unctuous
            bathrooms   you may squat
                part time
on different-colored glaze

tile city
                several of de painters dere
are handformed   dese painters (&
photographers)
                        had made number
of shapes   the tiles
    are Sousa's relatives
        from the interior
                                on the half shell

                        subtle
                    old men
                with slight
            irregularities
                        (things
            were on the surface
                    peculiar)

        just pick them off
        the half shell

sousa himself
had been enamelled
& shellacked   takes
about 3
months   an order
            can be filled

back country city
                              forced to let
him be glazed   was out of work under
the name of job de Sousa was set
in a loose pattern of brown against gray ground   It is mad
but he tried very hard   eating at all   in the country of
was a long story   The diet of dese painters is desgusting
dey infest de back country & are carriers of out-of-town
                                        deseases
in search of man   Life expectancy shrinks
to the glazing of tiles on special order

It took de Sou months to Die
with symptoms
of little stupid designs
in relief

asked why de sou refused the known locales the keeper said:
He was proud   and a little stupid   But he is back in the
                              Who's Who
of man's efforts   Yes he was better off on the bathroom
                                        floor
in a loose pattern of
mauve blue shit
against a paradise design
of tomorrow

                                             paris/ 1962

americans

i see you now
                    frightened but bland
a multi-headed mask
                    with rigid eyes
staring from a white hood

as once in alabama i saw you
                    in steel helmet
building liberty ships.

a sudden commotion

draws us
out of sheet metal
                    into the yard
tufts of hair/black
            flesh/blood
                        on lead pipes
i'm swept into the crowd
                        i scream
"stop!"
        my white face
                        unseen
lost
        in the fierce
                    hate

paris/ 1959

dirty words

irresponsible   failure
                utopian   outsider
noncomformisthairypovertypersonaltruthpoet

                                    queer
                emotion   negro
                satori   jew
hungry   bum
crazy   wisdom
emigré

            junkie   god
                                    silence

                                peace
                freedom
    love

athens/ 1966

between two fires

a fire in my brain
    burns
the slag & trash deposits
        of my century
i walk out the window
i fly in fresh dawns of gray walls
cats are dreaming fish heads
the monastery floats in the sky
    & i am
            free
                of stupid laws

above a thousand islands above water above crowded pleasure
                                        boats
monasteries mountains cities prisons cemeteries
shipowners & communists   panorama of all greece
above the sweet eyes of donkeys
                        faster than jetplanes
my sixth sense immune to dimension
i zoom thru frontiers without visa
i visit sleeping bodies & whisper in their dreaming ears
            kiss me
        break the evil charm
you who are bewitched by bread
enthralled by scraps of paper
time has shut your skull
from your mouth stones fall
& truth is a bloodsmeared ikon

    ah quit flying
    come off it
i'm really sitting on a terrace
& the scrubwoman has stolen my pen
her nearsighted child is crying
& now she is stealing my razorblades
        her lazy husband beats her
            for not stealing more
tho she has left me very little
i am free of these minor matters
only when free of myself

& now from a balcony a housemaid is shaking

handkerchiefs & dishtowels
over the railing
where her bare legs gleam
above eyelevel
she is young & hot
'you don't need a wall of words to raise your truth'
    truth
        has just now
           raised
                its burning head

                                   athens/1966

anthropology lesson

among the Arapesh of
    New Guinea
  children play
with their lips they
    bubble them
& run their tongues
    on the insides
    getting ready
for sucking

they
    laugh a lot
      never say
  sissy or tomboy
  to their kids
& have no queers
    among them

  they borrow
    & import patterns
designs pots dress
    & think to make
  anything or draw
    or paint
      is funny

they never

gather around
      another Arapesh
in awe
          & submission

they share their children
    equally
        everyone mama
            everyone papa

        affectionate
they rub against
          each other
    like cats
    the wet cold world
made warm
            by constant
    touch

athens/ 1964

viareggio

i hope it wasn't where now the hotels
    block the view
        of these mountains
or among the *stabilimenti* with
their stupid umbrellas
where the well-off families
    from turin & milan
sit stuffing themselves

the beach laid out
    in precise rows
    of deckchairs & parasols
        like a formal garden
& not a seashell or hunk of driftwood
    or dirty seaweed in sight
but every hour on the hour
    a nasty little boat
        hurls loudspeaker ads
    for niteclubs cigarettes candy

                    gelati gasoline
            & other useless poisons
                        into the air
                of the tyrrhenian summer
& the *bambini* crying
        for sweet poisons
            to the fat mammas
                with purple blotches
                    on dead thighs
who talk of family
        matters—nothing else
                        can exist
not wars nor poems
                nor poverty-stricken multitudes

CERTAINLY NOT DEATH

    i hope it was here
where i am lying
                        alone at last
                        on the
        lone level sands
                    stretching
                                down
                        to livorno
with the slanting *pineta*
                in the background
here i hope it was
they found & burned his body—

            the
                mythical
                    magical
                        heart
        signalling
                    thru
                        the flames

                                        viareggio 1960

between proton & neutron

i live in the space between proton & neutron / between left
& right nostril / between community & self /
i am from inner space / the loneliness of a cat / my mother's
loneliness / dumb bewildered looks of need / they seem to say /
i want to be more than cat / more than woman / i want to be you /
i am thinking of style! / how to contain within my empty spaces /
rockets / ruins / guns / images purr in my ear / the mute
powerlessness of need /
where i live / in that space between two electrical charges /
neither cats nor mothers can enter being committed by need to
the sovereignty of matter / i am a sort of freak /
the only law being: DO WHAT THOU WILT / i am sure they would
worship a turd left with the proper incantations /
the scientist says / something unknown is doing we don't know what /
both man & god have ceased to function with meaning / what can i
worship? / function without meaning? / the stance of science /
salting the tail of time / fishing for the now-moment / forever
is never /
better emptiness than ideas / the stance of knowledge: a bag
of facts can never / ever in the most brilliant mind / be filled
with the Sea of Life /
the stance of money / i pass a fine house where the landlord /
arms akimbo / haughtily supervises a beautiful band of sweating
laborers / (their armpits emit gold) /
wearing my seadog cap / wondering will i be arrested for disrespect
as everybody stands at attention / i ignore the bugle's notes
from the naval academy on the wharf / & the flag's erection /
i ignore the tongues of animosity & benevolence / i shift like
the tide / between ebb & flow / between male & female / between
the hissing flares & the silverblack sky /

hydra 1965

inscrutable as a croupier

inscrutable as a croupier
time in a hollow palm
accumulates poisons
has no conscience
has no soul

a lie of peace
　　has no soul
　　　has no friends
　　　　has no soul
　　　combines the lyric with
　　the neon ad
　　combines the polemic with
　the psalm
　passions explosions
irritations
has no soul
has no conscience
　all he has is
　a nice pair of craps
　　inscrutable as a croupier
　　a little time
　　　no bigger than a lifetime
　　　a little chance
　　　　no bigger than the bones
　　　　shoes fingers
　　　　horrors
　　　　　things
　　　　　fall apart
　　　　　　the relative
　　　　　has no conscience
　　　　grass
　　　　shapes
　　　strange vigils
　　calico money cats
　　throat cuts
　　the mobile the artist
　hang him
　from the ceiling
　gesture of independence
final dissolution
resolved
　blown up
　revolving
　　from the ceiling

athens/1966

dust poem

here's this little silly world
       going so fast i look up
       red ceiling cracked plaster
suitcases full of dust Sun appears
    & disappears   full of dust

in the court the dog barking
somebody cooking cabbage
                 i feel lousy

"unless you have faith & love
you will always be sick"

quote refugee doctor in clamart
among his weird inventions
crazy as a bat but will cure
anything with 'faith & love'
aided by a mineral machine
    bombards you with gold & silver
     manganese copper magnesium zinc
& Bach on the pickup
in the background the doctor
dancing like a hassidic loom

what meditation shall i do?
     i'm lonely
i frighten myself—anyway
we're only a speck of dust
on the underslip of a long platter
           among bigger
galactic platters
where life's superior

they haven't discovered us yet!
i'm looking at the red ceiling
    writing a dust poem

now just what is a dust poem?

it's an infinitesimal microspark of mortality
writ by an invisible & soon-to-be-extinguished hand
whose brain for one wink in the chiliastic flood of

                    endless kosmos
connects with Universal Mind & Eternal Breath
exhaling the preposterous
& absurd
beautiful moment of decay
        & nothingness yes
that's what i call a dust poem
dust dust dust dust dust dust dust dust
poemdust goldust sexdust
chinadust bluedust   westdust
earth a mote of complex dust
in the galactic swim see
that fly on the ceiling
among the dustflakes

the whole world on the dustbeam!
a mote winking
                among cosmic
                            squish

                                        paris/1959

another form of junk

it's supremely unintelligible

the maziest maze   NO EXIT
writ large over the mind
over the dawn curtains
slatted by unwelcome light
        announcing
another sleepless struggle

how can i give up the cellular need?

i will now say a few words
to god & the sun
the sun that i keep out with closed shutters
the sun that begrudges me revonal dreams
the sun that chews my brain & sabotages my energy
it's the fantasy
        deep in mind's hidden
        darkness

will have its perverse way
you may try to exorcise it
with your rituals
fish around inside the aquarium skull
or mumble prayers to imagined deities
    it will come back
    it's the plague
    Ego the demi-urge
    no urge can cure
        the great boyg
        the lost button
        the memory
it is myself
overexposed negative
drowned by light
on the ritalin terrace
of hydra
        clicking typewriters
        mad cicadas
        in the pines over
    a houseful of
    junk people
    playing guitars
        in the mazy labyrinth

hydra 1965

hellas time capsule

        gray shutters open to chickenwire
     umber islands float
   in rough sea of plaster
       your parthenon slumwall o greece!
shards and fragments
    of thy mad heraklion moan
        eternal recurrence
      in ancient collage

     sick of words crushed in circus blood empire
        wild decay designs
       of helpless beauty
knossos-pinned-butterfly
     Time repeating a cracked image

sleepless violence drained
of meaning
                    o capsule of cycles proclaim
            eternal danger and illusion flickering round the
                    flame of vanity
no escape
                    planets collide
            earthquake and war erupt   comets
                    plunge thru engendered steeples of reason
                            racing round the
                    sun and return in cosmic power of sprung stars!
history-squeezed brains and nerves accelerate Death pushing
                    thru mournful hopes
            tho' nothing can rivet whole the smashed brainmaps of madness!
no blueprints for
                    millennium's pure voids!
            no more nights! no more
                wisdom! no
            paradise products of lost mystic roads!
the moment cancelled
                life threw away the key
in this war of all
            against all
                    Death writes on the skin
his silent poem

icarus loses his wings comes zooming out of cosmic dust
            cunning dædalus weeps
                too late among the ruins
                    his science hands tremble
mountains
                    crumble as seas torn
                    from their beds and continents ripped
                        like paper leave moony craters

lemuria has sunk mu has sunk russia & america will sink
            the pope walks wailing
                    thru the engulfed cathedral
                        over drowned and charred
                            cadavers
the scalped earth bleeds
                the sun
                    beneath the sea
                        everything

in its place
how can it
be otherwise?

even

as the roar of summer
spreads
under this city hill

gold

hits the leaden air
a voice curses & mutters
boys bray on slopes & sparrows
trill in telephone wires

i tense

for the lonely thrust

hydra 1965

future tectonic catastrophe

able to hear colors   & see sounds   his mind flipped back   & for
words in   as he spoke the dimension on which   he lived
not the same as you   century followed century   mixo   neo
lithic codes   to cro   magnon   mutated out   mongoloid   eyes
HOMO AMERICAN
us   millet & barley of the nile valley   into maize potatoes squash
tool of the pithecanthropi   the stone celt   vast spaces of earth
menfilled
giant fuegians   naked   wrapped in guanaco skins   thru forfeit tundras
"patagones" on firebound land   evening land of the andes   cord
illera music of mountains   skyscrapers thru the sun
cafes under the orinoco spacecraft under the amazon gobi desert secret
trek of jews
black stone of phrygia
television jungles span
broken mountains
belching volcanoes
quakes
rockhard world of machinemen   into   space
into dreams

                                                        code music
           in static   of small transistors
                                              belief is animistic
good & evil in vast   wildernesses   prairies   steppes   rivers
      keeneyed tepee dwellers   cysts of hyperborean regions   cancers
         of environment   glaciation   of northern hemisphere   in
            AD 5,000 & AD 90,000
                                              ice sheets   over boston
seattle chicago ice sheet over canada   oslo in deepfreeze   copenhagen
stockholm leningrad frozen under vast sheets   of ice   cities only of
historical interest to contemporary archaeologists cancer of ice run
      wild ice teeth in thick thighs sabretooth tigers hunt in greenwich
village rhinoceroses in paris hippopotami root in moscow mam
      moths graze icicles in peking longtusked brownish wool giant hair
         animals in siberian prison nightclubs
               anthropoid poets
                        timetable of future
                                              tectonic

                                                          catastrophe
         advance of polar ice   purely as
                              tronomical   eve
                    nt
                                   o endless
                trudge of tribes
                                   thru wideranging danger
            of
                  un
                        i
                          verse
                                                    paris 1961

showdown: athens hospital

         in the middle of a football game
                  rasping on the radio
         nurses charge down the halls
         dragging tables & chairs
                  & patients by the hair
            like harpies
         on a mission of torture

nearby a hunchback farts
      cackles & belches
& looks looks looks
     at me
day and night
    staring belching
       his scrotum
big as a bull's
    on a midget body

   I turn my head
     to the wall
       *

wheezing like an old man
tho' young in the green ward
I'm stuck with needles & enemas
among Eleusinian mysteries
    & Ottoman sloth

'Byzantine decadence'
    no idle
or bookish term
  IT'S REAL!

nurses steal my pens
     & roses
peeking under the sheets
     snakebrained nurses
with the wrong medicine

they laugh & joke
     & slam the doors
while fragile old ladies
    gasp for breath
tubes stuck in their throat

     *

    outside
a hill
trees
     framed
   by the window
     like a triptych

& multi-leveled houses
with white walls

a small robin's-egg blue
   pueblo house
      above a large
         banana-colored
         pueblo house

            next to the blue
               house a brilliant
                  plant
             spray of yellow
                    forsythia
          in the middle
         panel of the
           triptych
             the window
               makes
at dusk
    on top of the hill
what you take for
    a cypress turns out
    to be a man
        curiously sharp
    & thin
        etched
    against the sky

       *

this quaking bag   of skin and bones
this poisoned liver   these yellow eyes
this draining gut   this flesh this flab
this irritable rage   this bullet-proof pride
this wasted body   this whispering voice
this liverish gloom   *is this me? is this ME?*
I stare at the walls   trapped by horrors
harsh transistors   pulverize my ears
among the moans   & all-night groans
no sign no sign   of humanity
no warmth   no warmth

       *

choked with rage   and indignation
having faced death   faced the void
        I saw nothing   nothing
process of blood   process of breath
process of roots   process of death
birth   death   being   not being
the light at the end of the tunnel
        the near-death light
                *

welcome energy of warm skin
reality of gravel & yellow dust
green leaves   welcome again
welcome light on white stone walls
welcome noise and screaming in the streets
welcome bells of Easter   welcome monastery on the hill
welcome flares & rockets   & cannon booming on the mountain
the mountain did not crumble   the rocks did not fall down
the asphalt did not crack open   & snap like jaws
there was no shock   no quake   no collapse
only the power of time   of zenith & nadir
everyday reality   of flashing fenders
motorscooters   gunning the silence
winning & losing   knowing   not knowing
nightmares & ecstasies   everything inexplicable

        *

        something comes
only a moment
                in an ocean of moments
                    over my head
            a moment
        I can't nail down
                I can't arrest the moment

            of death
                        or life
            always something flowing free

    what I am when I'm not what I think I am
            or what you think I am
                    in the dance
            of chance

the rolling dice of change
in a morning vision

Athens, Easter 1966; revised 2001 SF

notes from neanderthal city

1

nothing exists but energy

am i this static black-&-white
foto speared like an eel thru the gall
on the floor on a
pallet in Heidelberg?

dust rats garbage scraps Schoenberg quirky sounds
life is dirty

post office regulations
clocktime   generalissimo   junta moustaches

JEDER KANN MIT JEDEM

europa   gook rot
crooked sacs of pus   bloodyminded   usa   paranoia

dealing themselves contracts
okra
copra
tungsten
bauxite
bodies

they
slice into slivers the bodies of ordinary asiatics
with sheer evil weapons
sliced daily into slivers
evil
cuts the planet to pieces
nobody will get away with it
everybody's got to pay
for every unjust remark

for every unjust action
                    building good or bad karma

                    it's hard being dead

                    to perceive a little reality

          especially when the self
     even in the mirror is so hard
               to grasp
          to dust off jewelry of living cells

                         walls of Pain obscure
                         kaleidoscope cosmologies

which is the way to renewal?
          daily guide to inscope
     into cosmic dance
               of interpenetrating scintillations
               when furies eat the liver?
          when at night the fantasy turns on one note
               screaming
                         irritations in bloodstream
          ACID MOUTH BITING THRU WALLS

          endure these corrosive fires?
o angry waves of greenish slime!
detonate the fuse of your powerpacked warhead & explode that ugly
scene you've been preparing   generalissimo   don't keep the planet
in suspense   dangling   wide open like a yokel's jaw
o hard realistic weary nightmare   monsters   i offer you
free trips   to hexagram connections   i offer

                    ABANDONMENT

                                        ABSENCE
          cold stare of magritte
                    deserted piazzas of chirico

IN LONG DARK NIGHT
          MAMA TRAUMA
               WALKED OUT WITH SEASMELL
                         & POWDERED CHEEKS

leave me alone
you Wrathful Demons
something acid & yellow
regurgitating
can't keep it down
diarrhoea both ends now

what subtle unspoken transcendent real ache
between us hitherto unexplicit
with yr thick reddish warm
eyebrows
above the nervous tic
of scholarly wary eyes
hornrimmed mask hiding large soft
unique spirit of brüderschaft yearning
to breakthru demonology
of Third Reich cauchemar guilt
paralyzed you to speak
of self
Karl
what grim inhibited cut lines
cutself
no self to speak of
now

ach i'm back to the infantile bastard
crying against the fire hydrant
on NY curb in the night
for Mama Trauma
done left me
with skim milk
vomiting
stingy Mrs. Eichmann
screams "eat yr oatmeal bastard!"
long ago. . . . .
it flashes
on the inward eye
tho not "recollected in tranquillity"
flashes back
feeds on itself
in this predicament
of childish helplessness
in Germany   high on revonal   exhausted   sleepless
insomniac stasis neanderthal city horrors

am certainly *not* APOLLONIUS OF TYANA
             nor Jakob Boehme
       didja know Dr. Faust was busted
                   for being queer?
          juicy bit of historical gossip
we are all speared saints who know that darkbright dream
             Einsamkeit and Gedult / the meat of poetry /
       while Russia Reaffirms Stand
bubble mass of bodies
                   miniminds running the planet
                             thermonuclear incineration
                             death fifteen minutes away

       yellow skin & sense of doom
       earth's magnetic field disappearing
                        dwindling
             day by day

'I am going to Heidelberg on a raft. Will you venture with me?'
       sun on the banks of the Neckar
    thru which Mark Twain rode a mythy raft
             caring little for accuracy
                of fact or grammar or syntax
                   shocking the reader
                                  whenever he cd
       by 'wrong use of erudite phrases &
                foreign words' etc.
       from Heilbronn to Heidelberg

    those were the days
             'deep & tranquil ecstasy'
naked kids   motherly dames   knitting under a tree
fireworks at the schloss
                   . . . arrowy bolts . . . rockets . . . vomited skyward
       out of black throats of the Castle towers. . . . ..

October sun on gray walls   my hair is damp
       cigarette butts in a dish   i am watched by shadows
             wondering how long O Lord Lord
                in this yellow hell
          when from the hall there floats
     a vivid smell
          explodes in my brain
       whole episodes
                   explosions of hashish music myriads

                    of flutes
               fibres of sound
             strands of incense
          keen filaments of wire
     zambomba
                    Socco Chico

                         inch'allah

                              a million years ago

sipping mint tea facing the Djemaa el Fna in Marrakech snakes squirm
at my feet a monkey's wrinkled face blinks turbaned storyteller squats in
center of huge crowd of beggars A Thousand & One Nights in broad
hot daylight of dust & bargains & good odor of katami pervading whole
pattern of experience the tall tales of kif enamelled pipes &
soapstone bowls aladdin lamps from tin cans & raffia souk of rugs
djellabas music & magic stalls of sheep's nuts dried blood withered
paws evil eyes skulls bones hair
                         down in joujouka
       pan pipes of bou jeloud
                    white moonlight   white djellabas
               white white walls
          adolescent Father of Skins
               stomping his ancient
               PANIC RITUAL
                              convulsive

movements of a fucking goat
you can smell this boy

                              lean curved thighs
                              almond eyes
high cheekbones
                         possessed

               in trance
               dance
                    frenzy of flutes
       mad oboes
          frantic drumbeat
                    HU HU HU HU HU HU HU
                    HU
                    HU
          huhuhuhuhuhuhu HUhuhhuhuhuhuhuhuhhu
                    HU
                    HU
                    HU

huhuhuhuhuhuhu huhuhhuhuhuhuhuhuhhu
HU
HU HU HU HU HU HU HU

huhuhuhuhuhuhu   chopping the air
                     with a stick
          he'll beat you if you come close
               8 nites sustained orgasm   unrelenting
                               pandance
               grunts
                    cries
                         fucking
                         goat
                              floppy
                              mad wild ancient
good odor of katami pervading moonlight
          song & dancing boys   slipping snakes
                                        dust magic
                                            hashish film
not to be touched
                    by reason
                              right or
                                             wrong

out of Taroudant
     you breathe for the first time
          desert air ignites in the skull
               its message of silence & stars

                    ecstasis

will the streetcar clang forever on all the streets i live on?
oh god! they're changing governments again! they'll get me for sure!
the extreme right moving in!   swastikas in the air!
we'll all be busted for zooping around in convulsive delight
for throwing every sense into new relationships
for opening every eye of the skin to look at cellular light
ah no but i'm stuck   in static yellow   moments
up the street drifts modern death   canceled inner space
neutron ash   all that's left   soft skin tattooed with terror
slander of dead friendship   sort of vegetable machine
cuts a sinister path   signaling you
with electronic page
                    from coast

                                        to lunatic coast
throwing every sense into
                              cellular light
                                        under the influence
of   ENERGY
                    nothing exists
                                  but   ENERGY

BUT where is Pistis Sophia at this moment when i need her?
            o Lady/Divine Wisdom
          my mind is in the moon
                my crab birth in the 12th house
                  soma   soma   moonthink   of thee I Ching

              ultimate reality   oh god   i smell only that secret
                  rancid sadness of parks & thighs
                      dissolve in blue shifty silence
                  memory film under
              a rusty shell
              horseshoe crab filled with maggots
                on the beach
              i smacked it with a stick
                  & the maggots teemed
                    in the sunlight
                      7 yrs of age
                            now charged with memory film
                                in time of real fantastic scripts
                                    clearly mutation time

& knew then too on the beach
            perfect recall of future events
                traveling electroakashic web of mind
                      out of time
                        spoken word on the border of
                awareness. . . . . . . knew the undulating raga
                      exploded long time ago
            in ciudad neanderthal on the moon
                      against international space speculation
                          stench of ego areas
                floods mirrors of powerstruck dinosaurian monstrosities
              scorpions playing space roulette
          with red rhythms & white rhythms & brown rhythms
                third eyes between thighs
                    cohere in Ultimate Brain

cosmic din   skull keys twang   jazz fur
cosmic cells write World in meat
deep down primal
crash gling
lyptic
ping
gong   pong
tea metal
Flame thru
struct
you   me   all

ENERGY
radios
cameras   staring into slotmachine
tv   mirrors
crutches   whistling to dogs
                    dodging pickpockets   playback
automobiles   swans   chance factor
wristwatches   tinfoil   dancefloors
barometers   wrappers of the city   kaleidoscopes
decibles   lake traffic   memoryfilm
teeth   under neon blue   rusty shell
lipstick   sky glass   ultimate O
washing machines   steel corporations   soma
                                        sophia
trusses   hermetic moons
memorybanks
feedback   energy
glug   energy
sex   energy   energy
sex
sex
sex   horror
x   violence
man star   crystal   clairvoyance
supra universe neuroblasts hunchbacks   crystal
                                        cocks
god jails   breasts
winds   diamonds   blood   blue jeans
sacred neurons   skulls   teenyboppers
jetplane psychopomps   hair   epidemics
world sensorium   bones   hepatitis
icarus heliotrope microfilm   wars   suicide

snowjobs   doctors   kisses
   blowjobs   panic   monoxide
   photosynthetic ecstasy   hysteria   murder
  syzergy   insanity   airpollution
  violence   infirmity   poetry
   violence   skin   visions
                     happenings
  violence   parapoetry   spermatozoagyzmspunk
  vio   lence   horror   reincarnations hallucinations
W AR RAW A R   A W   horror   hereafternowhereeverywhere
 W A R   horror   secret dreams inner
  R A A   splendor
  W
  A
  R

                            heidelberg 1966/67

christmas on earth

for anselm hollo

     snow
   wind
thru shutters
     & cracks of doors

       acropolis slopes
       the color of columns
      creamy architraves
         windy interstices
       of erechtheum

    parthenon
   sleetclad
  greek frieze
     in deepfreeze

all trees are xmas trees
     goats graze
   as in a crib
      on a mountain

                    of cotton

in white
    tasselled gnaoua
                taguia
            from moroccan mountains
                            halfboots below
                                    the knee
                    austrian peasant jacket
                            chocolate brown
                flat beat silver
                            buttons
i'm taken
        for a serb
            or yugoslav
                café owner scratches
                    his dome
                when i say "american"
                    he don't get it
            jukebox bouzouki bams
AH   AH   AH   AHHHH   AAAHHHH
        into fluted ruins
                    by old clothes stands

stirring tinfoil
from cigarette packs
                shiny metal paper
                    around & around
                        in the brasero
far from the "shadow streets
            of childhood"   the
                        "hairy menace
        quaking
                under the bed"

i can't forget
can't dissolve
the nightmare mother
on my back
                heavy
as a trunk
or skyscraper
she weighed

i couldn't cry out
                    my right
            arm over
                        bed's edge
frozen
            deathshead stuck
                    in the door!

announcement:
                    poet's violent
                        flight from mystery
                            glare of abyss
        to red eyes
            of madness
                owl eyes
                    of death
muttering
            of moons & magic
                    mad
                    as the mist
        & snow
            nobody listens
            nobody knows

        then
to create entities
                bodies
                        out of words
(whitehaired spectacled
            embirikos booms
        fantastic sex scenes like
                man sticking big prick into
                    12 yr old girl's rosebud
                        mouth   when he comes
        comets & shooting stars
                Z000M
            across the roofy sky
        (poems not yet read
                    in anglia))

hot coffee in a taverna
watch the "flippers"
            no tv yet
            only backgammon

exquisite child
dances   sings   scrawls
              greek letters
                          awkward
                  on a page
          fair features
                burning lips
                    carnations   nunaraks   opals
                    a shift in its face

    i want to strangle the child

no logic
    only creative spirit
              blasts the world
                  at its core
        to reach
                      self

he did not try to be beautiful
                  rimbaud
            he hated beauty
    old pinched bitch
        had seen to that!

                  beauty you want?
Goooooold!   she screamed
& he fled to the
    color of vowels
        the diamond body
          the borderline
                  of the snow mountains
                  the primordial pass

      having strangled beauty
          played stinkfinger with
              the virgin mary
pissed
    on the holy
                  family
on all families
seen thru the barricades
their phony gods   no truth
having taken

a good crap
           on literature
                    "one-eyed intellects"
     & turned against the whole kit
     & kaboodle of bullshit
     he cried:
                author! creator! poet!
                that man has not yet existed!

           one voice
        of many tongues   if it be
                    universal image
                            of true self
     united with creation/destruction
           the PARAPOEM

     stale minds
  in the drunken boat
     sinking
                                   like the pequod
                                in sargassos
                             of wordblubber
                                            down
                    thru wriggling slick
              adens
           hells
                 of mistrust
        controlled dualities brainwash negative
           flickers radar vultures scoop
                 the brains of wellread zombies
                       in brainhellholes
  war is the god of all
                    gunfire echoes
           from all buildings in long
           strips of sound

almost every desire a poor man has is a punishable offense
to trust in man is to let oneself be killed
to philosophize is only being afraid leading nowhere
but to cowardly make-believe

           the whole planet quaking
              boiling over
        ready to roll thru space

               like a tennis ball
                    armies of ants everywhere
                         producing mounds of dirt
               below which their fascist labyrinths
                    with intractable order
                         arrange
          a muddle of money
                    the universe a savage animal
                                        devouring itself

ah li po   your pool
nerval   hart crane
cheap wine drowns you

                  WHEN WILL WE GO
          TO GREET THE END OF SUPERSTITION
                              CHRISTMAS ON EARTH?

     the day of universal language
          linking together all thought
                              will come

meanwhile
                    this amputated trip—

i'm on my back dribbling stars from foamflecked lips
in a field of flaming chrysanthemums

bizarre beasts dance
mescaline moons melt into diamonds

the seal of solomon bursts

the electric river flows

streams of holiness gush between my legs

i give birth to a white narcissus

six wands spring from the ground
lotus leaves sprout from the eye

Absolute Poem like a meteor streaks down
crushed by the earth in a swift instant

fiery chains of rubies flood the indifferent cosmos

i'm soaring out of my blood

athens/1964

how can i reach you?

i call across space my antennae are astral
you hear my words across space

we do not reach each other

      reach me

we cannot know each other

motor purrs outside
i see car without looking
then question do i see car

my chest is heavy
my head is full of smoke
my head is nodding like a doll's

      boo   i'm smoking boo

i wait the obsidian bird on smoke of a wing

the voice is alterable the body is alterable
the mind is alterable

life is alterable

one of those mornings

& everything is suddenly a beautiful garden
with birds in it & angels & trees
                    made out of wings
a crazy doodle of a garden
& you don't understand anything
        but there you are
making a poem of it
the most hopeless poem in the universe
        oh god how my toe itches!
that beautiful garden
            friends
                    it is not there

parapoem

in the wombdream bloody vision you cried
        in the newborn moment

a moon of thighs
like a wall in riverbright light rises
the moment writhes
into a man king come

he shall run in the sores between the legs
of a vain kiss

slain in taxis
in tortured corners
the saint flows into the dream
of the sun's way

the womb that bore little deaths
        & the dazzling holy
        center
concealed my own
where i hear the wheat cry

the mother with sex pierced by the thorn
        of dark loins

bore the slashed lone
         motherman
& rocked him
in drenched silence

war builds
its bloody room
& the mother
      is doom

landscape of cruelty

      jazz musicians on the nod dream of international joy
while a rat is transpierced by a grinning grocer thru a crack
                  in the pavement
      Chagall says good morning with pink hair & sapphire eyes
                  shopwindow dummy bites
         glass dust in evening dress
      broken glass & cufflinks spew diamonds
                  grotesque in rivery weeds
         corpses fished from the Seine
            the captain questions me at gunpoint
                  but death is still far away

      the Préfecture at the Panthéon is scary to pass
leaden-caped cops on their platforms tremble
            their fingers shake on machinegun triggers
         for long hair odd clothes & a manner of walking
            you have a mad urge to rush at them with bare hands
            you can barely resist
      the boulevards jump at backfiring cars
         the Dôme & Coupôle vast deserts of icy talk
            congealing the heart
                  communication lines cut
         the rue Mouffetard in hiding
               clochards smashed & limping
         kicked into vans on the quays

under a black sky
the Place de la Concorde is a laboratory
      for emphysema & carcinogens

in gray light like fluorescent tubes
    the city sickly   face-lifted
        tough old cathouse madam

    landscape of cruelty & the absurd
      cold stare of deserted being

I sat with Henri Michaux under carbonized trees
    while he drank orange juice
      saying 'I have given up everything
        even coffee

    I nearly died
    I nearly lost my mind
    no more mescaline for me'

sipping orange juice
        like hemlock

Blaise Cendrars lay dying
    across the street from the Santé
      the prisoners waved at us from their bars with
        sweet obscene gestures
          spit drools down his chin
        tongue lolls in helpless mouth
          eyes glazed & frightened

no more Trans-Siberian Blaise
no more little *poules* with a dose
it's a very long way from here to Montmartre Blaise
it's a long way
your illness a drag
your wife a real bringdown
your destination clearly the final asylum

morning vision

to approach a meaningless death &
    survive it
        on the verge
          to draw back

having faced splitting apart
looked into the drowning
diamond face of the blue void
in the funnel of ether
no pinpoint of light at the farthest
end
          nibble of nothing
process of blood laughter silence
process of stone snows roots bones
process of planets spiders microbes
moles crystals spheres wheat
petals suns

          i'd have welcomed the dark
          yielded to the shadowman
          without a fight

but for you energy of warm skin
& you whiff of the ram &
truck full of reality
growling real gravel
at the construction down the block
& real yellow dust on the road
i will walk again
& real green of leaves
vibrating again
all welcome again hail light on white
walls
loud noise even
welcome interruption & screaming in the streets
& bells of easter blue
& vermilion flares & rockets & cannon on the easter mountain
the monastery in the sky
on the mountain that did not crumble
on the rocks that did not fall down
on the asphalt that did not crack
open & snap the feet like jaws
shock & break of collapse
under the power of time & the power of persisting in time
zenith again not nadir down from the cross down from pain
dying & living in their place in time
where the cloudy the overcast
had taken unchallenged positions

o motorscooter gunning the silence

    o empty phrases
        drifting your everyday
          absurdity

    o blue flashing fender
        you burst & puff of poison
           o voices of win & lose

        you are process
        released from your poles
        demons or ecstasies
        weak or strong

          something has come
        only a moment
          in an ocean of moments
       over my head
              sliding
        a moment
i can't nail it
      down
arrest
      the water
        not death nor life
           but something
flowing
      free
              in between
whatever i am when i am not what i think i am
  or what you think i am

      in the dance
        of coincidence
    chance orchestration
           of genes

the drunken dice of change
in a morning vision

refuge of the triple gem

for Maretta Greer

the air being very charged
eerie winds out of the north like nerves
blowing thru the bones

        'the next few days may see
      some terrific earthquakes here'

& i saw
        my little acropolis pad
leap & tremble
           swallowed up
the erechtheum hurled into my bed
  a caryatid in my w.c.
    i'm buried at last with spiders
       shaving cream poems typewriters
            greek shards
     in moroccan slippers
              birds
   crushed among my books
    *   *   *

a square of purple cloth from the head-lama's robe
a crayon drawing by him of a half-eaten dog
& a weeping kneeling man in a deserted landscape
  of barren mountains
         chewed by the sea
  & within a circle of blue   seated upon a lotus of rose
    the Buddha   in a bubble
       this she had left me. . . .

  now it is up to me
to act again within the dharma & overcome
    'the misery begotten
          of our emotional upsets'

behind the glass wall

behind the glass wall
        fluctuant   i see blue limbs
    crumble away   black fungus noses
        thighs kneecaps

                                        "i have the taste of the infinite"

ylem
            primordial squinch   the universe crushed into
                                                        a seed
nothing will satisify me
                            i write green ballets & hollow
                                                    journeys
caught in the etheric web of yr crotch
                        a hairy ocean of darkness

                        dawamesc doors of pearl
                        open to fiery radiance

majoun madness
                    down marrakech alleys
        the   djemaa el fna
    squirming   with snakes
        in carbide glow

black gnaoua dancers!   lash sword!   flash teeth!
        under the barrow
            broiling in sleep   mouth
& nostrils buzzing with flies

                                            genitals thick swollen out
        of big tear in pants

                                    derelict 14 yr old street arab
            cameras   snapping
        like teeth/great souk
            swarms for dirhams

and who
        are you little arab
            i shared my visions
                            and ate
            black hasheesh candy with
the doors of yr body   flung
        open we twitched in spasms
                muscular convulsions
                    heavenly epilepsy on the bed

                    in the hotel of the palms
                       prolonged orgasm
                          uncontrollable joy
                             of leaving the mind

athens/ 1965

follow no leader

        they followed the leader into the mountains
        sat at his feet in a Swiss canton
                  as they decayed
                       like rotting fish

        and he looked at them
        and said:
                    turn off the ventriloquist's voice
                    flush out the snakeoil in the blood
                       your bible
                          your gita
                             your gems
                                your guns
                                   your flags
                                      your death

        and at night they went to the nite clubs gobbling and soaking
        up the suds
        while that thing
        between the legs
        became
               more urgent
        they dished up the cold turkey
        of what he had said
              and nobody felt too good
                    nobody felt

        so they took the train the limousine the rucksack
        and went back home

           next year
        they followed him to India
        and again he looked at them

and said:

             follow no leader
                    guru
        nobody is living
        everybody is dead
and again he told them
              told them

and again that thing
between the legs
        and between the ears
             got in the way

                                  athens/ 1965

it is

it is the zinnia-colored sea
it is the light on the dazzling chrome of the horizon where the sun hurls
    its yes
it is the foam of asters where waves make lazy petals on the khaki shore
it is the muttering mulch of shells protecting the groans of sandcastles
    hoarse with poems
it is the mountain of mica refusing to turn into sliderule numbers
it is calabria bony peak feeling the anarchy of its means
he sits saying The Absolute is a sea of blinding flowers
saying The Absolute is not white but only NOT
it is the lotus-covered ALL
he sits on the toe of a continent whose foot is wrapped in rags
saying I am Illumination when lightning lust scissors the crotch
he is moving across the cities with a rucksack full of visions
he is hitching thru the smoke
he pats the bomb of love thru the holes in his pants
he comes like a prophet to explode the truth when it is too late
at the volcano's lip he hears intolerable secrets
a diet of snails & capsicum seeds makes him adore simplicity
it is the ionian pressing its damson grapes on his dusty palate
it is the myth the cave the raving rock of electric mysteries
it is madness it is dancing
it is building a shrine of tears
he sees miracles when he picks his teeth
he will be a sage one day

he is weeping for the god that sits on his ass scaring little children
he beholds the invisible world where angels speak Blue & Violet
bibles in his hair he dreams of beauty under cycles of myriad suns
he is the race that came from the east
he is the sound growing out of the wordy night
the sound of fire
the sound that surrounds us in our silence
the sound that never ends
he is the agony of our flight from ourselves into the Other
he is crime appetite of the cosmos eating its way to Self grinding
    space in his jaws
he is the wolf of the world howling at the universe
he is death
he is sleep
he is waking
he is why

                                   paris/ 1959

revelation by
electroencephalography

the umbrella that he opened spread into a long black
canopy that could accommodate a thousand people
he called my attention to the handle
of carved yellow ivory
bigger than a man's head
                  & very flat

it was a chinese or indian demon
whose hideous features
distorted in a terrifying grimace
had something to do with me but what
very disturbing but what does it mean
was this a dream of kathmandu
& what about those spiders on LSD
who madly spun their asymmetrical webs
in abstract patterns

something to do with me but what

somewhere a knife is waiting

to vivisect my images
my fantasy
charted on a blackboard

my dreams are lab experiments
    with electrodes for meaning
        emotions are glands
            test tube fluids my happiness
                my anger

tell me who i am

i am salt whistling a tune from tosca
i am water discussing water
i am calcium
singing a freedom song
a system of neutrons & protons
    on a white terrace
    with a calcimined wall
        i cannot define
            or know

feeling a firm delusion

hydra 1965

hydra*

                you are a nest of snakes
            asylum of white walls
        dazzle of windmills
            empurpled by
bougainvillea

        you're bedlam-by-the-sea
        ballet of tight exiles
in port cafes

            jasmine & syphilis
        flourishing
        side by side

donkeyboy
      with the fixed starving stare
          of mountain lust
your shrunken lips
      frail clumsiness
dreaming of rape
      good morning
to your larger-than-life grotesque
          world-wonder
      only the donkey can
               accommodate

      all i ask
    is a bit of sun
      pure blue
around the rocks & poppies
      & no sea urchins
  to stab
      my hands & feet

a flat smooth sea
      texture of worn green
        bottleglass
a pair of thighs

*A Greek island

past present/future perfect

my white wall, nailpocked, holds
a poster: STONED TOUCH; a Greek ass: Hermes of Prax; 3
lean satyrs with hard ons, quite ancient, from Pompeii
supporting a brazier (postcard); a byzantine ikon; Mr. America
poster from Hollywood, beefcake busting out all over; Dante;
an ape on the Acropolis, or the present state of Greece;
photo of Krishnamurti 1927;
pencil drawing of me at 16;
German movie posters;
announcements of poetry readings;
15 years of Europe in photos I took there;
lions fucking;

my friends on the wall;
my friends who are dying like flies,
my friends the poets
now of the past
and maybe the future? not
to have said goodbye; not to have
met again; somehow
it all seems more futile than
death itself; we
never did say
what we wanted to;
now the changes
are irreversible.

three for the microbes

God, I'm in trouble again, sick!
the singlecelled killer that changes shape
the protozoan beast
sneaking thru the blood along the portal vein
like a thief, a maniac bug, threatening my vital organs, my life!
ah, what's left of this life, o Lord!
protect your boy, Harold, for once
help me thru the infected wilderness!
it is love that brings me down
love that fanatics call lust.
now for one night of lust
(why should I pay with suffering)
this dread bacillus wastes me.
I ask that I be spared for so light a sin
that harms nobody in the world.
              the love I gave
              I pay with plague.
are you so jealous that you must forever punish me
for those few hours snatched from boredom?

                    *

visibly wasting I go to a party
where they are drinking and singing
smoking and eating
of these I do nothing

but gobble up bodies
with my insatiable eyes
and cling to a kitchen stove
like the deckrail of a sinking
ship while the young
and healthy shout
and laugh
and I sad captain
knowing shipwreck

*

on the way to the party
I listen to a dead man speak
and recall when once he lived
his brilliant bitter conversation
and soon—and soon—

in that anarchistic erehwon
nobody has to worry
about money, sex, health or politics—
Paul, do they fly the black flag there?

i wait in the long corridors of public suffering

I wait in the long corridors of public suffering
in the San Francisco General Hospital
where a black man with a badly cut hand
sits rather jauntily holding it over a plastic basin
that slowly fills with blood
and he smokes and looks around with macho unconcern.

I am not so heroic, I wince
at his hand, at the squirming groaning emergency cases
wheeled in on metal tables
while the interns laugh and joke and the bored
attendants go about their business with indifferent faces
thinking of dinner or dates or movies.
I sit clenching my teeth
in horror and helpless defiance
raging silently.

a man with chalky pallor
clutches his groin on the stretcher, choking
and gasping with pain; one is led
from a ward with tubes in his nose, a bottle
feeding him hope and his chin moving
rapidly in prayer under a metal
plate; a black whore gets her bloodied eye
patched up and a biker with broken head
sits in glum smothered violence
wrapped in leather and hate; a wino
bleeds and laughs and coughs; the wards
are full of animal mucous, the slime
of our lives; I wait
to be put together again.

the statue of liberty is a tourist in the alps

6000 ft. up
slopes freaked with snow &
cold mountain water
gushing from pipe
in mossy cattle trough
         & the world still with me
         (bundle of L.A. Free Presses
         over the cowflop &
         God's own creation
         the cartoon
             shows poor raped
             Liberty fucked in the ass by
             Pigs

peaks & valleys
in 3 pm August sun
look immortal

but
>
> I've seen them
> go, friends
> that time & booze caught up with
> women & junk & boys &
> fame & dollars
>
> > gone!
> >
> > > they screamed
> > > of loneliness &
> > > injustice &
> > > got older
> > > talking
> > >
> > > > to oblivion

not even this
mountain will
last
shaking in quakes, sliding
and dipping into
the sea

> like Tibet once
> flat against the ocean till
> the earth slipped or
> got hit, collided maybe
> with another planet
> & the mountains
> rose

* * * * * * * * * * * *

> after an hour
> even a mountain peak's a drag
>
> tho I hate to see it go
> the planet will not
> survive
> > greed
> > & hate

* * * * * * * * * * * *

Kerouac you're nothing now
only a name—I shake your ghosty hand
we'll meet in oblivion

I'll be in the void soon
but in San Francisco
I type yr unpublished pomes
Allen gave me, his beard gone grey

> my image stared
> from TV the other
> night & I
> stared back
> shocked—who's
> the strange
> guy??

went home, to bed
                    thinking

Jack how's the void? we'll meet!
there!
          nah, we'll never meet!
we're victims, destroyed
by everything,
by time, by politicians,
psychiatrists, doctors, bad air, bad food,
booze, hunger, sex, lovers, no love, no money. . . .

> flipflops of planetary woe!
> > no time in the abyss
> > no time to play with form
> > as we scream in the dark

when void is formless
what's form?

* * * * * * * * * * * *

san francisco preview performance 1972

I always thought
it would be like this
like my dream long ago
of great tides hurling
upon the land
myself engulfed
with struggling masses
screaming
choking
fighting
for air

now this strange
prophetic dream
seems true
as I watch the waterpipe
shaking
and the lamp on the night table
and the bed with my body
in it shaking
as the earth shakes
night after night
in warning

cold turkey

red ants were crawling under my skin
in my brain, in my armpits.
I could not sit or stand
or lie down without fire.
I tried to shed my skin
like the flaming tunic of Greek mythology
but it was no good . . . the ants remained
I called on God, I screamed his names,
the one, the many, the all
starting with Jesus Christ and Jehovah.
I prayed to Buddha and the Lord Krishna
got down on my knees to Allah

but had to get up again I was shaking so much.
I tried the Greek and Roman gods, Christian saints
and the saints of every religion I knew
but still it was no good . . . the ants cavorted
and frolicked in my crotch,
they jabbed their needles into my penis,
I howled till the walls shook,
ripped my flesh with my nails
till I sank swooning to the floor
bloody and dying
and swore I would never
get hooked again.

then after eternities
the insect demons disappeared

I drank water
took some downers
and slept it off
for 3 days.

three parapoems

       YOUR NIGHT   must come
in   your   nightsheds   everywhere
frozen   crocodiles   under
     the   skin
   bloodfoot   burn   in   the wind
insomniac   devour   the
     rooftops   in   a
yellow   wind
     mirrors   &   owls   within
sight   of   dawn
in   your   nightsheds
everywhere   your   night
   must come

CRABS   GOATS   SCORPIONS   LIONS   &
        what   bloodstream   of   the
        consciousness   of   IS
heavenhouses
            rule   conscious   cells
of   world   brain
        F L A S H I N G
        c o m m u n i c a t i o n
dreamheads   pulsate   signals   to   each
        other   thru   chaos
        commercial   worlds   bequeath
world   could   be   such
        streaming   vast   jewelfire
equators   howl   to   green   ice
        &   polar   flares
    snow   becomes   grass
        NOTHING   BUT   FLOW
                    thru
morphine   seas

CHEMICAL STRANGERS feel
trembling
        the melting bubbles
              of the sun
for the roads darken
in your night
in your land
of ashes
        blood thru corn
the spirit
        turned
                to trade

o hollow AMERICA
        youth in holes
must escape

we shall enter
                the ocean-of-eclipse
from aqueducts & graters
& kitchenware prairies

        millions flee
        the lightning

of your deaf ferocity!

american girls
beneath bestial bellies
     lay
a thousand muscles strain
  volcanic vulvas
  puddled moons
     in windblurred skies

hotel nirvana

1

if only by pronouncing SHIVA
  if by repetition of the mantra
     by endlessly chanting a delightful phrase my liver spleen
       heart intestines
    could suddenly be restored whole

if all the vicious circles of resistance & violence could be
dissolved by the powerful sound of a universal OM uttered
from the beginning of the kosmos to the end of the kalpas

ah my god watching the white smoke of the locomotive in the
valley at night the gloomy cliffs the lights of the village
ghostly veils of milky silvering blackness gone in a puff

watching my fright & panic on waking in darkness with a terrible
dream of loneness like death coming on

watching the soothing effect of a mantra repeated till the
sound reverberates thru all my cells turning them to jewels
of momentary glinting light

watching myself in all my manifest mazes

watching a tidal wave of giant stars & flowers & flames
  & wheels whirling disks in the sky
  space beyond space endlessly
    opening my human head
    past all limits with body still on earth among houses & trees

                    & the sun the sun
                    with calm full gaze
                                        & the moon her lunar eyes
                        stillness raying
                                    astral influences

watching medieval woodcuts viols flutes hautboys flageolets lutes
pure voices of faith & holy peace & plaques
        mottled faces the barrows loaded with corpses
        nuns with habits over their bellies flung on the ground
                getting fucked by monks
                    they all have eternal expressions
                        emotionless faint smiles
                            of passion as if posed in monalisa
                                noncommittal
                                    disinterested mystery

o benevolent passion that lifts us on magic carpets out the
windows of middleclass tenements! that raises us on waves
of our own minds
                        out of our mind limits

o molecular rainbow!
o carafe where tiny sperms swim!
o lies of love & brotherhood!
o emotional bullshit!
                        leaving only the cold fact
                        the desert
                        the child crying again
                            man betrayed again

            if only by pronouncing a syllable
                if by casting a spell
                I could hold off
                    the bold girl who stole
                        flesh from my flesh

who tore my spirit up
and left me with knocking knees
heaving guts
and gagging throat
threatened with void

            my break with a thousand loves in one

2

i am gnawing the bark of trees in hunger
    i am getting furious at everybody
        i am the screaming kingdom of torn up streets of earthquake
            i am hate which i call love
                i am the poet of potential murder
i am the post office of athens losing important letters
    i am tying up millions of lives in knots & vicious circles
        i am kafka midas labyrinth of lost souls with no thread back
i am death destruction annihilation emptiness ignorance dreams evil
    i am smoking & drinking myself to death
      i cannot learn my lesson
        i am a nasty prolonged illness
          i am a whitehaired old lady who thinks she is god
i am the terrible endless persecution of the individual by the state
i am red tape cancer cigarettes blackmail lying theft disgust
    i am white light breaking thru gloom
      i am gloom breaking thru white light
        i am my cat lapping her nounou
          i con myself with cynical ruthlessness
i steal cars & rape children & run an eternal racket to grab while the
        grabbing is good
    i am available in small doses only
      i breathe the poisons of noisy overcrowded cities
        i am contradiction separation loneliness
i am the soul yearning for god who does not exist except in myself

3

bumming thru all cities
        they flash thru my mind with monstrous speed
  i see the pampas the andes
        a claustrophobic trap
where an evil sun shining like an aztec mask of hate
      tries to burn down all life
flushes of vapor from rock
            threw me
            face down upon the ground
streets reeled   the earth quaked
rome   athens   new york   my mind
blown
      i could not rise to the god or demon
        of a dying planet
       corpses try to contact each other
        with helpless gestures

lovers go mad in cannibal beds
              gnaw each other's flesh

                dead mouths dribble worms of sound
hips explode
                hot membranes into throats
              that grope the crotch for god
lipstick passions breathe into blue carbonic fumes
        streaked with tobacco haze
            as macedonian helmets of the police
              glitter with hate
      the international cripples huddle together
              dying
                  of universal butchery

seeking the light
        the way out
poets sell their poems in the black market of the soul
            in the muddy wave of ruin
        in atomic winds thru olive groves
              madness riding the winds
                  riding the brain

      words   images   fotos

          a vanished universe
              with memory of you
        in departed rooms
              your tongue
                  in my mouth
              in another city
                  without you

                      4
swami under mt. lycabettos
        seated in the lotus posture
        among the philodendron leaves
              with gentle mind
                  two grayblack braids
                      behind your ears
                          jokes & parables
                              slightly naive
                          devoted to the vedas
                              also science & bible

with flashes of illumination
near the funicular
where the peasants in yellow dust
stop to gawk at you & laugh
just flown in from paris
with your white turban
your flowing robes
& sandalled feet
just arrived to unravel
a personal western crisis
between husband & wife
(metaphysical jetset)
with your life of peaceful meditation
with your dark skin of asia
with your voice of white clouds
with your breath of yoga
with your healing eyes
what can you tell us
from hotel nirvana?

5

they followed the leader into the mountains
sat at his feet in a Swiss canton
as they decayed
like rotting fish

and he looked at them
and said:
turn off the ventriloquist's voice
flush out the snakeoil in the blood
your bible
your gita
your gems
your guns
your flags
your death

and at night they went to the nite clubs gobbling and soaking
up the suds
while that thing
between the legs
became
more urgent
they dished up the cold turkey

of what he had said
and nobody felt too good
nobody felt

so they took the train the limousine the rucksack
and went back home

next year
they followed him to India
and again he looked at them
and said:
follow no leader
guru
hero
nobody is living
everybody is dead
and again he told them
told them

and again that thing
between the legs
and between the ears
got in the way

the business of poetry

the business of poetry
is the image of a young man
making music and love
to a young girl whose interest
in love and music coincides
with an enormous despair in both
their inner selves like a plucked
guitar in the dry hot sun of
hope where savage and brutal men
are tearing life like a page
from a very ancient
and yellow
book

zombie fix

i saw gardens & fountains with sufic script on columns like palms
between mouldering lanterned walls of Granada sunlight Alhambra
lattices of star moon crescent lotus & diamond
casting their patterns into pools & floors

i saw sadfaced heraldic lions & mosaic saints in ceilings
chanting forever of heaven in words of purple & blue & gold

the beast & the angel of Europe alive on riverbanks
or meditating in cloisters acting their dedicated roles
going with prescribed postures to a prescribed destruction
& then to a prescribed creation

under the grilles of Seville i walked thru plazas of porcelain
with holy images plumed horses & hearses & baroque dreams of ebony
with carved chimeras gargoyles balconies
with flowers madonnas bleeding hearts

i saw caves & guitars with remnants of Lorca's gipsies clicking
castanets for busloads of tourists & singing & wailing soleares
for pesetas flashing their teeth in rehearsed routines of corn

& the bullfight in Alicante full of blood & spunk & buttocks
tight silk flaming olés in dust of broiling corrida in the
blowtorch sun & blaze of mobs with an ear a tail a groin a horn
handkerchiefs & cushions hurled & everyone
crazy wild for *cojones! cojones! cojones!*

& the blind on streetcorners screaming *para hoy! para hoy!*
sad broken chant of lottery tickets by miserable shepherds of chance
stuck without mercy in their current of rags & death

in sulphurous Andalusian landscapes sizzling colors of soil
mineral landscape of rainbow nitrate nickel & ferrous landscape
rust of blood where flamenco rhythms grew harsh
with gitano cries of ancient poverty & buried magic curses
the malagueña erupted out of the flesh in furtive
glances of lust in the johns of Malaga in Cordovan alleys
dark rustlings in doorways off the ramblas
fandangos of fuck in hotels that stank of fish

all over Spain i shook the clammy hand of executed souls

kissed sweet mouths of corpses spoke with the vanquished
spirit of revolution walked with unspoken fear
that looked out of peasant faces watched the zombie
movements of bodies that could not speak their need

then back to Manhattan's gray glow of glass & steel
vapid saurian heights of shiny nightmare script written for all
with breakdown nerves of power mad executives
running the world on alcohol & sex
back to the two-dimensional
automatic scenario of the zombie fix!

as the t'ang poet said

for W.C.W.

as the T'ang poet said
　　the scene
　　　　of a poem
　　　　　　is like the smoke

that issues from
　　fine jade
　　　　when the sun
　　　　　　is warm

it can be seen
　　from a distance
　　　　but not
　　　　　　from close to

the distance grows
　　greater in time
　　　　but you
　　　　　　have the touch

that makes the poet's line
　　come true
　　　　as the T'ang poet
　　　　　　said

nobody
    can learn
        this difficult
            art

and who
    but a few
        can see the smoke
            of fine jade?

expatriate party

The plump young lady
        with the resonant voice
                from Michigan
                        was writing uh
a novel, she said she had only written
                        television and radio scripts
                                before
and stayed all night
            in a corner of the room
                    in the same
                            chair
the thin yellowhaired boy
            with the waxen face of St. Germain
                        des Près
was trying hard to control
                his shoulders
and hands
        and showed an interest in
                    the plump young lady's
                            uh
novel
    while his eyes traveled
                around considerably
                        to
hairy chests
    which
        this being a warm island
                of the Peloponnese
                    proved rather stimulating

Zoe managed not to belch
            but her laughter was almost worse
                        Poor Zoe!
                              high IQ
                                    horse teeth
but she has got God
            and poetry
                  Dick speaks of explosives
and chemical engineering
            5 months in the army
                        and thinks only
of the precise date of his
            discharge
                  meanwhile indulging
                              in smack & speed
Tony still plays the role of cocksman
                  no woman too old for him
                              but he can't get it up
the kraut beatnik poet bullshits as usual about Buddhism
      and wears a gold earring
                  that should clamp his lips
                                    together
the T'ang poets
      his models
                  have driven him to despair
"When two masters meet
                  they laugh and laugh," he says, laughing
and weeping on the whitewashed
                  terrace as the moon
                              comes up huge
"the trees, the many fallen leaves"
                  and passes out
                              while guitars rage
and a breeze whips the
            hashish smoke
                  and kerosene lamps
somebody crouches on
                  the coping
                        as the blonde Australian starlet
                              staggers across the terrace
                                    in search of her
personality that a NY book reviewer is willing
                              to help her
                                    find

he shoves her
                    down among the pine needles
                                   beside the house
                                            and
         socks it to her like a lesson
                              in mathematics
          this girl is always open
                         to culture
                                      the moon
      is high and full and
                     the cicadas have quit
                                   their racket

night piece

   the sea & the wind & the rain
      are battering my house
         tearing at the cliff's foot

   the bad ocean dumps
      its tonnage ashore
         breaks on rock
            all its mean force

   inside the house
      in the center of the storm
         a lone mind far out
            a single conscience adrift

   I lie awake recording
      the tremendous monotone

quanto sei bella, roma!

tenors yelling I LOVE YOU to fountains
arias in railway stations
umber & gold piazzas
rippling facades
piazzas & pizzas!
restaurants sprawl white as spaghetti
tablecloths under Egyptian obelisks
Verdi! Puccini! Mastroianni!
vespas barf
below umbrella pines
& marble steps flare high
in the sun
among baroque angels on bridges

                                 (lavish vision!
                                 the city an eternal
                                   adolescent made for love

Quanto sei bella, Roma! the waiters sing
in Trastevere where
Belli the obscene
                 poet of *verismo*
sketched immortal monologues—

                              your bridges, Rome,
aqueducts, roads, satyricons, palaces, colosseums,
         orgies,
                     muscular hot boys
& monumental mammas—

                             (Muse! *must* you
                           forever remind us of
                             fleshy matters?

a city like a poem, a sculpture, a
sweeping signature, cupids
for punctuation marks, rococo artifices, the
mind of Bernini in each stone flourish, slums
of white marble, Rilke's city of flaring streetstairs,
La Dolce Vita, haunted flesh, Fellini's freakshow
of timeless ruins, layers of time. . . .

                         (white
                         travertine & ashen tufa

                              & salamanders skittering
                              in the rubble

                         *

at the Palazzo Orsini, by the 14 ft. fireplace (quattrocento)
the old count nervous as catgut,
twitched; weekends it was quartets;
& they talked of Dado Ruspoli who made headlines
for taking dope—*stupefaccenti*!
                              & could they
under the eh circumstances—well, *invite* him, the young prince,
to their musicales?
                    no, one must wait, *pazienza*,
until it blows over—one can't be *too* careful; &
besides, hadn't Mohandas, their favorite guru,
been detained by the *polizia* on suspicion of lacing chocolate
bars with hashish, attempted seduction? & the Finnish soprano
collapsed, near death; at the hospital (floating kidney)
the drug was discovered, the guru held
for manslaughter; a curious turn of events—but
she pulled thru & he was deported,
dear Mohan! he sang Tagore so beautifully!

l'americana, by this time, had got her languages boggled:
        "I am here since 25 years—
            25 years with *Italians*!
        and not ONCE been robbed!"

& the Princess Caetani: "Sì, sì, *endless* money, *l'americana*. . . .
        she (la principessa) was a Biddle,
                              a Philly Biddle,
& founded *Botteghe Oscure*, the noted "little
                    magazine"
                              ran over 500 pp. (biennial).
to take her mind off her only son,
                    who'd been shot down in Musso's Air Force
& her daughter at 45, tall bony angular, went off
        to marry the Duke of Marlborough
& poor old Ruggero, the Prince
            having composed an opera
                    that had taken 50 years *or sono*
heard the first performance
                    on RAI (Radio Italiana) aged 94

& expired shortly thereafter
                & had known Wagner
                & Debussy
                        & Verdi

& at dinner once, after being damn brilliant
at the palazzo with liveried servants
on the street named after his family
passed his hand over his eyes
& there was a hush at the table
& when it was over smiled wanly
saying,
        "What a *bore*, old age!"

& at the castello at Ninfa:
"My wife tells me you've translated our Belli!"

he was then (on the death of his brother)
                         Il Duca di Caetani
                           e Sermoneta—
                    "impossible! I mean,
um, certain *words* used in the *best* Roman society—
they simply are NOT used, are they?
                    in English-speaking countries."

                  servants slid about.
                    the Duke resumed:
"Take, for instance, our Roman word—*fregnaccia*. . . .
how, I AHSK you, HOW would you translate *fregnaccia*? ? ?
To us it's just *big bad cunt*."
                  (that would be 1955, *più o meno*,
               when he was 94, slightly stooped
                     at 6'4")

"Cunt," I said.

They had known Valéry
                  who edited their Paris magazine, *Commerce*,
in the Twenties.
& Gide, I think, was on the payroll.

                *

obelisk

I AM AN OBELISK OF EGYPT
I HAVE COME TO CHANGE ALL THAT YOU KNOW
I'VE BEEN WAITING 5,000 YEARS
UNDER MY SCRIPTURES RIVERS DIE
PRAYERS RUST AND FLAKE
I SPEAK SYMBOLS
I GIVE OFF IMAGES LIKE SMOKE
I KEEP SECRETS
I AM ONE COOL STONE

now

the bottle of mineral water is guillotining the trees
        i tighten my scarf

in cap & hornrimmed specs
i'm superimposed on italy
                speeding north
into rain & winter

9 years
knocking around the mediterranean

far from redskin curse drunk air race clash

soon paris (again)
black bitter & wet
        winter
everyone's cold & jumpy

machineguns are bursting

outside
it's becoming switzerland
                full of snow & chocolate
        darkness clean almost white
presses against the window
        & steams it

everybody asleep
        only me alone in the rushing corridor

i hear the expiring hiss
of everywhere i've been

nobody-noplace-night
   NOW   NOW   NOW

I have no address
     no property
let the customs men come
     i have nothing to declare

only the present
   of cold   crises   & war
timetables   whistles   brakes   signals
hungry   tired   needing sleep   & i drink
i drink to you now to your passing like music
     to your rhythm & flow
i pour words on your head i smoke you
     i eat your peanuts

i read your novels & write your poems
i meditate on your dirty socks
i discuss your violets with a beggar
i stare absorbed in your mandalas
     from china & india

and the train like thought outleaps the night
floats from timebound tracks of steel
     everywhere & forever

     because of her wheel
because she feels unbound to the earth
unbound to gas air metal mineral
beyond airfire where the seed begins

she is a wise train
she is not fooled by spaceships
she has a mind of her own

she outleaps fields of chocolate sleep where watches grow
no switzerland can hold her long

because of her wheel because of her go

o wheel

you burn thru my mind as the train burns thru the skin of night

now france

now france   yesterday italy   & it's fall
special paris light   slant on treetops   gray
buildingtops   clear   hard   like french eyes   bulge
of intellect   chalcedony eyes   slightly
          inhuman no?   & how
architecture creates   the sky

          will someone stop me in the street   saying
          how wonderful!   we don't know each other?!
                    just walk arm in arm
                    & never ask our names!
make love at sight!   anonymous as monks!
                    esperanto lips!
          africa in my arms!   near east!

but how to slow down   i'm running away
          are those my arteries   or steel tracks?
                    stations in the dawn   old man
sourly pushing letters   in huge sacks
          are they my unfinished plans?

               paris of leaves   beards   duffel coats!
          am i interested in radio telescopes?
          the kind that look inside the moon?
          parabolic mirrors?   limits of the solar system?
izvestia follows me around   sneers at my life
                    no wonder i'm feeling blue

i'm here to tell you of a finer fate
          to explore trees
                    listen to colors
                         pick the golden flower
                         feel under someone's duffel coat

for the clear light
of the void

down on your knees!   pray to the holy human body!
    worship god in the fork of the thighs!
        i can't blow the 'socialist victory'
    nor raise any flag but my lilywhite ass
to all the silly nations who want me to choose sides

I've chosen   orgasm/feeling/smell/soul
freedom of dream   who is freer than when he dreams?
    i choose the light of the sky   over the boulevards
        & the bookstalls   full of sexy pictures
            & occult prophecies   THE EARTH

believing in the absurd

writing a poem
& feeling absurd
about this useless activity
I went to the window
& saw a scraggy nut
beret mothy beard
groucho moustache
grinning
muttering
to himself
staring
at greeting cards
in the window
of the *imprimerie*
gît-le-coeur
suddenly
in a swift
handwriting on the wall
laughing secretly
& shaking his old head
(lonely weirdo
in priestly garb
ratty & black) he
wrote

& I had to see
& ran downstairs
& read

WE ARE SEARCHING
FOR RATIONAL REASONS
FOR BELIEVING
IN THE ABSURD

now i'm in vence

Now I'm in Vence where Lawrence died
his grave ghouled by three arty harpies
who spirited his remains to a phallic tomb in Taos
and lightning rips the hills of the Azure Coast
quake destroys Skoplje in Yugoslavia
as ancient prophecies work thru vast Illusion and Dream
the worst yet to come as Man knows not to govern his own House

and a Firefly lights on my dirty bedsheet among such omens
its body glows in the dark
it is a Star on my bed as other Stars float on the floor
with Moths & Spiders at their work
and I see flashes of Illumination and want to live to tell it
yet this morning I bombed a giant Spider in the bathroom
sprayed him with Flytox because I was afraid
afraid of huge hairy tarantula tentacles
composed and wary dance of his body
I watched him curl, shrivel and crawl on the porcelain shower floor

and I thought, will I meet Death by Heavenly Flytox
sprayed on me for my hairy Lust?
burning in agonized death throes
on the floor in insect pursuits?
mountainous Silence answers with trees and moonless Flowers
as I spin under the cartwheel chandelier in country house
knowing no mescaline molten jewels of Sun and Star
no laughing gas no kif can turn me on come final crackup of this World

I demand in silent prayer never to fear earthquakes nor violent men
and kiss the young red mouth beneath the figtree at my cottage door

where we stand in the dark clutching shoulder and breath in summer
        night
speechless and aching in our wordless Flesh

the inside of a poem is red

at 5 A.M. a bomb goes off.
rue de Buci. broken
windows on both sides of the
street, all the way to the top
floor. downstairs the Italian
restaurant is littered
with dead spaghetti. next
door, in gutted display, a
magician frozen forever in black
silk cape and evening dress gestures
to the shop-window floor where
chunks of glass gleam at his
feet, crushed.

at the Hotel Jeanne d'Arc
and the Café Mabillon burst
beer mugs, sandwiches, cats.
Beauregard, the black
painter of yellow, got fished out
of the sea, half-drowned, starving again
in Paris. St. Clair the mad
English poet jumped into the Seine
naked and, feeling cold, climbed to the
bank; a *bateau mouche* slid by with U.S. tourists
taking photos: he stuck his middle finger
up his ass and waved it at them.

"I'd like to help him," confided Alexis, noted
Greek sculptor who shaved his head and wore
black leather coats, affecting a
criminal air, "but I'm very delicate
inside. this kind of thing
upsets me. he is always coming around
and it is getting me depressed the other day
he ruined my work for at least an hour. tried

to commit suicide in front of me—pure theatrics—
and grabbed a saw in my studio and started
to cut his wrists. it is getting me
down. especially since I have
2 commissions to fill and
am behind."

gas fumes. smog. streets
bomb-filled. the sky is black
in winter. the Paris light
that artists praise is gone.
the sky is wet
and black. Beau tried
to end it all again.
rain.
fatigue.
if silk could sing.
oh jesus.

St. Clair sneaked out of the hotel
(owing rent) with a mattress
to sleep on the quai
among the bums. I slash at a poem,
the inside of the poem spills out,
stains the room blood red. the
inside of a poem is red. this
is dangerous. I start to throw paint
on canvas. it explodes in all
directions. a wash of blue,
violet and green a skyey ground
for a big green question
mark that becomes the center
of the painting, with red
drops scattered
everywhere.

i'm at an impasse

i've been around
i'm at an impasse
i say no instead of why
i'm in the red
my books don't balance
words mean less
i forget what i wanted to say
no matter
images rituals
are meaningless
shallow excuse for
empty minds
i've been around
looked for the Master
poked into Mysteries
a lot of words
to escape into
sat on a riverbank
meditating endlessly
squatted on walls
stared at ceilings
had moments
of leaving the body
& all that jazz
where are you
whom i loved with my bones
the only meaning
my life ever had
where are you
i'm at an impasse
believed in visions
love & brotherhood
deceived myself
right down the line
ended in lone
crazy despair
chewing my nails
eating my liver
frightened
wanting to die
wandering rootless
with empty hands

who invented this brain
this nervous system
runaway cells
where a tune gets stuck
and images go wild
i'm at an impasse
you're gone & i'm lonely
facing the void
of habit & death
hooked on the chain
of stupid events
nipple & lip
hot mammal warmth
these come first
then whiskey
cigarettes
a joint
a spike
some head
some tail
then
nothing
nothing
old primal suck
first urge
repeated endlessly
more & more
soulless & dead
i'm at an impasse
what do i crave?
i walk the streets
of each new city
in keen expectation
i've been around
what's it all for?
cold stars & the void
fear in the throat
you are gone
i'm at an impasse
can't break thru
the wall of words
i've been around
seen it all
power & failure

ecstasy
horror
revolution
despair
oh where are you
i'm at an impasse
i've been around

all the artauds

Hundreds of Rimbauds everywhere
at coffee galleries laundromats bars
at streetcorner intersections
they demand immediate recognition
speak with telepathic intensity
end by panhandling a quarter

There are more Rimbauds per square hectare
than Baudelaires in the bohemian sector
but when I arrived at the poetry reading
I distinctly counted 365 Artauds
one for each day of the year

France does a brisk trade in Artauds

Every Artaud accuses the others of being an impostor
each shows scars on his wrist grins toothlessly with aquiline scorn
wearing feigned madness like a Purple Heart

When I began reading they rose as one man and screamed
denouncing me for pederasty black magic and catholic spells
all the Artauds made one hell of a noise
I could hardly continue

When it was over I shakily left for my favorite café
found myself alone
ignored by about a dozen Artauds at the counter
who communicated with each other in some kind of cabalistic jargon
made up of medieval Spanish academic gobbledygook and Bronx
    Yiddish
plotting the overthrow of the King of the World

who was the only one in their way

Laughing loudly they praised each other's genius
staring forcefully in the mirror
where they saw themselves multiplied infinitely

the last bohemian

in memory of Maxwell Bodenheim

I used to see him on MacDougal Street bouncing a ball
and clicking his teeth in a crazy grin

Sometimes he spun a yo-yo
and sold old sonnets for a buck each
muttering "Bee-yoo-deeful pome. Signed. . . . "

He stank of cheap booze
lushed out in subways
with a bloody head
under his faded ratty hair

He was the Dante of Greenwich Village

Sometimes he beat his wife in Washington Square
and they screamed at each other

> "Fuckin BASTARD!"
> "SHUDDUP YA SLUT!"
> "Goddam BITCH!"

Everybody stopped to enjoy the scene
familiar among chess-playing Italians
and bull-dykes with pekes
faggots cruising the meat rack

Maxie always carried a briefcase
with hidden important messages
about the Revolutionary Girl

He was a wiggy prophet who yelled at the air
        "FAS-SIST SWINE!"

Once he pissed at an audience from the stage thus ending
his performance unexpectedly

He couldn't have arranged a more artful death
murdered by the mad cat with the flash bulb grin
yelling: I KILLED A COMMUNIST!

He died with *The Sea Around Us*
in his folded arms

invisible beast

            the peasants are right
carrying radios in the streets
            counting their money
without a thought
for the mad scientist's lab
            or the prophet's gloomy cry
kissing their ikons with incense
up their framed and gullible ass
            taking it easy
as they starve on dazzling coasts
            marvelous islands
& sundrenched fields where
they shit on the lettuce & tomatoes
            they're right
they are not so dumb
wanting to get rich
            & have big cars
& diamonds big as ulcers
            they go on talking
of bread & wine & bills
            & the weather
in the next room they are dancing
            to bouzouki
            & singing like bulls
they laugh when I speak
foreigners are funny
& I don't tell them
            of the voice
I hear thru the music

rasping a prophecy
or the invisible beast
        hunching
its terrible shoulders
            against the wall

manichean vision

a woman with scratchy voice
screams at me—
I pissed against her window!
she must have narrowly escaped!
ah, music. . . .
music's therapy for mangled nerves.
slunk
down to the oily port
outside the yacht club
where an obscenity, a bleached turd
or serpenthead Kandinsky
bobs in the waves.
it twists, it turns
in the Greek harbor.
I reel by the hawser
play it by ear
with weed awareness in fierce moonlight.
I follow ragas on a lone cithar
up the donkey path white as skulls.
listen! raw strings
twang on white terraces,
a folksong scene,
myself sunk in cortical trance
while eyes—*whose?*—search me out—
WHO'S THAT LOOKING AT ME? oh, damn you!
it's myself! and then
a BLACK TURD falls
from the sky over the shops
and sloops! it stains
the bright cafés
messing up woven shirts
and creamy thighs; it creeps
into the Aegean sea and air,

into the coffee and conversation,
over the fleecy rugs; it sneaks
within the rucksacks and schnorkels,
between the pages of the book of poems . . .

oh god-it's GOD!

cocktails bugged by washington

(From a news item, 1965.)
                    for Philip Lamantia

the rose is a spy   the vase an agent
the martini olive has ears
transmitting cocktail code messages
toothpick aerial picks yr brain
WATCH THAT ROSE!   long-distance bugs
snoop fingernails and pubic hair? ?

Axis Rose
Tokyo Rose
Cocktail Rose

no flower is safe no blade of grass

we walk the streets of athenian spring
two poets screaming silence
                        in golden dialogue
Silence is Golden so who can bug silence?

mannekins watch us from shop windows
wax transvestites with torn neon breasts
leaking fluorescent blood

we magnetize the city with thought vibrations!

                    signals flash
we smoke
bugged cigarettes and look
thru a one-way mirror

greece answers

for Nanos Valaoritis

Greece answers with rape and sodomy, a good answer
to all those xtian centuries poisoned with
conscience for having warped the bacchic kicks
of the soul

Greece answers with cold cells and swill for pot adventures
and cisterns full of microbial woe
olive trees condemn red tape
the umbilicus of the world at Delphi is a rotten egg of stone
who touches the egg touches the origins of madness

Greece answers with shipowners
mystic poets lost in bureaucratic offices
choked with crimes of customs officials
legally stealing cars from impoverished invalids
in nightmare cubicles of labyrinthine ledgers

Greece answers with lyrical lawyers quoting fiscal strophes
jacking up fees while tenderly requesting an old photo
falling upon your bed to the strains of ouzo voodoo
extorting the last drachma of devotion from trapped clients

Greece answers with iron rods smashing footsoles
crushing kneecaps and ankles
freedom gags on a colonel's moustache
electroshock to the genitals brings down the classics
lobotomy on the Winged Victory
deranges the Discobolus

Greece answers thru the mouth of Medusa, paralyzing
with concrete stars, flinging her serpent sting
into the eyes sput and the eyes go dead as the black hole
at the center of the galaxy where all matter ends
in the cosmic garbage can

Greece answers with junta tanks and tommy guns nursed by the CIA
answers with screams of peasant pain, drowned
in fabulous sunlight and jasmine, strangled
in galvanised gulfs of amethyst, glazed
in grottoes and olive groves, guillotined

by dances in tavernas, fingers snapping
mustachioed murder official as passports
by horny secret police insatiably dreaming of orgies
answers with short hair, long skirts, dead newspapers,
dungeons, broken statues, torn pacts,
battered remains of civilisation, destroyed works,
poets howling from ruins of bleeding parthenons,
tragic muse in a bomber, gods in the sixth fleet

Greece answers with a Texas accent
with a tongue of tungsten with a larynx of gas
with orange smog with lizards in the agora
with computers wrestling the abacus in wineshops
with a heart of missiles
with blood of marble
with 8 million electric eels
entire population of Greece
writhing under 3 or 4 miserable minds
U.S. agents in Constitution Square
investigating sex habits for sexless files
bugging dolma vine leaves and cocktail cherries
books armpits genitals
so that not a thought shall be free from New York to Piraeus
and the rubber octopus of steel and oil shall inherit the earth

Greece answers with islands with suicide
wells of loneliness white walls of flowers
myths of monsters prowling everyone's labyrinth
memory overwhelms us in Greece the statue falls forever thru time
abandoned Delos aims Apollo's broken cocks at eternity
Rhodes hurls cockroaches large as sparrows at the coast of Turkey
the frogs of Aristophanes croak in the brakes of Crete
Plato's boys roam hissing and snapping their fingers in rhythmic dance
the minotaur flirts with the trojan horse in the fleamarket of Athens
the dollar has raped the drachma on the abdicated throne of Constantine
and now little draculas are the debased currency of Greece
Tsaruchis the painter says 'There are no men anymore'
he should know, he has had them all
Minos has fled to London to play Che Guevara in his imagination
Zina has gone to Nepal to become Madame Blavatsky
Nanos in Oakland exile plots the surrealist overthrow of the junta by
        poetry
nobody's left in Greece except American Express
what good are the cafés now only the dead inhabit them

corpses reading guidebooks
cadavers aiming cameras
mummies poking in ruins
the Acropolis bored with skeletons
caryatids consider moving to Hollywood
they will rival Melina Mercouri in personality ratings
I don't want to lose you Aegean
o amethyst sea come back
what will we do without you
where can we go anymore
I am desolate
who will comfort me who will magic me

Greece answers Know Thyself

these fears are real not paranoid

I am walking in Silent Spring and mourn the loss of birds
I do not feel like a million
I feel like I've been hit on the head and robbed
I feel cheated
my cells are crying for oxygen
each breath of air is deadly
I cannot trust water
poets are jumping from bridges
dying of bad faith
nothing seems true
love seems impossible
poisoners in high places
shove death down our throats
my spirit is flagging
I want to crawl into warm snug flesh and forget these monstrous
crimes, political crimes
whom can I turn to?
did Rachel Carson live in vain?
O insecticide department
my life is yours
the display is homey and cheerful
with pickles and olives across the aisle
and the bath and laundry soaps adjoining
rows and rows of insecticides

which do you choose? shall it be DDT for baby?
shall we anoint our skin with paint remover?
these fears are real not paranoid
brain and nerve damage from homey sprays for the garden lawn
and the American table would delight a Borgia
o zen masters! o positive vibrations!
o flashes of beauty and starlight and swift flowing visions!
my death awakes me
and is my life

words from the wall

i tell you
        this city is finished
it IS
     god they will not listen!
i have only just returned
         my friends
& therefore can see
         clearly
it is late   too late   & the city
  listen!
        don't run from me
   shaking your head
     it is you
who are mad!
       but under
the streamlined saurian beasts
with steel-embossed hides of glass
   i walked
        anonymous
while the people
   laughed

polemic

hiding behind his heaven where nobody can get near him
the Almighty who takes advantage of the sick & the dying
who gives no reasons his power is absolute
who need confess to none although he kills us all
making little children to suffer
and the aged to stumble like overworked beasts into the grave
who fritters away kalpas playing with worlds in his hands
as boys play with balls & marbles
shooting comets & planets novas & solar systems into space
rolling them like billiards down the alleys of the firmament
the cosmos in his hands & probably bored
having to invent angels & then growing tired of them too
because they were probably too solemn about being good
so that he expelled a perfectly decent one
no better & no worse than the others
but who had the tough luck to be chosen to be kicked out of heaven
to be told to go to hell
a really indecent act
(how can anyone respect such behavior)
then after inventing Evil & giving it a home
to invent man   to invent woman
to place before their morning eyes a temptation
something really irresistible   o it ain't my fault
i didn't put it there myself
and then on his abstract haunches to sit back in a cosy seat in
the sky
watching a comedy forever after
and when things got tiresome
to invent new hopes   new possibilities   new despairs
for the luckless miming actors starving & illpaid
killing his own son in cold blood
giving as an excuse the salvation of mankind
double-crossing everybody   EVERYBODY
including his own son who saw the deception in his agony
and for all we know he is laughing his cosmic head off
then yawning & looking at his watch that ticks away the chillicosms
about to retire about to call an end to a bad joke

at the trieste

the music of ancient Greece
or Rome did not come down
to us
but this morning
I read Virgil's *Eclogues*
struck
by the prophecy of a new era
"a great new cycle of centuries
begins. Justice returns to earth . . .
the Golden Age returns," he wrote
30 years before the end
of his millennium, describing
the birth of the infant god, "come down
from heaven." Jesus was 19
when Virgil died at 89. . . .
will the Golden Age never come?
same faces
thrown up each generation
same races, emotions, struggles
all those centuries, those countries!
languages, songs, discontents!
they return
here in San Francisco
as I sit in the Trieste
— recitative of years!
O Paradiso! sings the jukebox
as Virgil and Verdi combine
in this life
to produce the only Golden Age
there'll be

california will sink

I woke and looked around—
same old curtainless windows
torn shades thru which the sun
easily broke mornings. roaches romped
in brown paper sacks of garbage
and the pink fridge held
its hopeful vitamins
that would save me
from smog and the Food Conspiracy
and the dawn crept
across the windowsill
like a sick bum
and I thought: *all this will change*
and dressed and shaved and went down to the beach
and ran along the shore
nodding to the yogis in the lotus position
contemplating their acid navels
—the sun could not rise without their help—
and returned for lunch
and napped in the afternoon . . .
when I awoke it was evening.
I went down to the beach
and the whales were dying on the shore
and the sea lions perishing
and the fish uneatable
and the gulls choked with oil
and the plants withered
and the air brown
and the people irrelevant
victims of enterprise
denied, denied, denied
by the politician, the industrialist
and there was nothing I could do
but wait for the prophecy to be fulfilled:
California will sink overloaded with deathliness
into the Pacific
and what is the coast line now of many a land
will be the bed of the ocean. . . .
the oceans are dying
all pollution goes to the sea
they are not dying of long hair and nudity
but the people cannot understand

they cannot draw sane conclusions
the people are sick
they have been too long poisoned
by lies, by flags, by slogans,
by counterfeit nourishment,

they do not know
they do not see
they are with the gull and the sagebrush,
the ocean and the spider,
the sky and the dove.

o swarm of bees

o swarm of bees with fixed ideas

will you never change   will you never wake up

is there no way to shake you
from your stupor of habit
your coma of commerce
your insect marriage

must you always murder imagination

o mass of insipidness

who can believe in you
who can save you
will you always choose the wrong way
        are you the future
        are you hope

will you never be more than a maddening hum
in the throat of space
& time

she talked of debussy, van gogh and the rain

her name was Marcia
and she played The Golliwog's Cakewalk
after school. Marcia
wore a red wig
and hornrimmed glasses
to hide the lack of
eyebrows. her lips were white
and very thick. her brown eyes
laughed painfully. Marcia
played Debussy one rainy night
when I was fifteen. somehow
her ugliness got lost
in those cool chords.
it was impossible to touch her,
tho' in a black tight dress she . . .
well, I decided then
as I listened to her talk
of Debussy, van Gogh and the rain
that if I could not play the piano
or be six foot tall
and very handsome
I'd write
poetry. . . .

a terrible night in the closet

It's a terrible night in the closet.
Moths are gnawing at dead souls.
I smell rain, said the heel.
Spiders are prowling in the corners.
I want to get out! said a sad voice.
Me, too, pal, me, too.
It's dark in here. I'm suffocating.

The key! the key! Muffled laughter.
It's coming from outside. *We're in here!*

Beasts crouch; teeth are bared.

What if a fire breaks out!
Fear crawls along the crack of the door.
A giant stumbles, begins pounding.
Let me out! You can't keep me here!
The door shakes but does not open.
Everything shrivels inside.
The rivers in the closet dry up.
The mountains are barren.
Underwear withers. Pants collapse.
Bathing trunks gasp for air.
We'll never get out.
Break down the door!

whatever happened to yetta weinberg?

what am I doing hating a symphony by Vaughn Williams
    that's infernal my cat doesn't mind one bit curled up asleep
on the rough wool of my candystriped Moroccan blanket from Asilah
    her taste in music's informed why doesn't somebody
                                    come I'm going nuts
    pretending I'm real I'm not no sir I'm weird
                                        there are too many of me
I've never been the same since age 13 when I used to peek
    from the bay window of my room thru the trees overlooking
        her bedroom where she exposed herself on hot summer evenings
    by a reading lamp tho she never read a book those bubs
        in lamplight and me with my nose over the sill like Kilroy
            breathing hard babyfaced kid beating it
        I wonder what happened to Yetta Weinberg the landlord's daughter
        this symphony stinks I'd pop off in my knickers sometimes
            without touching it at the movies

                            some frightening
                        man would put his hand on
                        my thigh when I was 12 or
                    less and when I got up he'd grab me
                        by the seat and I said my mom
                    was in the back and I'd
                        tell if he didn't stop
                        she warned about

taking candy from strangers
she warned about everything
so it didn't mean a thing
when I grew up I became
that man
which ought to mean something

it's amazing how much poetry you can write just waiting for a friend
to ring the bell they're always late thus securing
posterity's gratitude
maybe the person from Porson did us a favor Kubla Khan
couldn't have
kept it up much longer it had to break off to get back to my life
I'd press against her as we kissed she'd wiggle her ass
and squirm
"Let's do it sitting down" which always mystified me
I'd ask why but get no answer and *very* worked up pressed
harder and when she squealed I twisted her arm OUCH!   she was
in tears
OUCH! OK! OK! I'LL TELL YOU! BECAUSE—BECAUSE—
we're not MARRIED!!!
stunned in the 1930's parlor that was the end of my childhood
a flashbulb lit up in my head and I understood my hard on

true confessions

momma
because you could not believe
he loved you
you ripped the shirt off his back.
blood ran down his arm
and face as Steeplechase
grinned beside the brilliant sea
with ferris wheels and dodgems
in Coney Island once.
I stood beside the freakshow
shaking in the street
with shame and fear
while people gaped
and you, momma, screamed: LOUSE!
SONOFABITCH BASTARD!

and the waves kept dancing
and the beach gleamed, it was always the same
no matter where we went,
Harlem or Brighton; dirty words
went sailing thru the air like turds
and roaches romped
and neighbors neighed
and faucets plunked
mad music in the sink
of furnished rooms
where you got slapped for nagging
and I got teased for being
and never knew what to be.
on headachey Sundays, momma,
you went around with a turbanned head
playing dead
in a cold wet towel or dishcloth, clutching
your breast with suffering—
Sarah Bernhardt! he'd sneer
while the radio yapped like a pack of jackals
hysterical ballgames, shrill, raspy,
hell on the nervous system. *he*
was listening. the Dodgers ran
homeruns thru our mealtime wars.
thru the stink
of rancid mazola frying.
and the corncob I caught in the belly
from clear across the room
for speaking out of turn—at least
I was seen and heard for once: I gagged,
turned blue. HITLER!! you screamed
at him. GOLEM!! MURDERER!!!
between the two of you
I was squeezed like a bedbug, crushed,
done in. age twelve
I grabbed a breadknife when he hit
you hard, and stood on the bed and stuck it
at the center of his paunch: "Do
that one more time, you bastard, and
I'll kill you!" Max, you never did it again.
Max, you rat, you scum,
hated stepfather of my childhood, bald
man with a pot, fat slob, one eye
on the landlord, a step ahead

of the rent, jobless in attics,
basements, transient rooms—I cried
my heart out each time we moved, never
had a home or friends, while he sang
East Side West Side All Around The Town and laughed
and read *The Saturday Evening Post* and died
of fat around the heart, a cigar
and a bottle of beer, the last
pinochle in his pudgy paws,
and I was cheated out of killing him.
have I ever told you, mother,
what all this meant? have I blamed you,
threatened you, killed you?
old woman, you're lonely
and can't remember
and have not changed
one bit.

out of my head

Lucia is stabbing her lover again, she's mad!
I admire tuneful suffering
but god, I'll become a True Believer, I'll
pray, give thanks, anything, if only you, thou, thee
help me—shit! melody flows from that damn opera
like my diarrhea—OOOhhh!! I'll write a poem,
Muse, don't get pissed off, rescue me
a little, *do* something, can't you see I'm in trouble?
the bitch won't give me a tumble!

Sunday tedium stretches back
to terrible afternoons
when the opera could not save me
from nervous fatigue, dumb squabbling parents, emptiness. . . .
ah that coloratura with flutes . . . sweet style, I envy you!
& grow nostalgic—for what? musical erehwons?

Italo friends, old streets, Brooklyn, come back!
she's doing the virtuoso thing to a flute—
sharp silvery scales, *con brio*,
arias sexy as olive skin—

Mafalda of the Budding Breasts, Anna of the Juicy Lips,
Frankie Zelitto of the Hard Ons, Joey of the Thick Thighs,
Giuliano of the Muscles, Giosuè of Soft Smiles—
SANGUE they sing SANGUE!
I see blood spilling
out of the opera
out of my head!

a poem for pound

I

came up from Black Mt.
to meet you at St. Elisabeth's
& the receptionist said
"Mr. Pound cannot be seen / he is not well today"
I protested that you were expecting me
& she plugged in the doctor
"There's a young man here
who has traveled all the way
up from the South
to see Mr. Pound"
but the doc wouldn't allow it
& I couldn't stay overnight
with $2 and an oilburning Packard
to get back to NY in
& the leaves falling
chill in the air
so we never
met

II

too late, doubting his touch
his life, stupid like all lives,
irreversible, all mistakes,
too late, too late—

"I do nothing—I know nothing—and the biggest idiots are
those who believe they know something. . . . "

Pound,
for this   "certainty of the greatest uncertainty"
I mourn, relent for you, for me,
for Oedipus, for King Lear, for the Devil himself—

"I would like to explain to you . . . oh, but it's so difficult,
                        and all so *useless*. . . ."
whom were you addressing whitebearded bard?
    did you really speak so?
more moving than the nagging rant
        of your arrogant days—
    you thought you had the answers
        but you lived long enough
    to know there are no answers
        intelligence
            never enough
    pain paid with pain

our insolent blindness. . . .

did you pay your dues?
        grow saintly towards the end?
did Mind burn Ego up?

millions of innocent dead want to know. . . .

once I received a message from you, Pound
one word, what zen simplicity,
drawn like a Chinese ideogram across the page—

                    WHEN?

                    signed   EP

Pound, *if not now,*   *when?*

address to an angel

Men cut tears out of diamonds
making crystals bleed

Stones weep on fat fingers
making nooses of gold

The rivers are swollen with Death
rivers of oil & blood
running thru the streets of the world

Prayer turns to a sneer
& the nerves of my head burn like coals

Angel, when will this end?

all american poets are in prison

—written by Harold Norse and Jack Micheline
at 185 Marina Blvd., San Francisco

Yesterday
I sent a secret letter
to a Russian poet in prison
by carrier pigeon
Guilty of publishing
a mimeographed magazine
of young Russian poets
who said fuck you
to the establishment
In America such a silent murder
The pigs of commerce
want to control your mind
the cash register joins every cause
Nor do they want
the fire of the soul
Fuck truth they say
over the gray ashes of America's living dead
Thank God for my mother's Rumanian heart
my grandfather carrying stones to keep warm

my father jerking off the iceman in the Bronx
Thank God for my father's Russian Hard-on
I'm sick of America let's leave it out of this poem
What has America done that I should notice her
Notice the girl peeing in her pants next to me in the 6th grade
and the Jewish teach with the self-conscious eyeglasses
weeping tears of borsch for the labor movement
and Father Coughlin blowing Joe Louis in his dreams
Fuck America give it to France
I got to go to the next course
Rotten lettuce in the ice box
Spread the word like butter
we're sending our poems to the Chinese laundry for lichee nuts
The Grocer's daughter poor nymphomaniac
with legs like lox and lust for cock
she was a real intellectual with 194 I.Q.
hustling sailors on Times Square
O silent Russian poet in prison
All American poets are in prison
Jails of the soul
Blocks of the brain
Streets without deliverance
Murder in their shoes
Deceived by rotting molars
O instinct where is the ash tray
Old urinals on the Russian Front
The beer is no good
The printer's ink sucks on the page
O Comrade in Russian tea rooms
They have killed my pigeon
My brother

August 2, 1969

it really doesn't matter that your socks don't match

I stick a poppy in the parking meter
And smother timetables in drugstores
I nurse at the nipples of a flying saucer
Unidentified objects find me weird
This is the last time I shall address you
Between empty pages filled with light
Between your muscular buttocks
Where vine leaves shriek like the pulley of a clothesline
And I make love to you

russian river

When I got out among the redwoods
I thought I was happy but I smoked too much
and the houses were dark
so I tried to get back to the city
but got stranded
between an opera singer and a doublebarreled shotgun
somewhere I lost my voice
forgot where I was going
and didn't know where I came from
I had always been suspicious of the country
but this time—well, the opera singer
was off key and the rain endless

don't argue with the sun

against the stars, the universe,
no therapy for sagging flesh,
the poem will not save you,
music can't solve the dilemma,
the devil will win, finally,
youth will rot like a can of sardines
in the garbage, don't argue
with the sun, just go
like an idiot, like a fly,
like a rat in the wall, like a millionaire
in his Cadillac, like a ballerina,
legs gone in a furnished room,
like a madman, a genius, a saint,
like a leaf, like a whore,
like a broken liver, like snow.

the astral country

for Julia Chanler Laurin

my aura can't make up its mind what color to choose
whether the primrose yellow of intellect
or lilac blue of lofty spirit

a scarlet cloud floats in the astral sky
    threatening storms of irritability

here comes someone who's going to make me mad
& i might as well say goodbye to the lavender
        strip across my chest
i've been developing so long
flashes of red lightning
        are starting to cut thru
            the top of my head
it's a damn nuisance
                        i want the lovely violet
    of the psychic faculties
golden stars
        on a lilac blue ground

seen only by clairvoyants
    who know what i'm moving towards

some boddhisatva i think it was who said
  "In the white light
      no ray predominates"
don't worry
i'm still down here with you all
trying hard to get out of the gray

once i had a bright light in my hair
i walked shining thru the blackness of gossip
what's brilliant wit down here looks greenish-brown mud
   to somebody higher up

don't think i have invented any of this
each word we speak is translated into an astral language
whose colors are more precise than our words

when will we stop crawling around on five paws?

don't you think it's time we quit this monkey cage?
we've become so attached to the openings of the body!

when i'm in a crowd my aura begins to shake & tremble
like water colors running into each other
my astral mix in a cloudy ferment
i'm no longer as clear as i was
this is because of the combined worries & fears
& the foolish desires of everybody
getting into a collective tizzy
it ends in bed with a headache or a pickup
is this what you really want?

if i told you i have smelled incense growing out of a small garden
& oozing like syrup out of a tree called "Henry"
would you believe it? well i have —
& heard teeth grinding in the drawer of my desk
& footsteps on the stair after a person had left the house
& seen a magnificent circle of radiant light with my eyes shut
& buddha himself came to tea & gave me a friendly pat on the shoulder
& an ancient coptic necklace of copper wriggled out of the ceiling
     & fell at my feet
       & i presented it to a girl

& seashells & roses squirmed out of the arms of an old medium
   in a trance with brine on the shells
                    & dew on the roses
& they smelled not of the old woman but of the sea
            & gardens

the empty plate

               the empty plate on the kitchen sideboard
               as unromantic as the moon
                    glistens while in the courtyard
               a colored infant
                         makes a catlike sobbing sound

               mailboxes are banging locks
               in the hall the lights are down
                    my pulse is ticking like a bomb
                    1959 shoves on

               the cleaning woman with cataracts
               comes slowly up the broken stairs
               leaning dry wintry hands upon
                    the louis treize bannister
               & the odor of garbage
                              follows her
                    when she appears

                         * * * *

you didn't recognize me when in your dream early this morning i arrived
quite naked except for a snake wound round my loins—like a bikini . . . in
a husky unnatural voice, 'look! it's hermes!' you mumbled . . . dazzling col-
ors . . . feathers . . . plants . . . flamingoes in red flannel . . . everglade nights!
we were sipping like bees at the eyelids of an idol about to open a crack in
the universe thru which the final secret of reality would be revealed . . . we
found ourselves in the catlike sobbing gray areaway of parisian dawn—milk
bottles of eternity gleaming on cool ledges of tears . . . our tongues raw with
the evidence of empty sidewalks . . .

in the mailbox a letter from the police requesting that i register
my dog

but i have no dog
another from italy saying how much i am missed & would i send
some thought
genuine modern thought
from France
wrapped in a small parcel
duty-free
& a postcard from tiruvannamalai
BE SELF REALIZED NOW! ONLY THE SELF IS REAL
& a letter from flatbush—"eat well don't trust strangers
        love   ma"
& a french ad worried about my sex life
& from a swiss painter in alicante
"i've had another vision: GOD IS ALL!   why can't i paint?"
& a lover in new york: "it's snowing, i think of you, send me
        your smell!"

i see america daily

I see America daily
in the Paris *Herald-Tribune*
& the rest of the planet, too—
a family in a rowboat
escapes from a flood
in Indiana
with their drenched dog
smiling
& the suffering look of the poor
on their stricken faces
while an African Premier complains
that he can't bring Stonehenge
to Nyasaland
"to show there was a time
when Anglo-Saxons had a culture
that was savage"
& Art Buchwald, sinister
enemy agent
reveals military secrets
in his column
in code
under the guise of

good-natured humor
but after all the people know
he's a Jew
& the White House
is picketed daily
by those who know,
the red-blooded
Americans
of senile dementia
—things have really
gone to the dogs,
boxer shorts for
boxer dogs,
elastic jockstraps
for horses
& a bra for the cow . . .
one look at the pickets,
their parched grim faces,
& you know they mean it—
meanwhile a Frenchman is doing the tango
with an amorous seal in Paris
where a bank president
kisses his wife goodbye
on the way to his dishonest job
& doesn't know it's forever
as the chauffeur opens the door
of his limousine & a man
in a snap-brim hat steps over
& empties his revolver
into him, a nice
spring morning in March
n'est-çe pas?
ç'est la vie . . .
& they have torn up the pissoirs
of France
for the sake of decency
& closed the ancient whorehouses
of the Mediterranean
& a fat Communist wheel
tells American newsmen
"Get rid of the United States"
between mouthfuls of *gnocchi*
alla romana with darker
threats dropping

from his sullen features,
addressing a thin capitalist
reporter: "Tomorrow
you will be rudely
awakened. It will be a great
surprise."
& the United States goes on
in its innocent euphoric pursuits
of alcohol, psychosis, suntan oils,
bingo & decadent jazz
unaware that soon
Castro will sit in the White
House running the Western
Hemisphere, Mao Tse
Tung in the Kremlin
running the world
& Krushchev beside Stalin
running the daisies
tomorrow—
& a giant ad of a girl
whispering dreamily into
the smooth haircut
of a smooth man's head, "Harry,
let's do it now." but she
only wants a flight
on TWA,
while unemployment in the USA
reaches a high
of
72 million
more than the entire
population of Italy,
a nice healthy state
of affairs
in a nice healthy country
enjoying the benefits
of democracy
where queers are busted
daily
beat up by cops for the crime
against nature
of keeping the population
from exploding
tho 3 billion people

in the world
will double to 6 billion
by the year 2000 A.D.
most of them starving
and nowhere to lay
their hungry ass
while birth control is preached
by America
against the religious
scruples
of the Catholic Church
which feeds its constituents
on the nutritious diet
of the wafer
& the wine
altho meat & spaghetti
are harder come by
& an editorial tells us
that celestial music
is in danger
picking up stellar radiation
thru the radio telescope
tuning in
on the Word, the logos &
the angelic choirs singing
UHF or UGH
on Channel 2
or Channel 82 —
haven't the angels anything
better to sing? but I don't
blame them, the scientists
say that singing commercials
have drowned out
angelic voices
all over the world, bouncing
off the moon
& back to earth
while sexy basketball players
exhibit their naked
thighs
over which solitary fairies
drool & whack off
staining the sheet
with gyzm

of wet dreams
imposed on them by
Mammy Yokum
& Bouncy Belle
as Pogo wisely comments
on society, "Lissen,
you go makin'
a internal revenue letter
CLEAR
and they is gonna
think it's a FAKE!"
& the tall blond
teenager fumbles
in Jonesboro, Ga.
& tells of committing
30 burglaries
& 10 murders
(his family, of course)
as high school pupils listen
in shocked silence
at a meet of young jailbirds
with parents & teachers
on "Operation Teenager"
designed to understand
our juvenile delinquent
problem
(not
our senile delinquent
problem)—
the poor kid just didn't
feel *secure*
without his yo-yo . . .
O America! I see you daily
in the Paris *Herald-Tribune*
at a fairly safe distance
overseas
where I find it easier
to sing your democracy,
America,
I'm afraid to go back and find
all the animals clothed
or castrated,
decent babies getting themselves
decently born from test-tubes

like real Americans,
antiseptic
hygienic
untouched by human hands
or dirty foreign
un-American ideas
like SEX,
America. . . .

uroboros

whoever he meets on his way he eats raw
he eats the lungs of wise men
he is content to live upon hearts
he rejoices if he can devour those who are making love
he lusts after couples who press against wall posters in the subway
he lurches by the Left Hand of God
he picks his way thru the ice on the streets
past computer signs and movie marquees
past staggering drunks
he cuts a shadow like a figure skater
he rubs his penis against his shadow and spurts out of his own mouth
his boots make a crunching sound against beautiful young teeth
he laughs as he cracks the skulls of young men and rips girls up the
        middle and gobbles their intestines
his face re-occurs like a phantom's in the windows of locked buildings
he passes a man washing vomit from the sidewalk
he passes a man pissing against a bank
he passes a man weeping in a bar
he passes himself without recognition
he swallows himself and chokes
he is the tail-eater
everything becomes food for him
he spits and sweats and vomits
he screams and weeps and shits and pisses
and eats it all

i attend a poetry meeting

I attend a poetry meeting.
they eat canapés, gossip,
drop some Big Names, drink a little.
they are not young. the host looks bitter,
wags his short white beard,
calls on them, one
by one. in a circle
round the comfortable room
they read their little poems,
their voices subdued,
barely breaking the silence.
comments are murmured. they
seem afraid of something
or someone. maybe they know
this is not poetry, this
un-happening, what
can shake them into life?
a gray Angora cat strolls in, makes a
pathetic sound. it's too soft. my turn.
I produce a manuscript. I am new here.
I read, in a hoarse creaking voice, with a
head cold, a long
apocalyptic prose poem.
I take risks.
turn violent phrases.
kick a few sacred cows.

all hell breaks loose. I am attacked.
the poem's banal, pretentious, disgusting.
one calls it crap he's a dried up poet.
indecent. immortal. cliche. show-offy.
cries of Rape! I have RAPED poetry!
the host looks unhappy.
"in all the years we've met, **this**
is the first time," he bleats,
"the very first time we have—uh—STOOPED
to—ugh!—anger—" he looks daggers
at me. I sit almost smiling, taking
it all in, why are they so incensed?
have I ripped them off?
exposed ugly secrets?
the rain of labels keeps falling

rules I've broken.
taboos violated.
then, quietly, I tell them:

I wrote the poem 20 years ago.
hungry, lonely.
to purge myself
of rage and powerlessness,
academic restrictions.
if I have offended you
by handling big themes
with the craft of a
bungler who puts feeling first
(To you a romantic myth)
well, tough shit.
your myths are not mine.

I made them feel again.

for the first time
they snarled at each other

east wall 3711

Anna Pavlova, where are you?
East Wall three seven one one
in a London crematorium. . . .
so much for the Immortal Swan.

When I hear the music of **Swan Lake**
how can I feel immortal?
who will lead the Dead Swan
across a tightrope of velvet gut?

Oh, Anna Pavlova!
come out of the wall!

uncles

1

bootlegger, bookie, boxer, tout
uncle Joe the bighearted tough
once he beat up 3 armed hoods
singlehanded, without a gun
twice married, twice burnt
towards the end he played the horses
and faded out broke
in a Miami motel

2

my uncle the taxidriver called Big Red
was a tall doughboy in World War I
returned shellshocked with a stammer
and vacant denture smile
more afraid of my aunt than the hun
no smoking no joking no children
dead at 40, mustard gas

3

uncle Lou had lank blond hair
confusion and shyness drove him to drink
his Irish wife kept up with him
they expired under the table

4

uncle Mike had 12 kids
a mortgage and a fat German wife
a lifer handyman barkeep
went bald, got fat, drank up the dough
and died on welfare embracing Christ

5

oh blue-eyed Uncles
who taught me to box, to drink, to be fair
who left me with nothing but lost cousins
didn't you know that Jews
don't fight, don't booze
Jews are not big and handsome
Jews are not poor and dumb
UNCLES!
what's wrong wit youse?

the guns from the rooftops

The guns from the rooftops.
are aimed at our hearts and genitals
with deadly accuracy

*

There's Someone out there, I tell you,
   who's the answer
      to your prayers

laughing all the way to the grave

Theo Sarapo,
when you married Edith Piaf
she was crippled and bent with age,
46 and 4'7" tall.
Theo Sarapo, handsome Greek,
your towering height and youth
ridiculous and touching by contrast.
I watched your romance in the papers
at the Café Mabillon
over morning croissants and coffee.
When Piaf died of her own drama on your honeymoon
France went mad, you were blamed
but I knew from your photos
that you were as good as your good looks,
"A good boy," said her closest friends
and they should know.
You died in a car crash a year later
like her other husbands who died in accidents.
You were the last in her Greek tragedy,
26-year-old Oedipus with sexy legs,
just the kind to send old stars to the grave laughing.
15 years later I watch the Piaf story on television
and admire the spirit of that little sparrow.
Her eyes glittered when she looked at you,
her lips greedy for your mouth,
her features straining for your youth
across a gulf of time and suffering

and the madness of fame,
the separation from touch.
I dream of a young lover like you,
Theo Sarapo.

San Francisco, 2.xi.76

i am fighting on the lone front

I am fighting on the lone front
fighting propaganda with poetry
fighting booze with marijuana
fighting noise with silence
fighting television with vision
they're fighting me with underarm deodorants
buying my mind with soap flakes
cleaning up my speech with mouthwash
poisoning me with miles of video venom
polluting the food and the head
but I'm fighting back with poetry
they hit me with nuclear reactors
and I throw them a third eye
they deck me with put ons
I bang them with hard ons
they're fighting cut-ups with shut-ups
they're fighting literary symbols
with status symbols
they are fighting sexual freedom
with vice squads
fighting gay power and pecker power
with the zombie of the hour
I want the International Man
but all I get is the local yokel
they are fighting on the cold front
against reality
I'm fighting on the pubic front
for my everloving sexuality

Venice. Calif., 1969

the gluteus maximus poems

I

Aha, sir, what are you fondling so fondly
   under the spray? you think you're
   unobserved but your half-hard belies
   the macho pose—and you, sir, there
   secretly in a corner at your locker,
   twisting your rod from view
   under a towel, a stiff curved bow
   of anxious meat—and you in the steam
   room glancing over soggy newsprint,
   black and beautiful, fighting down a
   rising tool, it's no use, sweetie,
   desire will out, don't try to hide!

In the locker room naked men sashay
   from shower to sauna with steaming skin,
   undercover agents of lust: erections
   point like index fingers
   in a mass wet dream where wetness
   ignites uncontrollable fires
   fed by dumbbells and parallel bars
   and sweating armpits and pectorals—
   muscles communicate like the blast
   of a shotgun, thrust of missiles
   whose launching pad is a crotch!
   the gluteus maximus is more
   than anyone can stand! I'm a casualty
   of powerful curves, the lissome hip,
   male mounds of maddening joy!
   and then those parts "men love
   to gaze upon"—how to survive
   flames of sinew and joint?

San Francisco, 10.ii.74

2

Tough butts and beauties by the ton—
but none for me? Ow, what lousy
luck! If I were smooth instead of hairy
my chances would be better.
But no one wants to be called a fairy
and that's why their assholes are uptight.
It's the way of the world—real men would rather

bash in your head than suck your cock.
But every man has tried to suck his own
and wondered what it's like to get fucked
up the ass. Which makes them walk and talk
as if they've shat themselves, the butch
walk so sexy and ridiculous—
the speech tightlipped, sphincters shut
both ends, closing sweet holes
to other men's meat. But you
can have them drunk or stoned
or pretending sleep—then it's heaven
until they wake and, sullen, go
as if they'd spent the night with a whore.
But you both know who stuck it in.

San Francisco, 22.v.76

3

Your ass has given me insomnia
because of your ass I can't sleep
your ass intrudes in everything
sits plunk in the middle of my lunch
sits on my mouth and eyes
spreads its cheeks over the poem I am writing
winks its asshole at Ravel
muzzles Krishnamurti
obscures the white light
your ass your incredible ass

The *gluteus maximus* has always seemed to me to deserve at least as much attention as the more dramatic male generative organ. I had hoped to begin a cycle of paeans to the penis and maximus muscles but never got further than the above, with a nod, of course, to Olson.

i'm across the street
in the cemetery. dead.

Charlie was throwing poses
into the mirror like a contest winner
raising his arms over his head and
flashing a Mr. Big Bicep
and then a fast latissimus shot
in the old John Grimek manner.

The gym stank up a storm
of armpit and crotch and male ego
the hustlers with their golden boy good looks
strutting like they owned the place
powerful and lazy with muscle

throwing Mr. Universe poses
every chance they got
and sipping honey from plastic bottles
or raw milk between sets.

The competition was coldblooded
and the conversation hard edge
like who had bigger pecs and
were Rick's abdominals more cut up
this year and did Joe really get 200 bucks
off the faggot who phoned the gym
from Pittsburgh
halfway across the country
just to make a date with him?

It was uplifting to work out
with intellectual giants!

Charlie quit taking immortal stances
long enough to come over and say:
a funny thing happened this afternoon
where I work, you know, at the Federal Bldg.
downtown L.A.
this car comes charging up the road
onto the curb and crosses the grass
and smashes into the Federal Bldg.
and when the cops get there
they find

this note:

I'm across the street in the cemetery. dead.

They found the guy there. Killed himself.

Maybe he had placed second
in the Mr. Venice Beach contest,
I suggested.

Venice, Calif., 1969

let the dogs hump in the streets

Let the dogs hump in the streets
I'd do the same if they'd let me
those guardians of public morals
who fear the horrors of pleasure
more than the horrors of war

We've grown used to our daily murder
give us this day our daily dead
our daily rape, beatings, swindles
by the law-and-order boys—
their God cannot stand Love
or Pleasure—their God is Death.
—We are crucified by Him . . .

Let the dogs go berserk
running around in dog packs
biting their owners when they
come too close—earthquake:
it makes them leap upon each other
humping away the fear

Meanwhile we wait for the big one
that will rip off the State, smash
the City like a toy—"Is
this it? will I die?"
we know and the dogs know
and the cats and canaries and goldfish know

But it is too big, too monstrous, too
forever for the mind
to handle . . . which is why
we stay and tell ourselves:
what will be, will be—
like the sour old ladies
at the sea's edge, turning
their faces from the sun

Venice, Calif., 1971

spidery interpol spreads
a dirty web to the moon

Au nom de quel dieu me défendez-vous de vivre selon ma nature?
—André Gide

the police the wars the depressions!
horrible parents and wizened minds!
vicesquad sex! underground! made to sneak!
who's injur'd by my love?
in the name of what God
do you prohibit me from living
according to my nature?
Police!
the police invade my emotional life
they make me fearful and jumpy
they give me influenza colds insomnia
the police who outlaw sleep and pleasure
the police drive their big black bugs of despair thru my dreams
the police whose spidery interpol spreads a dirty web to the moon
the police who snare the circle of stars and God in dragnets of blood
the police who put Imagination on trial before ulcerous magistrates
    farting catarrh and gloom
the police who protect the State from the most dangerous enemy, you
you, the individual, waving the Bill of Rights from the quicksand
where you are rapidly sinking out of sight
the police who watch winking and scratching their nuts
(this is called entrapment) saying. *We got the goddam queer this time!*
and somehow as you go down the police
are part of how you die
waving the Bill of Rights from the quicksand

New York, circa 1952

two madmen

i am a war between two madmen who never win
this weird nervous system cannot change
time or pain

or memory nibbling survival

a lunatic wailing *love love*
with all the evidence shored against me

i float on a bedsheet to the stars

the sun burns in my belly

at fantastic speed i race
to the expanding skin of the bubble
of vanishing space

i am thermonuclear entropy
running down with the universe
on a golden horn
on a seismic kick

i am a cosmic tick
living on a small cold by-product of the delicate pressure of
starlight
with a glowing anus

Athens, 1965

follies of 1966

the poet descends the jet runway
his attaché case full of hexagrams
while the hammers of morning explode in the walls
& need transfigures his dismemberment
he strays in creepy hotels
watching tight pants with floral designs

the amazon princess kept talking all night
obviously trying to get him upstairs

she had a haughty compulsive air
and talked on and on about castles and children
while pneumatic drills
     airbrushes
        motorscooters
ripped her monologue
like civilian counterparts of napalm
     & lazy dog

all right I have taken my sleeping pills
and knocked myself out of pre-frontal lobe insomnia
bedroom scenes may have adverse effect
on international relations

Geneva, 1966

loner

I was made to be a hero
   but there were no causes
& besides I was too short.
Nature, that bitch
on wheels, never quits
   tormenting me
with her gay jokes!
She covered my skin with black fur,
painted my jaws blue,
stuck a barrel chest on
legs like tree stumps
and hung a fat salami
   between them, I'd laugh
about it but a foolish
lust for men drives me
   batty. Well, curse
and fuck out your brains
in your fist. Nature
   is one damn bitch
you just can't beat.

San Francisco, 1975

bastard angel

for playing a cubist guitar with lavender strings
for needing you
for sniffing paradise cottons
for eating you
for masturbating on a subway toilet
for hating you
for exposing myself to a gay dwarf who went up on me
for loving you
for pockets full of inadequacy
for wanting you
for being a secret agent of Earth
for teasing you
for daring to leave my body without notice and the ether police maced
    my dreams
for despairing of you
for flying to the moon in astral projection without permission from the
    State Dept.
for dreaming you
for sweeping into a perfect orbit around the Pentagon with peaceful
    intentions
for undressing you
for behaving scandalously at my own funeral by lecturing on life after
    death
for scaring you
for wallowing in my own pederastic imagination
for blowing you

Madouri, 1965

the bedsheet is stained
with wet dreams of you

The bedsheet is stained with wet dreams of you
with fantasies of your skin that I can't get enough of
Every night I leave testimonials to your beauty with my cells
with a colorless blob like a Rorschach blot like spit
which shows that creation and waste go together
If I really had balls I'd have long ago ripped them off
like those wiggy priests of ancient Rome dedicated to Cybele
my balls have caused me nothing but trouble
and made me bitter as piss
Yet nothing can stop me dreaming of you
in your moldy jockstrap in your boxer shorts
that I'd like to tear off and eat.

San Francisco, II.iii.74

to a young man in torremolinos

I want to pull your nipples
and make them explode
I want to shove between your legs
the live firecracker
of my needy flesh
and blow up
your hairy ass

I want to push my heavy artillery
down your throat
and silence your verbs

But no, you go on
with a mouthful of dead pricks
with a brain of bank accounts
with a heart of spades

you smell of fried air
and polar ice caps
of passports and social security
numbers

Torremolinos, 1962

crouching in the corrida (madrid)

I stand at the window by the Puerto
del Sol watching
evening fall
on the big crowded shops
and shining hair.

From the shabby lobby
comes the odor of fish
and roses,
steam clanks
in the pipes.

I face the full-length mirror in the
dark hotel and masturbate
to a flamenco guitar.
I follow the bullfighter in my
imagination,
he flashes his crotch at me
like a sword and
I go down, bleeding.

I am a stranger, spying
through keyholes,
I am a sex maniac,
waiting to pounce on a fly.
I am a gored bullfighter crouching
in the corrida of empty
hallways, bleeding
out the moment
of truth.
I am the bullfighter and
the bull, dancing
the sexual dance
of death.

Madrid, 1956

return to pompeii

pushed along burnt out tufa streets
in a breeze of departed bodies
urgent ghosts & twisted lips
   sculptured scream of the lava dog
      back among triglyphs & rainspouts
         the ashen cornice
   like a childhood disease I'll never outgrow
on the stained walls their red rites
      House of the Anchor
        the Centaur the Faun

wrapped in my human fur I prowl
   the lupanar once more
      to the two cocks of divine priapus
    —obeisance & awe!

when the volcano shot
his hot lapilli pumice beans
   into fleshy air
did you know in your niches
& pinkwalls & oilsweet baths
   from temple to cathouse
     latrina to prison
       you'd be a crippled god?

   & I return to these brown ruins
      kitchen utensils scraped from rock
        two-thousand-year-old bread
          under glass
      in museums
            —tourist fare!

Naples, 1958

priapus at pompeii

evening all awash
        with moonlight
the bay charged
      with crinkly tinfoil
           of starry lights
outlining ships at anchor
     vesuvius
        standing guard
           over all
at its feet
     antiquities
        & souvenirs
    forget-me-nots
          of flying cocks
       remembrances
        of Priapus
   a deity
       nobody
         can
           forget

Naples, 1958

florence/brooklyn/the world

Dante lived here
   & got kicked out
now he's worshiped
     like a saint

I saw a plaque on Cranberry Street
    in Brooklyn once
       to Walt

garbage
grew in heaps
that stray cats picked
    by the diner
       where it stood
     on a torn brick wall

here
      damp logs smoke
        & spit
      thru casing cracks
a mist
      twists in
         downstairs
        a tv blasts

along the Arno at night
     the world is
         running jewels
         adorning
     upsidedown
   statues
where palaces shimmeripple
        in mossy light
  of Quattrocento air

I walk
to the *Cascine*
     under trees
     by the riverbank
        watching
        pickups in the dark
          humping in the reeds

a voice yells
        HEY DIVINE LOVE!
      DIVIN' AMORE . . . .
then snickers
        HANGMAN GOD! NO QUEERS
        WITH CASH ON 'EM!

   Dio boio! nessun' froscio
   con soldi adosso!

   it's a boy with a bike
     (a Donatello)
his sexual beauty found in museums
that he wouldn't think of entering

squeal
        of tires cutting
                curves
and a fishing canoe afloat
        among the rushes
                no oar no rudder
with a bird chirping
        on a dead winter bough
                snow gleaming
        from the hills of Fiesole
                above the piazzale

the couples are gone
        in loud cars
                as a cold wind springs up
        listen to the reeds!
                a soft roar
                        the gravel paths
                                choked with débris
what am I doing
        in this wet mess?
                                well if I wanna sit
                                in the rain
                                        why not?

Florence, 1958

meditations of the guard at the belle arti academy

I watch them every day—they
never change, any more than these statues
change. They say stone speaks to them
but it must be another language I don't
understand like English. What does David say?
Ask Michelangelo. But there they go, those tourists,
head in the clouds, seasick with awe, whispering,
Great, great! What's so great about a naked man
in marble, I'd like to know? I'm bored with all this
heavy stone, these horny fauns and coy hermaphrodites
that play the syrinx while a dirty old goat keeps trying
to put his thing in them (although they've got balls, too).

Meanwhile I catch these queers who grab a feel of the stone,
of David's legs and feet or a satyr's prick.
Nothing much goes on and the pay is lousy.

Florence, circa 1958

a question of identity

i cannot walk
down a street
without
some uniformed creep
questions my identity

WHO AM I?

poet?
    spy?
        junkie?
            fag?

or saint maybe?

my american passport??

the eagle lays
a rotten egg in my adams-apple

the fears of european fuzz
raise the issue of forgery
        i'm looked at
        more closely

where do you live? what are you doing here?

they handle the document—loath to let go.
        might slip thru
                    their hate's red tape

well move on! we're looking for someone
who COULD *be you* . . . .

(why aren't you better dressed? they think)

i smile

    as cool as i know how

Paris, 1960

the boy, the birds, the concierge and verlaine

the sweet young thing is passing around
the hat and the French cat sings
AH AH AH lalalala with his guitar
and the asses of St. Germain are firm
blue buds in the sun and the cars
are stinking up the air and screaming
and everyone drinks beer
and eats
caca-
huètes*

and it's all a mimic movie of lips and tits
and swollen jeans padded in the right places
while copcars cruise like leprosy
and plastic bombs shatter windows
cufflinks and shoelaces
and fat flies buzz at café tables
in the white sugar and ham sandwiches
left by those whose security
is threatened

and I leave too
for a quiet little square
Place de Furstembourg
with 4 planetrees and a streetlamp
Delacroix worked here STUDIO CLOSED
TEMPORARILY FOR REPAIRS says a sign
it's been closed 8 years
they work slowly here

and on a bench flat on his belly

a lotus boy with radiant tan
and very dirty feet
dozes beside a huge green
cardboard folder thick with promise
from the Beaux Arts Academy
on Rue Bonaparte
suddenly the budding artist
looks up drowsily
and everyone stares
at him

the concierge at the window
on street level, her leathery old arms
folded on the sill
and the birds stare
as she sits very gray
very sad
one hand against her mouth
elbows like knobby staves
and I stare
like Verlaine discovering
Rimbaud

it might have been a painting by Delacroix

and I remove myself
to hold the picture in time
but next day I am back
for the boy, the birds, the concierge
and Verlaine

nothing is there, not even the trees
only 4 great gaping holes
where they had been

*peanuts

Paris, June 1961

gay party

one stares at moonlit roofs
looking for himself out there
where the stars are howling

in the middle of the room
wobbly with beer and grass
among a thousand shifting faces
where worlds combine & planets collide
I turn on my axis
rolling in space like a whale

the night is full of colors
and the electric smell of hair
armpits crotches feet
in a welter of warmth!

Jackie the spade moans Loverman
by a lamp that turns the wall to snow
his/her lips full of suck and assholes
singing in a voodoo voice Loverman
but coming down goes into a corner
of the room to cry

then the unspeakable thud of the world
on my head
and we're off to Les Halles by dawnlight
Gregory Corso
Jean-Jacques Lebel
myself
among onionsoup & trucks
bananasorangesapples   vegetablespilledstreets

o drag queen Jackie!
your metal gown has stopped glittering
your magic paraffin tits sag like hotwater bottles

                  & the party is over

Paris, circa 1961

rusty smog sky of evening . . .

Rusty smog sky of evening, bodies heavy with exhaust, trees drip gas . . . movie marquees & cafés do their utmost to create pallor even turning to black silver the cheeks of les noirs; exhaust & smog carcinogen air bleaching every expression deepening eyesockets of pithecanthropus erectus waving spongy ectoplasmic nostril hairs in the direction of human culture GIANT F U E G I A N S half naked shlep thru the Flore or the Royale feeling anthropophagous in television jungles pissoir pong roasted chestnuts by the church of St. Germain.

Giant fuegian monster emerge from long highcheekboned swish with jet-black eyes & vegetable face, animal stage, his body puts me off & turns me on (that's because I'm not made up you should see me when I am) . . . he was nineteen & as far as one could make out had no personal feelings, called Jacques or Jean talked a queer kind of animal french . . . his body had no nationality invested with a mind belong to that kind of prostitutional life which was a mush. He & this language of his may have been something almost extinct.

We were soon obeying the promptings & stirrings of a pair of skins contriving to get together with if possible the gizzard.

Wrapped in skintight guanaco hide his body presented edible portions of human anatomy an adolescent of the type makes you water to devour the muscles, devour him whole, his mouth wreathed like the rays of a starfish in mandibular ecstasy he reared the one thing in a man comes in a spongy ectoplasmic substance for which women are clearly not constructed.

This lovely cretaceous creature fell on me shifting the Earth's crust.

i rotated about the sun in primeval slime consciousness a molten spheroid surrounded by thick atmosphere of subatomic energy, radioactive phenomena supplying light & heat from this parent body of intensely hot matter a scorching gas continually exploding within my subliminal:

> his hot primordial prick filled all the universe
> my body peeled away
> first the skin slimed off like a waterlogged rat's or a victim of
>   radiation
> then the bones melted like tallow & became sticky & gooey like
>   loukoum
> pink loukoum

utter slime gushing fast
from vegetable bodything
queer kind of animal nationality
his body had no corners invested with a mind
language thru the farthest side of mush
an adolescent dredging up crimes
his mouth wreathed with muscles

i lay still unmoving slime talking french! belong to that kind of mind-language may have was a mush & he something soon obeying instinct stir-rings of get together with skins if possible gizzard, adolescible portions of type makes muscle devour him you water his mouth wreathed starfish. He reared come in thingman substance, godly gland! saurian boy!

•   •   •   •   •   •   •   •

Paris, circa 1961

archaic age long forgotten

Hothouse Jurassic atmosphere of intense heat. Low in the orange sky, an infrared sun spits flame over the firebound land. Delirious monsters crash thru woods & marshes in sexual frenzy, snatch at giant ferns & mosses to staunch their lust. The Time of the Great Dying. There is only one sea-son—summer. Eternal summer. Millions of years of summer. Scalding temperature boils reptile blood to flaming pitch. In the saurian cauldron only relief for frantic monsters is fuck fuck fuck. Sexual dance of death lead-ing to racial fadeout.

With schizophrenic lunacy, a roaming holocaust, fantastic giant Diplodocus spreads terror—equipped not with one but *two* sets of brains: pelvic brain serves to direct fulltime fucking program. This character is so huge & unwieldy he needs two control systems for that vast area of meat. Anyone can gnaw away a good hunk of his tail before the message gets thru to sluggish Pelvic Brain. Weighing around 50 tons & reaching lengths of 100 feet from stem to stern, the monster is forever cruising to score a piece of ass—& when he makes it he shacks up for months until running out of sperm & strength. Armor-plated love affairs of this sort bring down giant horsetail trees, rock the earth with seismic shocks.

So Diplodocus is permanently on heat. Upper Brain complains. "Well, let's eat. I'm hungry!"

"Eat?" cries Low Brain from deep in the cockpit. "Don't be a shmuck! Dig what's nearing from that club moss yonder!"

Sure enough it's a young chick not more than fifty foot long, tipping the scales at a chic 40 tons—with the cutest ass you ever smell. He reels (Low Brain vertigo) and without another grunt mountainously lumbers through the fiery day, knocking down trees & crushing boulders. He jumps her, hurls her into a carboniferous bog with a crash that can be felt round the planet. Displaced masses of hot earth fly into space like meteorites. Wigging with saurian lust, he unzips fifteen foot of metallic cock (by 9 ft. around) which he blindly stabs like an iron stake into the toppled struggling mass of plated flesh, not giving a shit whether he hits a hole or makes one. In this case he makes one—the slick chick is male. But what does our hero care? He rams the torpedo in as far as it will go—up to his basketballs. The victim is stuck for at least a month. Time snores. Four brains & legs, long bony spines like spikes, all mixed up but good in a steamy mess of blood & dinosaur spunk. The whole earth blazes, spitting out fires & rainbow-colored gasses like one huge volcano—under a sky of infrared or ultraviolet blastfurnaceflame.

Time snores. One month later Diplodocus wobbles uncertainly to his feet. The marsh is a horrible bayou of reptile blood jaws teeth spikes jism flesh. He leaves his silent partner motionless in the slime . . . armored monsters fuck like tanks in radioactive air life forms drain thru armored cocks schizzy monsters jump each other blindly stabbing spikes of plated affection bringing down worlds bringing down armor city split with seismic lust bomb of lust convulsive shift to hate the dinosaur sinks slow armored brain-slime cry of dying meat in rusty cities iron fish climb trees footlong eyes shut the dreamdoor slow over hushed gray land gray sounds foam hate germs spit gray tears whisper gray pain in rustgray air

•   •   •

Paris, 1961/62

Rusty smog sky, & *archaic age* are cut-ups, but the second is spontaneous flow with cut-up ending.

vespasian ballet

On the Quai du Pont Neuf opposite L'Institut de France and above the riverbank where the young pompiers of the Seine live and exercise and probably fuck each other in the ass in their grayblanketed bunks, which you can see deserted if you walk past by day, stood the memorial to countless ballets of desperate pleasure—wired and boarded up like a stage set of better days, a rare antique ingeniously preserved from collapse.

For months it stood like that, a museum piece, a monument—and a mirage to unsuspecting tourists whose acute anticipation plunged them headlong to dashed hopes. Like my own bitter look of astonishment when I appeared, one Friday night in autumn, to keep a date with a young Arab who worked the urinals Mondays, Wednesdays, Fridays and Saturdays.

His bicycle, chained to the nearby bench, was the high sign of his presence. In the 'presidency', the middle urinal, he would fondle his big meat lovingly, showing it steaming in the dim glow of the pissotière to prospective clients.

On either side of him, when I first entered, stood wary fairies who nervously fled at my approach. When I glimpsed his face, a cautious inner voice (one which I hate but have learned to obey) had silently screamed: BAD NEWS! BAD NEWS! I left in a hurry.

I knew I would return. That primitive face was a magnet drawing me to the shrine.

After hours of fruitless cruising, for the remaining pissoirs had become furtive and panicky as a result of police terrorism—and so reduced in numbers that it had become difficult to score—I flew back to the cozy cottage to find a reckless daisy chain in progress, which I instantly joined having made my presence unmistakably 'felt' by entering the full house with a raging hard on.

Soon the Algerian and I were alone, the others presumably having got what they were after. The face that had scared me earlier—flat-nosed and negroid, with powerful jaws, a sexy killer in a news flash foto—now leaned over and grafted a tender kiss on my lips, his dangerous good looks softened by reassurance, the fierceness of his scowl erased by a tumultuous smile.

His large calloused worker's hand felt under my pants until he managed to insert several fingers up my ass. I ran my hands along the dark gold-colored muscles of his thick shoulders and chest and down under his balls along his thighs. We were now old lovers as he murmured softly, "Drop your pants!" With one hand in my money pocket, that also served to keep my pants from falling below my knees into the slimy urinal floor, and the other guiding and squeezing his great circumcised cock, while he kissed and licked my ears and neck, I shot a long pent-up load into the reeking sheet-iron where it was immediately flushed away into the sewer beneath. Although he cleverly made sounds to simulate an orgasm, I knew he had held back: for business reasons. I slipped him 500 old francs, which he accepted with a grateful smile and without the fuss I had half expected, and then nostalgically left him to his harmless hustling.

Only once I heard his voice, husky and guttural, straight from the balls, when we made our date for Friday night. He told me of his work hours there, in a serious matter-of-fact tone, and then we kissed goodbye.

I named the pissoir: THE PASTORAL URINAL.

When I returned on Friday, the pissoir was bandaged like a wound. And so it stood among the bouquinistes for many months before being demolished forever by the spiteful and jealous guardians of the law.

Paris, circa 1961

Vespasien in French, *vespasiano* in Italian, meaning urinal, immortalizing, no doubt, the emperor of that name who first inaugurated street pissoirs: the "ballet" is the gay scene.

pipe dream of arabia

sipping mint tea facing the Djema'a el Fna in Marrakech
I watch snakes squirm at my feet a monkey's wrinkled face
blinks as a turbaned storyteller squats in the center
of a huge crowd of beggars & tourists
narrating A Thousand And One Nights in broad daylight
full of dust & bargains & good odor of katami
beyond the reach of the western world I sigh with relief
listening to tall tales of kif in a language I don't understand
watching enamelled pipes & soapstone bowls filled with hashish
naked boys asleep covered with sticky flies
aladdin lamps made from tin cans glinting in sunlight
everywhere music and magic stalls with sheep's nuts
dried blood withered paws evil eyes bones hair on shrunken heads
I sigh with relief & soft contentment
what I understand is sensual
as when I set foot on non christian soil in the casbah
those first unwinding minutes in Tangier
I shed like a rotten garment the guilt for pleasure & sodomy
dropped the stinking cloak of the western world
& was taken up in the endless pipe dream of Arabia

Heidelberg, 1965

from an old tangier notebook

For Paul Bowles

• • • • •

Eroticism of their music . . . long twang of sitar . . . throbbing
string of Eternity . . . nasal wail of stars
in desert nights . . . sweetness in the air . . .
jasmine and donkey dung. . . .

• • • • •

I wish that boy had stayed . . . then there's no death. . . .
only intertwining motifs . . . music . . . merging mouths. . . .
the figure in the carpet . . . mosaic in the floor. . . .
and smiling in the eyes. . . .

• • • • •

Thought will never fathom the smell of the groin!
Thought cannot grasp the musk of a male!
This is the mystery . . . the holy spirit come. . . .
"Nothing is more beautiful than the commonplace."
The Universal Poem between the legs!

• • • • •

I want to write the poem of muscles—the animal poem!
Tenderness . . . rage . . . lust. . . .
bowel and anus open to the giant penis of God!
the poem of muscular thrust and the sweat of flesh. . . .

• • • • •

When I'm high I'm in touch . . . erect phallus heals all. . . .
this is the savior . . . the animal . . . the tender cruelty. . . .

this is the mystery
this, the priestly task
this, the fertility rite
this, the hallucinogenic vision

THE SELF IS AN ANIMAL

THE UNIVERSE IS AN ANIMAL

Being is no more than the bark of a dog

Tangier, 1961

pan pipes of bou jeloud

For Hamri

down in joujouka
pan pipes of bou jeloud   white jellabas
white moonlight
white walls
adolescent Father of Skins
stomping his ancient
PANIC RITUAL

convulsive
movements of a fucking goat
you can smell this boy

lean curved thighs
almond eyes
high cheekbones

possessed

in trance
dance
frenzy of flutes
mad oboes
frantic drumbeat

HU
HU
huhuhuhuhuhuhuhuhuhhhuhuhuhuhuhuhuh
HU
HU
HU
huhuhuhuhuhuhuhuuhuhuhuhuhuhuhuhuh
HU
HU

chopping the air

                              with a stick
                    he'll beat you if you come close
               8 nites sustained orgasm   unrelenting
                                        pandance
                    grunts
                       cries
                          fucking
                             goat
                                floppy
                                  mad wild ancient
          good odor of katami pervading moonlight
               song & dancing boys   snakes
                                         magic
                                      hashish
          not to be touched
                         by reason
                                   right or
                                            wrong

          out of Taroudant
               you breathe for the first time
                    desert air ignites in the skull
                       its message of silence & stars

                              ecstasis

                                        Heidelberg, 1966/67

in the broken mirror . . .

For Jane Bowles, in memoriam

In the broken mirror my ass has 3 cheeks.
There's mouse shit in the quaker oats.
The day I left Tangier I munched it
thinking it was nesselrode, then panicked.
2 hours hunting a croaker with Jane Bowles.
Visions of some terrible disease:
dying in convulsions, vomiting green.
That was the room of empty Eukodol bottles
Burroughs left behind
—the Villa Mouniria, run by a French
ex-whorehouse madam from Shanghai.

Never did find a croaker
but managed to survive
mouse shit and Jane's laughter.
The croakers had all vanished
because of the heat
that time of day.

Athens, circa 1965

monoxide morning

For Nanos Valaoritis

Cutting graveyard capers
with Turkish coffee
like ghouls we dig up ancient shards
hoping for a big haul
among the tourists in creepy flocks
clicking cameras at caryatids—
outlandish lumps unsightly un
gainly they stink
of imbecility among the dying
cypresses pinetrees grassblades
choked by diesel and transistor
poisons green
chemical dust
of Athenian smog

Everywhere
machines invade the flesh
yet cats continue basking
in the hazy sun
and the chained goat sways
on the hillside
in ecstasy
while the Parthenon looks down
from creamy heights
as lichen and rust nibble the pediments
and tourist feet break the spell
of antiquity's vibrations.

And I am looking at rusty orangeade caps

when the grass hits
like a bardo rainbow
like Outer Mongolia
like thighbone trumpets
roaring in the blood!
O blessed grass!
burn down the Parthenon
and all the corn of Greece
and Egypt!
burn the frigid witches
digging ancient sculpture
their stony loves
inflexible patterns
hardened by habit.
burn down the jails!
their stony laws!
free the holy prisoners!
burn the polluters of the earth!
burn atomic stockpiles! burn munitions!
jetliner! telstar! intercom!
burn all destroyers!
the earth is great with grass!
who needs NUCLEAR APOLLO?
THERMONUCLEAR MINERVA?
NIKE CRASHING WHITE FINALE?
burn winged idiots who burn down the cosmos! burn MONEY!
intergalactic destruction for MONEY and the GOD OF MONEY!

Around the corner the anti-Christ
probably playing football
will bring the millennium
of soccer athletes making love to us all!
the anti-Christ believes in the phallus
he wants us to be happy
he doesn't want us to suppress hard-ons
for the sake of respectability
the anti-Christ is a sweet boy
who used to be called Eros
and it's time he returned
we've suffered enough for two millennia
bring back the carnivorous saint!
The anti-Christ's mother is no virgin
she's the little old lady of peace movements
to ban the bomb and clean up the air

she will shake her umbrella and change the world!

Everything is possible when the grass hits!
everything new, shining, reborn!
I believe salvation is immediate love!

Old worlds burn down and new worlds form
in flaring clouds of brown
monoxide morning.

Athens, Jan. 1964

dancing in piraeus

            turning
              & turning
                the greek
              boy
            writhed
          a sinuous turkish
        dance
      at the waterfront
    taverna
  light
  fast
    & feminine
      everybody clapping
        & hissing
          keeping time
            & laughing
            & overexcited
          someone
        threw an empty
      beerbottle
    under his feet
  & he slipped
  or leapt
    on it
      with the grace
        of danger
          like a flamenco
          dancer

&
                still dancing
                snakehipped
                into the kitchen
              right arm
          spurting
    an artery
      the floor
          wet & sticky
            with it
                while the jukebox
                  kept right on
                    like a floorshow
                  that couldn't be real
              but some kind of
          extravaganza
          except nobody
    was laughing
    & the waiter
        taking advantage
          of the situation
              overcharged
                us

Athens, circa 1963

violent lemon sun

opening and shutting its beak
here's a big bird
waddling
upon the pebbles, a small boy
scales stones at the bird
who moves without haste
among café tables
as the sea churns
under a violent lemon sun.
Greek urchins flop in the water
screaming
then lie flat on shiny bellies
the color of chocolate,
their bodies hard and supple,

the aloof bird coolly surveys
their grimy shorts
and underfed bodies,
takes in the foreigners
with voices of dead ends
filled with lust and money,
on this pitiless claw of rock
the young Greeks splash and yell
looking across to the parasols
where whitefaced tourists
like pancakes in the sun
continue facing upwards
catching the light
and darting swift glances
at the brown young bodies,
they will not get together
until night falls, then
under cover of darkness
there will be quick transactions,
drachmas will change hands,
addresses flutter like leaves,
the bird opens and shuts its beak,
stabs at a piece of rotten lettuce
as the sea churns
under a violent lemon sun.

Athens, 1965 / San Francisco, 1972

dream of seeing through my asshole

Dream of seeing through my asshole:
holding sacred the disorder of life.
My mind is oceanic, follows twisted waves of words,
to-fro tides of all-night sleepless tape recording of words
till light of dawn breaks through marble (Akropolis
under which in a cave-apartment of Anaphiotika
I watch the sweating cold stone walls)
and write paranoia poems of a paralyzed generation,
paradoxical saints monsters demons self-divided inspired
madly pursuing assholes and eternal come of heavenly pricks
stuffing ghee up the ass, pulling strings through nostrils
at the feet of gurus, the feet of Raihana and Meher Baba

purifying themselves each according to his ritual eyewash
sitting untouched by compassion, parabolic minds that do not touch
having come to Greece
to seize a live tradition out of the stone.

Athens, circa 1965

carnival in athens

For Charles Henri Ford

Thighs, confetti and lips showing through masks in a preposterous display of sexual quicksand sucking you into this Greek orgy for several nights, milling youths winking and nodding at each other . . . boys wild with horny glee, blowing horns, flexing muscle, sinuously shuffle in this churning frolic, here a snagtooth ape, there a blackrobed witch, a Texas cowboy . . . What a mob of masturbators and sweet sodomites! stoned, high, ripped, drunk, wearing purple pontova wigs, some with transvestite charms, many wiggly butts. . . .

Here is Achilles in his stetson, tight, bluejeaned and blond, his bowlegs grip an invisible horse . . . and Spyros weaves homeric hips through the crowd as Ares kisses Socrates by the yogurt parlor. . . . Then, to no one's amazement, stately Death appears, skull eyes rimmed in white circles, like the one in Black Orpheus, his painted mouth close to mine—ça va, monsieur?" he hollows, then vanishes in the sexy crowd. . . . A tall queen screams, "Ciao, bello!" and cruises on through streamers flung like spunk, like hotshot paper gonads, multicolored cum. . . .

Gorillas, guerrillas, dictators, career women, we act the fool, dreaming awake, circling round and round to music and laughter all night, letting off steam but not hysterical enough or mad enough . . . the great jag ought to vomit up a century and get lost in the distant past of bacchanalian roots, orgy of genitals and lust in the gutter. . . . Costumes and clothes should pile up like barricades in the streets against war and regimented sex. . . . Ah, anal Dream! No such luck!

This is as far as we may cross the barrier of global unlove.

Athens, 1964

love-junk

waking after 3 goofballs
with vague hardon directed
at nobody
             I reach for 2 more
& gulp them hoping
they won't be the final
apocalyptic darkness

your image keeps probing
with sharp insistence
like a rotten molar's dying nerve

I cannot uproot absence
& sleep is no answer

       •

I am at the end of empty roads
that stretch for years
(humming a sad tune) to you
unknown identity who
               takes shape
to fuck me into paranoia
of losing
       you

my body weakens
with terror
& hatred of all desire
knowing
         how hard to destroy
persistent need
that kept us
       (once)
so close

2

another country
& what is left
of the few familiar
possessions a

handful of old jazz &
françois couperin
        on the old
portable philips
1 lamp
a few unmatched socks
        some fotos
of you & other ex-loves
whom now you have
joined

I sit fumbling in a
tiny kitchen
stumbling
over garbage heaps in cartons
dreaming back to
our best times together
knowing
my blood cannot discharge
what poisons have
gathered there

3

waiting to swallow me
THIS BIG BLOODY BLACKNESS

an unknown language
drowns my ear
LANGUAGE OF BLACK
impenetrable
snowfall of gutturals
BLACK SNOW OF NO
SOUND
I am engulfed!
sleepless & unawake
I stare at a hawk's feather stuck on the wall
        from New Mexico
snow slips over the hill like a bandage
        falls & falls but no relief
goofballs turn me on awhile
then I sleep sleep
restless like screaming
but wake too soon in a rush of doubt
BLACK POURS IN FROM THE COSMOS! VOID-BLACK!

my yellow eyes fall on black newsprint
it crawls towards me like an insect
on a pair of black boots
       thru wax ear plugs
          STOP
STOP   STOP
               S T O P

4

I have been thru orthodox halls
of hospitals
stinking of men dying
of errors
& clinical madmen with the best reputations
in white smocks of ignorance
the unorthodox too lack the magic
the inside information
for none of them know anything
of the fire that I have stolen
none of them hold
the instruments that can measure feeling
the apple has nothing to say
about good and evil
about isolation and broken vows
but only reminds me
of something that is not health
that is not money
that is not success
something that once held a little truth
in it
something I let slip
out of my life
& has now become a long-distance call
ending
in silence

5

the tape recorder sings: *her sin*
is her lifelessness by Dylan &
again I'm running running
like hell from city to city
thru freezing streets
of shut-in faces & garbage cans
& the latest news full of chaos & futility

& love is a punch in the mouth
no attempt to communicate
words rasp like a scratch
tearing skin from bone
raw meat torn
cut off from self
as metal birds burn down the skies
into a rubble of cripples
exposing a gap where the face should be

what fire & lies have done
to second-hand people!

I look at them & see
myself
camera shutters & dead tongues
clicking

6

there is only the one
fix? why?
the whole world heaves
like a dream reeling
down the street & in spite
of kissing couples & lonely
pad with postcards of Blake & Bosch
there's surely someone who'll show
with the works—strip down
at the right time w/out too much fuss
& maybe even share this
isolation
—fill it with laughs!

I throw 3 coins to know
when it will happen
& hang in like an old pro
against the ropes
refusing
to be counted out

Heidelberg/London, 1966/67

the underdog walks alone

at night he wanders thru piled-up tears
& nerve-wracked skulls
dawn finds him nailed thru the heart
he wrestles in a coffin with mirrors
draws blood in the meat of hell

the spike glitters
stabs his double who walks among crystals
dreaming of cones & cups & shimmering shark vaginas
opening nuclear lips in the sky

a desperate girl has slashed her wrists
in the alps a man took an overdose
machines go haywire at his approach
he screams against the mounts
& the sea withdraws from the coast

the sea withdraws from the coast
& the sun is brown in the darkness of noon

we are computerized
with alpha signals & beeps of brainwaves at this
mutant moment to overcome
the leap from the window the speeding car
blood spattering
guitars & breasts   pariahs weep
in apartments never to be abandoned
lone self unable to face
lone self

new sciences
slash & rip the dream
dig pain & disruption from torn brains
it is not satori it is murder it is lies it is crime
under rhythm's
hypnotic spells that burn the nerves
in the beast's suicide flight
in the flux of endless change
in the burning books
of ancient knowledge whose keys are buried
under walls of words
where primitive shibboleths still grip
the vaginal kiss the clutch & ripple of masks

where divided selves
break against blind walls
in refusal
to see in oneself the Other
the wound under bandaged words
the gifted maniac gone wild
in the last embrace the last wet dream
of the child whose memory nails him
to the mast of paradoxical dung & gold

angelic
forensic
tantric
magnetic
assassin with monumental thighs
of steel & ivory
in the circle of his maledictions

gnomic
empiric
vampiric
mystic
galactic   mad   denied!

the underdog walks
alone
but will return again & again
to the vomit of repetitious beds
the vacuum of troubled children
who enslave without knowing
the roots of possession
possessed by the spirit
of negative foetus
pre-mental morphic spells
our double
whose lies are
ours

London, 1967/68

The key to this poem is contained in the section "Mystical Aspects of Gay Love" in Mitch Walker's *Men Loving Men* (Gay Sunshine Press, 1977), notably the section on the Double, which I read ten years after I wrote "The Underdog." My poem deals with the consequences of rejecting the homosexual spirit source by the younger partner and the evils unleashed by turning off the Anima.

young mr. america

YOU CAN DISCOVER A GREAT NEW MUSCLE
DON'T LET JUNK WRECK YOUR DUMBELL CAREER

Here's How To Broaden Your **SEX** Build And Mold

THE LARGEST JOCK IN YOUR AREA!

EARN MORE MONEY PICK **ANY** BROAD OR SAY

. . . Are you getting enough? . . . MR. PROFESSIONAL DUMBBELL

the man with the cut-up muscles

TAKE A TIP FROM THE CAMPS!
        The tougher your workouts the
        more YOU need S U P E R S T R O N G M A N
                             SEX

   "HOW

  M
    O
      D
        E
          R
            N
               MASTURBATION
HELPS
    B
      U
        I
          L
            D   !
              N   S
           A   R
         E   E   use it as a
       L   D   back & arm builder
     U L
    C   U   use it as an
  R   O   adjustable squat rack
 E H
H S   use it as a
                     chinning bar
                 USE IT AS A LEG

discover your complete self discover your world . . .
                 you need no PARTNER . . .
           dedicate yourself to PRIVATE GYZM

        SPECIAL
for the young man with a S-T-R-E-T-C-H   MAN!
                         BOMB-BLITZ
                         AMERICA
        with your JOCK

                      Athens, 2.xi.64

la drogue/voyage

NON STOP   Ethiopian
                    service,
FLY
    away to the birth   of GOD
    aboard
        a power-packed   ETHIOPIAN

you'll enjoy a reliable performance

   Jet
        FLASHES
                   from
    secret ball

Pluck

       LIFE
                baby   FROM ICY DEATH

DON'T
be
VAGUE

         TAKE A TIP FROM THE CAMPS

time   weeps   The Truth about   Red, Green, Black, Yellow, White
                                 MEN

Brilliant liar
DAZZLER   MISTER BEAUTY

    THE UNSTEALABLE   ULTRA   HEARS

"Sorry* . . .   end of   THY ETHIOPIAN
                           DOLCE VITA

    SPECIAL LOW WEEKEND RATE

Athens, 9.xi.64

seventeen

same streets same faces
every day of my young life
same tasteless food
dished up by a nagging
baby mother
whose blue eyes gored you
with innocence
making you cry
some kind of holy idiot
"Eat your soup!" she commanded
"Finish the mashed potatoes!
Drink water! water is important!"
I felt like vomiting most of the time
no one to talk to
reading made matters worse
the Russian nihilists almost destroyed me
each day the houses grew
more monstrous
the streets more blank
the sky more impenetrable
I was going crazy
I started to cry
I cried in the subway
wept at the movies
sulked in classrooms
stinking of chalk and sperm
my notebooks grew damp with sperm
in the boys' room I masturbated
and was masturbated by other boys
I fell in love with their asses
then suddenly it was too much
I threw up in the toilet bowl
came out shivering
next day grabbed a freight
south

Heidelberg. 14.xii.66

el amor brujo

below 14th behind bamboo blinds
    in the mexican restaurant
we had chili with red wine
        & the mexican girl
    came to our table
to the two *guapos*
           with a terrific grin
   & dropped her handkerchief
into my lap
        the flag of her *amor*
& i was cherry & blushed
& my friend said You're in & there was
      a backroom

later
nothing sadder than cold streets
    of abandoned warehouses & lofts
garbage cans empty trucks
& from topfloor studio of modern dance
    el amor brujo
        reflected
            mirrors of sound
in my head in the dark lofts in the silence of my friend
                    New York, 1941

after-hours

   Only the blue law stops the flow
of infinitely sentimental guitars and
mouth-organs. Blue music, also,
   cut off, leaves the stragglers
   blue and vociferous to the
      last-ditch rendezvous.

   Here, dazed as owls shaken from
a tree at dawn, blinking they gather
in the vast fluorescent barn of the
   cafeteria. The pillars like
   Egyptian temple columns

receive the frantic packs

To coffee and pastry and the
pretense of a good time that
is kept afloat. Chairs creak
   and scrape incurably, but tables
   secured, as on a ship, won't give.
      The roar of emptiness is

Deafening. Displacement glitters
from faces like fake jewels. All
seek noticed anonymity—rough
   hoods and painted boys, their
   arms round each other, grunt
      and lisp in babyish

Displays of *amour propre* (that
never convince). Forced by pressure to
this caricature of pleasure, borders
   of loneliness devise an L.C.D.
   in sex. Strutting above their dates
      with shoulders like shakos, the truculent

Females brandish their difference. Though
music is missing, the energy of
dissonance has a rhythm, percussive
   as Varèse; a tortured atonalism or
   sounds that slide up and down
      the spine like a twelve-tone row

Of Berg. . . . Unnatural as grammar, the
fierce glaze of the after-hours
joint, like a klieg finger, selects the
   focal points of distress: the false
   posture, frozen grin . . . grotesque
      tumors of response, and

Witticisms grown wild like
a sudden growth of tissues; and
desires, morbid as clinics, spreading
   a *guignol* of invalid contact. This
   weekend terror of isolation
      confides in alcohol

For swift reprieve. . . . Morning hangs
out weak pale streaks of
blue, like ragged denim. The air
   blows sharp and cold as I move
   to the subway down the street. Immersed
     and part of this like a germ

In a deadly culture, I cannot leap
free of the bacilli—the
mould that breeds such lethal
   negative cells. Not yet . . . I descend
   with a burning fur of smoke
     on my tongue, my throat

Muffled beneath. Underground
ads and faces add up a like sum
of automatic data. The way home
   lies through routine tunnels, revolving
   doors that reflect headlines,
     empty buildings and my eyes.

New York, circa 1941/42

photograph of an athlete

A pale sky,
an abandoned tower,
two huge gulls,
gold sand, and
the beautiful stance
of an athletic man:

classic thighs
straining
over the witchgrass like
the discobolus.

New York, circa 1949

angel of last summer

Remember the angel of last summer?
Today he came to the roof and spoke.
I was bathing in tar, sun and smoke.
He said, "I want to beat this rug, but not dirty the wash."

"So, beat the rug. Keep your house clean."
The angel smiled, his muscles gleamed.
He beat the rug, I read my book,
The washing flapped and the chimneys shook.

"It's hot," he said and disappeared
Through the aerials—for another year.

New York, 1951

three songs from "penny arcade"

(A cyclical melodrama for voice and piano, set to music by Ned Rorem)

I

Test Your Skill

The rifle chatters to *Vienna Woods*
as violence waltzes boys to each attraction.
One kills and kills—the pinball enemy
will not die, but leaps back for a penny!

The aerial bomber, riding his tightrope
of thrills and spills, must shout *Geronimo!*
each time suburban boys approach to spend
their dreams (small change) at the electric show.

Who is the dangerous-looking boy whose fist
grapples an iron lever like a throat?
His fingers close securely, his big wrist
bulges with veins of power—the machine is choked!

Who is the boy with hair dyed sunset orange,
with midnight caverns where a face should be?
He moves among the others like a ghost

hungering for a life that can never be.

Who is he with eyes of cellophane,
eyes that enwrap some priceless, living toy?
Who is this monster with the clicking brain
mechanical as a wheel? Who is this boy?

2

Song of the Third Duck from the Right

There is a breaking in the air.
I'm shot in the heart; let me drown, Despair!
He had violet eyes and yellow hair.

I don't want to rise and be shot again.
I'm tired of all these hunting men.
Let me drown, let me sink down like cement.

3

Goodbye to Penny Fate

It's goodbye to the dice and poker games,
    Goodbye to radar and pinball.
It's goodbye to the girls with pretty names
    That hit you like a skee-ball.

Tom has weathered the sly machines
    That guess anything about you.
Dick has emptied out his jeans,
    Will try to live without you.

Goodbye, goodbye to Test Your Strength,
    Goodbye to Guess Your Weight.
Will try to carry on at length
    With height and age and state.

But now goodbyes and more goodbyes
    To Make-Believe-You're-Great,
To handsome, popular and wise;
    Goodbye to Penny Fate.

New York, 1950

ballad of beautiful boys

Whatever became of Hans, the German,
tall and pale and hard as an oar?
And where is Bruce the college freshman
who made a javelin look small?

And the Irish boy in the Merchant Marine
whose body made us drunker than wine?
And Mario with the olive skin
and thick black hair on muscular thighs?

And where is Ibrahim the Egyptian
with the bull neck and powerful hands?
And Ahmed the Arab with the sexy grin,
hung like a donkey and mad for men?

Where's Henry with the barrel chest
matted all over with fur like a bear?
And sweet Eugene, smooth as marble,
with balls like ripe, heavy pears?

Black Albert, giant of ebony,
who never tired and who moaned and jazzed?
And Per the languid blond from Sweden
and Nick the Cretan shepherd lad?

Where's Joe the lifeguard from L.A.
with massive shoulders and wasp waist?
Where's David the beautiful Jew from Brooklyn
that Michelangelo might have cast?

Where are the sailors, Tom, Dick and Harry,
cruising and hot in their navy blue,
fresh from farm, lumbercamp and prairie,
following a dream too good to be true?

Where are they now, the wonderful ones
who flowered on streetcorners and waterfronts?
Where are the beautiful boys I knew once
whose greatest dread was the touch of cunts?

New York, 9.xi.51

a party of albanians

A party of Albanians—no, Greeks—
in native holiday dress

on the grass in Central Park
outspoken in gold and red—

the males in frank white tights and
sashes, woolen tunics open at the throat
—soft slippers with pom-poms like peonies
on the toes . . . the girls
lavish with ornament—

Now I cannot sleep. . . .

When they left, the onlookers
remained, numbly bewildered, drab
grays, browns, blacks—
                              dirt
unpleasantly piled round the hole
uprooted flowers leave!

New York, 1943

monsieur fenelon

While lathes were rasping and motors whined
Monsieur Fenelon sat in the sun
              of his kitchen window
fingering his hairy tits and
watching his unwrinkling penis
              thick as a zebra's
swell between his hard fat thighs

Smoke from three chimneys
              tall as buildings
also unwrinkled into the morning . . .
the clattering of drills
tore down old walls and
              new ones were soon
              erected

But Monsieur Fenelon (always
the poet) having seen
            the dawn
from the safe approaches of the night before
watched drowsily with equine eyes
            his own erection
            in the sun

New York, Winter, 1943

christmas card, 1941

Hello   New York   hello hello
You smart and bitter babies
Hello 52nd Street
You hot-lipped number at the nite club
Hello   Joe   hello   Greek
Grand Central   CBS   crabapple trees
In the sunken plaza under the RCA
Building   hellooo
Sunlight on sanctuary birds in Central Park
Slant on the service table in the penthouse
Of Mrs. Rich and
the WPA   keeping alive
For years those who have been painting
Dead images in "dynamic" murals
The starving artists
Hello there
I am trying to see
Trying to focus the confusion

        How beautiful the city shines
        White Indiana limestone over
        Noguchi giants the telephone and
        Typewriter and Prometheus lording
        It over the penguins and parasols

I am trying you painted bitch
To see your scared pale running
Bodies breaking in waves of terror
Into the subways and cellars
To believe you are really

Ochre and green under the
False rumors of bombing planes
Heading coastward for death   hello
You pampered lode of culture
Ballet boys kissing sailors
On 42nd Street   with ballerina waddle
Harlem hysteria   Brooklyn brothel

    Now the breakdown places
    Torn earth on the breakfast table
    A foot in the boudoir drawer
    Burning photos of Oahu
    Pearl Harbor   Waikiki
    As the nightly news report
    Assassinates the ear

    Can we make a move without thinking
    Of shattered limbs
    Can we take a step without fear
    There are those who went to jail
    For writing pamphlets
    In Oklahoma, Alan, you went to jail
    For the crime of owning *Das Kapital*

    And before we die let us not overlook
    The "nigger" Neal who ate his testicles
    And penis and said he liked them
    And had to because he hoped to live
    But the blue-eyed girls
    Cut off the rest
    His fingers   his toes   his ears
    And took them home as souvenirs
    What state was it
    What's the difference   it happened
    Nor the last to get his photogenic figure
    Hacked by mobs
    As he hung like a dead branch
    Or moss on dead cypress
    In the deep South

Oh anyway hello
I am trying to say the oratorios
Will be sung this year and
Peace and good will

Et cetera
And there will be much asking   Will it be
A White Christmas and my aunt
Will continue to send me gifts
Which on the warm sand
I shall examine
And quip about with friends here in Miami
A place of hideous homes
Whitewashed and square and pink
With coconut palms over card tables
On clipped lawns with bulbous matrons
Who cackle with lobster-red lips
Talking of weddings
While I lie watching their sons
Admiring their muscles and youth like my own
But secretly wanting to marry them
If they only knew
After all I'm a 4F
That's why I'm lounging the war away
A disgraceful pacifist

Christmas greetings
Ding dong bell
Hello Christ   hello manger
Hello Magi   hello lamb's blood
We may certainly need it
We're bathing in it already
But now I watch my body change
From youth to firmer manhood
As the Florida sun pours tan
Evenly on my face and skin
They'll be after me with khaki and leather
And buttons if I look too healthy
But nevertheless I send reassurances
Home to mother
And am totally confused
And see nothing good
But a few dreamers and teachers
All I can say from this sugary beach is
Hello   New York   hello   hello
Peace and goodwill
Et cetera

Miami Beach, 1941

from all these, you

from a gull's oily breath
from a Greek letter
from 2 snails around foam
from seaweed
from imminent destruction
from the corpse of a seal
from blood
from the night sky
from a joint of marijuana
from four walls of despair
from an urge to shout
from a need to expose myself
from the thighs of a bodybuilder
from a fat whore
from the empty pockets of my boyhood in Brooklyn
from the vacant blue eyes of my mother
from her cracked factory hands
from her shopgirl life of persecution
from the swarm of roaches in the kitchen of Harlem
from the nervous breakdown in the attic
from the circle of light in a vision
from anxiety, dreams, paranoia
from moist lips and erections
from giant vaginas and promethean pricks
from my lovers in 15 countries
from dreadful loneness in my own country
from the karma circuit that joins us, divides us
from the rose I wept at from the void
from the beat hotel where I cut up my life
from nostalgia for the soul cashed in long ago
from endless need of sex/love/$$$$
from insomnia, broken vows, exhausted adrenals
from the anguished cry of flamenco guitars
from feeling, desiring, laughing, strangling
from the ebbtide, the flow, the lone mind, the sea surge
from the years, the years, the years
from the tube sticking out of a boy's body in Viet Nam
from Amerikan war crimes madder than any poem
from smog in mucous membranes, DDT in tits and the govt in your bed
from the chemical feast of Deathsicola
from Marrakech nights of hasheesh and majoun
from the burnoose I slept in near the Sahara Desert

from white trees in moonlight, Pan pipes of hysteria
from the crucifix, the Mogen David, the crescent, the comet
from the nada and dada
from the way out which is the way in
from the Dance of Shiva, from the tongue of Kali
from vibrating colors, the rain, the sun, the stars
from rawness of emotion
from déjà vu of a face or city or passage
from the Waldorf Cafeteria where we dunked pound cake in coffee till
     5 a.m. with nowhere to go
from New Year's Eve parties full of beer and clairvoyance
from standing room at the opera where we got groped by aunties and the
     Götterdämmerung never had such a climax
from the earthquake that shook me up at the sea's edge before dawn
from the brick and mortar tenement rocking to wild chthonic music
from all these, you
     my poems

                       Venice, Calif., circa 1971

in the city forsaken by the angels

in the city forsaken by the Angels
a million people seek refuge.
made homeless by earthquake
they run into the streets in nightclothes
or stark naked, clutching
an old photograph or a drum.
buildings shake and fall apart
into a heap of glass, plaster, concrete.
shattered cars, buckled bridges, dams
broken and gushing over a suburb.
old ladies weep, traffic signals
don't work, children scream.
a naked youth in an overcoat
carries a sign hastily improvised
on cardboard: REPENT! THE END IS NEAR!
he speaks to no one. his hair is golden
shoulder-length, his legs perfect.
I approach in awe, wanting
to touch him. . . .
but as I think of the Angels in Sodom

he vanishes. . . .
to go down in a heap of rubble
with 100 twisted old ladies
sour, insane, hating life
is like dying in a bombed ghetto
like TV alone in a room
with commercials.
dying of irrelevance
for a god of adding machines
for a dream of envy.

Venice, Calif., 1971

gone gone gone

discs of lost america!   1934 gray pearl
saxophone riffs of body   & soul & smoke gets in
your eyes   duck soup   stardust lapping lobes
of memory   boyhood pavements   roamed in
musical comedy sadness   of wanting to be
beautiful & great!

let the tenor sax dig deep   o funky jazz   in proustian key!
mouldy sneakers!   lockerrooms!   pubic shadows
in chlorine pools!   my life & loves   in backyard cellar
coal garage!   o body & soul!   static of worn
old platter!   fiery crackle!   patina of sound!
you send me   BACK!

america?   or just a school of   budding flesh?
soundsmell   filtered thru   fresh high
pubescence?   touch wakes   painful
pleasure-petals in the crotch   hot pants
reek in toilets   stained   underwear   swollen bare
boythighs   tense   o spasm shudder!
discovered   thrill of   shoot!

all gaul divided   down willoughby & clark
sweet coffee bean smell of   dusky dock   i cover
the waterfront   where are you?
gotham blinking diamonds   over tugs & winches
steamy trucks
anaconda river   crawls across my page   heading for
crab eyes   horseshoe nose   snakemouth

Athens, 1965

nocturnal emissions

You may go to bed a poet but wake up a jackoff.

· · ·

My sex life is none of your business unless you share it.

· · ·

A little sex is a dangerous thing.

· · ·

A limp cock is like a phone off the hook.

· · ·

If God is Love, Sex is my religion.

· · ·

Seventy years in the closet—the average American's life-span.

· · ·

When we kill our desires we stink like any corpse.

· · ·

He who binds to himself a Boy
Doth the Wingèd Life enjoy.

· · ·

Genius, like money, is usually in the wrong hands.

· · ·

Money is an IOU drawn on the blood of the people.

· · ·

Racism is a disease of the blood.

· · ·

The body politic suffers from a terminal social disease: money.

· · ·

Revolution is major surgery on the body politic. The patient usually dies.

· · ·

The only revolution that has a chance of success is the sexual revolution. All other revolutions are based on hate and can only fail. You must physically love your fellow-man.

· · ·

Conservatism is for the well-fed; revolution for the fed-up.

· · ·

The law, not homosexuality, is a crime. Sex is natural.

· · ·

Sick people create sick laws that create sick people.

· · ·

When the first Christian pervert, St. Paul, made nature a crime against Christianity, civilization was finished. Had he been handsome instead of hideous, the whole course of history might have been happier.

· · ·

If God is dead, he died of shame for his followers.

God is come, the cock divine.

"Join my Church and your golf will improve." (Newspaper headline)

We are searching for rational reasons for believing in the absurd.

San Francisco, circa 1973

allegro vivace
or
now it can be told

Thanks to the biblical scholar, Professor Allegro,
who deciphered the ancient Sumerian tablets
and found that fertility cults
were centered around psychedelic drugs,
now it can be told: Jesus Christ,
the cross, the mushroom and the cock
are one. The Christ of Christianity
was a sacred mushroom.
Let all gay men proclaim their holiness.
They've worshiped the sacred mushroom
for millennia. THE COCK IS HOLY!
Let men and women proclaim universal allegiance
to the only true religion: S E X. . . .
Make it *allegro vivace!*
Let the death-cult of suffering die!
Let J O Y and P L E A S U R E take
their rightful place! that's
as holy as you'll ever be!

San Francisco, 1973

adult bookstore

A cute boy is obliging his friend who's putting the whole 9 inches
      up his ass
while a young girl is trying to suck a huge cock but not quite making
      it, which is very touching, so to speak
like the sweet innocent look of cattle grazing or cats licking each
      other's fur.
O innocent kids! Don't stop!
I've got a hard-on, I'm coming!
And they say Nature is dirty?
O polluted century!

                            San Francisco, 27.xi.71

do i think he's normal

he finds all cocks but his own
    disgusting, can't understand
what men can see in one another,
    guesses he has some kind
      of inhibition, says
that cock & cockroach
   have the same effect
     on him, goes
so far as to imagine
   a cock is like a spider,
     the effect is similar—
he grins & asks me
   do I think he's normal.

subversive activity for commies

BIG RUSSIAN COCK
GUARANTEED
TO UNDERMINE PEOPLE
EVERYWHERE
IT'S THE MOST POP
BECAUSE IT TASTES
SO GREAT
STRAIGHT
AND THE MOST MARVELOUS
GOURMET FLAIR
A DELICACY
WHICH WE SUGGEST YOU SELL
MILLIONS ALREADY

This poem is a cut-up, Paris, 1962; it surprised me by its not so mysterious message once I could read and re-arrange some of the words and delete others. It came out with a Jewish accent in the end.

the true brotherhood

when the young truckdrivers unload
below my window I stick out my head
& yell hello!

they look up grinning
groping themselves
& carrying their load
as I carry mine

when clearly it should be distributed
from each according to his ability
to each according to his needs—

the true brotherhood
foretold in prophecy
from ancient days!

San Francisco, circa 1974

pierre

God, how I miss you! Since that night
In Barcelona, in the drab hotel,
Your image keeps returning, your height
And blondness that went so well
With the conversation, like an inner light.
Nothing happened. But it might have, it might!

I never saw you again. . . . Still,
Does it occur so often, on the move,
That one meets, hoping he will,
Someone who fits like a groove?
Next morning, on business, you were off to Brazil.
I can't remember when I've felt so ill.

Barcelona, 1956

les sylphides

All that bombazine and swan stuff—
moonlight and mothballs!
The silky male in white tights
pushes his crotch around
like he stuffed it
with a ballet slipper—
an old dancer's trick.
Nureyev and Nijinski
could get away with it but—
no, I'm sorry, *this*
is the kind of ballet
that gives fairies
a bad name.

San Francisco, circa 1973

lady in the dark

O Lady in the Dark, come dance with me!
I'm the handsome leading man
waltzing down the stage in lights
to a burst of applause, my smile dazzling!
Everyone loves me, the golden tenor,
I put a catch in their throat
with my looks, my voice, my charm.
I'm a dream, a beauty! what a hunk!
But I'm really going home to my lover
who is a truckdriver with big muscles
while women fight each other
to tear off bits of my clothes. . . .

San Francisco, circa 1974

strangers

If I have puffed eyes and a lifeless expression
and my body starts to sag and my lips commence to curl
it is you, beautiful strangers, I'm thinking about.

San Francisco, 2.i.75

last night at the party

You're only 20
& I'm old enough
& jealousy
is ugly
at any age
but
I did not enjoy
all that kissing
& fondling
you did with the boy
you picked up
last night at the
party

to which I
brought you
you might have spared me
that
to make matters
worse
I had to go
because of a head
cold
without even a chance
at the pretty
boy
who had eyes for
me
I think

San Francisco, 14.xi.76

to an ex-lover who ripped me off

This rage I feel towards you
it's so strong it makes me ill
I want to slash hack cut
people & things
maybe this way
I can break out of imprisoned
pain
break down walls
I've built around me
hack thru isolation
& ruined sleep
I realize
I'm talking to the dead
about the dead
I understand that
but there's nobody else
to talk to
since you left
like the thief you are
taking my things
& my last feelings
of tenderness

San Francisco, 19.xii.72

blood of a poet

For Paul Mariah

they sent him up for 5 years
set bail at 100 grand
& he did time in the hole
for making love
to a boy of 18
who wanted it
both lonely in Illinois
& he came out with an education
in pain
& breaks down when he tells it
& you feel ashamed
& dumb.

San Francisco, July 1972

adadadadada

I scan the People column
ADADADADADA
in the *Berkeley Barb*
I LIKE TO SHARE FEELINGS and
ideas with sensitive creative
people . . . no, that won't do, I'm hot. . . .
PRICK MEAT FOR HUNGRY MOUTH
that meat's too raw. . . .
MUSCULAR LATIN BISEXUAL 23
seeks muscular males for
sincere relationship, must
be discreet. . . . hmm, all right
but wants photo and letters
and I want *action*
so onward & upward
LONGHAIRED HUNG MASCULINE
dude needs steady servicing
by masculine oral expert
under 35, no S&M, wtr sprts or
discp . . . but I'm over 35. . . .
INEXP YNG M desires to learn &

make friends whatever Ur bag,
willing 4 anything . . . OK but no
phone—ah, here's a likely number—
2 GAY GUYS WANT HAIRY MASC
guy to 50 for trio, phone. . . .
soon I'm tooling across the freeway
to Castro and pull up before
old Victorian sprucely painted
and the 2 gay guys talk and talk
about the weather, Watergate, Deep Throat,
they're in their 30's, soft
around the middle and show a porn
flick of 2 teenage boys
trim & dreamy, 200 ft.
of cocksucking & buttfucking
& I almost cum but these gay guys
don't look so good when the light goes on
& neither do I
so with polite excuses
we separate & it's chug-a-lug
back to ADADADADADA
& jackoff time
but before I've gone 500 ft.
a longhaired kid near the freeway
eyes me as I cruise by
I pull up & the kid approaches
my god, is it a girl? it has a blond beard
and smiles into the VW with a hard-on
in beat-up blue jeans and gets in
& GROPES me!
so it's back on the freeway
to my place, perfect,
no hang-ups, a quickie
& he's gotta go, his lover is waiting
so at Mission & Van Ness
I drop him with a kiss
& back at my pad I tear up
ADADADADADA

San Francisco, 12.v.73

the love song of an old beatnik

1

After you left I missed you so much
I began to floss my teeth wildly.
There was nothing to do.
The sunflower seeds you put in a jar—
don't worry, they'll keep
much better than me till you're back.
I think I'm catching the flu.
And it's raining—no, it's fogging
and Georg Philip Telemann is doing his best
to cheer me up with a little baroque,
not German Romantic. And
I might feel better yet.

2

But I don't. I pick myself up
and move from room to room, wading
thru tides of old newspapers, seaweed
of laundry, transistor tangles, strange
torn fauna beached and gasping. Upstairs
a hi fi stereo rock
breaks thru the ceiling. Giant retards
stomp in hobnailed boots over my head, dropping
hammers, breaking bricks, blowing glass!
When I complain they hint at paranoia and bad karma
advising meditation. They go
back to mu tea and brown rice, aiming
kung fu kicks at the door.
I nibble sunflower seeds (they flush
fallout from the system, according
to Russian scientific researchers)
and pass the kitchen sink absently
searching thru books, unanswered letters.
I single out old photos. You float
to the surface of a burial mound, smiling
on a technicolor shore. I tack you
to the wall. You'll stay
fixed in hypo light years ago.
Then the picture becomes clear. This
is all that I'll be seeing of you.

3

Outside, I feel myself breathing —
or is it someone else breathing?
I don't know. It's the same face
looking back in the glass. But
is it me? People
no longer pause as they used to,
catching my eye in the reflection
while I windowshopped too. Now
these reflections are
like a broken mirror, a child
howling in the dark.

San Francisco, 1975

in the sun on a warm
november afternoon

For Winston Leyland

in the sun on a warm
november afternoon a vast
synthetic paved
square with a
fountain from which
poisoned city
water flows it's
the Embarcadero
Plaza & I'm
flat on the curved
cement
benches thoughtfully
laid out for the
recumbent human
form by the recumbent
city planners thoughtful
but not aesthetic
& businessmen in
money uniforms
rigid
walk by
with short hair

mad-looking among
the freestyle young
they pass with scarcely
a glance

the kids
mostly black &
brown scream &
play in the water
splashing
while 2 young
men beside me dart
furtive glances
at my bare
hairy aging
albeit muscular
torso
as they munch
lunch
always these signals
of restless quest for
ecstasy, freedom
under
the humdrum
externals
as life goes
on
secretly beneath
the noise and
speech that exist
on broader daylight
terms
of falsity

San Francisco, 1971

working out

For Ken Lester

What a fine pair of obliques!
your body restores, in the old sense
the meaning of *gymnasium*
          —the true learning!
you glow like an aura
                    such whiteness
                    such hardness
and above the pleasing "pump"
                              a mind

                                        San Francisco, 24.xi.73

labor day . . . in the vegetable kingdom

For Howard Schrager

A family of diabetics in the arboretum
(under the conifers near "Pink Beauty" and "Prunus Armeniaca"
which turns out to be plain apricot)
—they're all skinny and tightassed and you mustn't stare at them
they make sure by staring at you
with anticipated hostility
and a girl's on top of a blond boy
kissing by lush viburnum
while a mad whistler in beret, beard and pink corduroys
passes and glances to see if you're staring and thinking he's nuts
which he is, whistling loud and syrupy.
Meanwhile naked babies coo in the fountain like pigeons,
one blond baby looks like an old man
and keeps diddling his penis—dirty old baby?
and here's a big baseball game, the parks haven't changed much in years,
Golden Gate Park could be Prospect Park, the earth's a little sicker
but will probably pull through
as frisbees float like flying saucers
creating a nuisance if you want to meditate
and be left alone.
This is a vegetable poem.

If you're not a vegetarian go read a carnivorous poem.
Chicano kids start a softball game
and a sexy bottle blonde outfields like Mae West,
first base is her spiked shoe, second a tampax, third a brassiere.
The boys laugh like hell.
And in the Men's Room a hermaphrodite hysterically screams:
"OUT! OUT! NANA STAY OUT! THIS IS THE BOYS' ROOM!"
his/her gray hair and smooth worn features leaping with traumatic rage
and the little girl starts wailing, trauma officially begun/dykehood surely
as powdered old ladies with trembling hands sit in the shade
dumbly seeing nothing
and a dachshund rushes away from a black man who calls, "MINNIE!
        COME HERE, YA BITCH!! I'M GONNA WHIP YO' ASS!!!"
and nothing is really happening but breathing and whistling and looking
which is the way I like it
because it's the least history can do for us,
I mean, just leave us alone.

San Francisco, circa 1973

kid, it wd be nice

kid, it wd be nice
if you & me made it
but you're cuntstruck
        & tho' well hung
        you're hung up too
& make a mess
        in the toilet
that you visit every 5
        minutes for god
knows what
        mysterious
compulsion & yr nails
        are too clean
    yr head's with poetry
        & the Empress of China
            on some private cloud
but kid you don't
    know how dollars &
        Time
                eat the soul

& have never missed a
        meal & you've lost
3 coats already
        "don't know where or how"
& I can't lend you mine
            on no trust fund
        yr laugh's infectious
but kid, only lovers
        crash here

San Francisco, 3.viii.72

o furum optime

(*after Catullus*)

o slickest thieves at the Turkish Baths
Vibennius and your fairy son!
the right hand of the father is predaceous
and the son's behind remarkably voracious!
so beat it, both of you, go to hell!
since everyone knows of the father's filching
and your ass, boy, is too hairy to sell!

1977

get your big fat wings out of my face, billy

When I'm feeling down
nothing can bring me up
but money
            or a good fuck

Why are they both so hard to get

Sometimes good dope can make us forget
the fall of the dollar
and the pain of America

Merely the act of speaking Italian
gets my juices flowing again

A city like Amsterdam
not a parking lot in sight
braces my spirit
like the absence of Los Angeles

Little cigars from Sumatra in brown wooden boxes
and a quarter kilo of old Gouda
make me more mellow than a hamburger
on a formica table off the freeway

The poetry of Blaise Cendrars
seems closer
in a hotel room on a street called Sarphatipark
    in Amsterdam
than among the rednecks in the redwoods
and the Dutch language that is so much like brillo
scrapes my ear
gone flat like automobile tires
like American history
gone flat in television
like commercials for shitola

And when I talk to Franco Beltrametti
or Harry Hoogstraten
or Simon Vinkenoog
or Joanne Kyger
or Ted Berrigan
or Ira Cohen
or Tom Raworth
or Tom Pickard
or Anne Waldman
or Carl Weissner
or Vernie February
or Jessica Hagedorn
I know we belong to the same country
which is *not*
the fatherland of Jimmy Carter
or Anita Bryant
and the gravel voice of Allen Ginsberg
is sweeter than Billy Graham's

Get yr big fat wings out of my face, Billy
If you're goin' to heaven
that's one place I don't wanna be

14.ix.78/Amsterdam
For Harry Hoogstraten
& Poetry 78

transcendental meditation

★   key ring   ★   key ring   ★   key ring
key ring
        actually I prefer your recommendation
    key ring key ring
it wd carry more weight key ring
     key ring coming from you key ring
key ring key ring key ring key ring
   it seems self serving
             key ring
coming from me   key ring key ring key ring key ring
    keep the words away
            key ring key ring
    keep the music away
            key ring
   key ring
       the vocal chords are loosening up
   key ring
wish I cd oil my vocal chords key ring
   key ring key
      ring key
        ring
          key
          ring
   keep
   thoughts
      away
       at bay key ring key ring
   It seems so long ago
          key ring key
          ring key
           ring
Nancy was alone

                    key ring key ring
                                        nothing
Looking at the late late show   key ring
                                        nothing
          key   ring
                              key ring
          tram car clang
                         key ring
                                   nothing
      ★   key ring   ★   key ring   ★   key ring
massage   key ring   cd use a good key ring massage
      key
                ring
                  key
                                   ring
no thought
no form
                  key   ring
through a semi precious stone
                                   key ring
          they sell you the word
                                   key ring

14. ix. 78/Amsterdam
For Franco Beltrametti
& Marcello Angioni

bullets

Outside the Plaza
on the Ramblas
bursts of machinegunfire.
It's the police.
People dive into shops and bars.
Shutters slam shut.
13 truckloads of Civil Guards
roll in. The streets fill
with them, tommyguns ready,
fingers on triggers.
They question civilians
emerging from hidingplaces, stick
guns in their bellies.

These were your killers, Federico
García Lorca. We're not allowed
to take their photos. Whom are they shooting?
Are they shooting luckless ordinary men
who have sat too long empty-handed
in squares like this, watching the pigeons
among gypsy songs? Are they shooting
students who do a little shouting
now and then because they are young?
Are the bullets rubber or lead?

I pass the Guardia Civil on Calle Fernando
and on the Plaza de San Jaime.
Their faces are tense, closed like iron gates.
Their fingers never relax on the trigger.
No use to say: Señor, we are only tourists!
It is not safe to look into their eyes.

the poem must be as modern as strategic rocket carriers

The poem must be as modern as strategic rocket carriers
equipped with nuclear warheads

Rockets can reach any point on the planet
atomic submarines can fire nuclear warheads
from any point in the ocean

ACTION! ACHTUNG! NEW WEAPONS! EN GARDE!

The poem must reach any point on the planet
with deadly accuracy

Words are weapons

A giant helicopter force of angry poems
releasing mushroom clouds of warning
will destroy anybody's serenity forever
from any point on the planet

dalivision dalivision dalivision

explosions
in the poisoned   blue   mineral
SKY
blue   of depleted   armpits
Sienna   and   olive-green
explosions
of a see-through
molecular
madonna
in the calm   of the bright
fleshy   folds
of
a
skeleton
creaking
like   an   immense   peeled
bone
blood-pink
gnarled in eternity
in the   foam   of   thighs
in the   double   image
of
S
E
X
melting
into
a
soft
w
a
t
c
h
drip   ping
T I M E
on dissolv   ing faces
devoured
by
ants
in the   splintered   atoms   of
her
jagged mercy
with the

SUN
in her solar plexus
BOOK
in one
&
holy phallic
BABE
in the other
hand
shooting
among the planets
his unthinkable
rod of gold
hot
SEED
into her immensity
killing
TIME
in the rush
of
creation
in the SUN of her
W
O
M
B
where the light
spatters
and becomes
BODY   MIRAGE   MATTER
MIRACLE
IMAGE
soft contours fusing
with
the world
landscape
in one body
rotting images
held by crutches
by his penetrating gaze
refusing
DEATH
SEE-THROUGH FLESH PIERCED
IN THE BULLRING
MOMENT OF TRUTH
in   the   center of   the

282

WORLD
at Perpignan
in   the   center of   the
multiple image
VENUS
L O V E
triumphant
Madonna
Christ
Mao
on the nuclear

C
R
C R O S S
S
S

of
genetic angels
Galacidalacidesoxyribonucleic
self-portrait
Assumpta Corpuscularia Lapislazulina
Kropotkin
Bakunin
a
dream of cosmic
unity
ah!
hallucinogenic   Dalivisions!
Take me!   I am the drug!
the illumination
of pleasure!
the lion of desire!
the skull sodomizing a grand piano!
Garcia Lorca
with figs & boiled beans!
starting the revolution
of butterflies
and dreams
!
★

13 April 1983
San Francisco

after reading jessica hagedorn's *dangerous music*

Your poems are like mangoes
They make me feel
                    sexual and tropical

They are also like motel rooms
in Southern California
with honeysuckle and freeways
and sounds of creaking beds thru walls
hot clean rooms near the beach
with flushing toilets
and wino voices

Your poems are like voodoo
they cast a spell
young latinos sniffing mirrors
gardenias in a corsage
at some late night party in Puerto Rico
                    where I've never been
or in Manila as I
                imagine it
full of equatorial chic

Your poems are   like pearl and ivory
fans from China
                        like a bongo drum
        an acoustic guitar
a San Francisco rock beat

Ah, Jessica
        what magic
                to make so much
                    happen

                                19 Sept. 78/Amsterdam

mysteries of magritte

"Attempting the impossible" he
created a woman
using his
brush as a penis
spurted
P A I N T
into the room
&
her body
formed
before him

N U D E

almost
finished   but   not
quite

Holding his palette
in his left
H A N D
he dipped his brush
&
began to finish
her
shoulder
as
she stood
with her smart 20s bob
like

V E N U S
de Milo

He named her after his palette
P A U L E T T E

There is no whoopee here
only "brooding eeriness" and
haunting "poetic"

D   O   O   M

He created her
each day
hated travel
&
F A M E
preferred to remain at
home
&

P A I N T

She survived
him
& gave interviews
kept his studio impeccably
neat
a final painting on the
the easel
where he
left
it
unfinished
when
he
died
It   looks   out
on   the   next
h o u s e

A   friend
once
asked him
why
there were no paint
stains
on the carpet

THE   PLACE   FOR   PAINT
he said
is on
C A N V A S
not on
R U G S

16.xi.78/Barcelona

the spanish painters

outside
my window

(it's really a door)

the green
palm
against the marine
sky
framed
by my French
door

(it's really a window)

&
iron grillwork
balcony

(it's really Miró)

myself
on
the flowering
counterpane
an odalisque
with
a
moustache!

the green
sky
frames
the marine
palm
&
iron grillwork
balcony

a
purple
plant

extends
its leaves
like crutches
o
f

B
O
N
E

holding
a

F
A
C
E

melting
in the green
afternoon

(it's really Dalí)

ah, señor!
what a truly
Spanish
day!

(it's really Juan Gris)

27.x.78/Barcelona

in the museum of modern art

I stood   sweating   before   the world
of   exploding   wheat
&   shuddering   suns
churning   paint
of the   mad   Dutchman   who
ended   up   in   a   tree
with   lead   in   his   brain
SCREAMING
&
H
O
L
Y

!

Thirty   years
after   my   vision
of   heavenly   hell
in   vibrating   yellows
&   stormy   blacks
I'd   weep   if   I   could
but   my   head   is
shot   up
with   decades
of
painkillers
&
jackhammers
blast   the   wheat

1972?/San Francisco

non-objective painter

to break thru   walls of conduct
    with a tube   of pigiron
   he juggles   colors   like indian clubs
       hairbreadth curvilinear weave
          in mazy motion
    the eye sinks
      an amazed boat   beneath the weight
             of a swirling   ocean
past uncharted poles   of vision
          past the deep iceberg's thunders
              the whales
    of watery childhood
      he plunges
  into   w h i t e   S P A C E
where   the   great   blank of being breathes
        &   each   soul   sails
then
    from the falsely shaped   he shapes
     changing multiforms   unknown presences
       the   dream beneath   the   surface
       of
          sensation
                   suffering
           joy

1956/Rome

in rousseau's painting 'la guerre'

In Rousseau's painting *La*
    Guerre a mad
      child with a
sword
    astride
     a black horse
unable to stop
      feet off
the ground the
    child wields a
      torch

                 over
bloodbeaked ravens
        black
                boughs blasted bodies
fallen
   in the
            foreground
        stupor
                in the shorn
faces
                    SEEN
                    from a
distance
            it might be
                        a dance
        the clouds
                seem
fresh & bright
                till
                        a close
view reveals
                they are
                    bloodclouds
a sick & human
                hue
& the girl
            arms
                    aloft
       in jagged
                    joy
turns monstrous
                the animal a
                        horizontal
stretch of
            tail
                &
mane
     eyeless
                her
                    hobbyhorse
                            not
playing exactly
     tho' clearly
            a kind of

game
      her grin's a
                 horror
      the field with
                   its detached
        forms
            clods of
                    dummy
limbs the
            ravens
                    shear
        La
        Guerre
            a
              primi
tive
      kind of
            stroke
                 there
le
   douanier
            with a clear
brush like a
          wing
             has flown
   us
into
         the dark
              force
where
         words   blear   in
the unbearable
              nightmare
       core

1963?/Athens

van gogh's eyes

In John Peter Russell's portrait of
Van Gogh
at the Stedelijk Museum
in Amsterdam
the eyes
of Vincent
burn
thru the mediocre pose
tho' we get a likeness
more than Vincent's wild
impressionistic self
depictions

Gaugin and Lautrec
in the 1880's
looked dull
beside Van Gogh
who took it up up and away
into the churning
atomic spheres
behind the hospital
at St. Rémy
the strangest wheatfield in history
where 'the black of the crows
dominates
the chaotic landscape
at Auvers-sur-Oise'   July 1890
with swirling bloody paths
and lurid swaths
that cut thru turbulence
of violent earth
and the dark ultramarine sky
crows like M's
for madness
slashing thru the vision
of this world

prophetic in 1890
for the century to come
of shattered reason

and I walk like a blind man

            in the museum
        feeling my way
            thru vibrations
                    and emenations
            of electric currents
                from the canvases
            shocking me
                        like cattle prods
            out of this drab
                            day
                into the coup d'état
                    of Van Gogh's eyes

21.ix.1978/Amsterdam

conversation in color

    You ask me where the sky begins
            here under my feet   you say
    it begins for me   but where
                do you begin?
    in your birth   your body   your soul?
            in your blue eyes?

    The Arab selling peanuts
    the waiter bringing beer
    & the traffic on the boulevard
    are all entering you
            by eye
                    & ear
    Where does anything begin
                    anyway?

        At the cafe table
            my eyes registered blue
    wherever I looked   a flash
    of blue striped every face
            the signs
    were blue we drank blue
    beer smoked blue
    cigarettes a blue
    haired redhead passed

My head is radioactive
how else
        gather so much blue
for our afternoon
                at the *Bleus Magots?*

I mean the magical change
that my rods & cones
invented
        is it so physical?
            are you sure?
        or a psychic state?
                        yeah
like when you look at somebody's aura
    & see emotions as colors
        & the world has suddenly
            changed forever—
                animations!
                    vibrations!
                        dimensions!

& you begin once more. . . .

I talk to you as painters do
in rainbow language
        saying BLUE!
and you answer: VIOLET-RED!
                PUCE-UMBER-CINNABAR!
and I reply: GOLDGREEN!

                                            1959/Paris

the ballad of marc chagall

Blue diamond eyes and snowy hair
A Chaplin man smaller than me
Chagall bought his newspaper every morning
On the Rue de l'Ile St. Louis.

I watched him from across the street
Where I lived and wrote poetry
Or we bumped into each other

And said politely, "Oh, pardon me!"

Chagall bought bread at the *boulangerie*
And I watched him and knew that he watched me
With those blue diamonds that cut through time
Beyond the Rue de I'Ile St. Louis.

One morning we stood eye to eye
As he bought his newspaper and looked at me
I felt like a painting about to be born
From that appraising look, wary and free.

Then the shopkeeper spoke, a splendid man
Who had been a boxer and had won the Grand Prix—
"Three champions," he said, "meet together today
In art, in sport, in poetry!"

Chagall smiled and said to me,
"You're a poet, then?" I said, "Oui."
The diamonds flashed. "I knew it!" he said,
And vanished on the Rue de I'Ile St. Louis.
Then he appeared among chimney pots
On the roofs of the Rue de I'Ile St. Louis
Playing his blue fiddle and dancing with
A yellow unicorn delicately.

16.xii.82/San Francisco

was it florence or venice?

Was it Florence or Venice
    canal or river
milky green water
of scraps, sedge, canoes
    afloat
            on wrinkled palaces
like a burning film
        in sunlight

Going between the two
    cities, their
differences less as one grows

familiar with pure Italy
   although there are
      so many, as many
as the eyes of the
   beholder

a face, irreducible
   worldly, yet rich
with light of other worlds
takes shape definite as
   lion's or rose's, fills
      the beholder with
content as of living
   in the real

As of living in a
   landscape, prepared by a
master hand, the details of a
painting where violence
   struggle, bitterness
      have carefully been
resolved—not as
      irrelevancies but

transcended like a slime
   the flower or man
grows out of—Venice built
on palings and
   flowered from rock Fiorenza
      which crumbling in the final
hour will have
   left their sign

1956/Florence

monet's venice

From flatness
    of marsh, seaweed
and mollusc, moss and mud, a
view of the heavenly city, as
    if in air
        suspended
over vapor
           beginnings

Stared at too long, it
    evaporates
cannot be held
by the mind, all light
    rising
        vibrant
color from the
        seed of sea

The foreground only
    attaches
us, by darkness, to the
plane from which
    inexorably
        we look. It's
the dark, dark
      of struggle

lacking which all
    cities are
abstract—from the implied
solidity fo caves, rocks
    and sea
        such gold
trimphally
      aspires

1954/Venice

color scheme (naples)

Out here above the bay
on a crazy perch
my cottage hugs the cliff.
I watch the ship
white on a lead sea
or single slant sail
in the wind; my bedsheet
makes another on the terrace.
The gull's wing
cuts white arcs
over slate waves.
On the volcano's flank
a smear of snow;
my window
tufted
with cotton wads
plays its part
in the still life.
I am aware of
dominance of gray, so white
merely smudges sea & sky
irritatingly, like stains.
I stare
at wing flap
& sail   & snow & ship.

1958/Naples

the gallery

In the Uffizi country
goldflake images
of scarecrow Christs to frighten us
up cross and crown to Paradise!

Past walls of flesh and haloed hair,
immolations, battles, hells,
we range our mythic dreams.
O murderous, all these slain!
The beast runs at the lance,

the hunter runs at the jaws.

Then out. Out! Then blue.
Infinite blue! Absolute white!

1956/Florence

the worst thing you can say to him is i love you

(*for Charles Bukowski*)

he does the things a real man should

playing the horses
winning crap games
sneering at fags
women
vegetarians
librarians
poets
sucking at 6-packs
getting drunk
and mean

oh boy what a great writer!
what a smartass clever bastard!
what a bleeding scarred snarling smashed
GENIUS!

shake your fist
at that old kike in the sky!

step on everybody's toes! hard!
                    GENIUS!

throw him an orchid
                    bloop!
he'll shit on it

this hatchet man
heaver of meat

cleaver of bone
bitchy butcher
he'll puke in your face
laugh at your pain
and his own

for humanity consists of a quite stupid and dull majority
(this is perfectly true)
humanity is a conspiracy
of dullness
but HE is a conspiracy of
GENIUS!

I say leave him alone for Chrissake
leave him alone
don't go writing articles and pieces about him forever
in the "littles"
it only makes him run off at the mouth
the badmouth
attacking his well-wishers

he's a kind of Mayakovsky in Los Angeles
as if they need one there
noisy flashy brash
allergic to himself
and others
colossal hulk of rotting flesh
decaying and charred
like the old Venice pier
crusted over with barnacles and warts of raw experience
in love with collapse

oh leave him alone
he will never accept you
he will betray you
piss on you
belittle and destroy you
                    plop!
with those squinty sneaky narrow distrusting monkey eyes
tearing at bleeding piles with little mean fingers
those tiny hands on a big gorilla
mutilating
mortifying
dismembering

a man with a face like a close-up of moon craters

making poems of self-pity
hate
disgust
suicide

and
the worst thing you can say to him
is
      I
           love
                you

inside out

Wearing myself inside out
like a coat put on in a rush
in public I seemed ridiculous
to the outside in.

It seems I revealed too much.
The lining of the self
and certainly the label
gave me away.

But in broad daylight
on Main Street. I ran
among the crowds
and the traffic policeman

like a circus bear
with a gold ring in my nose.
I caused a great sensation
among the outside in.

New York, ca. 1940

ymca lounge

Behind the daily papers and cigarettes
they relax. Some read, most sit
and stare at *The Three Fates* on the wall
while Tschaikowsky's *Hamlet* overture
grieves. Eyelids droop. Talk rises, falls.

In the corridors boys leap
clutching small bags with the odor of keds.
Old men rasp to sailors stretching jersey thighs.
House phones ring at the desk. The Spanish motif
of hanging iron holders for flame-bulbs sheds
an embalming, funeral glow, reflects
the baldness of one with a turquoise ring
and pointed black shiny shoes. Odors
of hot athletes pervade the lounge, armpits
tangy with musk. The young men watch
each other with studied indifference, rise
and leave and return under stained glass
windows and porticoes. Eyes sometimes lock
and, with significant glances, the youths go
into the hall together murmuring
and ride the elevator to a room
or lavatory. The grieving overture
switches to *Gaîté Parisienne.*

New York, ca. 1941

tantalus

So many bodies have passed him by
virile limbs that tantalize
in scant clothes clinging
tight—it's a wonder he's not demented!

All day about the city
he padded the pavements, looking

Now he stands by the low wall
a wailing wall for his desires
which he conceals so carefully

you would not suspect them

He is mild, youngish, grave
and obsessed with passing
as anyone else

But his greatest obsession
sends him into the parks and streets
and will not let him sleep

New York, 1943

stratagems

This simple painter of walls
during the noon hour
squatted before a laundromat
smoking and being
excessively smiled and talked at.

His hair, dusted with plaster, curled
on his forehead, blond sculpture.
The dust made up his lashes
whitely, thickened like a
detail of eyes on a Roman bust.

His lips were fresh and full
and red. The forearms
bulging slightly, tan
and powerful, bore strange tattoos.
He did not smile.

The smiler crouched
nervous beside him, spoke
swiftly, searching his face, darting
anxious glances at the
paint-smeared overalls, the arms.
the lips, the calm blue eyes,
then left.

Now I know his name, his taste, his touch
more intimately than the nervous boy

who could not act
and talked too much.

New York, 1.vii.53

roman bar

Beside it the Forum
of Augustus

within
a steady flow
of life

lived in wicker
chairs

ranged round the
windows
letting
in the sun
&

views
of ancient ruins
At

tables young
men play
cards, joke

about each other's
rear ends, make
obscene gestures—they
drink

espresso, wink
suggestively—a
beggar strums a

guitar
the backroom is

for games—an old
dumpy grayhaired

grandma
dressed in
black takes out
pen &

ink—
laboring with tongue
& thumb she
writes a

letter
children peer
at candy

cigarettes are
sold

Rome, 1954

island of giglio

we sailed into the harbor
all the church bells rang
the main street on the crescent shore
hung iridescent silks from windows
stucco housefronts gleamed
rose, pistachio, peach
and a procession sang
behind a surpliced priest
carrying a burnished Christ
when I set foot on shore
a youth emerged from the crowd
barefoot and oliveskinned
and we climbed up rocky slopes
till dusk fell and close to the moon
at the mouth of a cave we made love
as the sea broke wild beneath the cliff

✻

skeletons of fish, boats
on the beach, granite
boulders, juniper trees
and the town with winding
alleys; old men suck pipes
as the full moon leaps
like a flying fish &
shrinks up the sky; we
merge on the rocks
where waves run
up & down

Rome, 17.vi.54

syracuse

The theatre of marble and moonlight has smooth steps like milk on stone. In the city the nymph is a green pool among papyrus and electric lights around her fountain. Half-nude boys squat on the rail, in the heat, cock in hand, inviting male tourists with smiles and nods. What else, prying at columns and fountains, can you ask but that the metope should live? It was here the fantastic wombshaped cave became a listening horn of licked lime, ear for tyrants; here the whisper of the condemned was borne upwards, past dripping walls; echoing lips of water, moans, midnight confessions, conspiracies. Outside, not so secure as a god, yet nearly, to the people monstrous, Dionysius, tyrant, at his ear of stone overheard the enormous cavern unsheathe its secrets.

Sicily, ca. 1954

etruscan fresco (tarquinia)

Was it against Nature when the bull
seeing the young men couple in the wood
pointed his huge horns and charged
the naked youths, bull's blood
storming his erect hot pizzle?
Three thousand years ago
the men who painted frescoes
to commemorate the dead

knew that lust was all that stood
between themselves and them.

Florence, 1954

on translations of catullus

Catullus, you'd bust your balls laughing!
For 2000 years they've fixed you like a horny cat—
the pedagogues can't take you straight.
Old pederast, they'll never make it
—not while they teach you how to write!

Rome, 1955

catullus for real
(translations)

LV
The Search

Oramus, si forte non molestumst

If I may look for you without offense
I beg you, darling, where's your hiding place?
    I've searched each corner you frequent,
The lesser Campus and the Circus tents,
And in the Forum bookstalls where your face
Over some verses, by intelligence
Made more desirable, is usually bent.

But you were nowhere; from the hallowed white
Porphyry of Jove's temple, like a dog
    I ran, my tongue hung dry, a sight
For everyone to see. I stopped mid-flight
In Pompey's portico; the women gagged
With laughter when I quizzed them: "Spent the night
With me? Catullus, are you well? are you all right?"

But still I kept on asking for you: "Give me

My Camerius, you bitchy girls!"
     And one, baring her tits for me,
Says, "Look! He's hiding here, can't you see,
Between my hefty breasts!" Well, seeking pearls
In oysters is not harder, dear, than to be
Patient with you, nor the tasks of Hercules.

No, not if I were like that Cretan jailer
Brass-wrought, or bird-footed Perseus
     Or Ladas, or a heaven-scaler
Fording cloud-currents like that fleet sky-sailor
Pegasus, or the snowy team of Rhesus,
Could I catch up with you; add to my failure
The speed of gods and winds, my skill could not be frailer!

Though, Camerius, you yoked all these
Into my service, I should be worn out
     To the bone, fainting, on my knees
Hunting you down. O my sweet friend, please,
Do not deny yourself so proudly, flout
The love I bear. Don't mock my miseries;
Out with it, you can trust me—where are you apt to be?

Do the dove-white girls detain you? I'm above
Fits of jealousy, but if you keep
     Your tongue tied in your mouth, love
Between us will be wasted. Will you prove
You hate me? It pleases Venus—talk is cheap—
To hear our words. But if you're firm as Jove,
Let me, at least, possess a small share in your love.

Rome, 1954

XXXIII

O furum optime . . .

O slickest thieves at the public baths,
Vibennius and your fairy son!
The right hand of the father is predacious
and the son's behind remarkably voracious.
So beat it both of you, go to hell!
since everyone knows of the father's filching
and your ass, boy, is too hairy to sell.

Rome, 1955

C

Caelius Aufilenum . . .

Caelius for Aufilenus, Quintius for Aufilena—
    One boy is mad for the brother, and the other boy for the sister,
All of them the finest flower of Veronese youth.
    Here's the sweet brotherhood! Here it is!
The brotherhood of man! Which shall I vote for? Caelius, you:
    Your friendship was beautifully shown me—it was unique!—
When a mad flame scorched my genitals. Luck, then Caelius,
    May you be successful and potent in your love!
                                   Rome, 1955

LXXXI

Nemone in tanto potuit populo esse, Iuventi . . .

Of all these people is there not one handsome man,
    Juventius, you might have chosen for yourself
Besides that friend of yours from the sickly area
    Of Pisaurum, paler than a whitewashed statue,
Who now is dear to you, whom you presume to prefer
    To me, your Catullus, not knowing what a rotten thing you're doing?
                                   Rome, 1955

XV

Commendo tibi me ac meos amores

I am entrusting to you, Aurelius,
all I love most in the world, this boy, and beg
only a small favor, if you've ever valued
something beyond price, to be kept chaste and pure,
then guard this boy for me. I don't mean from strangers;
it is not the man in the street I fear; he's busy
about his own affairs. it's you,
you and your big prick
lusting after boys, molesting good and bad alike.
when you're outside you may waggle your erection
as much as you please at anyone you please, but spare this one,
it's not much to ask, but if lust
runs away with you, if your dirty mind runs amuck
and you betray me and my lover, you'll suffer,

I promise you, a terrible fate.
before the whole town's eyes, with your feet in chains,
I'll shove radishes and mullets up your ass.

San Francisco, Summer 1976

XVI

Pedicabo ego vos et irrumabo

I'll fuck and rim you both and suck your cocks
faggot Aurelius and fairy Furius
who believe I am immodest because of my verses
which, admittedly, are quite voluptuous.
but though the serious poet should himself be chaste
his poems are under no such strict necessity.

San Francisco, Summer 1976

XXI

Aureli, pater esuritionem

Aurelius, father of famine,
not this one only but of all hunger past
and future—you want to make love to my boy,
not even secretly: for you're always with him,
joking, sticking close to his side,
    trying every trick to tempt him.
    no good, it won't work.
while you're scheming against me,
I'll bugger you before you know it.
if you had a full belly I'd be quiet,
but as it is, what worries me is that
my darling will starve to death.
    so hands off
if you don't want me to *fuck you*.

San Francisco, Summer 1976

after belli
(*translations*)

LOT AT HOME

With their stout staffs in their left hand
Two pilgrims at the hour of *Ave Maria*
Were looking for the hotel in that area
Because one had a pain in his leg and couldn't stand.

There they met Mr. Lot, and he threw wide
The door, saying: "My house. Step inside."
And they answered him: "By gosh, tomorrow
You'll be the white-haired boy of this rotten borough."

Those were two angels, brother, whose tight britches
When the gay Gomorrhites saw them pass
Straightened all the dicks in the whole city.

And they arrived shrieking, those damn bitches,
"Lot, send down the pilgrims to us, so we
Can oblige each other by putting it up the ass!"

Rome, 1955

Ave Maria: after sundown; since all Biblical events took place in Belli's early 19th century Rome, as far as the speakers are concerned, time is reckoned by the Italian system, according to its Book of the Hours (translator's note).

lot's refreshment

So, already at Sodom and Gomorrah
Everyone was roasted and baked like mullet
And from so many families in that horror
The only one that escaped was that of Lot.

Without ever taking a breath or pulling the reins
The Patriarch kept running the whole day:
But then, as it usually is, to his daughters there came
With dusk a fantasy to want to lay.

But because on that far border they were sunk,

Not even one cock with a spark of life,
They said: "Daddy is sexy!" and they got him drunk.

   Then having thrown two glances at his dumdumdangle
Those randy sisters happily all night
Divided between themselves the bang-bang-bang-o.

Rome, 1955

Dumdumdangle: in the original, *dumpenmente*, a portmanteau word Belli
created from *dum pendebat* from the *Stabat Mater* (translator's note).

prick poem

Well, call it the cock, dick, prick or peepee.
crank, dork, joint, pisser, sweetpea,

tootsie roll, lollipop, weenie, piece of meat,
sausage, salami, banana, somethin' to eat,

peter, boner, codpiece, flute or fife,
snake, cucumber, dingus, staff-of-life,

dong, prong, schlong, wang, hardon,
weapon, tool, piston, ramrod, gun,

shaft, stiff, bone, bishop, wick,
puddin', pope, pud, French tickler, joystick,

pipe, rod, knob, rolling pin,
John Thomas, stretch, grow-in-hand, stick-it-in,

what the old doc calls organ, member, phallus,
and his withered wife calls penis, thing, priapus.

Rome, 1955/San Francisco, 1985

ti voglio bene*

on the terrace
with cactus and geraniums
under the dome of Borromini
in the sun
wiping sweat
trickling
through thatch of bodyhair
I read and broil in   the olympic summer
as the date
gets buried
under a mess of days
and unmade beds
and nights
of sexy numeros
and I get stuck
in a vise of stone
of swirling angels
domes
fleshy frescoes
brown bodies
in Roman light
among marble fountains
saying *dove vai?*
and singing
*ti voglio bene**

Rome, 1956

* I love you

victor emmanuel monument (rome)

The marble typewriter or "wedding cake"
is large enough to shelter in its side
several armies; as it is, they keep
a squad of *bersaglieri* there, the hand-
picked of all Italy, the flower to guard
this monsterpiece. In scarlet fez and blue
pompom halfway down the back, like birds
of paradise they strut, their bodies hard
and flashing flesh by sunlight or moonlight
with all the brilliance of the male panache.
And this is all they have to do. What else
on seventeen cents a day, in Italy?
Any night by the white marble ploy
discovers them in whispered assignations
picking up extra cash, from man and boy.

Rome, ca. 1956

massaccio

I think of you, Massaccio
        in the city
    of feudal gloom

apprenticed
to Ghiberti
        laboring on those dazzling doors
    that swung to paradise

hungry helper, hard up youth
you held the birth of man
in your hands

then, on your own, you worked
on the tabula rasa of a thousand years
    (blank wall of the church)
with figure, form, shade and light

you worked with Christ
your brother, like you

315

with no place to lay his head

color flowed as never before
form fit content as never before
still broke, anonymous
you gave to those worse off than you
and went to your death
    in Catholic Rome
starved in that Heaven of Christ-on-earth
        at twenty-seven

Florence, 1956

the singing gallery

On a cracked wall in Italy
I saw something the bomb passed by
in a dark church aisle:
Piero della Francesca
set his seal of light
in colors that speak yet.
And Luca della Robbia
made thick marble sing
his joyous song
of Renaissance boys.
They sing to me.

Now it's rockets to the moon,
we change sex like underwear,
we believe in science.
All right, men must have myths.
I'll take The Singing Gallery.

Florence, 1956

the secret pornographic collection

In the National Museum of Naples
on this hot afternoon
lamps, braziers, jugs, caskets,
kitchenware—ancient food
from the buried city of Pompeii,
fixed in cold lava, a world
of naked pleasure: tripods
holding basins or braziers—one
mounted on marble, goat-legs forming
three ithyphallic young Pans
with tilted erections, raised hands
while dark young men
browse languidly and stroke
themselves
joking, touching their past
as they touch their sex
in sensual recognition
as if the church
and two millennnia
had never happened

Naples, 1958

La Raccolta Pornographica is the secret pornographic collection of the Museum, so-called because it houses the erotica of ancient Pompeii and Herculaneum, from which the bronze tripod was liberated, by Alexandre Dumas *père*, I believe, who became curator under Garibaldi in 1860, and to whom we probably owe its open display in one of the galleries, although I cannot vouch for the accuracy of my scholarship since changes of moral climate have constantly affected this collection's accessibility. During the Fascist era, for example, it was made off limits to the public.

piccolo paradiso

For Giorgio

let the age hang itself! we've had
four marvelous days together
        no news reports   only music
        & no serious discussions

plenty of wine   the best
from the islands
         white
            falerno & ischian
               & lacrima cristi
                     we've made up
                  for months
               of loneliness
                  hard work
               nastiness
                  of 'superiors'
            we may not live
            very well or long
our mistakes are perhaps too great
      to bear correction
         at this midpoint
            of our lives (you're somewhat younger)
                  surely too great
to make up for the lengths we go to
         hide them
                           è cosi . . . that's
                              how it goes
                  but at least
                  we're ahead of the game
               we've stolen a march
                  on the dead   the herd
if the return to grayness
sharp tempered weapons
of those who force life
into corners
      is more than we can bear
      remember this
         the wine
            the ladder
               of stars
                  climbing vesuvius
                     outside my window
               the waves
                  banging into
                     smooth tufa caves
& the opera
      as we lay together
                  remember

Naples, 1958

i am in the hub of the fiery force

red for fire red for lava red for blood
   red for the savage meridional sun
      for the walls of herculaneum
         the mouths of nymphomaniacs
            the gums of satyrs their monstrous pizzles
            their dreams their bestial dreams
               for the villas at the volcano's foot
                  the scorpion's sting the dying screams

red for hibiscus rose amaryllis
   red for phallus red for yoni
      red for pompeii red for stabiae
         for the naked men fucking in frescoes
            the cymbals of shrieking priests of cybele
            their orgies eunuch rites of castration
               for drums and pipes of loaded bacchus
               for snaky jagged tongues of fury

red for pain for raw for wild for bull
   for wine for lion for kill for hell
      for suck for lust for whip for drug
         for high for bust for crime for thirst
            obsessed with red as the universe burns
            i am in the hub of the fiery force
            the red heat of the conflagration
              o cosmos turn! turn! thy flaming wheel!

Naples, 1958

green ballet

For W. I. Scobie

    overhead
    on the bridge
trucks are speeding under angels

parks are empty & leaves are falling

    erect in mud

their shoes slurping
on the riverbank two people
are breaking laws with their hips

at the top of the steps a sign reads

WORKERS ONLY   NO TRESPASSING

one is in rags
he is 16
he has red lips

the other is a man
who sees god as he looks up
        at the boy who looks down

the boy is thinking of the whore with the man
he spied on in the shadows
        by Hadrian's Tomb
as he clutches the man's ears
                tensing his thick
thighs
        & they come

the man thinks *god god*
        & the terror!
any moment all's reversed
only the world's uniform **THUD**

all this time the Tiber sucking
        sucking
the fat mud

Rome, 1960

In Italian the title, *balletti verdi,* means gay scenes or scandals, in the ver-
nacular.

the pine cone

the insane police
    dog yelping
for a pine cone
to retrieve from the
        waves
    his reflex joy
        mad anguish
when it is not thrown
WOOF!

    he rolls
over the cone
       tearing
at sand
    with forepaws

as Spanish fishermen
    watch and
        laugh

    I chase the flesh
as that dog chases
    the pine cone
       o Christ!
the earth
    and sea never
looked so new
    so perishable

    I walk
up streetstairs
Carrer del Gats in
        Benidorm where
           highstepping ringdoves
spread fantails
    in cotes like César
Girón approaching
    a bull
    ass and head stuck out
       arms like
banderillas
    my god what swagger!

I stand looking at the
    Spanish night
of shimmering suns and
        galaxies

my blood
    throbs in black gulfs
      a car hoots
down the road

Benidorm, 1956

gothic quarter, barcelona

A shopkeeper kicks in the head
of an old beggar, a thief holds a knife
to a tourist's throat, a woman screams
raped by a drunk in a doorway
of marble and puke, young macho studs
attack 2 drag queens in full view
of cheering crowds shouting *Olé*
as a birdlike woman on a barstool
with unblinking eyes and flourwhite face
like a mime or a clown
stares
straight
ahead
immobile for hours
and a hunchback begs and insults the crowd
while sailors from the Sixth Fleet wander
drunk and horny under Moorish balustrades
and rotting stone columns
where Arabs in burnooses check out
bleached whores under stained glass windows
while gipsies howl flamenco
under festooned city lights
forming graceful loops overhead
and a dog farts
and a cripple waves his stump
and a landlord with a dead rat face
cruises a sailor who rubs his crotch
with the look of a striptease artist

and under the portico the whores
stand on duty
a whore who walks like a truckdriver
a whore who writes poetry
a whore who looks like a drag queen
and a drag queen who looks like a whore
and there's a macho stud
who turns gay when he's drunk
and burns cigarette holes in his hand
because he hates what he is
although everybody loves him
and the students sing and drink wine all night
under the lamps of Gaudi in the Plaza Real
the crucible of Spain
where the whole country ferments like wine
like cheese like painting like music
like birth
or death
or dreams
or war
or love

Barcelona, November 1978

the barcelona girls and boys

They look familiar
out of the Thirties
where I left them
back in
Brooklyn
long ago

But this is Barcelona
after 40 years
of the Generalissimo
to keep them on ice
to stop the clock
and the heart

Now Spain's a democracy
and these young women

are madly in love
with social ideas
and with their young men
who wear leather jackets
and rough beards
and carry books
for the revolution

They touch one another
in streets, cafés and restaurants
with much tenderness

But I would ask of them
only this:
make your revolution
for the freedom to love
either sex
in any way
as need demands

Do not become the pigs of the future.

Barcelona, 6.xi.78

france

now France   yesterday Italy   & it's fall
special Paris light   slant on treetops   gray
buildingtops   clear   hard   like French eyes
bulge of intellect   chalcedony eyes
& architecture creates   the sky

     will someone stop me in the street   saying
     how wonderful!   we don't know each other?!
       just walk arm in arm
         & never ask our names!
make love at sight!   anonymous as monks!
         esperanto lips!
     Africa in my arms!   Near East!

but how to slow down   I'm running away
     arc those my arteries   or steel tracks?

stations in the dawn   old man
sourly pushing letters   in huge sacks
      are they my unfinished plans?

      Paris of leaves   beards   duffel coats!
      am I interested in radio telescopes?
         the kind that look inside the moon?
      parabolic mirrors?   limits of the solar system?
Izvestia follows me around   sneers at my life
            no wonder I'm feeling blue

I'm here to tell you of a finer fate
      to explore trees
         listen to colors
            pick the golden flower
               feel under someone's duffel coat
                  for the clear light
                  of the void

down on your knees!   pray to the holy human body!
      worship god in the fork of the thighs!
         I can't blow the 'socialist victory'
         nor raise any flag but my lilywhite ass
to all the silly nations who want me to choose sides

I've chosen   orgasm/feeling/smell/soul
freedom of dream   who is freer than when he dreams?
I choose the light of the sky   over the boulevards
      & the bookstalls   full of sexy pictures
         & occult prophecies   THE EARTH

Paris, 1960

chez popoff

melo chez popoff
melo at the monaco
melo in storyville
melo eating pink loukoum
melo with one gold tooth
piscean melo digs the hidden poetry of death
turns on in my room with words of crucifixion

betrayed by pinball machines
telling tales of three-day hard ons
having it rubbed with hot cantari in french guiana
he offers himself for coins
he gooses tourists on the boul' mich
his chocolate chest startles the quays
the quay of pont neuf & le petit pont
sheathed in mirrors & lies
his look is telepathic
his kisses are black lightning
he paints dark blobs of pain
in his room dark with death
in his room light with laughs
in his eyes dark with light
o unreachable bird of smoke
black swan of sad jazz landscapes

Paris, ca. 1961

place de furstemburg

the sweet young thing
passes around the hat
and the French cat sings
AH AH AH lalalala
with his guitar
and the derrières of St. Germain
are pink and blue buds
in the sun and everyone
is drinking beer
and eating cacahuètes
in a mimic movie of lips and tits
while bombs shatter windows
next to the cafés
and flies buzz in the sugar
and wine glasses
and I leave
for a calm little square
with 4 plane trees
and a street lamp
Place de Furstemburg
where flat on his belly

a lotus boy
with radiant tan
and dirty feet
dozes beside a thick green
cardboard folder
from the Beaux Arts Academy
as the concierge at the window
her leathery arms
folded on the sill
sits very gray
very sad
very old
one hand against her mouth
looking out at him
and suddenly he looks up
from the bench
drowsily
and I stare
as if perhaps at a painting
by Delacroix
whose studio is closed for repairs
in this same square
and next day I am back
for the boy the birds the concierge
but nothing remains
not even the trees
just 4 gaping holes
where they had been

Paris, June 1961

from the 6th arrondisement

(*Paris journal, September 1961*)

Paris, you have ceased
to be the *cité*
plein de rêves. But you
are still the satyr-city, kissing
couples in the streets, young
bodies & fantastic
styles of dress —

the *youngest* city in Europe!
half your Frenchmen just kids.
I'm envious, have a
toothache & a hard-on
and feel sorry for myself
in Paris in the Spring.

        *

9, Rue Gît-le-Coeur (the Beat Hotel)

armpit odor of bearded boys—guitar
riffs, bongo drums, voices & candlelight
up at Milt Mezzrow's, Room 30—swinging
real nice . . . but at 10 p.m. the concierge
warns: "the cops are coming if you don't stop!"
"Yeah, man, like if you're happy, the fuzz
comes. If you're living, the heat shows.
Man, let's get to the Andes . . . gotta face
reality . . . the bomb is here & there ain't
no room for us both."

        *

He goes from hurt to hurt.
"The thick veil of Maya
that must have covered my heart
is not so easily removed."
His devotion is impressive.
He wants to be "self-realized"
yet seeks out suffering
& cruelty in his men.
We hit bottom, touch
silence.
Poor F. will you ever
know what you feel?

        *

Chlorophyll & blood . . . and the sky
with bars at the end. Paris, old whore. . . .
I limit my life. Fatigue.
All them germs!
Police! Eye contact

is dangerous. But couples still kiss,
walk with linked hands—clutch
each other. I'm
the odd one, a small time Genet, haunting
pissotières (like Gide) and even those
have been torn up by de Gaulle.

*

Masturbate wildly. 3 a.m. A knock.
Throw open the door, naked.
Arab I used to know. No place
to stay, Crash here? OK. Shows
me his boat ticket. "I return
to Tunis in a week." Removes
shoes & socks, revealing huge
dirty feet, swollen from tramping. Asks
for scissors, slowly cuts
all his fingernails, then toenails.
Removes gray houndstooth suit.
Climbs into bed, mutters, "Je suis
très fatigué." Loud snores.
Next morning, without a word, he dresses
& laying a cold hand briefly on my arm leaves.
Masturbate wildly.

*

Rue Bonaparte. 8 p.m. Paratroops
in scarlet berets at pinball "flippers"
with whores of both sexes. Smoke & coffee.
A paratroop winks at me, his whore frowns.
Around midnight, police wagon pulls up.
Out jump the keystone cops, tommyguns ready.
About to go thru the usual spot check when
there's a shot from the rue St. Benoît, around
the corner (probably a paper bag). The fuzz
turn white, awkwardly tug at pistol holsters
(very strange because their tommy guns are ready)
and disappear on the run, Mack Sennett style,
tilting at all angles. We laugh and pay,
whores, paratroops, hustlers, pimps & crooks,
& move on, in leisurely fashion.

*

Fishboy

Fishboy knocks. He is 18
with powerful smooth thighs.
Stands holding a cigarette
between two flippers,
honey hair sleek as a seal's.
Unforgettable aroma, musk
of something wild as wet seaweed. But
he's just French farmboy hustling
in Paris. Asks for a 'loan'
of 5 francs. I nod and help him
drop his pants, like peeling
a layer of skin. He bends
to plant sweet lips on mine, grinding
his hips as we pant and grunt.

Later I light 2 Gauloises,
give him 5 francs
and off he floats.

*

French Country Boys. . . .

French country boys have rigged themselves a simple primitive contraption, a fuck machine to bugger themselves, says my friend Van B., who ought to know as he is a rich American of French descent who owns a castle in the country, where he has spent some 50 pederastic summers. Fishboy, when I ask about this, calmly agrees.

The thought forms: to bugger Fishboy is the answer to all men's most cherished fantasies (in Morocco they would kill for him), for not only has he the most extraordinary buns I have ever seen (and I am an aficionado), white, smooth, flaring, voluptuous, perfectly calipered by a Blakean God—but his thighs must be the world's most desirable.

(Yet he wanders around Paris with his clean tight pants, peddling that gorgeous ass for a few lousy francs—thank God!—and many nameless assholes are put off because of this anomaly.)

Many years later in San Francisco I came across Margaret Mead's statement to the Washington Press Club: "I think rigid heterosexuality is a perversion of nature."

The newspapers did not report the reaction of her audience; but any man gazing at Fishboy's naturally flushed hairless cheeks and crimson lips, not to speak of those nether cheeks, must surely feel the same or be a pervert.

Think of the tremendous *unnatural* effort at suppression of homosexual urges, largely unconscious (the common state of the world), that most men make all their lives (except gay ones, who are really the most heroic because they do what others merely dream of doing.)

I regret to report that Fishboy disappeared from circulation before I got around to fulfilling my desire. A moral of some sort must surely be implicit here (strike when the buns are hot?). . . .

Paris, ca. 1961

a gay night

I drove them out last night
to a gay club where faggots dance
16 kms. from Paris.
we found a few desolate queens
seated at tables in a large room
with copper pots on the walls, a loudspeaker
played sentimental tunes from the Thirties.
this old dyke in a tweed suit
runs the joint. we order beer.
things picked up after awhile.
soon everybody was dancing
like 'normal couples'. two bald queens
clasped each other round the waist,
the short one in a white turtleneck,
his ass stuck out, danced
spine arched, head coyly tossing
from side to side. the place
became a barnyard: shrieking freaks,
cackling falsettos to Viennese waltzes,
plucked eyebrows over thin moustaches,
goosing and horsing and oinking.

have you ever seen a freakshow dancing?
André danced with everybody
while Mustapha sat and smoked my Gauloises Bleues.
they were drumming up trade.
"See that grayhaired old one?" a sheep
with glasses, a few tables away,
looked over and grinned. later
they disappeared in an Aronde.
I drove back with André, who never shut up for a moment
about the lousy bunch of cheap fairies.
at the Mabillon around 1 a.m. Mustapha showed.
"What happened?" I asked. "Nothing." he spat
in disgust. "You made nothing?" "Nothing,
I tell you! He wouldn't pay. He owns 2 cars,
the Aronde and a Studebaker,
and he wouldn't pay. Merde!"
he smacked his fist into his palm.
"Well, that's what I told le petit André," I said.
but it served him right.
he never said thanks for a free lunch,
free beer, nylon shirt, broke dates,
stood everyone up, basking
in the aura of his looks.
as for his pintsized pal, André,
with the big droopy Arab nose,
he has the nerve to charge
100 francs. Demented bitch!

Paris, 1961

the death of 9 rue gît-le-coeur

For William S. Burroughs

a bat flies in thru the window at 3 in the afternoon
slides under the table and disappears . . . postcard from chinatown san
    fran
suddenly drops from the ceiling out of nowhere
everything is normal, nothing is strange
black bat flits slow motion to the table's bottom
where it vanishes

everything is permitted . . . nothing is true

indo-chinese lady in silk parts bamboo curtains & glides downstairs
giant spade from french guiana slips thru mirrors turned on
dreamachine spins shapes & colors round & round
opening up visions as it crashes the sight barrier & alters the brain
a great american writer receives whole episodes in his sleep
for the novel of new consciousness

> prophetic utterances
> nameless assholes
> agonized angels
> end of poetry
> huge genitals
> buttfucked boys

sad movies on the sea wall
drowned islands float up from adolescent place forgotten
drifting croon of shrunken ether heads
iridescent bubbles of shifted consciousness
it is over . . . finished . . . a dream
workmen hammer & plaster in halls full of tools & cement
old spiral staircase white with wind
no more army surplus parkas
no more guitars
no more horns
the old café FERMÉ POUR TRAVAUX
ghostly espresso machine gapes on dusty shelves
    chairs gape
nobody now where we used to gather & talk
"very uncool to carry a piece"

mirrors of 1910 kept nagging me
flashing nails in your cheating naked brain
kept seeing America dying in swamp green smiles
a bat flies out of your eyes
dreamachine turns on the boy's agonized cells
the room flushed out by your mouldy expeditions
took possession of his falling flesh

"Beat Hotel," Paris, 1963

A threnody for the hotel in Paris internationally known as the "Beat Hotel"
where H.N. lived with Allen Ginsberg, William Burroughs, Brion Gysin,
Gregory Corso, et al., and where the Cut-up method was born and *Naked*

Lunch assembled for publication. Everyone decamped, so to speak, in 1963 when the motherly old woman who owned the place, Mme. Rachou, sold it to retire to an apartment across the street, and some years later died. In her youth she was a waitress in a restaurant frequented by Monet, Pissarro, Picasso, etc. At the hotel she ruled with an iron hand, a legend in her own right.

vence

Matisse and Chagall painted church walls
and D. H. Lawrence died here
lightning rips the hills of the Côte d'Azur
quake destroys Skoplje in Yugoslavia
and prophecies work through vast illusion and dream
a firefly glows on my bedsheet a star in my bed
and I bomb a giant spider spray him with Flytox
fearing the wary dance of his spiderhood
I watch him crawl and shrivel on the shower floor
thinking Will I meet death by Heavenly Flytox
lightning bolt or shift of the earth crushed
in agonized death throes caught in insect pursuits?
here in this country house no mescaline jewels nor laughing gas
hashish or kif can turn me on come crackup of this world
I kiss the Sweet Young Thing at my cottage door (he is sixteen today)
where we stand speechless and gazing in the summer night

Vence, 1963

cannes

Near the Croisette the jeunesse dorée
glitter in nylon briefs.
They cruise among deck chairs,
lotions and parasols,
taking in suntans
with swift expert appraisal.
To watch them, you'd think
they had lost something in the sand.
They glance quickly

at sprayed hair and coppery thighs
with an air of boredom, shifting
their attention as if waiting
for someone who doesn't show.
Like yachts they twitch and strain
at anchor. A well-contrived
apocalypse would hardly disturb
the routine. In the evening
dressed with casual care
they fish around café tables
checking out seafood, styles, breasts
and muscles with equal zeal.
Whatever they talk about it's flesh
they're stalking with such élan, though
hinted at in slick repartee. It looks
like a fun game on this hot
Riviera—but the casualties
are high. In bars and hotels
when the fleet's in, the atmosphere's
international and gay. When
the gobs leave, there's a kind
of business-as-usual ennui
in town. Picasso had a villa
here. I recall mainly the heat,
cream-puff façades, chic languor.
And a gendarme who wouldn't believe
my passport and almost booked me
for strolling on the Croisette one night
impersonating an American.
I only half-convinced him parleying
French with a New York post-nasal drip.
When he left, grumbling, I muttered: Céline,
The 6th fleet lay in offshore darkness: chill air
warned of summer's end. A few girls,
drunk, flapped like beached fish, gasping
as they kissed their garçons. Cannes,
elegant and impersonal—a casino
of the would-be heart, spinning
a roulette wheel, like the sea
that rolls endless waves of chance toward lovers.
But not, to be sure, in a passionate way.

Cannes, 1963

to mohammed at the end

          the boat
               slid from the
               dock into
                    nothing
                      i
                    watched
                         the sprayed
                    wake
                    churn green
               silk water
          peaks till
               mist
                    twisted the
                         white town—a
                            face
                         followed
                    flashing sand
               & wind & cheap
          hotels—a face
     will follow
voices
     cities
          & after
               a year
                    or two i'll
                         grab a boat
                    on a water
               chain
               pulling
          me back
     to turn me
  on
again

Tangier/Torremolinos/Athens, 1962/63

djema el fna, marrakech

Ragged listeners smoke and are carried away on magic carpets
A storyteller squats in the center of a crowd of beggars
Narrating A Thousand And One Nights as I sip mint tea
Snakes squirm at my feet naked boys covered with flies sleep on the
      ground
Aladdin lamps glint in the carbide glow desert music everywhere
At magic stalls with evil eyes bones and monkey hair
Atmosphere thick with hashish kif and fantasy
And I'm swept up in the pipe dream of Arabia

Marrakech, 1962

carnivorous saint

we dig up ancient shards
clicking cameras
among the dying cypresses
choked by Athenian smog.

yet cats continue basking
in the hazy sun
the chained goat sways in ecstasy
the Parthenon looks down from creamy heights
lichen and rust nibble the pediments
and tourist feet break the spell
of antiquity's vibrations.

the grass hits
as I look at rusty orangeade caps
thinking Who needs nuclear Apollo?
thermonuclear Minerva?
Nike crashing to grand finale?

we need the anti-Christ
who is probably playing football around the corner
the sweet boy who used to be called Eros
and wants us to be happy.

bring back the carnivorous saint
whose mother is no virgin

she's Our Lady of Peace Movements
to ban the bomb and clean up the air
she'll wave her umbrella and change the world.

ah yes, when the grass hits
old worlds burn down and new worlds form
in clouds of brown monoxide morning.

Athens, Jan. 1964

under the night sky

Helen applies nivea oil to my crevices
you're beautiful she says
you have that lived-in look
and I like the white adobe hut
where we are at home
on the beach with the old gold mill
abandoned out front
near the "aztec" ruins
of Skyros
morning glory on the vine
two little fishes in a pitcher
muscat grapes ripening
sandlilies outside the door
of the cottage
that we leave tomorrow
I pluck some basil leaves
and gobble grapes
and think of the night sky
under which we sit
smoking too much
whispering together
of hurting
and being hurt
can love after so many
errors, after so much
pain and fear exist?
under the night sky

on the Aegean shore
on the edge of a precipice
we kiss

Skyros, 1964

giant cruiser

Giant cruiser with yellow funnel
and blue sign: RODOS
(Rhodes) glittering among white houses
like sugar cubes, white sailors
and white birds
while at café tables
tongues wag languidly
like the tide

sensuality nags the nerves
around the port
where sunbrown boys
with hairy legs and bellies
and creamy blond girls down from the north
sniff the air voluptuously
on an eternal cruise

then from the Naval Academy
on the wharf a bugle blares
everyone stands at attention
in various stages of uninterest
a boat horn breaks
the military ritual
and the pleasure boat—SARONIS—
floats into the harbor
as barelegged bathers float
into restaurants, cafés
and other lives

Hydra, 1965

conversation galante

"Mind if I sit down?"
   "Okay. Have a cigarette."
 "I could write a novel about my suffering.
   The whole town knows about me.
That boy has made me lose my self-respect."
"What else is new?"
         "Maybe I'll cut my throat."
            "What time?"
      "He won't let me suck him off anymore!"
"Humiliating."
            "What am I gonna do?"
                        "Well, wrap
a 5-pound-note around it—most powerful
      aphrodisiac in Greece!"
                        "You too!
         You're making fun of me. Oh god,
            I love him!"
                     "The donkey boy
   has twelve inches—"
      "Maybe I'll dance with him tonight."
"With who?"
            "The donkey boy—make Yanni jealous!"
   "Mark, you're a fool."
         "Thanks. I'm gonna get drunk
   on ouzo and dance to the juke all night."
"Oh, you silly Dutch queen!
   I'm gonna call you Wilhelmina."

                              Hydra, 1965

white terraces

To Princess Zinaide Rachevsky, in memoriam

1

Beautiful ruthless, dangerous, spendthrift, generous, selfish, violent, the princess tried everything from striptease queen, movie starlet, royal marriage, poetry and painting, to becoming a Zen monk with a shaven head in Nepal, where she died mysteriously, thus ending her search for impossible enlightenment, just as she was beginning to resemble Mme. Blavatsky in her forties, her spiritual double (but not her physical one for Zina was slender), half-charlatan, half-magician. Zina had been busted for dope and prostitution, among other things, cut off from three vast fortunes for her crimes, but in the end was a real artist, that is to say talented and treacherous. I do her homage as an unforgettable bitch with class and charisma. She held court on the island of Hydra and in Athens, where I last saw her.

2

guitars on white terraces
with cicadas and typewriters
and near-naked girls
and heavy stoned fucking in moonlight
and the island, they said, was magical
full of evil vibrations
(dogs were killed for sport)
an American scholar's Mom got raped
by the donkey boy
with the hugest dick in the port
secretly had by the scholar

who didn't know whom to be jealous of
and wrote a bad poem about it
and fell into the harbor
among the other jellyfish
and got fished out
moaning, "I wanna die!"

some did Greek dances with the fishermen
until they collapsed under the moon
brains rotten with retsina
passed out against whitewashed walls

some got busted for pot and spent 5 years in Tartaros
writing *Notes from Underground*

raped in their imaginations by Greek convicts

some became pop singers
some crouched with fear on street-stairs
their minds crumbled with breakdown
and the I Ching could not save them

some took acid and "saw the Light"
and went off to lick postage stamps in India
learning humility at the feet of gurus
giving up all possessions

some took poison and some blew out their brains
and Zen could not save them
nor Wu Wei
nor their name in a book
and their astrological chart was lousy

Hydra, 1965

a big fish

For Kostas Tachtsis

300 pounds of blubber
flat on her back in Piraeus
jellyrolls and squirms, shakes her tits
120 pounds of Yankee sailor
blond babyface puts it in
2 poets masturbate on him

the fat greek whore
got sentimental, heaving hugging moaning
as he made us do it everywhichway!

Renna the Great White Whale!
little Davy flounders as he sticks it in
leviathan—his big harpoon—we
stick it to *him!*

he shoves it to his orchids and we flower in one glooey
freakish ecstasy of momentary meat! everybody

kissing and hugging—it was great!

Renna
    whose life savings went
one night—her loverpimp left her
beached—gaping swollen mammal in the street—
big fish for the fleet!

Athens, ca 1965

karma circuit

pale boy of the north with the dark spanish eyes
and hebrew mind who crossed my path thru poetry i ching
talking of superconscious telepathic coincidental changes
of the eternal now

hitching thru paradoxical zen
circuits of enlightenment
malmo—hydra
helsinki—ibiza
speaking the passwords karma oracle paranoia hexagram connections

finland is white and you had need of moving into blue
of summer's southern gold to find the way
to cross the bridge

what bridge? the bridge you always come to where
you stop and turning back must ask the question where

and everyone you meet is really you—another you
on wavelengths without separation
no frontier between selves or lands—all you's and me's

we sit up half a night the lamp burns low the kittens race
in the garden scratch at the cottage door as donkeys sob
their animal heats beneath the window
in the rubbish dumps outside

you screamed your poems in rotterdam tore down the german flags
hoisted the flag of israel breathing flames of kerosene
and you were busted for it

wild as your lapland flute
   kissed by birds and fish
      with swinging dragon fire
         traveling to the point/no point

         you leave all words and thoughts
      for sound beyond sound
    silence beyond speech

i'm oxidized by your mouth

Hydra, 1965

addio

For Julia Chanler-Laurin

i have sat on the oldest throne in europe
     & heard the peacock scream in the ruins
i have drunk from the castalian fountain
    that the latin poets called
      the source of inspiration

& patted the umbilicus of the world in delphi
i have seen the sun
    on red columns
      & gold columns
        & blue monkeys
& seen the king of the lilies
  emerge
    from the flaming wall
      of crete
    feathered initiate
      staring tall & young
        from the earthquakes of time

& at the oracle of apollo
  heard the pythoness
    from the rock   :   CHOOSE

i knelt among the hollyhocks in the olive grove
    knowing these cliffs & chasms would once more shift

        && tumble down

i passed an enormous lizard being devoured among the
        shards.
      by black ants hungry & mean

a bat grazed my hand at dusk a slipper moon horned
      the mountaintop

& on the plateau
    beneath olympus the chairs & tables trembled in the hotel
    while the tourists chewed with embarrassed whispers

       && the shopkeepers mad with greed
    plundered their hopeless cash registers

the peasants rolled in dung beneath the peeling gold
where the mosaic pantocrator glared from the ceiling
with the jealous eye of the author

       && i have heard the ass bray & the goat cough
   && the mule fart & the cats couple & bugs bash
      && the boys hiss & dance together
        && the jukebox blast the sky

but the meaning will not break
    like light
the message will not come thru

the beast cannot follow the waterbearer
    into the upper chamber
      && the time
is at hand

                    Delphi, ca. 1964

zorba's dance

Four days before we met I wrote about your features, cast of mind.
I explored the journey of your psyche, hoping for a sacred union.
The balance was delicate, like a mouth gaping in a dentist's chair.
One risks exposure, an aspect from which I have had to suffer too long.
Gipsy, Wandering Jew, Elijah, I envisaged an actual love commune.
How could I know that everyone would end in broken vows?
To shatter the silence I play a Greek dance alone in my room.
I dance around and around on a Cretan beach.
There is nothing but the sand, the sea and the sky peopled with ghosts.

London, 1967

opera house in the sky

For Allen Ginsberg

a flock of pterodactyls picking their noses high above the snowy clouds
what gentle flight! there's Greenland down below—37,000 ft.—a
continent of ice
Pot-Au-Feu, says the *Tribune de Genève*, K.O. and many other trite
nothings—the hostesses *don't* smile
businessmen talk German, study indices and scribble accounts
air-conditioning and muzak clobber the senses—give me a cold—it's
night tho' the sun's still shining
we're getting a bit tippy while the queer Dutch ventriloquist, on his
way to the lavatory, says, "I am a very big strong sick man!"
and the Company Director passes: *Guten Tag!* everyone's so polite!
Big Mouth never shuts up for a minute, telling the world about her
operations, her age, her job—it's the talking sickness, she admits, as the
pained man listening chokes with anger and boredom
and she raps, "What is illness? is it real? I've thought about it all my
life. Is it Mind, is it diet, is it air, is it poison, is it feeling, is it conflict, is it
fear, is it not doing or not being, is it unused, misused energy? Please tell
me to shut up!"
and the man smiles and smiles and murmurs softly, "I'm really
innarested."
"What is illness but unused energy? energy crushed and shrunken into
small clots of gray lumpy snailish matter? energy drained, siphoned away
by misuse of feeling. misemotion."
"What will you have to drink?" purrs the hostess

and a potty little guru comes and croons, "There is Something Beyond!" waving his hand vaguely in the direction of the toilet—

Big Mouth looks up briefly, then back to Numb Listener: "I'll bet my guru is more tranquil than your guru!"

and a beach flashes a gang of bank crooks run by a master mind intermingling hot kisses with white foam

and Marlene Dietrich sings *Allein in Einer Grosser Städt* followed by *Horepse Me Mas*—Dance With Us—on the earphones

while Americans play poker in shirtsleeves

and I am reading Edgar Cayce's prophecies in **EARTH CHANGES** about the break-up of the North American continent—will Los Angeles be there when I arrive?

Space and Time have zeroed into my psychic fallout mind and I watch for signs and portents flying silver birds that skim the polluted skies

tsunami will reach 100 ft. to drown our outlaw country—slavic hordes will take over—Atlantis **RISE AGAIN**—and **MU**—the Hopi prophecy come true—White man destroy himself, broken land return to Red Man—

I am zapped by vibrations from 20th Century mosaic laws of simultaneous sense perception

in this science fiction return to America—a decade and a half gone and:

"They're all wearing their old age make-up," Judith Malina quips backstage at **THE MYSTERIES**—in Geneva—"except you!"

welcomed by Allen Ginsberg with a quick affectionate kiss: "I'm learning how to milk cows, I've got a farm upstate—it's like those last drops of jissom from a cock!"

as Scheherazade and Maurice Chevalier and Steve McQueen celebrate my return—

(in an emergency o my poems we'll go together in flame and water!)

meanwhile I'm a doctor with a stethoscope listening in on the divine heartbeat of the planet's soulsounds

over great landmasses and vast mountains—*C'est Magnifique* sings Chevalier—Great Moments In Showbiz—Magister Ludi—

the plane bumps—my pen moves across the page like a seismograph registering inner shocks and tremors of thought and feeling

speeding thru space toward President Arch **CREEP**—ah, there's Carmen taking over the Presidency, thank God! any smuggler band would make a better state than our killer govt. infecting the world like a cancer

with William Tell's pastoral sweetness before the storm

vapors clouds brown soil erosion—I'm an astral doctor—my musical stethoscope diagnosing Earth's ills—it's cancer I tell you! America eaten away in a kind of badlands virus disease of redneck greed!

I look at sulphurous gold we float above like gods—Fasten Your Seat Belt! Attachez Votre Ceinture!

great wasteland never seen on European continent! and now Verdi, Prelude to Act III La Traviata—all periods and sounds, all places and spaces merge—at the Opera House in the sky! violins! bel canto!

we taxi down into manic Manhattan of my birth and related mysteries!

New York/Geneva/Venice, CA, 1968/71

gone with the wind

I wake in the dark aching
Alabama! I can hear
old Mrs. Mitternight
in the sheet metal yard
at the rolltop desk
looking down from the wood railing

"Son, it will hurt
a whole lifetime—"
(the deep McBurney incision)

and it did, the war wound
a whole lifetime

In the Catholic hospital
with the crucifix over the bed
the horny nurse peeked
under the sheets:
"Whut y'all doin', huh?"
exploding in giggles
and she wasn't looking
at my appendix

Southern jokes in a gray ward
always about peckers
—stitches of laughter
and clamps over the drain
biting into cut flesh
yards & yards of gauze
with pus

"Handsome" they called me
until I stood up
then it was "Shorty"

and the old guy tottering
out of bed in the ghoulish
glare of sick dawn
couldn't be kept down
because death was upon
his huge bald head
and I heard for the first time
the death rattle

*

The midget and weightlifter
shared the same room—weird freak combo
of muscle and mite—

"his mouth
jest on a level
with mah fly—"

and in the steamy Mobile night
I saw the midget blow
the hot weightlifter
spittle gleaming
at the corners of his lips

*

Mr. Nil reading Rupert Brooke
belching
at the Alabama Shipbuilding Co.
where I wore a helmet
and muddy boots

and saw a black man
beaten to death
one blazing noon
fists and lead pipe
crashed into his skull
till his face went
beyond pain

MURDER! I yelled
"Shuddup!" they snarled
"or we'll lynch ya too!"

no one believed me
"It never happened!"
said the news desk editor
with an icy stare

              *

The governor's daughter had a green Lincoln
and a dogface—
at the mansion I was eligible
tho' the guv didn't believe me
when I talked of what I had seen
at the shipyard
500 white men gone mad
he preferred talking "classical music"
(Dance of the Sugarplum Fairies)
genteel Old South Monticello image

The guv headed a grocery chain
his wife was a pretty brunette
they had a French name
it was all peachy
but the daughter had a dogface

"Haow curm yew so blaaack?"
one of his kids drawled—
"Not black," I said, "dark—
sunburned—but your old man
is *real* black!"
if that's the word they wanted—
reason weaker than blindness
especially in a fine old Gone-With-The-Wind
mansion with corinthian wooden columns &
"darkies" in white jackets
(like a whiskey ad)
to serve us
smiling (only they didn't
smile—they looked
frozen)
everybody looked frozen

in some kind of deepfreeze
of the head

and back at the sheet metal yard
bewildered sharecropper fellow-workers
spat on the ground
scratching their nuts
unable to grasp
how I made "Southren sassiety"
and me just another apprentice
and damyankee to boot
(I could have taken over the state with my looks)

but the governor's daughter
had a dogface
not even a green Lincoln
could save her
tho' she tried pushing her boobs
against me
saying Tschai cow sky
and took me for rides
in the green limousine
and kept staring at me
saying, Doncha *luurve* Cho pin
and panted in the parlor
almost dropping her undies:
Ooh, tell me about Bee tho ven!

I preferred mammy shacks
sneaky honeysuckle sex
under wrought iron balconies
black ghetto red light nights
whisper & rustle of hustlers
raising of skirts
dropping of pants
quick! bend over!
hurry!
no   glance   back

*

I had escaped the fighting
in the Maritime Commission
among azaleas and rotten shacks

among men who knew how to hate
hate for the wrong thing
always the wrong thing
metal birds burned down the skies
out of sick visions
you couldn't run from Hitler or Roosevelt
or ratproofing
the world swarming with rats
and we ratproofing, caulking
building Liberty Ships
in the mud of the Gulf
with U-boat periscopes
like Loch Ness monsters
Nazis off Galveston
and Mobile
as we made the world safe
for vested interests

                        *

my cut side ached
and the blond kid I roomed with
drove us to "niggertown"
where the laundress made us wait
on the old batch. we hadn't noticed
the sunset
or gray shadows. in the dirt
and gravel
of a rundown funky bar
stood some young blacks. something
zoomed across the road at us.
"Bad news!" whispered the kid. I bolted
holding my right side, the kid
had disappeared. it seemed
I wouldn't get too far
without my guts all over
the street. I heard the black boys
closing in. a hand shot up
before my face. a streetlamp glowed
in my eyes like a third degree.
"a quarter, whiteboy, and yew pass!"
I dig in my pants, fish out two bits
and put it in the black man's palm.
he grins at me. with a theatrical

sweep of his arm he waves me on.
I found the kid's car just
as he was getting in, the
black boys about to jump us. I
don't recall
what happened to the laundry.

*

the first night in the boarding-house
the landlady puts me
with a fifteen-year-old boy.
I couldn't sleep. wanted to duck
under the blanket. he kept
thrashing and flailing, his legs
all over mine, one hand
grazing my belly. next night
she puts me with the blond kid: his
hairy legs remained on his side
of the bed. two nights later
it's his brother, the
handsomest boy in Mobile.
good Southern Baptists, both.
did sex exist?
I end up with a limping Spanish clubfoot,
the only ugly boy in the shipyard. we're
so horny that when he presses against me
we squirt and fall asleep.

*

in the steamy room with the blond kid
and the weightlifter, three of us,
each in separate cots, I hear
a strange flapping sound, starting
and stopping. the moon rises
over the weightlifter's cot and I see
his naked muscles white as marble
in the moonlight, his hand flapping
. . . starting and stopping . . .
the blond kid snores and I stare, making
no sound; the full moon reveals
the weightlifter's superb physique,
glowing fantastically. I creep

toward him like a ghoul, stealthily,
my hair over my face and whisper, "Warren,
Warren," hoarse with excitement. he
makes no sign of having heard
or seen me, with the wild
courage of desperation I reach
to touch him and he starts, his body tense,
glances at me, shifts his gaze
back to his burning moonlit cock
and I know it's all right.

*

Warren's asleep and Bud, the blond kid,
wakes and whispers, "Come here," and
I can't believe my eyes for he
is naked and erect; he grabs my head
and I go down. almost at once
he comes like a bull. then:
"Don't *ever* do that again, hear?"
"Didn't you like it?" I ask, incredulous.
"We don't like cocksuckers in Alabama," he says.
"It's a crime against Nature."
"It *is* Nature! You *wanted* it!"
"Never mind!" says Bud, getting feisty.
"Jest stay in yore own bed, hear? And leave
Warren alone." "That's Warren's business!"
"It's mine. If I catch you touching him
it'll cost you your job!"

*

In the Bellingrath Gardens
gray Spanish moss hung
from live-oaks in hazy tresses.
The scent of gardenias
came from beyond the boxwood
borders. A brown thrush
fussed among dead leaves.
I stood on a parterre overlooking
the broad lake; behind me
splashed a fountain into
a marble basin. My brain sluggish
I felt the moss envelop my senses

in the grillwork plaza with strange
iron benches, forgetting ugly
dumps, crumbling shacks,
shipyards, factories.

*

In China, Europe, Japan, the war.
Here, the shipyards, the airplane factories.
My nerves beat, drilled and hammered,
they pounded and tapered and punched,
they ratproofed and sheared. They steamed
with the loud exhaust from the gantry crane.
They hissed and rumbled with the clam-shell bucket.
They hooted with the locomotive, screamed
with the buzz-saw. My nerves
made a vast fire
in the stoke hold of freighters,
blazed in the furnace, smoked through the stacks.
I lost myself in blueprint and steel.

*

The old Chief's balls hung down to his knees.
Even the jockstrap couldn't contain them.
We laughed like hell when he stomped around
the flat we shared, growling and grumbling,
his balls swinging like some tired old bull's.
We were the young ones and joked
about everything, but mostly
about the old Chief's balls.

*

At Dr. Terrell's on Royal Street
a fat young man painted
"lahk Picassio," had thinning
fair hair and washed-out blue eyes
and an unpleasant habit of grabbing
my head and shoving it down
to his crotch. I forced back his hands
each time and would have slugged him
but he was too soft and would spatter.
He'd whip out his thin

purple dick and jack off, hoping
to elicit some response. But
a dog would have been more tempting.
"Picassio" stopped talking
only when he masturbated. He rode
the streets in an old Ford shouting
obscenities at blacks when he got drunk.
Dr. Terrell shuffled home
and sat in the old library drinking,
exchanging a few words with "Picassio"
and glaring at me as if the Civil
War had not yet ended and
I was a spy in the house.

*

Around the dead frame of the house
the street fell down below the gate.
The garden smelled of fish and roses
where centuries of pet cats ate.

What happened in the library
before the wind blew through the glass?
Coming back each night he sits
whispering "Frankie" as the hours pass.

Each night he shuffles up the porch
as pillars shake and dry wood creaks,
prepares his dinner, doffs his hat,
and ritually, softly speaks:

"Frankie! Frankie!" to the books
in faded jackets on the shelves.
The Twenties thrillers, loose romances
fail to implicate themselves.

Silent as the chokecherry leaves,
old Ambrose in the kitchen knew
his mistress when she lay and read
two lazy decades lightly through.

He hears the doctor whispering
the catechism of her name.
The evening sighs on Royal Street

like ghosts that drape the mansion's frame.

Now Dr. Terrell's dead; his gun
that never once had left his hip
cannot be questioned, nor the house
and Ambrose with the buttoned lip.

*

A cold wind blows through the world.
The West decays and crumbles.
The East destroys the Soul.
The threat to life grows greater.
The century wanes,
the world shudders.
Love alone pleases the Soul.
All the rest is waste.
Lechery, venery, sex, lust.
All the rest is waste.
Gay, bi, kinky, straight.
All the rest is waste.

Heidelberg, 1967/Venice, CA, 1970/San Francisco, 1976

let me love all at stillman's gym

freakshows. ferris wheels. rollercoasters, glittering thrash of surf. sea-smell. saltair. youths in openair lockers. sand. sun. nude bodies. they look up and see me in toilet window. they make obscene Italo hood gestures. up yours. *va fongool.* left hand pumping bicep in crook of right arm. shame. I blush with shame, they think I'm a girl! crimson shame. I'll die of shame. and delight. excitement pumps hot blood through my veins. chestnut hair over my eyes. I can see my bangs glint coppery red in the sun. everybody looks up at me. my cheeks and lips burn, they must be flaming red. I peek over the bathroom window ledge. *Hey! ya want dis?* they yell laughing. mocking yet sweet. they grab their dongs and wave and waggle them half-hard. their hips press forward. hump the air. *Come 'n' git it!* HAHAHA! sparks shoot out of my hair my skin. I am full of electricity. I grab the toilet paper cylinder. slide it in. pull it out. they can't see. they make farting lip sounds. the razz the Bronx cheer. *Hey kid wanna wop salami? c'mon down!* they collapse with laughter. slap each other's suntanned muscles. bend their knees on the sandy floorboards of the showers. helpless with excitement. lustful laughs.

they gleam gold. dance under the shower spray. wet, hot, salty, sea and sperm. froth and foam. salt of the earth and sea. *if the sandman brought me dreams of you*. I pick one out with my eyes. tall. lean. ample cock, he looks up. defiant. provoking, tender. sneers like a bully with feigned contempt. then slyly winks. (buddies do not see this, they see only the sneer.) then secretly points forefinger to breastbone, then points at me. together, us. him and me. I'm suffocating, scared. tantalized. breathing hard. what shall I do? I hide behind Auntie May's chintzy white toilet curtains. *I think I'd dream my whole life through*. minutes later I peer furtively over the ledge, they have forgotten me. nobody looks up. I feel lost. suddenly unwanted. they slap each other's butts, grab dicks, flick towels, yelp, make dirty gestures. yell with hoarse teen voices. sneak looks in my direction. pretend not to notice me. I flush again. I can almost smell the musk from their bathing trunks drying on sandy floorboards in the sun. the seabreeze wafts the musky odor in my direction. I feel faint with lust. they whistle. piercing. loud. tongue curled between the teeth. they slap each other hard. smacking sound. flat hard palms against flat hard bodies. they whip wet towels across butts with a smart crack like a gunshot. cackle. shadowbox. prance. HAHAHAHAHA. they do not look up. should I go downstairs? what will they do? call me dirty names and beat me up? I could not stand it. the one I love looks up. loud Bronx cheer with puffed out lips, then sneers handsomely. waggles it. long. thick. pointed. foreskin. lips curled. arrogant. beautiful. *for you brought a new kinda love to me-e-e*. . . . I duck. I hide. rouged with shame and desire. it's too much. in medicine cabinet mirror I see my face. like a girl's. roses and olives in my cheeks. flash of brilliant teeth. I grind them in agonized frustration. Calcium they call me at school. my teeth so pearly white. Handsome Harry they call me. pubic hair thick and shiny, and new, I am 13, I watch the young men under the silk spray, twenty-eight young men bathe by the shore. they do not know who watches and loves them. behind the curtains I make love to America. in the closet I make love to America. my love is bigger than the Atlantic Ocean. America does not want my love. America throws sand in my eyes and tries to drown me in the Atlantic Ocean. but my love is bigger than any ocean. over the greatness of such space steps must be gentle, everywhere sand and waves and sun flashing. superb young acrobats in tank suits. they build a throne of bodies. along the sand I crawl on my belly to the throne. I am a slave to the monarch of flesh. no god more precious than this throne of youth. let me love you all at Stillman's Gym. I am 13, I want to love America. America with its smell of gymnasiums and locker rooms. America with its smell of hamburgers and hot dogs. America with its smell of jockstraps and privates. America with its deodorants and disinfectants. America laughs at me. Steeplechase laughs. Luna Park laughs. the fat lady jellyrolls and laughs, the seal boy with black flippers laughs. Zip the pinhead laughs. multitudes on the beach laugh, under the boardwalk the lovers laugh, the bank director in a beach cabana eats the newsboy's ass and laughs. a great horseshoe crab rots on the sand with slimy maggots infesting its jurassic head and laughs. I poke it with a tarry stick. it dissolves into the sea's endless rhythm and laughs. I fade out in dumb relentless sea-surge. I do not laugh.

*   *   *

fingers delicately palpate hairs on backs of thighs

run gingerly along bulge of buttocks

rest gently on asshole

belly trembling—bands of muscle ripple—

suck in—waist tight—thighs arch—like bows—

arrow ready from quivering tendons

to shoot—

lower my head and grasp my feet—

tickle my toes with moist fingers—

bend down further—straining—

back and spine aching—

lips purse with kissy stress

towards pearly glistening moisture—

heart pounding—tongue darting—

hands clasped beneath thighs—

grappling—bending—snout burrowing—

pressed in musky nest—

aaahh! mmmmmm!

GULP!!

Venice, Calif., 1969

when law is murder

*"If the government becomes a lawbreaker it invites every man to
    become a law unto himself; it invites anarchy."*
                                        —Supreme Court Justice Brandeis

He took ginseng & mu tea,
worked out with weights
and resembled an anatomical chart.

He was not a monster on display
but a nice blond kid
at Muscle Beach.

He reached down
to a paper bag
& gulped some dago red
without removing the bottle.

"I've been drinking it all day,"
he said. "Helps me thru
a workout." He winked
and I felt a bolt of love.

Then I saw it, from
the underside of his biceps
around to the triceps. Worst
goddam burn you ever saw.

"Didja notice the pigs in the prowl car
waiting to catch me
taking a drink?" He took another.
Spat. "I'm 26, just back
from Nam. Legs burnt
by fire-bombs. Now
they want me to be a good boy,
no drinking, no screwing. Does
that make sense?"

His sinewy tanned back gleamed
in the sun. Everyone
wore bikinis, bathing trunks.
He never removed his pants.

Venice, CA, 1969

mr. venice beach

The gym stank of armpit and crotch and male ego,
the hustlers with their golden boy good looks
strutted as usual, powerful and lazy with muscle,
throwing Mr. Universe poses and sipping honey
from plastic bottles or raw milk between sets.

The competition was coldblooded and the conversation
hard edge, about who had the biggest pecs
and were Rick's abdominals more cut up this year
and did Joe really get 200 bucks off the faggot
who phoned the gym from Pennsylvania
clear across the country, just for a date with him?

Charlie was throwing poses in the mirror
like a contest winner, raising his huge arms
over his tiny head and flashing a Mr. Big Biceps shot
and then a fast latissimus in the old John Grimek style.

Then Charlie quit taking immortal stances
long enough to come over and say, as he wiped the sweat
from his obliques: A funny thing happened on my way to the
gym at the Federal Building in downtown L.A.
This car comes charging up the road onto the curb
and crosses the grass and smashes into the building.
and when the cops get there they find this note:

I'm across the street in the cemetery, dead.

They found the guy there.

Then Charlie started back to the mirror.

He placed second in the Mr. Venice Beach contest,
he said, flexing his quadriceps.

Venice, Calif., 1969

the queer-killers

Kick the fag in the nuts. Bash
out his brains; they're not
doing him much good. He's a loser,
a queer. Break the fag's
goddam ass. Shut his cock
sucking mouth for the last
time. He's a pervert, a sick
degenerate. Break his face.
The law won't touch us, chum.

Venice, Calif. ca. 1970

a warm november afternoon

in the sun on a warm
november afternoon a vast
synthetic paved square
with a fountain from which
poisoned city water flows
it's the Embarcadero
Plaza & I'm flat
on the curved cement benches
thoughtfully laid out
for the recumbent human form
by the recumbent city planners
thoughtful but not aesthetic
& businessmen in money uniforms
rigidly walk by with short hair
mad-looking among the freestyle young
they pass with scarcely a glance

the kids mostly black &
brown scream & play
splashing in the water
while 2 young men beside me
dart furtive glances at my bare
hairy aging albeit muscular
torso as they munch
lunch
always these signals of restless

quest for ecstasy, freedom
under the humdrum externals
as life goes on
secretly beneath the noise
and speech that exist
on broader daylight terms
of falsity

San Francisco, 1971

harley-davidson

I climb on the Harley-Davidson
behind him. "Hold me," he says,
"around the waist!" my arms
petrified as we hurtle through Brooklyn.
he glances over his shoulder.
to show appreciation I smile, thighs
numb with tension. the feel
of his lean belly under the leather
is soothing. Nick's slant
blue Russian eyes sheathed
in the Jaeger like that scene
of Slavs and Teutons on the ice
in Alexander Nevsky, he turns
into a knight, I his vassal.
we ride the lancing air,
one with the machine
alive and leaping, sailing
a concrete sea. words
had not brought us together, words
made us "comrades". we never spoke
intimately. teenage marxists.
slum intellectuals.
                    we shoot
by dazzling shores, roar
at the rocks—then back,
I pry loose. Nick grins,
removes the Jaeger. lank
blond hair over high
cheekbones. "Were you
scared?" still trembling I frown.
"Nah. Let's do it again next Sunday."

San Francisco, 26vi.72

on riverside drive

Under the Soldiers & Sailors Monument,
under Grant's Tomb, the pulse
of a city beats in the blood
of the boys cruising each other,
the trees & shadows give off
a sexual feeling, benches
extend a promise; rank
odors of leaves, damp
mulch of groins; they expect to
find each other after hours,
after the opera, the ballet,
after Lorca and Whitman and Stein,
after whiskey and Billie Holiday,
after everything has closed down
and the night is about to begin.

San Francisco, 9.v.72

i am going to fly through glass

For Anaïs Nin

Perhaps you do not remember the effervescence of the Rumanian girl in church waiting, it is true, for a mortician in groovy tennis shoes

perhaps it was so much like everyone, but more pederastic, the love I pretended when you were tearing the iridescent neck and the cab left the respectable houses farther down to where the crews were displacing the river

in the darkness we became even more aware of the Doctor who is soft as a bat in the green night . . . the narcotic fireworks . . . the softness she felt as she swallowed some of it . . . the inside smelled of sandalwood

I have lost count of the years of darkness, with the keen knife I cut the first throat I saw, I cannot lament the loss, and o, the night pleases us like memory

I'm busy writing a fantasy in verse to forget the victim who fell before the Cross, in vain trying to convince himself

I remember you danced in the labyrinth when I was tormented in different parts of the city fighting so many things

then I could do nothing but submit to a cruel dream . . . I saw trees move intravenously and flow through passageways where I appeared disguised as many faces and

entered a room whose walls smoked, burnt letters fell like onion skin, in Gothic script

at the top of the staircase a woman thrust her breasts sensually forward, struggling out of a chastity belt, and devoured the wallpaper depicting a muscular equilibrist in orange tights whose head resembled one of mine

my jaws ached, I had been grinding my teeth in the underground laboratory where the "King of the World" ruled . . . I held in my hands a crown of feathers . . . I could hear gold . . . music poured through my fingers . . . I am going to fly through glass. . . .

San Francisco, 1972

dreams

Tell me, dreams, will I find a new lover?
How do you feel, dreams, about my taking a new job?
What are my chances, dreams?
Will I get rid of my backache? will my luck change? will I travel?
  become famous?
Dreams I want to know. I have given you my best years and what have
  you given me?
I sacrificed everything for you, placed you on an altar,
  invoked your images, burned my bridges for you.
I whispered of you to my best friend. I followed where you led.
I consulted you, took dictation from you, I was a faithful servant.
  I listened reverently when you spoke, obeyed when you commanded,
   studied your moods.
I puzzled over your riddles, divined your symbols,
Nobody has trailed more closely in your wake.
I saw decayed interiors, stone mazes, wild horses plunging into the
  sea. . . .
I went through outlandish metamorphoses.
How have you rewarded me for my fantastic pursuit?
Come on, dreams, let's level with each other!
I am just where I stood at the start of this journey, dreams!
Brrrr! oh fucker! this thought scares the piss out of me!
I mean, everything I've thought and done, dreams, *everything* has been
  thru you, and now you're leaving, walking out! I'm getting older,
  more tired, catch cold easily, and, worse, growing forgetful, not
  remembering you! this is dangerous. . . .
Don't, for god's sake, leave me, dreams! You're all I've got.

If you go nothing's left, only the dull puke of everyday "reality" that
    dreamless gloom! Glub! I'm drowning! shopping and dollars!
    election speeches! dirty laundry! kitsch! schlock! AAARGH!
pollution. statistics. data processing. shriek. racism. computers. gulp.
taxes. war.
    I'LL THROW UP!! Don't leave me, dreams! I'm nothing without you
       . . . shit . . . just shit.
You're my everything, dreams, my oracle my guru my divine right . . .
    my cock my cunt my year-round asshole . . . my boy my joy my
    cookie my nookie my groovy suck!
San Francisco, 21.ix.72

this has been happening a long time

For Gerard Malanga

someone very familiar
tho' we've never met
fumbles around with his tool
shed while I crouch beside him
I request machine oil
for my squeaky bicycle
he hands me the oilcan
I notice his black velvet pants
with a flower design
our pants are identical
I reach up to tell him
with my hand that caresses the soft
material under which the hard
teenage thigh grows
more familiar
my hand explores his calf
the muscular buttocks and
something swelling in front
my mother calls Lunch Is Ready
he may be the brother I've wanted
we chat like blood relations
comfortable with each other
my mother rides a snow sleigh into the kitchen
she is having her problems
we laugh at her worries

we share an inner knowledge
he responds to my touch
with no visible emotion
I am growing upset
I reach for his penis
I hold it like an electric eel
electrons come in my hand
he seems to melt into the snow
and sound of sleigh bells
this has been happening a long time

San Francisco, ca. 1972

underground love

old man mutters under dogwood
as 3 straight suited exec types
cross the street looking brainwashed
i.e. stiff prejudiced unloving
their money uniform looks wooden
cars flow by to freeways
Oakland hills like Fiesole
Tuscan panorama from downtown San Francisco
I've left part of me in Tuscany
part of me in Sicily
pieces left in Rome Paris Tangier Athens NY
with boys in the international
underground of love

San Francisco 2.iii.72

reading my poems at universities

reading my poems at universities
dazzled and stimulated
by muscular bare legs on campus
hairy young studs and clean-cut smoothies
when will I fill this sexual void
audiences just waiting to get at the liquor
I dazed and wandering among them

supposedly free and loose
not drinking
not pinching asses
not groping crotches
the very model of an asshole
I want them to come to me
(delusion of grandeur)
I'll read that book on self-hypnosis
become a rampant bard
yelling: Down with your pants!
ah you creep, when will you tear the locks from the doors!

San Francisco, 3.iii.72

the bus

the bus lurches
thru underground transit co. construction zones
faces tempt me thighs make me giddy
PLEASE HOLD ON SUDDEN STOPS ARE SOMETIMES
     NECESSARY
what is poetry? BIT OF PARADISE DISCOUNT STORE
will I see you again?
FOR LEASING INFORMATION CALL AGENT
I think of you
HAROLD'S TERMINAL DRUGS
this is where I get off
but I don't get off
I think of a Mediterranean landscape
the twang of a Spanish guitar
sugarwhite walls
SORG PRINTING CO.
your legs are on my mind
oh, he hangs on to the strap
sneaking looks in my direction
I need him
I want to smile
he wants to smile
but he doesn't
he frowns
looks out the window
looks back at me

why don't I smile
I pretend I'm thinking
we lurch
towards somebody unattractive
ooops
the driver must be nuts stopping like that
smile goddammit smile
there that does it does what
he looks scared embarrassed
doesn't smile
and this IS where I get OFF
now he's waving he's waving at me!
now I smile now he smiles now we smile
now he looks rueful but glad
to show his feelings
as the bus speeds on

San Francisco, 25.iii.72

chicken

my legs? oh
they just came
naturally big

I'm training
for
the football team

I gotta lotta
endurance
(hot
looks in the direction of

middleaged
ass
in the grass

dark blue
circles
under his young
eyes)

I'm in shape
from running
(built like a
sinewy Renaissance
puto,* ripe
Italian buttocks
smelling of
parmigian')

I oughtta
be big
all over when

I'm 17

San Francisco, 18.vii.72

*Italian: winged cherub

we do not speak of love

For Alix Geluardi

we do not speak of love
but all are pushed & pulled
by it

taking all forms & shapes
twisted pounded burnt
by it

like sculptor's clay our faces
punched & pinched
made long or ripped apart
by it

eyes pained or deep or lost
lines cut in cheeks & foreheads
from it

we do not speak of love
our faces scream

of it

haunting bars &
running wild in streets
for it

we do not speak of love
but spike warm veins pop pills
burst brains with alcohol
for it

gods & demons wrestle for the heart
of it

I can't survive the lack
of it

San Francisco, ca. 1972

remembering paul goodman

1

As I cross a windy streetcorner
waiting for a bus
that never comes
in the wind and the rain
I remember
how Paul walked
with a shaggy dog trot
and half-shy smile
pipesmoking
toward a drunken party
where he ran
to hard young bodies
and handsome faces
tho' loss of balance disgusted him.
People fell
into the bathtub, smashed
and Paul stood as if amazed
at the madness of crowds.
And I recall once
when he stood at his window

sight-translating
Our Lady of the Flowers
how his blue intellectual eye
kindled suddenly
at a passing navy ass
and as he brought a criminal beauty
out of the French language
a revolver went off in his mouth
releasing
orgasms
of
light.

2

Now he does not exist
those parties are gone
the nights the lovers
gone
only the feelings remain
another here
another now
the written word will survive
somehow
in somebody's memory
this is the truth of poetry
to make it new each lifetime
Pound's gold standard of letters
Goodman's bitter faith

I write to make myself real
from moment to moment
how else do I know
I exist
if I didn't I'd go
mad with emptiness
and boredom I confess
Paul Goodman
helped us live
in the present
tense

3

Strange to hear your voice
disembodied on tape

lecturing at universities
over the air (and you're dead and gone)
less bitter than 20 years ago
some say more bitter
but you were diffident then
and shy
needing the sweet turned neck
and ear of the young
you pursued love and fame
for what? towards what?

    Lonely old Orpheus
       Romantic woodsy Wordsworth
          anarchist Shelley of coldwater flats
      on your bicycle over the bridges
        loving the pastoral urban scene
      dashing to handball courts for quickies
        blowing the boys
    in parking lots and doorways
    with Puerto Ricans on stoops
        secret jackoffs on East Side roofs
with shepherds of chance on streetcorners
      among traffic horns and coffee smells
        smells of urine and sperm in sacred latrines
         bus stations, bars, penny arcades
      42nd Street grope movies
        smoke and kisses
O Empire City!
      Soul-brother Socrates
        tugs at your elbow—
          Catullus declaims: *pedicabo ego vos*
            et irrumabo . . .
        You lived in sad neglect
          till late success brought dollars
            gray hair and heart attacks—
        your son Matthew dead at 20
            your wife Sally once applecheeked
              growing old. . . .

You wrote *The Facts of Life*
and we read our poems and joked
and met Edith Sitwell, noble scarecrow dyke
with birdlike mask
and Jean Cocteau signed copies of OPIUM

and *The Eagle Has Two Heads*
saying,
              "These English words . . . these are not my words. . . ."
and flirted with me
and you were jealous
biting the stem of your pipe as if it were the pin of a grenade. . . .
And when I said you were our Sartre everyone looked uncomfortable
                                                              in 1945

but when you died the other day
a famous critic called you that
and I bought *Hawkweed* for a dollar
and read those kinky poems again
—a voice unique and personal
caught as in rock for future years!

4

Patchen's slow death of bitter pain
    Jarrell stepped in front of a car
Sylvia Plath stuck her head in the oven
    Delmore Schwartz OD'd on booze
O'Hara struck by a beach buggy
Berryman highdived from a bridge waving
    Blackburn went by cigarettes
        & Goodman forgot his pills
these are the poets of my generation
    give or take a few years
Paul's poems kept growing bleaker
        with indignation & rage
    with every sleepless night
that went without love as age crept up
        who's next? the pattern's old
freaks of the western wilderness
between the bughouse & the bar
American poets live their lives
    some starve tho' you may not hear it
        others vanish into academe
to sugarcoat their hell, grow dull
    Paul with his "pretty farm"
tried the Horatian life, it didn't work
    in a black flag he draped his love
tobacco, wrong food, loneliness
    stopped his heart the American way

5

Writing *The Glass Menagerie* was no cinch, Tennessee.

"It's only a potboiler!" he said. "Wouldn't you rather see my poems?"

Julian Beck spoke of Gertrude Stein and the revolution of feeling.
He raised black flags in hell
and threatened the world with peace and saintly patience.

Jimmy Baldwin emerged from 5 a.m. mist into neon cafeterias
with watchcap and desperado eyes
placing his naked soulscript in my hands, his negritude,
and we had to choose bars carefully.

Paul Goodman sat on my floor listening to Auden—
their first meeting—both thought they were Shelley—

Ginsberg, high in the subway, red kerchief round his neck,
recited Rimbaud in eerie dawn of 1944
drowned by the IRT, flood of words across the aisle from me
and then departed for mad mindmusic after we greeted the future.

Death, sex and war . . . sailors everywhere . . .
jukebox romance of South Sea guitars . . .
we cruised the salty seas of love. . . .

I recall it all
through a scrim of decades
and broken love affairs
and rubble of dead friendships.
Paul was not sentimental:
"I do not eulogize dead men," he said.

I find that fitting.

San Francisco, 1972

a kind of immortality

Scientists predict that California will have a major earthquake of devastating proportions sometime within the next few decades. Now is the time to prepare yourself, your family and your home for such an event. *Do not rely on others*, it is your responsibility to be prepared. A major earthquake will tax local government and emergency response agencies, probably beyond their capability. It is imperative that each citizen be prepared for such an event.

—*Pacific Bell Family Plan*

1

I always thought
it would be like this
like my dream long ago
of great tides hurling
upon the land
myself engulfed
with struggling masses
screaming
choking
fighting
for air

now this strange
prophetic dream
seems true
as I watch the waterpipe
shaking
and the lamp on the night table
and the bed
shaking
as the earth shakes
night after night
in warning

2

From wine and dope and desolation
of taverns and bus stations
with pinball machines and video games
from waiting in vomit
at some forlorn forgotten place
and time
from the tiger of memory
from the loneliness of the last stand

with blood-torn twisted mouth
crying in a stunned alley or subway
like an exposed intestine
numbed by fluorescent tubes
from the sad choked scream
behind dirty curtains
in downtown tenderloin
where alarms go off with insistence
and hysteria
from lunch counters of donuts and coffee
with closed faces of bleakness of not knowing
anybody or oneself or anything
of being nothing and going nowhere
I want you to stop
I want you
to forget terror and suicide
for one small moment
forget earthquake and heart attack
I want you to take a deep
breath
and listen
deep inside yourself
and hear
what you heard before
you came to this
place of desolation
and tell yourself
you're not alone
it's really a dumb dream
on a mean planet
and you're going to wake up
and be somebody
you always wanted
to be

3

I saw a young man in my room
strangely intimate though unknown
yet loverlike and warm.
"I know this city well," he said.
"its hills and business district.
I'm a taxi-driver, 27, been thru
the big quake, the western hill
is safe," and vanished.

Was I talking to the dead,
some astral hitchhiker
between sleep and waking?
I fell back and heard:
"It is an exceptional time
and situation."

4

Night after night earth trembles.
stars sharp over the city.
Vehicles whoosh in the streets.
Scratching my armpits in the bleak bed
I fornicate with hot youths
in my imagination.
Why not go down with grandeur
under collapsing roofs,
pancaking floors,
coiled rocks roaring,
office buildings capsizing,
land-developers foiled.
greed smashed by Nature!
Ah, what a noble death!
This will be memorable, by god!
A kind of immortality!

5

in the city forsaken by the Angels
¼ million people seek refuge.
they run in the streets stark naked, clutching
an old photograph or a drum.
buildings shake, fall down
in a heap of plaster, glass and concrete
in a matter of seconds bridges buckle,
cloverleafs contort, freeways tangle,
dams burst, water rushes over suburbs,
old ladies weep, traffic signals
flicker insanely, children scream,
thousands die and are buried instantly.
a naked youth in an overcoat
carries a hastily-improvised sign
on cardboard: REPENT! THE END IS NEAR!
his end is beautiful and very near.
his eyes glitter, he does not speak,
golden shoulder-length hair glows

in the sun, his legs are flawless.
I approach wanting to touch him.
speak to him, thinking of
the Angels in Sodom, but he vanishes.

to go down in a heap of rubble
with 100 twisted old ladies
sour, insane, hating life
is to die in a bombed-out ghetto
with TV alone in a room
watching commercials.
to go down in a broken city
is to die of irrelevance
for a god of phantoms
in a dream of swimming pools.
to go down stupidly
in the debris of shlock and glitz
is to die of unreality.

6

Let the dogs hump in the streets
I'd do the same if they'd let me
those guardians of public morals
who fear the horrors of pleasure
more than the horrors of war

We've grown used to our daily murder
give us this day our daily dead
our daily rape, beatings, swindles
by the law-and-order boys—
their God cannot stand Love
—their God is Death

Let the dogs go berserk
running around in dog packs
biting their owners when they
come too close—earthquake—
it makes them mount each other
humping away the fear

Meanwhile we wait for the big one
that will rip off the State, smash
the City like a toy—"Is this it?
will I die?"

we know and the dogs know
and the cats and canaries and goldfish know

But it is too big, too monstrous, too
forever for the mind
to handle . . . which is why
we stay and tell ourselves—
what will be, will be—
like the sour old ladies
at the sea's edge, turning
their faces from the sun

Venice, Calif., 1971/San Francisco, 1972

embarcadero y

For Erika Horn

now the real estate pigs
have sold the old Y
I'll have to find another for my workouts

no more sweaty odors, jockstraps
everyone sneaking looks at each other
suppressing hard-ons
"Hey, man, you're in shape!"
talking of sports and women

I'll miss the showers
with a view of Treasure Island
across blue water the green hills
the Embarcadero Y will fall
to the wrecker's ball
for a parking lot
skidrow winos mopped up

   they'll tear down
   funky bars &
   burn the piers
   sending black smokerings
   to vanished Indians

dust and torn streets
highrises shooting up
black as the hearts of city fathers
hard as the hearts of "developers"

oh put them in wheelchairs!
push them over the roofs!
pull down the office buildings!

they have murdered the landscape
fouled the air
left us no choice

San Francisco, ca 1972

naked men in green heated water

Naked men in green heated water
float beside tropical fish
whose electric colors vibrate in a shock of black
light where greengray jelly waves
and something yellow darts through coral
Someone descends to the water
His perfect body stirs mind ripples
Eyes float on the surface
Music pours into the "minoan" pool

Striped fish are having an orgy with an electric eel
Snaky tendrils sprout
from the mouths of these young men
grabbing each other between the legs
where they explode roman candles of dazzling sperm

In this wetness feelings flower
like muffled dreams
like boats shot into the sky
like sweat mingling with tongues
like a rapist wearing his victim's skin

San Francisco, ca 1973

mysteries of the orgy

1
hands reach silently to touch me
mouths graze my shoulder like moths
fingertips palp my genitals
the scent and touch of my lovers
humming like moon rockets
launched into astral deeps
novas white dwarfs red stars
milky ways stream thru my breasts
white as Einstein's radium hair
my body awakes I'm resurrected I'm risen
watching bodies in stellar clusters
against the walls
in circular rhythms of planets
"each member an island universe"
I'm licked into shape again
in the darkness of this room
bodies give off light and heat
that may last a moment or lightyears

2
touching ourselves into blood's renewal
we wipe out many deaths
my soul comes when I lose myself
when I plunge into an ocean of touch
how long can I inhibit my profound empathy
without touch my feelings are twisted my spinal cord shrivels up

3
we are organisms like rivers
we are miles of flesh flowing
   towards the healing ocean of a mouth
we are seconds of a pulse
we are fields of flame
we are worlds shuddering in flight
we are unsolved murders
   committed by our secret feelings
we are corpses singing with our blood
you close my wounds with your tongue
thoughts dissolve in the meeting of lips
we wander in and out of each other
   as in unknown rooms of a hotel

the Hotel Universe where the owner
   keeps to himself
we will never understand this
powerful music shoots out of the walls
the walls that are equipped
   with Death-rays and Time-machines
and we fly out of imprisoned dreams

San Francisco, 14.iv.73

grateful

For Robert Peters

AND I AM GRATEFUL EACH DAY
Grateful to watch young bodies hard and swift
Rushing passionately after a ball
The crack of the bat like a sexual bolt of masculine thunder
Grateful to get through bullets, bombs and vehicle crash
Grateful to survive sleepless nights of puffed eyes
Grateful for reprieve from senseless annihilation
Grateful that even reincarnation is possible
As everything in the universe is possible
Grateful for love that may come in a flash
In a twinkling you're in the dance so you might as well live
Grateful for Spring, blue skies, bare thighs
Grateful for the wind and the world and the flow

San Francisco, 10.iii.73

old age does not happen slowly

Old age does not happen slowly
but all at once, in the head. The body takes its time
getting there, but the mind, clinging to youth
flashes suddenly—behaving as if it were still
careless!—flashes on sagging skin, discolored hair.
If you're a woman you probably cry.
Your face is set in sour lines about the mouth
at the corners, and you've an ailment that's killing you.
The ailment is Time.
If you're a man you joke about not getting it up
so often but doing it long and slow and women like it
better that way haha and you talk about the good old days
of football and war.
But if you're gay you're dead.
Nobody wants you, old friends think you're pathetic
and leave you alone with brief visits.
You eye the beauties like some leftover dinosaur
hovering in silence, terrified
of those hard men you used to have.
For if they go with you now it may be your funeral.

San Francisco, 4.v.73

the other

1

I am a drooling pythoness
crawling through rivers of mud on my belly
on my knees in the cosmos   on the prowl in the void
I'm the navel of the world at Delphi   I'm the oracle at Crete
back and forth on the time track   commuting through bodies and centuries
I love the taste of feet   I lick the crown of divinity
I'm the old in/out   always looking for the ONE
but finding only the OTHER

2

I'm on my back dribbling stars from foamflecked lips
in a field of flaming chrysanthemums
bizarre beasts dance
mescaline moons melt

the seal of Solomon bursts

the electric river flows

streams of holiness gush between my legs

i give birth to a white narcissus

six wands spring from the ground

lotus leaves sprout from the eye

Absolute Poem like a meteor streaks down
crushed by the Earth in a swift instant

fiery chains of rubies flood the indifferent Cosmos

i'm soaring out of my blood

3

i am a war between two madmen who never win
this weird nervous system cannot change
time or pain or memory
nibbling survival

a lunatic wailing *love love*
with all the evidence shored against me

i float on a bedsheet to the stars

the sun burns in my belly

at fantastic speed i race
to the expanding skin of the bubble
of vanishing space

i am thermonuclear entropy
running down with the universe
on a golden horn
on a seismic kick
i am a cosmic tick
living on a small cold by-product of the delicate pressure of
starlight
with a glowing anus

4

I AM AN OBELISK OF EGYPT
I HAVE COME TO CHANGE ALL THAT YOU KNOW
I'VE BEEN WAITING 5,000 YEARS
UNDER MY SCRIPTURES RIVERS DIE
PRAYERS RUST AND FLAKE
I SPEAK SYMBOLS
I GIVE OFF IMAGES LIKE SMOKE
I KEEP SECRETS
I AM ONE COOL STONE

Athens, 1964/San Francisco, 1974

never will get used to

never will get used to
    being alone at 2/30 a.m.
restless and wide-eyed
scratching my dome and wondering where is everybody
        where's the big colorful past
    can I bring it back by meditation?
the typewriter gapes like a wound the pinups curl on the wall
Krishna blows his conch into Eternity I am the taste of water
            the Light of the Sun & the Moon
        I am the sound in the Aether
    I have a very ethnic wall
an orgy of Dutch lesbians a Chinese mandarin calendar in lacquer
                        & gold
    a Tibetan silk tanka two Aztec lovers & Japanese calligraphy
        with a Russian May Day poster
        and I'm not feeling a bit mystic

            ah, just air from a lawn
    & trees—something I had forgotten—
myself age 15 running down the block in the wind
        a football in my arms. . . .

San Francisco, 12.i.74

breathing the strong smell

breathing the strong smell of each other
I want it to last forever
it is never enough
warming the coldness of the heart

we stood holding each other
two men locking eyes and lips
then your mind cut the flow
and it was abruptly over

yet I felt curiously healed
as if life were about to begin

San Francisco, 1974

masturbation

1

The walls of the madhouse scream!

(witness sex starvation
scrawled in blood & sperm)

The walls are raving

   (nightmares and fantasies
in the john's eerie light
and rancid YMCA smells)

Men wander, fumble
with themselves, search
    for touch
in stoned flight that ends

   down

  on their own genitals

2

In bar or baths or street
   (oppressing ourselves)
the past stabs us with memory
it glows with that lurid
nightlight of Van Gogh's billiard table
    and Bosch's hellish scenes
      jabbed in the nerve
resonating forever
   the early memory
     stuck in the throat, locked
in the muscles, crippling
          spontaneous joy—

So
   in sleepless years of quest
     we thrust
       from one lost love
     to another
thru aching scenes
    of need

3

In Genet's *Chant d'Amour*
the young convict sucks
his own arm in the
prison cell, blows
smoke thru a straw
thru a small chink in the wall
the only physical contact with
the other prisoner; this
sends them both into
masturbatory fantasies
of each other
from which they emerge
out of woods and grass
with a single flower
dangled between
cell windows

4

The machinery of government
hides the hearts of people
from each other

Gandhi said
and so love must appear
on walls
of toilets
in letters of cum

San Francisco, 1974

horns

For Lawrence Ferlinghetti

On the Chinatown corner of Broadway and Grant
an old man in skins and furs
with occult ornaments and symbols
is shaking a large cowbell.
In his other hand a brown lacquered staff ends in a two-pronged fork.

Around his belly a pair of bull's horns,
his fur-crowned head slowly swaying
from left to right
as in some ancient shamanistic ritual,
ceremonies out of the past.

Near him a Chinese boy locked in a deep throaty kiss with a dumpy
    blonde.

A white boy shoves the mouth end of a long horn
in rhythmic movements
up the Chinese boy's ass,
then blows the horn and inserts it again.

When the kiss breaks up the Chinese boy drunkenly thanks the white
    boy
who disappears with the still-dazed girl. The white boy's hand
grazes in quick succession four big erections
as a group of tall youths pushes drunkenly by in the tight-wedged mass.

          *   *   *

I'm pressed like a piece of paper in the mob,
like a page in a book.

Bodies pass through me and I through them.
Everyone wants to burst out of their clothes,
press flesh into flesh.

The streets are lined with blow-ups of naked women in topless
                                        bottomless shows.

The barkers scream: COME IN AND GET DRUNK AND HORNY!!

and the madness of crowds
is the madness of unreleased energy.

             *   *   *

I go home with images of bodies.
I go home with the imprint of smiles.

I go home with the dry taste
and feel of untouched skin.

I go home with the flank of the cavalry horse
and the horseman's boot grazing my cheek.

I go home with the stench of the cossack's horse
lifting its tail, letting go on the crowd.

I go home with the guns from the rooftops,
the deadly control of the State.

I go home sloshing towards others,
love flooding the curbs in waves.

I go home with the iron of separation
embedded in my life.

San Francisco, 2.1.75

thru the window unending cars

1

Thru the window unending cars
on the freeway; downtown buildings
in dusky rush-hour light;
a single tree
redeems the landscape. Flies
buzz on the murky pane. Upstairs
the neighbor's children thump. The
blank wall of the Pacific Gas & Electric Co.
cuts off the view of Treasure Island. Under
the wall a parking lot.

2

On Mutual Benefit Life
a flag is waving; flies skid
and stagger into the room
as if gassed. Streets
are empty, everyone gone
for the weekend. Bars
fill up with single
men and women, clotted
with lonely ghosts. Loud
music and voices won't lift
the sinking stone of loneliness.

3

Past midnight.
I pad the halls
of steambaths; rock
blasts showers and TV,
I pass up orgies needing
a single naked human.
In the half-light I step
into a cubicle
and with anonymous limbs
we come together. Then
without a word we part.
I reel home to an empty flat.

San Francisco, 28.vi.75

lost

I drove around
not knowing exactly
what part of town
this was, some tough
neighborhood
where they followed you
with their eyes. I did
a few turns, passing
cute little stucco houses
like candy boxes in the
sun, full of browns, blacks,
yellows. Finally, climbing a
long hill and taking a
turn, I
saw a gang of teenage boys
who stared with
eyes like electric
eels. Shaking a little
I slowed
down as if searching
for a house
number. My heart
beat crazily. The
kids in tight pants
ran up a driveway into
a schoolyard looking
back, laughing. I
disappeared down
the street
trembling.

San Francisco, 28.iv.76

the big banana

I want to liberate beautiful boys from false ideas about sex.
Sex is religious mystical healthy and nutritious.
It's like eating a banana.
The Big Banana in the sky.
I'd like to peel him and eat him, foreskin and all.

Fall on my knees and worship god's rod.
If he's Jewish or Moslem we'll eat him sliced, all creamy.
Big Banana Split with hot nuts.
Perfect Orgone Prana Orgasm.
There is no Banana but the One Banana.
All other bananas are bananas.
I am the Big Banana.
Thou shalt have no other bananas before me.
Yes, we have no bananas.

San Francisco, 1976

playing doctor

Cock in the ass 3X daily
and some hot cum before bedtime
was his prescription for good health.
If he missed one injection
he'd grow tense and irritable.
But at night his full firm buttocks
pressed against my prick
dissolved all tensions
in 3 or 4 hefty treatments.
Then a great softness and tenderness
transformed your features, Jim.
Like a sleepy child with tousled hair
you'd lean against me, sitting up
and gazing with enormous eyes
in love and gratitude.
At such times I wouldn't dream
of playing doctor with anyone else.

San Francisco, 12.vi.76

this beautiful young man

This beautiful young man, just 20,
brings himself and his poems
lazily one afternoon
a half-hour late

recommended by a famous poet
who told me how good he was in bed.

His looks being superior
to his poems, which imitate his recommender
badly, I am kind and tolerant.
But in one poem he speaks cruelly
of how he enjoys "making old men
cry" when he turns them down.

"Ah," I say, "would you turn *me* down?"
And the little bitch does just that!
He's *straight*, he says, has a girl
and makes it with *one* man only,
the famous poet. I fly into a rage
and scream, "If I'm not famous enough for you
go fuck Walt Whitman and drop dead!"

San Francisco, 12.vi.76

paper bodies

For Neeli Cherkovski

1

Everything I want is in this photo of a boy, nude, completely relaxed, his buttocks seen from a low angle shot. He stares placidly inviting and I fade into the picture with him. I wake abruptly from a fitful dream before dawn, knowing he is . . . unreality of flesh beside me in the lonely void of a bed . . . (it's only a paper moon). . . .

2

I spend long hours gazing at you
studying all the angles

My tongue roams your body
my mouth wanders
along your belly
breastplates armpits mounds

Tongue duels with tongue
my throat engulfs you

My hands stretch out to hold
a still-life fantasy of pulp

3

Don't you want to be beautiful
like Sandow? No, the gorgeous numbers
can think of nothing but their tits
and waistlines. I'm
growing beyond the pale of their power.
They're stunning and I'm stunned, numb
with unsatiated looking. I can't eat the page
with its bevy of dramatically edible boys. But
as an old goat, maybe I *can* subsist on a diet of paper.

4

For Adrian Brooks

There's Someone out there, I tell you
who's the answer
                              to your prayers!
Get off your duff, Heinrich, follow
those flashing legs disappearing
on the green lawn of the city park
in red shorts. After all, it's your own
future, nein? Ja, ja, ve must go
to the next whiskey bar
or ve must die. I tell you, I tell
you, I tell you don't ask why. A White
Line at an angle stretches along the sky
over the trees and into the roof
of the tenement across the square.
It's Election Day. We are choosing
between horrors. I tell you
ve must die. there's Someone out there
aiming his gun at your heart.
Meanwhile on Election Day a dog is howling
in the street, mourning freedom.
Down the sloping hill of the park a black boy runs
past the sprinkler splashing the grass
and the fire engines wail chug-a-lug thru the ghetto
to another burning life. O, show me the way
to the next pretty boy
                              or I must die.
There's

Someone
out
there
I
tell
    you
        who's
            the answer
                to
                    your prayers.
                . . . .

He may be in a bar   or baths
                or café
or in a bookshop
            or on the street

He may be in a magazine

Just show me the way

                                  San Francisco, 2.xi.76

to a hustler

As Boris Karloff marches to the electric chair in *The Walking Dead*
    you're jacking off
But when you imitate the mating call of the Double-breasted
    Yellowbellied Sapsucker
        out on the café terrace
You attract even the local birds to the telephone wires
            who answer with bird notes of love
                because you are wild
                and free
        and scream with the sheer joy of being 20 years old
            a giant of beauty and anarchy
    and when you play the guitar and sing
You establish the live connection with pure pleasure!
            Well is it love? all
              we need is money
            You say you will support me
We could bottle the perfume of your crotch and make a bundle
            You get hard ons for TV

that I'm no competition for
      but I could gaze at your lips and eyes
            forever
      browse in your pits
            explore those eyes
      that see only yourself
      in a child's shamanistic dream

                        There's so much to tune into
But when you break your word and lie
                              I'm unhappy
            you're breaking my trust
                  and love can't survive a hustle
            watch out baby
      cool the hustler's sleazy charm
            life's a bitch
                  the magic splits

Well this is a love poem
            Listen!
Joe I'm talking to you stop watching that goddam television!
      You'd stick your prick in the box if you could!
      Those cretinous phantoms
            make me puke!
      Is our love Mickey Mouse?
                  don't answer that—
      this is not a psychology lesson
                  it's a poem
      but when I'm stoned my mind is cinema
      the universe a lousy film
            and you're playing *Magister Ludi*
            just a-hustlin thru metaphysics
                  full of weed TV and "foxy chicks"
Hey you're jacking off again!
      (even tho' you've read Alan Watts)

      I'm not Elizabeth Barrett Browning
      This isn't a marriage of true minds
      just an old hustle
      with a dash of mysticism
      ESP and a high IQ
      and you've read some Beat Poetry
      and I introduced you to Tennessee Williams
      who was grandiose and arrogant

but all you thought about was money
today's hip hustler longhaired and lippy
able to talk about Siddhartha
and pick my pocket at the same time
a handsome kid of indeterminate sex

Well this is your friendly old poet speaking
The Good Gay Poet H. Norse who should know better
who's been around

> Ah, but the loneliness
> was too much
> for an incurable romantic
> too much
> and the beauty of illusion
> Two weeks of lyrical shell game
> was it worth it
> yep

So thanks kid
        thanks for the trip
(Now segue to synthetic ending)

San Francisco, March 1976

gas station

The young attendant is friendly
enough but his eyes turn away
from time to time like a dog's
unable to hold my gaze for long
although we're talking about
tires and prices and I don't
make any personal remarks or
switch from a strictly macho air
yet he's uneasy an animal
instinct warning him perhaps
that he is the hunted the prey
for he has the fresh robust look
of an ordinary healthy country
boy and I long to break through
all this banal tire-talk and

whisk him off in my car to give
him what I suspect he really wants
beneath the guarded self-con
scious unease but when I
stare at his pants and see the
slight thick bulge and two
stains there he shifts his gaze
again and I'm aware that we
have got to bring the 4-ply stuff
to a close or *do* something
so I thank him and he thanks me
and I disappear to write this

San Francisco, 19.ix.76

survivor

For D. W.

I want to make you laugh.
The long nightmare is over.
But you've stored the pain
in your narrow shoulders
and sunken chest
and small broken hands.
Survivor, child
from a Nazi camp in the suburbs
with a swimming pool
and limousines
there's nothing left
but you're still here
and I want to make you laugh.
Beaten daily till you were six
you understood
that even a brother means destruction,
that parents mean abandonment,
gone forever in the private plane
that crashed and left you in the closet
locked without food for days
as punishment for not knowing fear.
Now you're out of the closet,
20 years old

with a ruby in your ear,
with a flowing stride and long silky hair,
with a pretty face
and an eye for men,
with a need for chains
and stinging strokes
of a strap on your rear.
But you've come through,
you're here.
Poor little rich boy,
I want to make you laugh.

San Francisco, 22.xi.76

steppenwolves

A Sequence

1
Above The Pit

The rain tears down your defenses
slicing the grin from your teeth.
You retreat into the rainbow
colors of your guitar. Sadness of imperfection
changes miraculously into song.
Clutching the cliff of music you hang
from the notes above the pit. I come
wanting to share the sounds that transform
us, mouth snapping at love. My grin
grows back again as my lips
form words around the music
and our feelings rush
more gently into the space
from which the rain slowly recedes.

2
The Steppenwolves Are Howling

I suffer fools and madmen. This one's
invisible, magical, prophetic,
works miracles, goes

without food or sleep he says.
Muttering suicide, burning money.

All right. Steppenwolves
don't mix. But listen, kid.
delusions are a bummer. Fuck
the acid and crash. It won't
make you a rockstar overnight,
won't settle the pain. We're all
fools and madmen in our feelings.

FOR MADMEN ONLY:
                                        the caption
of your acid notebook melts
in wavy flames on washed out pages
where the mind has vanished
like invisible ink.

3

Insomniac Dreams

You're in touch with a UFO.
You're gonna change the world.
Your eyes zap people in the street.

POWER POWER POWER POWER

I didn't know you had such power.
We move toward the edge, you throw
your childhood in my face like pie
and everything gets sticky. The mask
of madness turns into a perfect stranger
feeding your fantasies —
                                        who are you?
extraterrestrial punk?
You threaten my life — punk talk.
A smashed nose, you say, will put
even a muscleman out — ?
                                        over and out.

I'm flapping in the flamy night
trying once more to reach you
but you're mad,
                                        really mad —

your dreams drip on me.

When the madness breaks will you come to?

4
Rainbow Sickness

I brace
    against the greasy morning
rainbow
        sickening in the trees. It's not
the first rainbow that's let me down.
There's a pot of crap at the end.

rainbow rainbow rainbow . . . I can't
reach your blasted mind, acid
has etched out the gray, leaving
rainbow colors of a rotting fish
and it's stinking up the kitchen.
You mean harm so I cover
my ass and scream,
your loony vibes causing convulsions
instead of orgasms, turned
to a punk dream of revenge. Well, I'm
    no fantasy but if I exist
as your idea of me I can still
heft a load of reality between
your fucked-up childhood eyes
    with a pitchfork
        full of poems. . . .

5
Will I Ever Wake Up?

I'm dingy with dope and rain
not to mention the passionate love affair
every night with the guy in the mirror
since you walked out the door
with your 56-year-old guitar
into nonstop flights to the far side
of yourself shooting to L.A. and back

stay stoned
keep moving

across the freeway 90 mph
like your freaked-out mind
that death-defying new persona.

Junkfood can't stop you now
or the marathon of bad health.

What does the windshield whisper as you race
across California through commercials
of death?

                    stay stoned
                        keep moving

6
Disturbing The Peace

My fingers flash in erogenous zones.
The spirit of Jeffrey curls out of the smoke
into my hand. But its no fun
with no body, so bring your butch good looks back
from the other side, Jeff, I want
your legs in the mirror!
I pick up a bottle and aim it at my mortality.
My spirit sneaks up my ass
and starts feeling illegal.
Can I be busted for raping myself?

7
The Glass Bead Game

Alone in Monte Rio
where the redwoods hold their counsel
far from the magic lantern
of your french-fried brains
I don't know what to say.
Hello? It comes out wrong.
Can you hear the connection breaking
like the end of a Johnny Carson joke
the audience doesn't get?
Something shorted. Well,
thanks. Perhaps I should ask
you to step on my toes again
in the kitchen littered with bones.

The garbage bags wrapped up our scene.
All those dirty words decaying on the floor!
Your notebooks and clarinet and Martin guitar
roared in the woodstove, lyrics, old songs,
old feelings reduced to ash.
Like your driver's license, your ID.
Hello?
Is this the party to whom I am speaking?

8

Relationship

It's like Gaudí's Sagrada Familia
or Guell Park, all twisted.
It's like the tortured agonized
Jesus nailed on wood
in the dark shadows of the stone
cathedral behind the noisy plaza.

It's like the matador with his pride
as he catches a horn in the groin
and it's over, they carry him
out, with the dead bull.

*

You sit on the floor
singing, strumming
the guitar and drinking Fundador
until 3 a.m. and you lurch
to the balcony over the plaza
with the amber Gaudí lamps
and the students drinking wine
and shouting and laughing
but you do not jump
you weep and moan
saying you want to save
the relationship
that is collapsing
like the peseta and
you don't know why

*

You smile when you're angry
you go to your room and play the guitar
you bang your head against the wall
and come out with a new song:

In My Dream I Fly

In my dream I smoke
and wake up feeling guilty
my resolve broken
now the sky
has fallen
how can I
face it? but remember
it was a dream, oh my

Ah yes, I'm Adolf Hitler
Generalissimo Franco
I wake up feeling guilty
wouldn't hurt a fly
everyone's a nazi
fascist maniac
children have no mercy
adults kill and lie

I'm young rich and famous
I will never die
I have eternal beauty
in my dream I fly
I wake up feeling guilty
you stare at me intensely
despair and accusation
in your eye

I do not wish to scare
any living creature
but the monster nightmare
grows to terrify
I wake up feeling guilty
you turn into a zombie
as in a horror movie
this is no dream, goodbye

9
Love Is a Homicidal Mania

We sit looking at each other
I want to touch you
but the distance grows
    greater
and I am powerless
to break the spell of such
numbness, such bitterness
that holds us, holds us
as if hypnotized, unable
to speak or move

Finally, we look across gulfs
    unbridgeable gulfs
in silence
    waiting for the other
to speak
    no longer trusting
our voices
        our feelings
and when one of us does
speak it is about
something trivial and safe like
    what café to go to or
        what books to buy
and the abyss yawns wider
    under our feet
as we yawn with boredom and
        paralysis

I cannot trust my eyes
which I keep averted
    from yours
knowing it's the end of
this deadly game
this so-called "love"

it is, at times, indistinguishable
from homicidal mania
involving 2 people who
can never be sane
around each other

We've come a long way to find
this out only to expose raw nerves, frayed
at the slightest hint of
differences
each sentence poised
on the brink of disaster

Whatever we say is wrong
we can only sit and stare
and grow paranoid
    suppressing
the need to hold each other or
    to scream

Are we forever pinned like writhing
puppets to the wall? must we go round
and round forever in narrowing
vicious circles of our own
design? If I could
answer this I'd be God
who, it seems, keeps making
the same mistakes
and even killed his own son
out of love

Homicide looks like hate
to me, but then I am not God
and do not presume to know
                    Barcelona/Monte Rio, 1979/San Francisco, 1985

third world

I understand those tales
of a sick aunt you must visit
in a distant town
or a big loan you must pay *at once*

I understand your situation
those 5 quetzals are necessary
there's no denying it

But something slips
between your gorgeous body and mine
sliding across the ruins of our need

It's not us but a third
invisible body
that comes between us
    a powerful drug
that takes effect quite soon

Guatemala City, 15.iv.79

the lightweight champion of santo domingo

A star among his compañeros
this handsome 20-year-old
in tight white pants

dances, talks, sings
shadowboxing under the streetlamp
outside his boarding-house

and offers himself
and the whole boxing team
of Santo Domingo

From fear and strange reserve
I hold back
although a dream is about to come true
Then wonderingly
I step
into the fantasy

Guatemala City, 1979

rubén

You speak of large sums of money that nameless gringos send you
of 6 months in Los Angeles where you picked up your bad English
with half-shut eyes droning on about the Big Affair
the Big Love who's rich and famous who'll buy you a Cadillac
and take you to live in Hollywood and other screen romances

This evening when you lay dozing in soft gray light
in my cheap pension room near Sexta Avenida
with the born-again landlord smoking dope on the patio
as dusk fell on your nude brown body and heavy genitals
we both knew you could not rise above films and fleapit hotels
torn shoes smelly socks diesel fumes comic books horoscopes
between the parks in Guatemala City
and I know you deserve a better script (and I hope you'll get one)
than the rich and handsome gringo of your wet American dream
Guatemala City, 11.iii.79

indian summer afternoon

I saw him in the supermarket
    hovering above the potato chips
       and candy bars

blue trunks exposing
    smooth thighs
    beginning to fill out

    mouth
  moist and parted
ablaze with ripeness

      of fourteen years

he stood submerging
   the needs
of that flagrant mouth

in candy and chips
unnatural substitutes

for what at this age

    nature
obviously intended
something so pansexual

that all the taboos press
    on him
and on the onlooker

a mask of casual make-believe
    of bland indifference
so that nothing disturbs the surface

    of the supermarket
on this hot Indian summer
    afternoon

Monte Rio, 28.ix.80

von gloeden

1

In this Von Gloeden photo
a nude Sicilian with white headband over short black hair
poses beside a decaying wall with time-etched designs

there's a cave or niche behind him and stone seats—perhaps the
Greek Theatre in Taormina, Sicily, in the
sun in the 19th Century when the boy lived

slim hips gracefully arching from the girdle of Venus his sex like a flame
but he's dead, immortal and dead of old age long ago
yet clearly alive and young through Von Gloeden
now

2

A fountain over his shoulder a Doric temple behind
his head with vine leaves in the foreground and
a dark shadow circling his neck
chin and nose like a boy's I went to high school with
and his sex like what I imagined my friend's to be

(one summer night in the Catskills I felt it press against me
in the cabin where we slept when we were 16)

now this boy who could have been his grandfather
presses his sex through the page through space through time

3

If I could join them and the baron—all those boys
a hundred years ago! clinging to Doric columns
or Ionic columns on the Ionian Sea, flowers and vine leaves
in their hair, young masons and fishermen
clinging to maleness smooth and hard on volcanic rock and stone
forever in a holding pattern older than Greece or Rome

4

This gallery of nude photos instantly on call
grows more unreal more remote mellowed by change
a shifting sea-treasure for old men's eyes
teased out of time beyond reality's grasp

Monte Rio, Oct./Nov. 1980

eric heiden's thighs

    grinning with exertion
arms flapping
            he races
    toward us from the green
            sports page
for his fifth Winter Olympics
    speedskating
            gold metal

    I wonder
        what it's like
to catch this prize
        as he skates
            off the page
        into your arms
    and you remove
        his tightfitting
            sleek gold suit

peeling
    the smooth fabric
        down
    from waist
        to ankles

  jesus!
one could lie
    at his feet
look up at that godlike body
  & ask
    nothing more
  than a little water sports
(without ice
    please)

Monte Rio, 21.ii.80

teenage redneck

a consciousness
lower than a
        slug's
dumb gloat and menace
in eyes and mouth

expression
like a third finger
  the letter F
blown between lower lip
and upper teeth
lingering
    obscenely

when he finishes it's

FAGGOT!

mutely mouthed

the finger's a
  .22

like the ones he empties
into birds
        and cats

hits   dead center
as he smirks
and checks this out
with his buddies

who shift uneasily
when I stop and glare
fists clenched
and stare
him down

and spit

standing my ground
his pals look
away

my eyes hold
his in a deadlock
he turns
chuckling
to his pals
they move off

I'm amazed that I'm ready/to kill

Monte Rio, 19.viii.80

the rusty nail

I go to The Rusty Nail
        where country lads dance
to thunderous rock rhythm

        shorts nipples baskets
    stinging odor of poppers
        cigarette smoke booze

    nothing happens
so back on   River Road
    headlights blind me
I flash   direction signal
to   truck behind
                and as I turn
into   dirt   road
            hoarse teenage voice
screams   from   truck

COCKSUCKER!!!

and   speeds   on

Monte Rio, 1980

about time

"You *homo!*" screams the blond kid
to the little girl in the dirt pile.

They are making endless engineering
projects out of gravel
                and dirt.
"You *homo-*
        SEX-u-
                al!"

The worst thing
            he can call her
but she doesn't cry
            or hit him.

She tries harder to please him.

The sun enters Gemini
the republic sinks into hysterics
the moon enters Pisces
not, certainly, a return
to the Good Old Days

and Venus turns her back
                             on us
while hanging in becomes
the burning question
                    of the moment.

Thanks a lot, lucky stars.

Monte Rio, 6.vii.80

double cross

He passes the hicktown ice cream parlor
where redneck teens hang out
smiles and disappears. . . .
he's worth taking a chance for.

I probe headlines
of newsvending machines
by the corner drugstore
and I'm just about to split
when he shows. We put out
weather reports . . . yes, it's
a nice day . . . his summer shirt's
open to the pubic rim
of his jeans . . . he's seventeen,
he says.

Eyes shift like gears . . . he's
hitching to Santa Rosa
he says with a tug
at his Marlboro
hand trembling as he looks
toward the mountains.

Too many fags in this town
he says.

I gaze at his hot features, the vein
pounding in his throat
as he preaches
against lust and sin.
He conquers them with the Bible.
Satan he calls it. I say
I'll see him sometime
and leave him to Jesus . . . who scored
first.

Monte Rio, 12.xi.80

the moronic plague

> *"I believe that homosexuality should be included with murder and other*
> *capital crimes so that the government that sits upon this land would be*
> *doing the executing."*
>
> —Dean Wycoff, "Moral Majority"

A deadly dullness sits
upon this land.   A fungus
    crawls in the pits of the body
infecting the crotch.
               It digs
deep, creating
a maddening itch and desire for release
which the disease inhibits.
               It works its way
from brain to sexual organs
taking over completely
till nothing's left of either. But
    the patient doesn't die.
          He becomes inspired!

In the grip of moronic fever
his eyes and facial muscles harden
his heart pumps ice-water,
he throws faggots in the fire.

The sound of professors burning
pleases the Moron soul.

God speaks on television
with a country accent: "Gimme
your money, suckers! And don't forget
your property. Sign
on the dotted line."
                            Electronic miracles
make the lame walk and the dumb talk.
But no miracle can make them think.

Millions fall victim to *Fungus Moronicus*.
Rival Morons shoot each other
in gangland style, warring cults from the **MORON CHURCH**
founded by Moroni, the soldier-prophet
who saw inhabitants on the moon
and sold moon real estate
                            to the faithful.

When hatred erupts in plague proportions
    the religious crazies rush forth
        in great numbers
            killing everyone.

Soon everybody's dead.
Nothing but the **BOOK OF MORON** remains.
They have hurled the H-Bomb
at pornography
trashed nature
wiped out sex.
At this point in his private
viewing studio **GOD**, who
has been watching the show
without a word, yawns and mutters.
"Well, damn *Me* if this isn't the most **BORING**
situation comedy I've *ever*
dreamed up! I'm glad
it's off the air."

And that's how the stupidest soap opera
in history
lost its ratings.

San Francisco, 8.iv.81

october

You drive to the park on a fresh fall day
cloud-and-sunshine, light and dark,
paths clogged with joggers and bikes,
stealthy cops stalking gays
around soccer teams on playing fields,
in latrines and behind bushes,
through Japanese gardens and Dutch tulips.
You drive to the seashore past stone windmill
where teenage surfer in black wetsuit
with yellow surfboard like seagod appears
mellow as peach under pastel skies
over flat beach rained on the night before,
pawprints of dogs, clawprints of gulls.

Prize Afghan frolics and rolls
in sand while master cries No, No!
snatches leash with a jerk of the hand.
The Farallones like phosphorous glow,
thrust of sedimentary rock from
frothy waves. Barefoot runners
puffing dash among cracked seashells
as white yacht among white sails floats.
Black man with thick black thighs
runs swiftly backwards then fast forward
unwinding self in a fierce sprint
knees chopping, hands sawing salt spray.
From dense clouds outbursts dazzling sun
stippling, dappling, spangling sea.
Young blonde lady rides roan mare
gently trots in calm curling tide
while fox terrier poops, prances away
with foxy look when I whistle to him.
Across beige beach cool breeze whips,
two tall young men approach, they're women
in windbreakers, slacks and short cropped hair.
Gulls patiently wait for apple core,
parliament of birds encircling blanket
peek and pounce when I heave it in air.

With faded jeans and bowie knife,
birdfeather in pocket, curly youth
stoops to forage pebbles on beach.
"You never know what you pick up," he says.

I nod and wonder: *double entendre?*
When time comes to change into pants
from nowhere people materialize
on horseback, foot, and helicopter:
out of the blue you're uncovered, stripped
bare when most free and innocent.
Dark clouds vanish, many more come,
variations on very October light.

San Francisco, 5.x.83

friendship

Are we living
in the same city?
Are we empty-handed, empty-minded
sacks of wind and dust? Believe me,
he writes, I'm your friend, in spite
of my failure to appear, my "broken"
promises. I lack
stamina to face
things. I answer: Ah,
yes, one changes, grows
bored, drops a lover, a friend. No,
he writes, he hasn't the courage to come
around. Vows to cure himself
of breaking his word. Signs, As ever,
Your Eternal Friend. Shows up
a year later. I
love you, he says sincerely, but
my fatigue is monumental. Can't
stay long, I have a dinner date. You
should grow your sideburns longer. I'll
come back in a week. A year passes.
Out of the blue he writes: If not
temporal, I'm your eternal friend.
Are we poets or what? Who are we?
Anyway, I miss you. I wish
I could see you, talk to you,
grow close again. I reply:
I feel much better now
that I've given up hope.

San Francisco, 6.v.84

rescue remedy

1

From now on I want each moment
of roses and Ravel like a surge
of sound and sea cloudburst of harps
catching a glimpse of feeling
    momentarily escaping
    into the psychic sense
that holds and binds us
    in music and touch

I saw you in the rainbow
shopping for organic flageolets
t-shirt and cutoffs revealing shots
of dazzling muscle as you bent over
    pleased to be living at this hour
    with so many of you laid out
    like a twelve-tone row
not a sewing machine or umbrella
        construct of need
    tingling my spine
        blinding creation
oh the felony of unbuttoned flies
assault and battery of good looks
    immorality of being alive
        orgasm of death crime of coming

2

I think these clouds are going to collide
with my thoughts. Will the Rescue Remedy
save me? the Star of Bethlehem? sweet
chestnut? the black pansy perhaps?
    will the mimulus help? for fear
    of known things such as heights
        or *other people?* will vervain
    protect me from those who have
strong opinions? and sweet chestnut
        from those who feel
they have reached the limit of their
    endurance? and
despite the larch that may guard me
from anticipating failure and refusing
to make a real effort to succeed

I'm thrown into reverse
by fear of gay massacre
and withering away
                before my time
    with a trendy disease.

3

Yes, poison is in. Everything
we eat drink see or fuck
        the air we breathe
        the sea we surf
even our cum gives birth to death.

    Brightnesse doth not fall from the Aire
    Queens must die young and faire
        Love, have Mercy on my Soul

All 38 remedies come in liquid concentrate form
    reputed to have a positive calming and
                stabilizing effect
in most stressful situations including
                nervousness anxiety anguish desperation
        just take a few drops of the Rescue Remedy
            for everyday stresses such as
                taking exams making speeches bad loans
                job interviews

    oak for those who struggle on despite despondencies
        olive for mental and physical exhaustion
            sapped vitality with no reserve
                mustard for deep gloom
    crab apple for those who feel something is not
                quite clean about themselves
    gorse for feelings of hopelessness and futility
        holly for negative feelings
            and a need for love

4

    organic rice cakes! unsalted millet!
        10 drops of chaparral! pau d'arco
    from Argentina! hawthorn berries and green
            Savoy cabbage leaves! will
        this remedy work for bad luck?
            bad dreams? will it heal

fanatic assassins on suicide missions?
godly nuts leveling
everything in sight
with hollow mechanical expressions?
will it free us to play
in sand and sun and swim
hot crotches together
with singing limbs?

ritual practices like
talking or praying to a plant
or making an offering before picking it
will raise one's consciousness

as we stroll on country paths
often a plant will greet us with a loud scent
shouting to us that the sense
of smell has a direct link with
the subconscious mind as Proust
has proven in six volumes
of memory and lust
such herbs can be used in dream pillows
for closer touch with our
emotional depths
aromatic herbs such as mugwort sandalwood pennyroyal
rose bay sage/make your peace with them
they will take care of you
herbs have feelings too
don't kill them take bits and pieces
and leave the rest
don't mug the mugwort
be sage
toxins must go

wood betony for self-loathing skullcap for feeling absurd
slippery elm for difficulty in believing in others or self
gota kola for schizophrenia lemon balm for paranoia
(finding ourselves in places and life situations
we can't accept)
smoke tussilago with cannabis for inflamed ego
cascara sagrada for anal retention chickweed for gluttony
calamus to quit smoking and calm the nerves
(also treats scabies lice and crabs)
fo-ti-tieng for premature aging ginseng for potency

fu ling for fearfulness and feelings of insecurity
    buchu with uva ursi for the prostate gland
    echinacea for v.d. and the immune system
        burdock's an aphrodisiac
kava kava invokes deep sleep and full-length epic dreams
    and goldenseal's good for everything.

San Francisco, 9.x.84

medieval spectre

The kid is cute (quite innocent)
but horrified at his deviate lust
he threw himself from a topfloor window
broke his back and grew a moustache.

A boyfriend deflowered him but
technically he remains a virgin
no penetration having taken place
in the years of the plague.

A medieval spectre haunts sex.

San Francisco, 1985

in a café-bar

(*After Verlaine*)

Remember the café-bar crowded with pricks
With their stupid morals and straight loves, —dumb hicks!
Where we alone, we two, bore the label "queer."
But didn't give a shit and whacked it right there
Under their noses in fact (what a great joke
We played on them discreetly, veiled by the smoke
From our pipes: like Io fucking with Zeus)
Until our cocks, bursting with love-juice
From our manipulations, like a bomb
Under the table shot great jets of cum.

San Francisco, 1985

high school lover

slant blue gaze
high cheekbones   pouting lips
in bathroom mirror admiring
his astonishing features
and first moustache
(pastel smudge on upper lip)
small upturned nose
and luminous wide eyes
that attract wherever he goes
longing looks for those
superb thighs and tell
tale bulge of pleasure

doing homework
nodding in rhythm to some hot
jamming earphones
thick hair standing up a little
framing forehead ears face
bent over geometry
perfect buttocks
partly exposed
he lies on the floor
white gym socks soiled   tennis shoes torn
from rough wear of power slides
on skateboard with fiery blue
dragon and skullsword emblem
surface smeared by the city

withal a cheerful cherub
streetwise tender tough
ray of sunshine breakdancing
nude and high in bedroom
with laughter and bad breath
(pot beer cigarettes)
mouth full of fun
and kisses
half-child half-man
balanced in wild abandon
of anarchy
and hotblooded joy

in search of never ending touch
at times of need selling
the firm young flesh
for immediate satisfaction
and dollars
to quell the hunger
in growing cells
he grows and gladdens the heart
of girls and fatherly
lone men

San Francisco, 2.x.85

lost america

discs of lost america!   gray pearl saxophone
riffs of body & soul   & smoke gets in your eyes
stardust   blue heaven   as time goes by
musical comedy romance   of wanting to be
beautiful & great

the tenor sax digs deep in proustian key
unearthing mouldy sneakers   lockerrooms
pubic shadows   in chlorine pools
bare boythighs   and buttocks of
secret loves in fiery crackle   and static
of worn old platters   that patina of sound

sound & smell filtered thru   pubescence
waking fearful pleasure-petals
in the groin   discovered thrill
of come

sweet coffee smell   of dusky docks
i cover the waterfront   where are you?
old songs stuck in the memory   desires lingering
the east river crawls   across the page

Athens, 1965/San Francisco, 1985

old black remington

Old black Remington noiseless, what shall we type today?
is there room among your keys? for real feelings? cool moods?
I stare out the window at Mutual Life; then examine my palm.
headline slopes down depressed but the fateline, ah, it's
still good, still strong, though at the wrist a chain of
snarled emotions tells the story, and the lifeline's still scary,
so much left unsaid undone, old poets dying, o river run,
Kerouac Patchen Pound, and yes they will stay fresh for ages
having pierced the dark with lasers of insight, cut through
black voids with shapely music, enlightened our doldrums,
lifted us, made us laugh and rage . . . oh, what about me,
mount of Apollo, am I immortal? hmmm, soon be worthless bone,
a book, a shade, a poem in secondhand bookstore, a bit dusty, sure;
some sexy youth will praise my name but I won't care, so here's
another poem, and thanks, old black Remington noiseless.

San Francisco, 1972/1985

unknown destination

1

Fifteen men are in love with him.
One is Ma Bell.
Another flies in from Switzerland,
heads a chemical firm.

"He just wants to see me smile.
I smile,
He gives me a Mercedes.
Flies back on the next plane
without touching me."

Fifteen men who run the world.
He runs them. They lick his toes.

2

In the house of glass you can see through
to the floor below. And the floor below
the floor below. All glass. You can see
down to the silver and gold plumbing.

On the walls are plates of gold.
You can't see through them.
The banker offers his house and his bank.
With devastating charm the boy barely
acknowledges them. It is his due.

Industrialists, tycoons, politicians—he
pisses on them. This inspires reverence.
They fall to their knees, content with a taste,
a smell, a close view of his "parts." They whimper
and lose consciousness.

3

Here is his leather pouch.
Bulging with green.
He will spend it tonight.
He will spend it on a party.
MDA. Quaaludes. Cocaine.
Brownies. Columbian. Boys.

Fifteen world leaders
are mad for him.
His nineteenth birthday party
will be an international event.

4

"The man I love must love only me.

I'll put a chastity belt on him.
Once a year I'll unlock the belt. Make love
for one night. He must wait all year
for this. Must not see anyone.
Must not jack off. Just pee
through the hole.

I'll make him rich. Seven thousand a month.
Just to wait for me. If he breaks out of that belt
and fucks anyone else
                              I'll scalp him.
I'll tear off his nose. Rip out his jaw.
Half a face. That's what I'll leave.
I have a fourth in Tai Kwan-do.
Learned it in Korea.

Listen.
A trick last week—
after we partied I fell asleep
My house boy wakes me. 'He's
got your billfold,' he says.

I go to the living room. In the darkness I see him
by the window. I switch on the light. He's removing the
green. 'I wouldn't do that,' I say. He grins. 'What
are ya gonna do about it?' 'I don't like that,' I say.
I rip off his nose. I hand it to him.

He stands there with his nose in his hand.
Screaming.

'Call an ambulance!' he screams.

'Get out or I'll rip off your jaw!' I say.

He runs out, bleeding all over my Persian rug.

I woulda gave him the green if he'd of asked.

He was beautiful. Flawless. His face *was* flawless.

I'm looking for just one man
who really loves me."

5

His striped t-shirt is in tatters.
Tight white cords smudged and stained.

He hangs around the café till closing time.

He will buy the café, he says. Hire
the most beautiful boys.
Wants us to know he is powerful.
The most powerful force on the planet.
He pulls the strings behind the leaders.
Governments wait for his orders.

Soon he must leave on his private plane
for an unknown destination.

San Francisco, 1.ii.8

homo

Amber lamplight on the
Green canal. Leaves falling
Into the ripples. Gulls
Settle on bridges. In Amsterdam
I lean from the attic window
Under the eaves in this
16th Century brick house, the
Trap door pulls up and
Conceals the bedroom, an Anne Frank
Dutch device that saved the
Lives of many Jews. The
Bedroom also contains
A meditation room with
Fine Persian carpets and glass
Roof, forming a triangle.
Beside me on the futon lies
The young student who followed me
After my readings and seminar
At the university. We
Made love all night. He is tall
With enormous gray luminous eyes.
Next day at the Van Gogh museum
Before the drawings of old peasants
In the Brabant he touches the glass
Frames: "This could be my grandmother. See
This old man — my grandfather!" He was born
There, his family still lives there. He
Explains that nothing has changed
Since Vincent depicted them. His
Grandparents still bend and
Dig up turf and potatoes, the
Faces in the drawings are
Suddenly alive, close, real.
Germans on the border in Holland,
Dutch for hundreds of years. He
Is the only one to attend a
University — vivid applecheeked
Skin glows, large eyes shine
With the flame of Rimbaud and Van Gogh.

We lean over original letters from Vincent
To Theo under the glass case and he reads
Them and translates for me as we attract

Mild stares of curiosity by our clearly
Intimate pleasure in each other and our love
For this moment together—older man
With gray temples, short and dark,
Extremely tall youth with shock
Of honey hair, enjoying each other immensely.

Richard, I want to fix you in this poem
As firmly as Van Gogh fixed your ancestors
In his immortal sketches. I pray for this.

On the border, speaking Flemish, Dutch and German,
The people in the drawings like those of Brueghel or Bosch
Before them are closed, thick-featured, earthen, suspicious,
The bodies heavy-limbed. They've never changed. We lean over
The letters and he reads them aloud in a
Resonant deep voice and translates them for me.

*

Teeming with youth these northern cities
Of Europe stir the nesting urge
Though not for the opposite
Gender, as one might suppose. Fresh-
Faced and enticingly well-
Made, with voluptuous
Lips and ruddy pale complexions,
Eyes the color of sky.
Young males with deep
Voices and applecheeked schoolboy
Ways have the flirtatious air and
Smooth skin of babes. But
Nothing girlish, believe me, or
Babyish about their hard
Bodies and often prominent
Protuberance between
Agile legs; the magic
Wand keeps them saucy, they
Sing in the streets of Zurich or
Amsterdam eager as kids
With darting eyes. Their trousers cling
Skintight to knifesharp thighs. Nothing
Can stem the longed-for same-sex need.
No matter what man-made laws may cause
In suffering. Wherever you go

The tide of sexuality swells
For same-sex love. With few exceptions
Most countries shut hearts and minds
Against it, slam a dike or dam
On nature. Well, this may work with water
But not the sexual tide. In
The Philippines blackmail attends
Each act of "affection," and
Extortion and deportation greet
The unwary tourist. Rackets
Flourish where unjust laws prevail.
Once the land of free and easy
Love between males, now it's a trap.
In the Moslem world where the Rubaiyat
And Sufi poems extolled boy-love
The fundamentalist police
Chop noses, hands, feet, necks and dicks
Off for this universal need.
In the Soviet Union and its iron bloc
Torture, exile and slavery
Greet "decadent bourgeois acts"
Like tenderness of men
For men, women for women, as if
Sex could be legislated and made
Politically correct. No head
Is screwed on straight. *Chez nous*
In the USA Gay men and boys
Are bashed and killed with impunity
In the name of *God*, no less. The world
Has gone berserk with politics
And sick, depraved religion. Murder,
Their lingua franca, prevails. Nuts
Quote the Bible and Koran
Convincing us we're better off dead
And try to prove it as fast as they can.
In Rumania if you're caught with your pants
Down in *flagrante* you can tell the police
That your Rumanian comrade was buying them.
The young men will peel for American jeans.
We live under dictatorship
Whether of God or man.
Stalin is said to have deported
All Russian homosexuals
To the Arctic Circle, Tschaikowsky
Murdered by the Czar

For an affair with a young
Prince. The imperial doctor injected him
With typhus—to avoid a scandal.
Swan Lake and *Sleeping Beauty*
Could not save him. *Eugene Onegin*
And *Pique Dame* could not have a sacred
Hair of his beard. The Czar wept.
No other course presented itself.
(The Empire must be maintained.)
Russia's greatest composer martyred
For homosexuality.
Gogol, "Mother of the Russian Novel,"
Also involved with a prince, died
Young, thus avoiding homocide.

    How many homosexuals
    Would Rexroth have exiled to Siberia?
    How many Jews would Pound
    Have gassed at Auschwitz and Buchenwald?
    How many Otto René Castillos
    Can Guatemala burn at the stake?
    How many Roque Daltons
    Can El Salvador liquidate?
    How many major poets
    Can condone mass murder and torture?
    How long can civilization
    Stamp its boot on the human face?

          *

Living below the poverty line
Having dedicated my life
To the Muse I travel
From San Francisco to Amsterdam,
Zurich and back (paid all ways
To read my poems, put up in hotels,
Third-class, grungy, cheap) and earn
Less than the cost of plane-fare—strange
Profession, or calling, rather.
Rewarded mostly by shy smiles, a
Schoolboy now and then with misty
Eyes and hero-worship who
Follows us to a café, writes
His name, address: "If you return . . .
Perhaps we'll meet again? . . ." He

Hopes you'll answer his letters. Will
Some dream come true, change
Your life and his? This
Happened to Auden and Verlaine.
In the wings waits some raw Rimbaud,
Some talented, arrogant youth who'll
Turn your life inside out with
Ecstasy and suffering. Yes,
Auden's Rimbaud did that
To him and me. After two years
He cruelly refused to bed with Auden
Who turned homicidal with rage
And jealousy: "I was forced to know
What it's like to feel oneself the prey
Of demonic powers, in both the Greek
And Christian sense, stripped
Of self-control and self-respect,
Behaving like a ham-actor in
A Strindberg play." How
Can biographers know the facts
Third-hand of what we felt
And did, and what we said or who
Loved, envied, undermined, betrayed
Whom? Who was the villain, who
The victim? The Superstar
Can do no wrong, the lesser shines
More dimly, fades, and sputters out
Into a black hole as time forgives
The one whose words still blaze with light
Into a future century
His life and deeds remote from truth.

*

"Mad, bad and dangerous to know,"
Wrote Lady Caroline Lamb in her diary
The night she first met Lord Byron. He
Had no use for prudes and said so—
He refused to compromise
With social reticence on sex.
(In Venice when Shelley asked
Why he was always surrounded by rough
Young men Byron replied: "What I earn
With my brains I spend on my arse." Shelley
Left.) Byron's memoirs were

Destroyed by his English publisher.
Too outrageous. Too obscene.
His journals and letters reveal that he
Had incestuous fun with his half-sister
And describe a party they both attended:
"Countesses and ladies of fashion left
The room in droves," he wrote. But many
More threw themselves at his feet—wives
And daughters of the nobility,
Governesses and servant girls.
He threw himself at the feet
Of gondoliers and stable-boys.
Today only rock and film stars compare
With his effect on the public. Shelley
Wrote: "An exceedingly interesting person
But a slave to the vilest and most vulgar
Prejudices, and mad as the winds."
By which, presumably, he meant
His undisguised love of working-class boys.
Shelley, alas, was a frightful prude
For all his anarchistic faith.
(And probably a closet-case, too.)
Byron in every act and breath
Was a flaming iconoclast to the bone.
Revolutionary for human rights
Centuries ahead of his time.
Of poor Keats he wrote rather callously:
"A Bedlam vision produced by raw pork
And opium." Matthew Arnold wrote
Of all three: "Their names will be greater than
Their writings." Their memory lingers on.
Byron practised what he preached:
"Ordered promiscuity."
He found it most in Italy
The most sensual and sensible
Of Western nations, the country of love
In all its forms, and the country of beauty.
Oppose this to England, the country of duty
And you will understand Byron completely.
In the Coliseum he once invoked
Nemesis to curse his wife's
Lawyer—with great success, it seems,
For later the man cut his own throat.
What all the biographies skirt
When they describe his exploits we

Can now fill in: when they write of his women
"With great black eyes and fine figures—fit
To breed gladiators from" they don't
Tell us how much he enjoyed their sons,
The gladiators he went down on.

*

Ever since Justinian
Who wanted more power over the Church
Fifteen-hundred years ago
Passed the first law against same-sex love
With the perfectly logical excuse
That homosexuality
Caused earthquakes, we have seen
Religion and politics
Condemn gay sex as crime and sin.
The law had no effect upon
The population; they behaved
As if the Emperor had gone mad.
But some prominent bishops lost
Their bishoprics and balls,
Were tortured and exiled. Many more
Churchmen were castrated and died.
The best historian of the time,
Procopius, states these harsh laws
Served as a pretext against the Greens
(The Emperor's circus opposition)
Or those "possessed of great wealth or
Who happened to have done something
Which offended the rulers." We know the empress
Theodora used the laws against
Personal enemies. When a young Green
Made some nasty remark about her
She charged him with homosexuality,
Had him castrated without trial.
Procopius says that this cruel law
Was invented chiefly to extort money
From the victims among whom were numbered
Pagans, unorthodox Christians, astrologers.
All Constantinople turned against
Theodora and Justinian
On this matter, as did other
Imperial cities. The Church itself
Was a prime target of the civil law

And played no part in its enactment.

Later the Church got into the act.
The Spanish Inquisition threw
Faggots into the fire to burn
Witches and other heretics,
Especially the unconverted Jew.
Thus for a mad millennium
Or two the world has been in the grip
Of the criminally insane:
Neros, Caligulas, Justinians,
Torquemadas, Savonarolas,
Stalins, Hitlers, Mussolinis,
Cromwells, Falwells and Khomeinis.

*

Turning the last page of the calendar
I read the quotation for
December 1984: "If
You want a picture of the future,
Imagine a boot stamping on
A human face forever." Orwell.
I've lived to see it. From
The Spanish Civil War to this
Month, witnessing on a global
Scale the March of crime, a
Technicolor horror worse
Than the sterile murders on
Your TV screen (cosmetic).

Antisemitism is
An exceptional folly
In the roster of lunacy

Wrote Kenneth Rexroth. On the very
Next page he commits "an exceptional
Folly" with homophobic rot.
Having criticized Pound's antisemitism
Rexroth erupts with equally gross
Hatred of "American Fairies."
"Homosexuality
is the revolt of the timid," he writes
With the same penetrating
Insight Pound showed for the "yids."

Rexroth has his "fairies" to kick
Around but admires the Jews. Well, what's
So timid about the Army of Lovers
Or Alexander the Great? What
About the drag queens who fought the police
On Christopher Street? What about
Julius Caesar? Lawrence of Arabia?

Homophobia is
An exceptional sickness
In psychopathology
Akin to antisemitism
And Negrophobia

*

Collaged bits of reality
From various points on the planet.
Testimonials to shame. Our poets
Contribute to oppression.
Ridicule the innocent. Our
"Enlightened" poets goosestep
With swastika or hammer and sickle,
Condescending and patronizing
While praising universal love.
Love in the abstract. On
Individual humans they spit.
Abuse and torture of the innocent
By verbal vivisection
Is cruel and wanton as
Laboratory experiments
On helpless animals
By well-meaning but dense doctors
Believing beasts don't suffer. Does
It ever occur to them they may be
Wrong? Ego blinds them. They're
Gods and demigods. Poets
And doctors dispense their pills
And nostrums for the good of the race
Often making matters worse.

Remember the drag queens in Greenwich Village
Who fought the cops with their fists and any
Available objects? They
Sparked Gay Liberation, an

Unprecedented event
Equivalent to the Warsaw Ghetto
Uprising of the Jews against
Vastly superior Nazi might.
Once ignited the spirit
Does not die. Israel rose
From the ashes of the Warsaw Ghetto,
Gay Rights rose from the ghetto
On Christopher Street. It
Is better to die fighting than
To live on your knees. Krishna was right
To admonish Arjuna when he refused
To fight his kin to the death. His brothers
Would have finished him off.
Pacifism does not work. I say this
Sadly. We're up against
Ignorant armies and must
Defeat them or die.

*

Love is not a crime;
If it were a crime to love
God would not have bound
Even the divine with love.
                    (*Carmina Burana*)

*

The Greek and Roman poets were Gay:
Virgil, Ovid, Horace, Catullus,
Martial, Juvenal, Tibullus.
Where would our culture be without them?
(Gay-basher Rexroth, Jew-baiter Pound
Through verbal abuse contributed
To genocide and fagocide —
Much as the Moral Majority
Sees God's punishment on the victims
Of AIDS, blaming the patient for
The disease. Who'll cure the Moral
Morons of terminal stupidity?)
Euripides at seventy-two
Spoke of his love for Agathon
Who was forty: "A fine Autumn
Is a beautiful thing indeed!"

Anacreon, who "delighted in
Young men" confided, "I'm old,
There's no denying it. So what?
Among young satyrs I can dance as well
As old Bacchus himself!" When asked
Why his poems were always about young boys
And not about gods he replied: "That
Is because young boys *are* our gods."
He was a pleasure-loving, wine-loving
Boy-loving poet. "Whatever Plato
May say it is unlikely that
Handsome Alcibiades,
After sleeping beneath the same blanket
As Socrates, arose intact
From his embraces," Lucian wrote.
Dying at eighty in the gymnasium,
His head on the knees of a boy, Pindar
Seemed happily asleep
When the attendant came to wake him.
Sophocles at fifty-five
Confessed that despite his age
He often fell in love with boys.
And Aristophanes wrote
That the favorite occupation
Of sophists and intellectuals
Was to make the rounds of gymnasiums
To pick up boys.
They went to their lessons
Accompanied by their little friends.
At twelve a boy already
Appealed to them, says the great playwright.
They considered him in the prime of life
Between sixteen and seventeen.
At eighteen he was over the hill.

*

To have a father of some handsome lad
Come up and chide me with complaints like these:
Fine things I hear of you, Stilbonides,
You met my son returning from the baths,
And never kissed, or hugged, or fondled him,
You, his paternal friend! You're a nice fellow!
                    (*The Birds*, Aristophanes)

*

And Addeus of Macedonia
(ca. 323 B.C.):

*When you meet a lad who catches your fancy, do not waste any time trying
to disguise your intentions, but immediately grab hold of his balls with both
your hands. Do not mince words, or say, "I respect you' or 'I would like to be
like a brother to you,' for that sort of thing will only stand in your way.*

*

Men are not gods
what you think
is somebody's
tall shadow over
your mind and
sometimes it looks
like a cross

*

Thought comes from the Devil?
   Good . . . to die?   "Thought
crimes" police
read one Book, distortions
       (5000 years of it)   brook
no argument.   Each word   beyond
Reason.   Beyond Thought.
      makes me puke.   hold views
of street-corner thugs   dumb hicks.
      Xianity for bucks. TV
evangelists screw   the simple-minded.

*

Zurich/Amsterdam, November, 1984/*San Francisco*, October, 1985

in november

In November I lost my food stamps, the computer said I did not exist

In November I lost my best friend who said I did not exist

In November I lost my manuscripts and felt as if I did not exist

In November I sent 2 postcards to my mother who wrote back saying she had not heard from me and DID I STILL EXIST?

In November I paid the telephone bill and received a final notice for the non-payment

In November my girlfriend accused me of unreality and infrequency with a tendency to dematerialize on weekends and holidays even Jewish ones and stormed out leaving a sinkful of dirty dishes and linen blackened by her feet, souvenirs of blood and tobacco burns

In November my checks bounced, mail stopped arriving, the toilet clogged, the cat choked, my poems were rejected, I got worms, the clap and psoriasis of the anus, all I needed was an earthquake to prove my destiny was not to be overlooked, and one was long overdue according to the latest reliable heavenly and scientific sources

In November I looked for all my published works in City Lights Bookstore and found only my early translations of Belli, I did not exist on the bookshelves altho' a thesis to prove that I did exist was written by some kid in Arkansas, 300 pages that nobody ever read called *Orpheus Unacclaimed: Harold Norse, So What?*

In November I gave a poetry reading which was so well advertised one day in advance that 5 people actually came, 4 of them drunk and cantankerous, the fifth had lost his way to the toilet, and one of the drunks kept asking, "Tell me how to win! I'm sick of being a loser!" and I answered from years of eminence: "Be invisible!"

In November when I crossed the street with the light a grayhaired man in a Cadillac looking like Spiro Agnew tried to run me down and swore because he missed me, something about Law and Order

In November I screamed at the neighbors upstairs who played stereo hard rock all day and night that crashed thru the floorboards but they said I was a liar it was music not noise and I was a fink for complaining and the one who practiced karate over my bedroom from midnite until 3 am said why didn't I take up yoga and gain deliverance from bad karma so they went on playing their rock and hammering on the floor and stomping in boots and breaking bricks until 4 am as if I did not exist and

In November I gave thanks for all my blessings without a turkey, with one good ear, high cholesterol, 59¢, 145 lbs, and 2 good balls.

your crooked beauty . . .

Your crooked beauty, Hugo,
maims us. You are all
that hurts. Taking us
off guard with your virile
grace, good looks. But
you're crooked, you're bad news.
So you brought in the new
year that already had no good
in it for me, exiled
from a loveless country, took
what you wanted from its hiding place
among dirty clothing—30,000 liras—
then ground your teeth. I saw madness,
Hugo, death in your heroic
stony features, bones more enormous
than clubs, murderous jaws, the unseeing
statue stare of senselessness. Now
what's the use? At that price
your beauty is too expensive, leaving
neither regard for feelings
nor the rent.

Rome, New Year's Day, 1954

in the cafés

(After Cavafy)

In the cafés, smoky and noisy,
and the loud bars with their screeching
and punk rock madness that deafens me
I'm bored. I've never cared for
these trashy joints. But they're good for drowning
persistent echoes of Keith. Quite suddenly
he left, without warning, for the proud
owner of two Porsches and a big house in Marin,
a hot tub and swimming pool. Keith, I don't doubt,
has tender feelings for me still. Yet I'm sure
he has learned to develop tender feelings
for a man with two Porsches. I live

in squalor. But what stays fresh
and sweet, what keeps me going, is
that for two whole months I had Keith,
the most desirable youth
on Polk Street. None
could compare with him. In my drab flat
with a view of trash cans and parking lots
he lived with me, a warm
affectionate lover—there was surely more to him
than meets the eye—mine not for a mansion
and two fast Porsches.

San Francisco, 29.ix.85

verlaine died here

How many times I have passed this house
watched the curtains against the shutters
and the plaque on the gray façade
telling the year of your death
Verlaine
in this room above the bookshop on the
rue Descartes—ailing street
of sad *clochards**. . . .
I have stood thinking
of your hurricane of junk and mud
the noise of cafés and buses and dripping walls
with that half-hearted paradise at the end
wondering who is behind those closed windows
a laundress perhaps
someone to whom your name is only a name
like you stuck on that sandbar where voyages stop

*tramps, bums

to walt and hart from hal

Your brown book stashed
beside my spear from Africa,
your book, Hart, with cryptic messages
of trade on rotting piers, of men
on lone patrol for kisses, gleam of bellies.
Your book, Hart, whose torn-off spine
counts the years, like ringed trunks of oak.
It was my bible. I kept it all these years,
my hand in yours, in Walt's, crossing
Brooklyn Ferry or under the choiring steel
cables of Brooklyn Bridge! Walt's *Leaves of Grass*
first printed there on Brooklyn Heights,
your street, Hart! Then to eternity—
from the *Orizaba* deck you leapt
into the sea. We never met.
Three years later, rapt with awe,
I wept as I gazed from your window
over the Bridge, where my professor lived
in your mythic flat! That year
I fingered Keats's hair in Morgan's Library,
curled under my touch! Your words, Hart,
were carved in *The Bridge* on the River that is East.
I caught the tune beneath the cabled spires
and harped the selfsame theme—the *Bridge!*

4/15/2000
San Francisco

This is a later-revised version of "To Walt and Hart," published in 1989 in
"An Ear to the Ground"

ready-made

I transport from the canvas unsteady dissonance in the blue!
I heard in a dream about Marcel Duchamp.
Was he speaking from the other side of the Great Glass heavenly Dada
    windows?
Marcel agreed to "bring a little intelligence into painting . . . this
    turpentine intoxication," he scoffed.

On Sundays friends gathered in the garden at Puteaux
Léger, Picabia, Metzinger, Apollinaire, Reverdy,
"with almost juvenile good humor. One almost forgets that
at that time nobody was anybody," recollected Duchamp.

"Fascinating frivolity and beautiful illusions!"
chortled Ribemont-Dessaignes. They behaved like schoolboys on
    holiday,
playing pranks, games, enjoying slapstick. Fame and public image had
    not yet arrived. Marcel could not stand them when they did.

Like Picabia he demanded unlimited freedom
hated groups and schools, repetition of style.
"Art is useless and impossible to justify!" declared Picabia.

    A wild ungovernable infant
      riding its hobbyhorse
    around the world, trampling
      the pompous beneath its hooves
    DADA was just arriving.

Marcel drew logical conclusions:
he painted a moustache on the Mona Lisa,
an act as pointless as suicide

to which he was utterly indifferent.
His heart belonged to Dada.
He painted all values into a corner:
the urinal is the good, the beautiful, the true.

Marcel was in love with bad taste:
he invented a way of being absent
that Rimbaud never suspected.
"Duchamp is destined to reconcile art and the people,"
said the unknown Apollinaire.
But were the people ready for ready-mades?

Marcel arrived in New York with a glass ball full of Paris air.
It was a gift for a friend. His "explosions in a shingle factory,"
as one critic dubbed *Nude Descending A Staircase* in 1913,
shocked everyone. Marcel was famous. With ironic humor
he detached himself on his condescending staircase
where with lofty vanity he observed,
"Without vanity we should all kill ourselves."
He had no other deadly sin.

In 1915 he exhibited a bicycle wheel mounted on a stool.
a bottle rack and a urinal titled *Fountain*.
The ready-mades became works of art, he said, as soon as he declared
         them so: looking at an object made it art.
He signed the urinal R. Mutt (the name of a firm of sanitary engineers).
The urinal achieved immortality.

> Meanwhile Gertrude Stein
> was busy in her own studio
> inventing Hemingway
> and Virgil Thomson;
> when she created Ezra Pound
> she frowned, screamed
> and threw the rough draft away.

"Remarks," said Miss Stein, "are not literature."

Stein and Duchamp took the 20th Century for a ride
on the merry-go-round of painted horses and calliope tunes
of childhood where they play in our memory still

The song of Rrose Sélavy.
The love song of R. Mutt.
The pigeons-on-the-grass song.
Song of unsteady dissonance.

Chanson of the urinal.
The pissoir melody.
Marcel Duchamp in drag
as Rrose Sélavy
camps through the studios
of friends and foes.

Marcel and Man Ray play a game of chess lasting forty years.

seismic events

Scientists predict that California will have a major earthquake of devastating proportions sometime within the next few decades. Now is the time to prepare yourself, your family and your home for such an event. Do not rely on others, it is your responsibility to be prepared. A major earthquake will tax local government and emergency response agencies, probably beyond their capability. It is imperative that each citizen be prepared for such an event.

—Pacific Bell Family Plan

1.

In Venice West on the Pacific Rim
I lived among palm trees and canals,
abandoned oil wells and *faux* Corinthian
columns for liquor stores, launderettes
and body builders in fiery sunsets.
Arnold Schwarzenegger, age 19,
jogs on the beach with me, we joke
as we jog and keep in step and flex
our muscles. Pumping iron at Gold's
Gym we define our *gluteus maximus*,
latissimus, pectorals and abdominals
—glutes, lats, pecs and abs we call them.
Superman biceps build Arnold's awesome
icon image like a great skyscraper.
The incomparable future Hollywood Herculcs
lifts the world on his massive shoulders,
head in the sky, mind over matter.

2.

Hollywood sinks in the sunset
with special effects, multimillion-dollar
productions with a cast of thousands.
Superman Arnold lifts tectonic plates
like weights and, with a mighty heave
of gargantuan muscles, he hurls them
beyond the Pacific rim to Antarctica
where they'll bother him and us no more.

3.

Earth strikes without warning, dishes smash,
dogs bite their owners and run amok
in packs gone wild. A hospital falls
like a deck of cards. A handsome youth
bears a sign: REPENT! THE END IS NEAR!

He's nude except for a long trench coat
slightly ajar, but he's no flasher.
His legs are hairy, his eyes are dazed
by religion, his hair is long and blond.
He looks like an angel. I smile at him.
In righteous horror of sin and crazed
by his faith he glares and runs out of there
to save body and soul in The Last Days.

4.

¼ of a million people
cry in the streets, clutching
family photos, heirlooms, kids.
Buildings collapse in heaps
of wood, plaster and glass.
Bridges buckle, traffic signals
go crazy, freeways crumble
as TV commercials squawk
on transistors their relentless ads
until death do them part.
They perish like smashed toys.
The Loma Prieta quake of '89
rattles our bones and shivers our timbers.
You can't say, "Seen one seen 'em all."
Every quake shakes you up forever.
I rush under a lintel and witness
a miracle! His head between
a paper tray and TV, my plaster
Jesus falls unscathed on the floor.
His virgin mother's aura slips,
her halo cracks and in a heap
of cheap plaster she litters the floor.
Brittle shards are all that's left.
I sweep her away as The Big One creeps
closer
        closer
                closer
                        closer.

5.

At age 6 I saw the Atlantic Ocean
spill into the streets of Surf Avenue
rolling over the beach in Coney Island.
I screamed when I saw my first tidal wave!

Mother thought our time had come.
Please God don't drown me, I prayed.
At age 8 I saw an eclipse of the sun,
darkness at noon in Scranton, Pa.
"The end of the world is near," cried some.
Beneath the Acropolis my cottage shook,
trembling and swaying at the foot of the hill.
On Mount Etna I stared at flaming hot rock
and survived 3 quakes in San Francisco.
Star-gazing in Brooklyn at age 14
I sailed out the window in the dark night
of the soul into a circle of light
to the stars in an ocean of swirling bodies
dying in one world, living in another.
It was like fainting and waking up
in a strange place with a déjà vu
or hallucination, to which I was prone
with intimations of death in life
and life after death. William Blake
was familiar to me at age 16,
with his swooning bodies and mystic visions.
I saw many through the mind's eye.

6.

Have no fear, saith the Lord, you have Me.
By Jesus we've been *had*—by His *Word!*
Words fasten in the brain like clamps,
like the cold stare of the shark's bold eye,
the great white bombshaped body of death.

7.

A ruthless dictator pounces
on a helpless country, seizes assets,
oil and women, raping them,
then dashing out their babies' brains.
Armageddon! screams the world.
Economies waver. Oil and gold
skyrocket, nations mobilize.
Fanatics howl: "It's the end-time!
Only *we* shall be saved! Sinners, *die!*"
I go home half-inclined to pray.

8.

In a convulsive shift of events,

holding a remnant of faith
on a sliding scale of disasters
unprecedented in scope,
I feel the ground move
under my feet. I reel
and cling to a straw
in the wind, a reed
in the sea. Is this it?
snuffed like the friend
whose coronary struck
him dead before he hit
the floor (he never knew
what hit him), drooling
in darkness. O let us depart
in peace! quick, quick—O Christ!—
from plague, quake, cancer, stroke,
accident or heart attack.

9.

In Greenwich Village, World War Two,
a GI wandered through late-night streets,
with tears streaming down his ruddy cheeks.
A farmboy in olive drab, distressed,
he cried, "Battle fatigue!" and wept like a child.
"I can't stand mom or dad or flag!
The Germans, Italians and Japanese
treated me better than my own people!
I must be nuts! I love the enemy!
I'm a traitor!" "Hush," I murmured.
"The only top secret you gave away
was love." He stared as if lightning struck,
then kissed me on the lips and fled.

10.

The sweet babyfaced GI didn't wish
to hate and fear and kill. He got
F-Reactions stamped on his record
(discharged for "Feminine Reactions"—i.e.,
"queer"). They drummed him out on his rear.
"You're no traitor, kid," I said.
"You gave no military secrets away,
only your heart, betraying none.
You loved your enemy, like Jesus taught."
That's when he soul-kissed me and fled.

"Even at the moment of its utmost splendor
human life hangs at the edge of a precipice,"
Sophocles said; i.e., in an *augenblick*
you're dead. The ring of fire jolts us
from our routine days. We jump
out of our skin and glimpse eternity
and fall back into our routine daze.

An old man listens to Borodin.
The Polovetsian Dances throbs in his blood.
He recalls his youth when he danced as a bowman,
clad in silk tights and a blue silk blouse,
arching his back as he leaps across the stage
in the Yakovlev Russian Ballet, New York,
at the Metropolitan Opera House.
Fire storms in his veins and slowly
he rises and sees himself again,
handsome, blackhaired, with sinewy thighs,
a muscular youth as he soars aloft,
cries out to his vanished youth and dies.

13

At age 7 in Scranton I pick up stray coal
in the railroad yard. A ragged old bum
with grizzled gray beard and bleary eyes
grins toothlessly as he bends down
and presses his mouth on mine and sloshes
his tongue around. I struggle and break
away and run home, retching and crying.
With the garden hose I wash out my mouth
again and again and wash away tears.
Sick with disgust I can't tell anyone.
In the evening smelling sweet soft-coal smoke
of the locomotive on the Erie tracks
I hear the train whistle wail and moan
and yearn to travel far from home.

14

"It's like being freed from a savage
and unruly master," Socrates said
of old age and the loss of sexual
desire. But it never stops for some.

It slips beneath the skin and lurks
like a cat crouching under a car, waiting
to scurry to another hiding place,
where it crouches and broods and sleeps.

15.

From a distance of years
he sees his old affairs
more clearly. He can't feel them
as he did in the heat of desire.
He views them through a glass darkly,
flickering like silent films,
tear-jerking and sentimental,
altered with mixed emotions
as though happening to another.

16.

Puberty hits like a tidal wave,
old age like a seismic shudder.
Tsunami sweeps us to creepy deeps.
Heartsick, achy, ach! Old bones,
I cry, you got bad attitude!
So what, you got pubic needs
you couldn't change. It was nature,
not you, when you started to stare
at other boys in locker rooms.
Nude, shy and scared, you knew
you didn't choose it. It chose you.
"I is another," said Rimbaud.

17.

Walt Whitman, William Blake, Hart Crane
flashed into my mind like Northern lights.
Rimbaud and Baudelaire swept into town
and Billie Holliday sang *Strange Fruit*
about black men swingin' from a poplar tree.
We might have hung there like strange fruit,
white, queer, straight, Beat, and I, half-Jew.

18.

Farewell, Rodney, you never reached 40,
handsome dancer, acrobat, snake-charmer,
ravaged by plague, your death was surreal:
your obit and photo beside the news item

of a woman who died at 104,
preparing to enter her first beauty contest!
You'd have loved it, Rodney! O ANGEL OF LIGHT!
RODNEY PRICE DIES OF AIDS-RELATED CAUSES.
We are left with Priceless memories.

19.

Arrested mid-flight with top-hat and cane
soaring onstage with effortless ease,
"He was meant to do flips in the air,
not lay in bed shriveling up!"
mourned his flaxen-haired fellow-Angel,
designer, dancer, collaborator,
who was always with him from the start.
The century ends with a holocaust—
contamination of the blood with love.

20.

quakes   floods
volcanoes   tornadoes
hurricanes   typhoons
fire storms   desert storms
genocide   homicide
ethnic "cleansing"
war   war   war
asteroids   humanoids
cataclysms   catastrophes
depressions   calamities
religious crazies
suicide cults
recessions
depressions
auto crash
plane crash
droughts
shootouts
killer kids
killer moms
killer dads
killer sons.

21.

Stripped in the morning sun I bask
and scan the papers, rub face and neck,
chest and arms with sunblock creme,

Sun Shade 15 Reduces UV
for aging skin. Paba protects you
(neck, brow, cheeks, legs, nose)
postponing decline and fall?
who knows?

22.

GOD MAY END UP IN COURT!
screams the headline about a gold mine.
Is it for all the crimes He committed?
Death sentence for every man and woman,
for children, lovers, birds and beasts,
for insects, fish, flowers and priests?
Who else would dream up such a world?
Was there ever a greater paranoid?
Believe in *Him*? a Nazi God?
No way. God may end up in court
for all his criminal indiscretions.
Ah, but the headline doesn't refer
to our white male chauvinist God
with a beard and dysfunctional family.
No, we're dealing with another God
of Australian primitives in a remote
Northern Territory where they
are undergoing seismic shock.
The elders of the Jawoyn tribe
have persuaded the government
to ban a mining project on their land
for platinum, gold and palladium.
Newcrest Mining Ltd. Co.
is suing them to lift the ban.
The government sided with the tribe.
The elders declare that digging the ground
disturbs the god Bula in the Sickness Country.
This sets off earthquakes and pestilence
and mass destruction, they insist.
Newcrest is therefore filing suit
in the Final Court of Appeal
which, mistakenly, it appears,
we have always believed to be God's.
God will be put on trial. Stay tuned.
This may prove to be a test case.

1993

Originally published in Journal, Contact 2 *(date unknown)*

the fire sermon

Those monks with matted hair
Those ancient priests half-nude
Who followed the Great One in his wanderings
They knew what childish passions keep from us
Who flex our fleshly intellect
Those monks   those ancient priests
Chanting in forests   disciplined in wastes
By roots of trees   by lakes
Calm in the dust storm   under the tiger's glow
Smiling at the long tooth   unmoved by the dancing girl
By raging thug   by elements
At the river bank   in the desert   on the mountain peak
Following wisdom   And at Gaya Head
The Blessed One gathering the monks around him said
"All things   O priests   are on fire"   and the world blazed
Eyes   lips   sex   blood   taste   birth   death
Liver   idea   pain   beautiful   blue
A huge bonfire of time and we in the center
"And the free man knows he is no more for this world"
O ancient priests   O countrymen

From Karma Circuit: 20 Poems and a Preface, 1966.

kali yug

        it's Kali Yug &
      the planet's expanding
    like a rotten orange ready to burst
the sun hasn't long to burn
& the asteroid
earthwards with deadly aim
            hurries to keep
its apocalyptic rendezvous
        the atlantic thrusts up
            an undersea mountain
pushing south america
& africa further apart
& bombs in the grip
            of lunatics

                    keep me awake
                       nights

what poem can influence
a munitions manufacturer?

poems can't deflect bullets
                    can't alter pain
or suffering
or make me for one instant forget
          that i will die

this is absurd i am not afraid
of death but the void i have not yet
filled with poems or
understanding

go
tell it on the
mountain
that the priest who mumbles a prayer
with soft waving hands
& jewelled crucifix
or the
proud grayhaired surgeon
                         indifferent
          to desperation
has more dignity
               or that you barely
               alive & overworked
with your thermometers & bedpans
& practical air
                    in your white
          nursecap
have less validity

man   man

is this a fantasy of ether
on a lifelong operating table?

Athens 1965

From Hotel Nirvana: Selected Poems 1953-1973.

the house is on fire!

Flowerchildren I'm with you   Diggers I'm with you too
    I'm with your frame of reference I'm with your Dharma
I want to share this Love that is pushing my Nerves out of my Skin
beating my head against the noise of London & the boys of London
        I want beautiful Personal Cities
no put-downs rules or regulations   throw the City wide open to Love
        Compassion not Walls of Fire
    not Philistine Hells
   no crooks fuzz sadistic Games
love communes need no moneygame to score Bread
    make lips available down on each other in final Twentieth
        Century gasp of Delight forget the Manufacturer's Label
    keep clear of the Gates of the Midland Bank
let's journey to Space beyond the London Planetarium
    travel on Astral feet
beyond Evil environment o love commune o god
                Freedom
will we ever make it? Freedom from Things & Persons
    Freedom from Thought if only to let Mind stop stop Time
        go naked freeflowing
        slip off our clothes
        act out our fantasies
        live out our dreams
but no
oh terrible lives spent in banks & offices & shops & soulless brick
    buildings!
    Dickensian solitudes of jails & basement kitchens!
   commercials of tube & poster!
    monstrous iniquities of a fucked-up century!
        heads of boys cut off from bleeding trunks in Viet Nam War!
          charred limbs of continuous war within ourselves
fedback to War fedback to Ourselves!
                    O CHRIST!
   WAR IN EVERY TONGUE! IN EVERY WORD!
I'M SICK OF WAR OF WORDS
     OUR OWN DOUBLETHINK MINDS
NOT KNOWING NOT KNOWING
     EVEN THE POEM A LIE!
   MAD UNDERTONES FORM JURASSIC SLIME IN OUR
    BONES!

    impossible Ultimata O Lao Tse!

have I alternatives under the Law
of Reciprocal Action?
stuck under stars
in Voids
in this nowhere Universe
I call my Self?

flaming naphtha & napalm soak the earth
    as I sit here writing poems in London
about the nastiness of Man
            THE HOUSE IS ON FIRE!

                                    & we go on
                                        talking

                                    London 1967

the gluteus maximus poems

Ah, sir, what are you fondling so fondly
    under the spray? You think you're
    unobserved, but your half-hard belies
     the macho pose — and you, sir, there
    in a corner at your locker, twisting
    your rod from view under a towel,
    a stiff curved bow of anxious meat.
    And you in the steam room, glancing
    at soggy newsprint, black
    and beautiful, fighting down
    a rising tool, it's no use, sweetie,
    desire will out, don't hide, let go!
    No one recruited you, forced you
    to love those muscular buttocks,
    smooth or hairy, those sculptured thighs
    you'd die for, live for, no one
    showed you how to crave with your soul
    the forbidden joy between the legs,
    to long for same sex, man and boy.
    It came announced by nature with
    pubescent awakening, born between
    your legs and eyes, your red red mouth
    desiring young brother mouths.

I remember still the young love laced
with fear and gnarled with shame.

In the lockerroom naked men sashay
from shower to sauna with steaming skin,
undercover agents of lust.
Erections point like index fingers
at collective fantasies; wet dreams
ignite uncontrollable fires
fed by dumbbells and parallel bars
as muscles communicate like the thrust
of missiles whose launching pad is a crotch!

The gluteus maximus is more than
any man can stand! A raving madness
in the blood! I'm a casualty
of calipered curves, of lissome hips,
male mounds of maddening joy!
Beauty of buttocks! ecstasy of ass!
Those parts men love to gaze upon!
What butts! what balls! what divine cock!
I suffer anaphylactic shock
when I'm deprived of it.

guatemalan entry

I stare at the young hot cock throbbing
in tight white pants on my bed.
How long can I go on about travel fares and news of the day?
Dark smoldering eyes, half-sleepy, gaze at me
from a face the color of café au lait.

I'm anxious to strip this 19-year-old down again
and expose the rest of that dusky, marble skin.
I stop talking and look at him.
He comes over and presses his huge hard-on
against my face and I turn my head
to kiss his pants there.

He begins to unbuckle his belt with the head of a bull
for a buckle and I smile and say *Toro*

and he smiles and says *Verdad*
and suddenly throbbing in the room in the sun
with chocolate skin darker than the rest of him
      his cock appears.

He grabs my chest under the shirt
moving his strong hands down my thighs
    white and hairy against his smooth darkness
    and turns me around so that my back presses
      against his cock
    that he pushes between my buttocks
as he kneads my nipples in the sweltering heat
    of a lazy afternoon.

And we both begin to hump in a tropical trance
    quickly reaching orgasm, he inside me,
      I in my hand, as the madness boils over
and splashes onto my fist and drenches
    the burning bed.

walt whitman called today

for jack foley

Walt Whitman left a message on my answering machine today.
He called long distance. I found him personal, enthralling.
His voice was vibrant, sexy, full of warmth,
Lusty in age, still powerful, still a natural force:
Centre of equal daughters, equal sons,
All, all alike endear'd, grown, ungrown, young or old,
Strong, ample, fair, enduring, capable, rich,
Perennial with the Earth, with Freedom, Law and Love.
Ancient artifact of wax, lone sample of eternal voice,
Early, imperfect, scratchy background of drowning din,
Roaring surf-like waves of sound rolled over his words
Like static from seas of Time, haunts of Spirit's mystical deeps,
Rising and surging, lapping syllables, cradling Space,
Reaching from 19th Century Jersey shores to me.
Many decades now since first I read your *leaves*, dear Walt
(a boy sixteen, rocking and rolling in your cradle of grass),
A century after your death you recite in my room,

From Edison's wax cylinder, four lines remaining,
Miraculously preserved, discovered, radio broadcast
Forty years ago, recorded, then melted away!
Here retained on cassette plugged into my answering machine
(O wondrous your Brooklyn accent, Walt, like mine!),
Close, familiar, at last in the flesh, your message received
And answered in kind, inspiring communal love,
Before I, too, am recycled in Eternity.

26 May '93

to mohammed at the café central

Tangier
sun and wind
strike the Medina mosque

Mohammed
seventeen years old
puffs his kif pipe
sipping green mint tea
where blue phallic arches
rise among white walls
and berber rugs

the muezzin traces ALLAH
thru the moon's
loudspeaker
over casbah roofs
of Socco Chico

moneylenders
sip mint tea
but Mohammed's eye
brilliant and black
darts among tourists
for a simpático friend
and glances at transistors
covetously
and tattooed mammas
you-youing
papoosed in laundrybags

peeping thru djellabas

the crescent sun
on lightning terraces
dries everything
in a second!

Tangier/Paris, 1962

to mohammed on our journeys

I was the tourist
el simpático
and your brother offered you
and also himself
I forgot about your brother
and we took a flat in the Marshan
with reed mats and one water tap
about a foot from the floor
and we smoked hasheesh
and ate well and loved well
and left for the south
Essaouira, Fez, Marrakech
and got to Taroudant
thru the mountains
and bought alabaster kif bowls
for a few dirhams and watched
the dancing boys in desert cafés
kissing old Arabs and sitting on their
laps, dancing with kohl eyes
and heard the music down in Jejouka
in the hills under the stars
the ancient ceremony, Pan pipes
fierce in white moonlight
by white walls
with hooded figures
stoned on kif
for eight nights
and the goatboy in a floppy hat
scared us, beating the air
with a stick, beating whoever came close,
Father of Skins, goat god,

and the flutes maddened us
and we slept together in huts

to mohammed in the hotel
of the palms

behind the glass wall
                                        i see blue limbs
                                        black fungus noses
            thighs knee caps
                            "i have the taste of the infinite"
ylem
        primordial squinch   the universe crushed into
                                                        a seed
nothing will satisfy me
                            i write green ballets & hollow journeys
caught in the etheric web of yr crotch
                            a hairy ocean of darkness

                                    doors of pearl
                            open to fiery radiance
majoun madness
                down marrakech alleys
        the   djemaa el fna
squirming   with snakes
            in carbide glow

black gnaoua dancers!   lash sword!   flash teeth!
    under the barrow
        broiling in sleep   mouth
& nostrils buzzing with flies
                                    genitals thick swollen
out of big tear in pants
                    derelict 14 yr old street arab
        cameras snapping
        like teeth

who are you
                little arab
                i shared my visions

                                        and ate
                  black hasheesh candy with
the doors of yr body   flung open
                  we twitched in spasms
                        muscular convulsions
                              heavenly epilepsy on the bed
        in the hotel of the palms
          prolonged orgasm
                uncontrollable joy
                                    of leaving the mind
                                      Athens, 1965

to mohammed at the height

        the moment widens—your voice
        VAST across the room—my
        head explodes into con
        scious speed an ache
        shoots along the
        nerve of my left eye pushing to
        the center above my nose—
        your browngold skin
        dance flute laugh
              yes
        everything lives
        because I love you
        ALL
        levels
        at once
        brain flickers
        nosebridge pinches
        bright cells full of happening
        this can not
        END

                              Tangier/Paris, 1962

to mohammed at parting

the wind hurls through the straits
        white ruffs on greenblue
   water I will cross
        to Spain

your bag is packed for the bus
      to Melilla
        back to the Rif

I see your mountain hut
the scrawny sheep
      rugged Berber tribesmen
        scrape in the fields
        you will scrape

      bye bye Mouniria
      so long kid

Tangier/Paris, 1962

byron alfonso

The dance you did in the mirror
the ancient Mayas might have done
      or the decadent Atlanteans
before the continent slipped
                  into the sea
the pagan dance
           that bypassed time
     (ancient disco fever)

A god entered you
           as you entered me

old satyr and young faun
      sharing the mysteries
        bypassing laws

drunken-stoned temple dancer
young male whore
    reviving the ritual
        with cannabis

rubbing your smooth body
against my furry one

smell of goats and satyrs

        gleaming sweat

with each step
        and bent thigh
the god rises
        and resurrects

the grunting dance
        of erections

Guatemala City, 1979

you must have been a sensational baby

1

I love your eyebrows, said one.
the distribution of your body hair
is sensational. what teeth, said two.
your mouth is cocaine, said three.
your lips, said four, look like sexual organs.
they are, I said.
as I got older features thickened.
the body grew flabby, then
thin in the wrong places, they
all shut up or spoke about life.

2

a pair of muscular calves
drove me crazy today.
I studied their size, their shape,

their suntanned hairiness. I spoke
to the owner of them, are you
a dancer? I asked, oh no,
I was born with them, he said.
you must have been a sensational baby,
I said, he went back to his newspaper.
I went back to his calves.
he displayed them mercilessly.
he was absolutely heartless.
men stole secret looks at them.
women pretended he was a table.
they all had a pained expression.
he went on reading the Sports Page.
his thighs were even more cruel
thrust brutally from denim shorts.
the whole place trembled with lust.

San Francisco, 1973

big thick dick

Big Thick Dick & Tasty Jr. Bear
Hairy & Sweet Delectable Indeed
And Dirty Mouth Showoff Awesome Gypsie Top
Big Irish Hung Like You'd Hope & Black Body Builder
For Muscle Worship Super Safe Mega Dick
And Creamy French Delicacy Horse Hung For Dessert
Plus Uncut & Hungry Fantasies Fulfilled
You'll Go WOOF! For This Smooth Blond Nice & Nasty Stud
And Rock Hard Professional Cleancut Gym Studs Waiting For You
A Man For All Reasons Bigger Is Better Indulge Yourself
All Scenes Considered Eat at Pete's Low Hangers
Or Bubble Butt Boy Toy Handsome Student Body
Or Prime Hot Rod Therapeutic & Erotic
Or Asian Dream Hairy Russian Rodeo Cowboy
French Marine German Master Rican Masseur
Eros + Agape Double Pleasure Body Magic
Affirm Self Love Sing The Body Mechanic & Surrender
Unravel With Stressbuster Deep Throat Man To Man
Warm Hands Warm Heart Warm Head Warm Butt Warm Rod
Nurturing Touch In Finest Tradition of Bodywork

Ahhh . . . Slow.Sensual.Complete.Ecstatic.Hot.Close.
Nips Aching For Touch? Call Bearcub or Dick of Death
Or Nebraska Farm Boy or Ragin' Cajun or Dungeon Dragon
Big Holiday Sale More For LE$$ You'll Feel Real Good

San Francisco, 1996

[This is a "cut-up" poem, i.e. the words and phrases were cut out at random from a gay newspaper, ads and personals, and put together as an invented "poem." HN]

elegy for st. matthew shepard

(1976-1998, martyred by criminal bigots blinded by hate)

Matthew, dear brother, sweet kid, a slip of a lad, 5'2", effeminate youth, your parents loved you and knew you were gay and were born that way like children all over the world in all countries, all times, barely visible in a child though predestined in puberty. Jesus never condemned you. But the Church hasn't heard the Good News: love is no crime. It's a force of attraction beyond choice or will. For this you were killed, lashed to a fence like a scarecrow, stripped, savagely beaten and left to die.

Crucified like Jesus who also looked like a scarecrow nailed to a cross, who most likely was not blue-eyed and pink-skinned with Breck-shampooed hair, who was also perhaps 5'2"—but awesome and wondrously gentle and holy. Jesus Christ didn't wear a white collar, preach sermons for hate crimes of violence versus the innocent. Perhaps he was always high on the mind-blowing sacred mushroom in his saintly Essene youth. He did not get uptight about sex. He preached charity, decency, love.

A poor Jew born in a manger, a stable on the outskirts of Bethlehem, he taught that each life was sacred, more precious than gold; and although he may have had dirty feet, long hair, hippie sandals, he made the ultimate sacrifice for his merciful teachings that conquered the pagan religion of Rome. O false Christians, you do not love Jesus, you love to exploit him, to sell him for profit, get rich in his name. "No queers or dykes welcome in church!" You laugh and you mock as you murder Jesus, Matthew and Dr. King.

we bumped off your friend the poet

Based on a review by Cyril Connolly, Death in Granada, *on the last days of* Garcia Lorca, The Sunday Times *(London), May 20, 1973*

We bumped off your friend the poet
with the big fat head this morning

We left him in a ditch

I fired 2 bullets into his ass
for being queer

I was one of the people
who went to get Lorca
and that's what I said to Rosales

My name is Ruiz Alonzo
ex-typographer
Right-wing deputy
alive and kicking
Falangist to the end

Nobody bothers me
I got protection
The Guardia Civil are my friends

Because he was a poet
was he better than anyone else?

He was a goddam fag
and we were sick and tired
of fags in Granada

The black assassination squads
kept busy
liquidating professors
doctors lawyers students
like the good old days of the Inquisition!

General Queipo de Llano
had a favorite phrase,
"Give him coffee, plenty of coffee!"

When Lorca was arrested
we asked the General what to do
"Give him coffee, plenty of coffee!"

So we took him out in the hills and shot him
I'd like to know what's wrong with that
He was a queer with Leftist leanings

Didn't he say
I don't believe in political frontiers?

Didn't he say
The capture of Granada in 1492
by Ferdinand and Isabella
was a disastrous event?

Didn't he call Granada *a wasteland*
peopled by the worst bourgeoisie in Spain?

a queer Communist poet!

General Franco owes me a medal
for putting 2 bullets up his ass

San Francisco, 1973

i'm not a man

I'm not a man. I can't earn a living, buy new things for my family.
I have acne and a small peter.

I'm not a man. I don't like football, boxing and cars.
I like to express my feelings. I even like to put an arm
around my friend's shoulder.

I'm not a man. I won't play the role assigned to me—the role created
by Madison Avenue, *Playboy*, Hollywood and Oliver Cromwell.
Television does not dictate my behavior.

I'm not a man. Once when I shot a squirrel I swore that I would
never kill again. I gave up meat. The sight of blood makes me sick.
I like flowers.

I'm not a man. I went to prison resisting the draft. I do not fight
when real men beat me up and call me queer. I dislike violence.

I'm not a man. I have never raped a woman. I don't hate blacks.
I do not get emotional when the flag is waved. I do not think I should
love America or leave it. I think I should laugh at it.

I'm not a man. I have never had the clap.

I'm not a man. *Playboy* is not my favorite magazine.

I'm not a man. I cry when I'm unhappy.

I'm not a man. I do not feel superior to women.

I'm not a man. I don't wear a jockstrap.

I'm not a man. I write poetry.

I'm not a man. I meditate on peace and love.

I'm not a man. I don't want to destroy you.

San Francisco, 1972

the ex-nun and the gay poet

They talked about meditation
and extra-sensory perception
as her eyes kept straying
to the black hair on his chest
where his shirt was open
and he talked of his new poems
as his eyes kept straying
to the slit in her crotch
where her slacks were tight.

They smoked Lebanese hash,
her first turn-on,
and she slumped a little
and said, "Nothing is happening,"
and he laughed, watching her

and she said, "I feel as if our bodies
are moving towards each other
like 2 sticks in a bathtub
of their own volition,"
and he reached over
cradling her neck in his arm
and said, "They are,"
and didn't wait
to remove his pants.

That night they drifted
in a twilight zone
with Adam and Eve
fish and amoeba
sperm and egg.

She spoke of the convent in Boston
where the nuns were in love
with the body of Christ
spreadeagled on the crucifix
and very naked.
The nuns did strange things
as they passed each other
silently in the hall
like flicking the habit
against each other's breasts
which made them horny
and quite crazy.
So she quit.

She dropped the habit
and went in search of a real man.
She worked at the US Army Base
in Libya, but had troubled dreams
of the Boston Strangler
and woke up screaming
because she dreamed of a man
under the bed.

One night he was *in* the bed
but it wasn't the Strangler,
it was a G.I. Then a cameldriver.
Then a string of cameldrivers.
Then a camel. Or was it a dream?

She felt the need of something
"more spiritual"
and having read Lawrence Durrell
she fled to Athens to find herself
but the Greeks had nothing
to say except "I love you,
50 drachmas please!"

So she drowned her dreams
in bottles of ouzo
with male hustlers in tourist tavernas
where they got money from other men
for services rendered
and gave it to her
for services rendered.
It wasn't very spiritual,
and she was losing her mind
trying to find a way
of giving and receiving
that wasn't physical.

It looked like curtains
for the ex-nun from Boston.
And then it happened.
"I met you," she said,
"I hit the jackpot."
She found her bliss
with a Gay American poet
from Brooklyn.

Porto Santo Stefano, Summer, 1970

william carlos williams

I want to thank you
   for the pink locust
   & the white mule
     for the keen
scalpel
   that carved
     memorable poetry

those silvery lines will shine on
like a harvest moon
thru infinite trees

     you pulled
     a jazzy native song
     out of the womb
       of America

meant to be heard
like a jukebox
     singing pop tunes
we can't forget
     your sound

I want to thank you
for being alive
although you're dead
& buried where the Passaic
runs by the parks
& Jersey dumps—your
bailiwick! thanks
for singing of used car lots
& the broken brain
that tells 'the truth about us'
your surgical cool fingers cut
thru formal literary crap
labeled PURE
           AMERICAN

I see you at the door
in Rutherford
clutching my shoulders
in welcome, eyes flashing

as we sit & talk
      till the light is gone
you wring your hands
      & paw the ground
like a racehorse
      on the skids
      smelling death

you pace and whinny   you are coltish
amazingly young   your high voice
agitated
         Jee-zus! what clean
hygienic genie inhabits your anguish!
old age
        disease
              the black earth
         in your throat

but that greeny flower
your asphodel
         still flourishes

Thanks for our famous garden party
in the backyard with roses

we sat hearing a concrete mixer
      the radio blaring
from the army surplus store

appropriate measure for
the language you never tired of
     —not English—but plain
        American speech
that you loved
as much as the stinking dumps
& immigrant women
of your landscape
           'I'll
experiment till I die'

what heaven
do you experiment in now?
is the asphodel blowing
in the junkyards of God?

                    abandoned
chariot wheels rusty & clogged
            with cloud dust maybe?

do angelic choirs sing
            in the 'variable foot'?

Athens, 1964

classic frieze in a garage

I was walking thru the city past umber embassies
            & pine-lined palaces
                palmtrees beside balconies
            the heat something
            you could touch

    past three kids with cunning
            delinquent faces
begging cigarettes
            from Americano sailors

—I thought of Nerval *Rends-moi le Pausilippe*
            et la mer d'Italie
while living on the hill Posillipo
    above a gangster's dance floor

                on the bay of Naples
                        in a stone cottage
            over tufa caves where the sea
            crashed in winter   sweet Gerard
                one hundred years
            have made the desolation greater

the tower is really down & the sun blackened
beyond despair   loudspeakers advertise
                from boats on the bay
drowning out finches & roaring sea-caves
            all in the hands of racketeers

I have passed my time dreaming thru ancient ruins
walking thru crowded alleys of laundry

outside tenements with gourds in windows
& crumbling masonry of wars

when suddenly I saw among the greasy rags
   & wheels & axles of a garage
      the carved nude figures
      of a classic frieze
      above dismantled parts of cars!

garage swallows sarcophagus!
   mechanic calmly spraying
      paint on a fender
observed in turn by lapith & centaur!

the myth of the Mediterranean
     was in that garage
   where the brown wiry youths
     saw nothing unusual
         at their work
among dead heroes & gods

but I saw Hermes in the rainbow
   of the dark oil on the floor
     reflected there
   & the wild hair of the sybil
     as her words bubbled
mad & drowned
       beneath the motor's roar

Naples, 1958

let go and feel your nakedness

Let go and feel your nakedness, tits ache to be bitten and sucked
Let go with pong of armpit and crotch, let go with hole a-tingle
Let go with tongue lapping hairy cunt, lick feet, kiss ass, suck cock and
    balls
Let the whole body go, let love come through, let freedom ring
Let go with moans and erogenous zones, let go with heart and soul
Let go the dead meat of convention, wake up the live meat of love

Let go with the senses, pull out the stops, forget false teachings and lies

Let go of inherited belief, let go of shame and blame, in brief
Let go of forbidden energies, choked back in muscles and nerves
Let go of rigid rules and roles, let go of uptight poses
Let go of your puppet self, let go and renew your self and be free
Let go the dead meat of convention, wake up the live meat of love

Let go this moment, this hour, this day, tomorrow may be too late
Let go of guilt and frustration, let liberation and tolerance flow
Let go of phantom worries and fears, let go of hours and days and years
Let go of hate and rage and grief, let walls against ecstasy fall for relief
Let go of pride and greed, let go of missiles and might and creed
Let go the dead meat of convention, wake up the live meat of love

at the café trieste

The music of ancient Greece
and Rome did not come down to us
but this morning
I read Virgil's *Eclogues*
struck by the prophecy
of a new era:
"A great new cycle of centuries
begins. Justice returns to earth,
the Golden Age returns," he wrote
30 years before the end
of his millennium, describing
the birth of the infant god, come down
from heaven. Jesus was 19
when Virgil died at 89.
Will the Golden Age ever come?
Same faces thrown up each generation,
same races, emotions, struggles!
all those centuries, those countries!
languages, songs, discontents!
They return here in San Francisco
as I sit in the Café Trieste.
O recitative of years!
O Paradiso! sings the jukebox
as Virgil and Verdi combine
in this life to show
this is the only Golden Age
there'll ever be.

dream of frank o'hara

I saw you being interviewed by a hysterical mob of followers
And, edging closer, got a good look at your defiant humorous face,
Quite flushed and ruddy as always, with a touch of contempt.
Only this time you didn't put me off, the haughtiness gone,
Turned to sheer madness, a venerable, daft figure.
You shot answers like a ghost accustomed to being right,
Coming from another sphere—yet the dead seem humbler,
Somehow, envious of us, though you made death a circus,
Behaved like a ringmaster, and the living who crowded you
Seemed left out of the real show, whose key you held so lightly.

I alone knew you were dead; the others, your "readership,"
In my dream were privileged for the first time to "see you
Plain." I was no less surprised when you chose to leave
With me, harboring no rancor for San Remo days, really nights,
Though I never knew why you should. We used to swap small
Talk over beer in the Forties, eyeing the service men and crew
Cut blonds. But you were guarded, as if you had a secret
You wouldn't share. Now, leaving together, you bubbled over
With vast, inspired wildness, spouting weird phrases,
The poetry of vision peculiar to schizzy types. Street noises
And pneumatic drills cut off the meaning, the city strange
Yet familiar. Cincinnati? I'd never seen it before. In a frame
House we talked to an ancient couple playing cards; you stole
A jacket and hugged it. We left, walked more paved hills, you
Spoke of violence. "All art is violence!" you said, still beaming.
I was afraid, not of you but the dimension you came from.

Our most intimate scene, this astral meeting, I can't explain—
Hypnotic, intense, stripped of vanity, and free of pettiness.
You were never more real or living. The whole day hung
In that tricky aura of dream and death and trivial things
That you made poems from: notes from the street, who died,
What happened in the bar and what the cat did,
Who fucked whom and where you went, some French
Thrown in for flavor, and all the time you're diddling yourself
With flashy rubbings from Life, gorgeous and bubbly Joy.

Just don't tell me that, except for dreams like this, dullness
Didn't drip into the spaces between sensation like Campbell's Soup,
Damaging New York, the sun, poems, music, like literary prize
        committees

Sitting, plop, all over your gay mood, with irritating power to ignore
The fresh and reward the stale. So when this dream is over I'll get up
And make some coffee not trying to capture the feeling of something
Happening. I know that the best as in sensation happens without rhyme
Or reason, and I'm going to let music speak for itself for a change.

(Sure enough your bibulous rhythms have swept like giant tsunami
With the riptide of your sound through the flat surface of meaning,
Soaring with a lilt of the voice and the color of orange (you loved it!)
Through drab grays and blazing blues. New pinnacles of pleasure!
Random freshness! Like this dream, this death, these oneiric things,
They're forms of my feelings, shapes of appearance, and maybe just plain
        mess.
But the messy earth breathes as we breathe, as animals breathe
And stretch and rush around and glow and emit sound, no need
To complicate the simple act of being, that merely consists of some
        oxygen and flowing.)

Together for the last time, Paris, a gathering you endured,
You remarked with blasting pupils ripping silky skies,
"All art is violence!" looking quite helplessly violent and angry
And quite drunk, too, spreading infinite bitchiness like a bruise
In the living room, made wet by bearded cocktail holders.
I retreated to New York, your first year, at the Remo
Where we put away the beer with John and gossiped profoundly
And joined the Marines. You played sonarman, the juke played Elvis.
Seized with immeasurable lust at the bar I rushed through a tunnel
Filled with nude sailors. I heard a whirring sound. My throat
Wrapped up in jockey shorts. It was the grunt's. And patriotic.
Your saucy images collide with foregone conclusions to be gone
Much too soon, for rococo joy hadn't worn out its ode.

picasso visits braque

Picasso flies into a rage at Braque,
screaming, You have stolen my jaws!
bastard, give back my browns!
my noses! my guitars!

Braque, puffing his pipe,
continues painting in silence.
Aha! yells Picasso. Roast duck!
I smell roast duck!
Aren't you even inviting me for lunch?

Wordlessly, Braque puffs and paints.

You know, says Picasso, more amiably,
that's a pretty good job you're doing there, Georges.
Tell me, isn't that duck finished yet?

Voracious, Picasso is ready to devour the duck, the
          canvas, the other guests.
But Braque only squints at his painting,
adding a dash of color here and there.

Disgruntled, Picasso slaps his mistress, boils his
          secretary in oils, casts a withering look at the art
          dealer trembling in a corner and

laughs,
biting the air
with 4 huge rows of teeth
blinking malevolently
3 eyes

i would not recommend love

                            my head felt stabbed
by a crown of thorns but I joked and rode the subway
and ducked into school johns to masturbate
and secretly wrote
                        of teenage hell
because I was "different"
the first and last of my kind
smothering acute sensations
in swimming pools and locker rooms
addict of lips and genitals
mad for buttocks
                        that Whitman and Lorca
and Catullus and Marlowe
                        and Michelangelo
and Socrates admired

and I wrote: Friends,
if you wish to survive
I would not recommend
Love

"i have always liked george gershwin more than ernest hemingway"

I have always liked George Gershwin more than Ernest
        Hemingway
    tho they both meant Paris when I grew like a tree in
        Brooklyn
            & the sun also rose
                            on my disgruntlement
with a loud clunk that could be heard from Prospect Park to
        Gravesend Bay
    a considerable distance
                        little did I imagine then
                    that I'd cross the Great Water and sit
                    sipping pernod with Gershwin's
                            sister-in-law and *Porgy*
                            excitement of brainwaves

i have seen the light
and it is my mind

the State has decided: who I am to love, to hate
what I'm to do in bed, with what and to whom

the State has made a military coup in bed
stop screaming: the world is a better place

we are now going to sing the virtues of mass murder
we will follow our religious leaders

our feelings are stamped: State Property
pornography is practiced by God
who has raped more souls than you can shake a prick at

Jesus Christ is a funny name
for an hallucinogenic drug

all those addicts like Billy Graham and the Pope
will have to account for their expensive habit

from his last words on the cross
I gather Jesus was begging for the ultimate fix

meltemi*

Meltemi
whitebreakers crash the shore
        wind whips sand & spray
& we lose our way without a torch
let the inner light guide you?
        how about those ditches
                    & gulches
that we stumble across the black sand into?
holding hands against the cold
we lost our way
                getting misdirected
in demotic Greek

meltemi

6 pm a veil waltzed over
    the sun   it's eerie
i felt the storm inside me
the sun like a paper moon over the mill
    behind the mountain

the meltemi started roaring
    after we took the beach route
into town—ouzo at the cafe—bus back—
    beach washed out by breakers
    & the back road thru the sand black
gulches brambles trees sheer drop into
nothing
    helped by native
    back
    sand whipping sharp

your fine hair tickles my nose
    when we kiss
making a lull
    in the storm

against destruction

+   +   +

small boy peers over my right shoulder
in the new beach house
awed by typewriter
fishing pole in hand
    scratches his crotch
    studies it like a strange fish
    the typewriter
then drags his tackle across the sand

+   +   +

the snoring sea
    the nightmare rumble sea
    over rock shelf
whole beach pounded flat
in the evening the meltemi died
    jewel pebbles
    by driftwood sculpture
little lone dog

                silhouette on hill
                   against the greeny sea
             sniffing dry branches
             hopeless takes a leak

Do you believe in a triune god?
         know or don't know
            don't believe
               my body on a cot in Spain
lying below me once—sailed
into the sea
      into the bark of a dog
         into the palmtree clack
         thru the skin of time
            Dhammapada

                   +   +   +

don't be destroyed by yr cock
      just screw
yr kefali on straight

         "This germ
became an egg"

      "they cut out my stomach in '45
i dunno what they put in me
a dog stomach i t'ink
mebbe a cow stomach"
      old Greek from Sprangfield
         Illinois

         playing pinochle
         made 200 bucks a week
in Hollywood once a cook
      lost it on the horses
horses dice cards
   spicy old bugger

& Mu was the Motherland of the Greeks

Heavily break the waters
extending over the plains

*Greek: wind, storm

greek islands

banners string on the quay green suns and pearly crescents
cool yachts
with spars like lances cut the sky
beyond the fanfare of the port

medusas burst bloodred, tarantulas shed fiery legs, stars hiss
a cannon ejaculates over soft drinks wines and meats

folksingers hikers the ageing young-at-heart the solitary the kept

what frantic quests!
scrabble of flesh on rocks and beaches
under the bushes beneath the trees

the jukebox brays on dancefloors choked with turbulent thighs
newsprint wars trampled

flares streak through dark like nova gonads
burn out quick
spray their flame and fade
into the black

parapoem—21

i'm on my back dribbling stars from foamflecked lips
in a field of flaming chrysanthemums
bizarre beasts dance
mescaline moons melt into diamonds
the seal of solomon bursts
the electric river flows
streams of holiness gush between my legs
i give birth to a white narcissus
six wands spring from the ground
lotus leaves sprout from the eye
Absolute Poem like a meteor streaks down
crushed by Earth in a swift instant
fiery chains of rubies flood the indifferent Cosmos
i'm soaring out of my blood

parapoem—29

Europe stains the poem
    I dance
    mad vigils

in the empty mirror
    silence
        moans in the mouth
            forgetting
to be reborn

an end to filthy pieties

    prophets
        let me kiss yr light

parapoem 35

      love rinses its hair full of starfish
     the frozen hotel wears a collar of lips
      we follow corpses into a lake
    of newspapers and dead flags
flowers scream, images sprout from their sticky leaves
    a voice proclaims: I ERASE ALL MEMORY!
     a man bleeds in the mirror
a radio scratches the sky with raucous announcements
    ice cubes take possession of Vesuvius
   chimneys write news items in Persian Rose Smoke
    a man comes out of the ground saying
    WE HAVE SEEN THE WRECKS OF OUR DAMAGED BRAINS

parapoem—37

white rain black noun collage of emptiness
telephone directory xmas eve paperweight flag
throbbing like the prick of a strange man
the bone beneath the skin the soul murdering itself

the Unknown beating against your freakish hole
the spidery power of Death whose luminous web trembles in space

a hard time to sing a black time to speak
suicide squads coverup lost footsteps
sensitive poets kneel before crimson eyelids
unsuccessfully dig up images in the wake of naked ugliness
we are cut to pieces by bursts of hair
the wars the Church screaming angels

pen pals answer bodybuilders in steel and concrete voids
gay cancer fetishists seek Greek pieces
words break my neck exploding into monstrous needs
charming female wishes encounter with discreet dwarf
erotic grandma tickled his little fancy with bare attack

aluminum lights the rage of the poor
poetry is the key to the karmic alphabet
my heart is an international museum of erotic art
with automatic recording switch in my leaking current
how sick I am! I must rape a gorilla!

black rain white noun collage of reality
days of steel flamingoes ordors of raucous meteors
o afternoons of endless ears!
I came to the edge of shimmering windows
I stopped inside out before you in dream
reality is a collage of lust rooted in emptiness

cyanide genocide

Wanna hear about the New American Revolution? Within one hour 100 of the top prominent politicians in the country will be liquidated. That is Phase One. Assassination, mass chaos. They know where the power lines are / the key points of the water system. They will put cyanide in the water supply.

What? You didn't think Flower People would do such a thing?

You're in the Wrong Revolution, Baby. Never heard of the Minute men? Well, you've heard of swastikas, haven't you? Und Adolf?

It's All-American now. The Commies, by comparison, are girl scouts. These Ultra-Rightists got members in top government places & far right congressmen / don't even bother to investigate / The FBI are on the same trip with agents who are Minutemen . . . Camp Middlevale? That was just a charade for the public which likes to be reassured . . .

So in a NYC raid on a minuteman apartment last year they found nazi flags & 50,000 bucks worth of arms and ammunition buried in the country. Thompson machine guns, C-1 & C-2 charges. For every one that the FBI apprehend they allow 15 or 20 others to flourish. The rightist coalition was put together by Wallace—a nice cosy arrangement of about 30,000 rabid mad dog fanatics who will act in the name of GOD/ FLAG/ & MOTHER.

Hot shit. If Hubert Humphrey had shown strong gains at the polls A special team was ready to assassinate him. These men are trained. They know their job & they know how to go about doing it. KKK. Minutemen. American Nazi Party. The only group today ready to take over the country.

This is not a dream. Anybody who thinks so is asleep. The Coup. Mass Murders. The Red Button. Before 1972. That is their time table. Get the idea? What can be done to stop them? The general public is very apathetic.

CYANIDE IN THE WATER SUPPLY IS GENOCIDE. ACID IN THE WATER SUPPLY IS GROOVY.

Yes, America is a country of extremes. So to balance the Nazi nightmare we have the benign spectacle of Dr. Timothy Leary running (on the ACID PARTY TICKET) for Governor of California.

The Politics of Ecstasy or Parapolitics, as Lawrence Lipton has dubbed it. Throw a lotus at a Klansman & watch him dissolve in green smiles.

In 1960 Leary first had his profound experience with the psychedelic sacrament; Burroughs began to cut language lines that control mass mind; & I acted as a medium for expanded consciousness in poems that I called PARAPOETRY, in the Paris Beat Hotel where I shifted mental planes & guidelines like a deck of cards.

Diamonds rained down from peeling paint & greasy hairstained gray walls. We stopped playing roles assigned by tradition & authority. No one expected industrial wastes to turn everybody in the world into a cesspool— all this & ugly green lungs—The only means of disposal is burial—now, with the planet's ecology on the line we are fighting to save our air water food & earth from total poisoning by money-mad industries spraying DDT over the world's chicken eggs butter meat fish igloos lettuce greens liver.

Industrial atomic waste dangerous for 250,000 years lies buried and air-conditioned (because of intense heat) in Montana—But what if it breaks out—Oh doctor—No baby escapes—DDT can find its way even thru protective shield of placenta—Mother's milk carries it—"DDT was mother's milk to me"—"Now darling, just suck up some of this shit from mama's nipple"—"Mmmm . . . good"—

The whole system which poisons our food & then polices the poisoning is built on madness—each individual in the USA has now accumulated 10 to 12 parts per million of DDT in his body—Doctors' fees have tripled over the past few years—UP AGAINST THE WALL MOTHER EARTH!—BIOLOGICAL WARFARE!—

Environmental pollution results from greed & moneytheism. "To Hell With Prosperity!"—a murderous conspiracy by ALCOHOL CIGAR-ETTES PESTICIDE MEDICAL LOBBY to wipe out Americans in a war of SLOW POISON—all these green & ugly killers—Dr. Strangelove hoists his phallic arm in stiff erection—"Mein Führer," he shrieks—"I can valk!"—He is still walking.

Venice, California

This prose poem appeared in an undated issue of the journal *Notes From Underground*, published in 1968.

catalan-talgo express

For Peter K. Wehrli of Zurich

After having read Peter Wehrli's remarkable little book, *Catalogue of the 134 Most Important Observations During a Long Railway Journey*, I had a few of my own to add. . . .

135. the luxury
    the luxury of the Catalan-Talgo 1st class Express out of Zurich, based on the mistaken assumption that trivial dreary muzak, softly but relentlessly piped through our carriage, is one of the distinguishing characteristics of superior travel.

135a. when in actuality it is an imbecilic imposition of taste, invading one's privacy and depriving one of free choice, such as silence or other forms of music that, at least, might be preferable.

136. the maître-d'
    the maître-d' who addresses us in Catalan, Spanish, Portuguese, French and finally English, asking if we would care for lunch, and who leans over solicitously when I request the menu and then, the moment of truth when I inquire about the price, and he answers softly, 68 francs, which in our collapsing currency in October, 1978, is $45 (forty-five dollars!) for lunch!

137. the reply
    the reply as, gasping incredulously at each other, my traveling companion and I, in sheer horror, chorus, "We are not hungry!"

138. starving in first class
    wondering if dinner will cost $100 (one hundred dollars!) and conjuring up images of cannibalism as we ride luxuriously through France in our first-class carriage starving and secretly eyeing the other passengers (and one another), our eyes falling simultaneously upon the pleasingly plump American girl from Berkeley seated in front of us devouring cheese sandwiches.

139. the huge tray of food
    the huge tray of food that just went by unless we are already seeing a mirage.

140. the ticket-taker
    the young blond ticket-taker who twice has asked to see our tickets, whose well-built body and healthy ruddy complexion begin to look irresistible.

141. the edible landscape
    the edible landscape with its chlorophyll green grass and fat white poultry and milk-laden cows, not to mention delightful cafés dotting the juicy scenery and an occasional restaurant, which we eye wistfully; France has never before seemed quite so good to eat.

142. the water of life
    recalling how shipwrecked sailors and those lost in deserts survived by drinking their own urine or that of others and the mysterious book I once received from an unknown person in the mail called *The Water of Life*, scientifically documenting the remarkable curative effects of urine, enabling one to survive all illnesses by subsisting solely on one's own piss for 40 days.

143. the arm
    the soft white arm of the American girl showing in the space between the seats in front of us.

144. the recognition
    the recognition that all my life, whether or not on trains, I have been constantly hungry, a hunger for experience, a hunger for knowledge, a hunger for love, a hunger for sex, a hunger for money, a hunger for fame, a hunger for immortality, a hunger for art, a hunger for poetry,

a hunger for music, a hunger for food, a hunger for pleasure, a hunger for beauty, a hunger for infinity, a hunger for the impossible, a hunger for fulness, a hunger for intimacy, a hunger for laughter, a hunger for emptiness, a hunger for holiness, a hunger for truth, a hunger for trust, a hunger for satiety, a hunger for mystery, a hunger for the marvelous, a hunger for awareness, a hunger for dreams, a hunger for surprise, a hunger for life, a hunger for death, a hunger for magic, a hunger for recognition.

145. the uneventfulness
the uneventfulness of dull stretches of flat green land after Lyon with power lines and small industrial plants, like boring stretches seen from an American train.

146. the look of California
the look of California for a few kilometers with Spanish adobe houses until suddenly switching to ruined medieval castles and ancient churches.

147. the wish
the wish crossing my mind that we could get off the train and stop overnight in a French village with marvelous wines and cheeses and old architecture so pleasing to the soul, not to mention the sound of real French, a voluptuous sound, corresponding in sensuousness to the taste of old wine and cheese and the vaulted delicacies of Gothic cathedrals.

148. the accident
the wish being father to the thought when a great shattering sound and a rending and tearing occurs, as if the train were suddenly bombarded by a shower of large rocks, and the train shakes and rattles and lurches violently on the verge of jumping the rails and the important-looking old train official pulls the red emergency brake and

148a. the train stops
the train stops. Passengers rushing to the exits in the warm bright day, a rural landscape peacefully around us, everyone urgently asking in five languages what happened and finally the answer. An overhead cable has broken, something about something called a *paraphrane*.

149. the joker
a tall blue-eyed old man with straight white hair keeping everyone in stitches in the exit, telling us he's an *artiste* (speaking French) and

when I ask, Singer? he says, No, comedian and when he asks my destination I say Barcelona, to which he replies, Perhaps.

150. the joke
the wry old comic telling us the story he had told the night before to an audience in Lausanne, of a man who consulted a palmist because he wanted to know if they played football in heaven; she tells him to come back again next day for the answer and when he returns she reads his palm and says, I have good news and bad news; the good news is yes, they play football in heaven; the bad news is, next week you're on the team.

151. the paraphrane
the rumor beginning to spread that the delay will last an hour or two as we wait impatiently for the new *paraphrane*, nobody having the slightest idea what it is.

152. the Star of David
undaunted by the seriousness of the occasion or by the prospect of boredom or hunger, himself having already dined on the expensive lunch, the old funny man continuing to entertain the small crowd on the platform, demanding of another oldster his nationality and, receiving the answer, Chilean, tucking his two gold Stars of David dangling from his neckchain into his shirt, but when the Chilean laughs good-humoredly, popping them out again and asking the same question of another who answers, German, at which the comic pops them rapidly back into his bosom with a look of mock alarm.

153. the virgin and the German
while we are laughing the comic asks, Do you know the difference between a virgin and a German? No? The German will always be a German.

154. the seats
the entertaining interlude wearing thin after awhile, everyone settling back into the seats, preparing for a long delay, some wandering idly around the tracks while others hop about, one even climbing to the top of the diesel engine to photograph the broken cable, this idiotic pastime not escaping the keen-eyed old French Jew who drily remarks, Americans.

155. the real problem
the real problem, according to him, not being the *paraphrane*, an object nobody can form a clear image of, but the closing of the toi-

lets, he says, making a troubled face and clutching his abdomen in simulated agony.

156. the return
pushed by a relief engine, moving slowly backwards towards the village station of Livron which has a tempting café and restaurant only about a hundred meters from the station, finally stopping and descending to the platform, but nobody is permitted to leave as the enigmatic *paraphrane* is expected at any moment now, according to the old official who had originally pulled the emergency brake, although we cross the rails to use the W.C., bringing us that much closer to the tantalizing café.

157. the mistake
speaking to the young American boyfriend of the sandwich-eating girl and learning that they too are from San Francisco, we mention the outrageous sum of $45 (forty-five dollars!) for lunch, explaining that we are starving, and discover that we mistakenly have reckoned this sum in Swiss francs when, according to the boyfriend, the menu was actually listed in French francs, making the cost of lunch about $16 (sixteen dollars!), expensive indeed but far less piratical than we thought, causing us to regret our stupidity as now we are ravenous although we all have a good laugh at our mistake.

158. the departure
departing at last from Livron with a new engine, not a *paraphrane* in sight at 4:15 pm, after a two-hour delay, vowing we'd gladly spend $16 or even $20 dollars for dinner, much relieved that inflation had not as we feared reached runaway stages during our journey in the Midi.

159. the paperback
passing Orange, my mind flashing back to the Duc d'Orange, recalling irrelevantly that we have no rhyme in English for orange, simultaneously noticing the curly-haired American from San Francisco reading a cheap paperback about Vivien Leigh by one Anne Edwards, two names that somehow seem even less relevant to me than Orange or orange.

160. the change at Avignon
preceded by a tinkle of bells, the PA system announcing in 5 languages that we are approaching Avignon where those whose destination is Milan, Marseilles or the Côte d' Azur are to change trains, the realization dawning that Avignon was the seat of the papacy during the time of the troubadours while the Roman pope remained seated

in Rome, and that this Provencal city was the center of a rich hereti-cal tradition of Gnosticism, romantic poetry and music, but still feel-ing the not so romantic pangs of hunger while being informed that dinner will be served after we cross the Spanish border, thinking of the terrible hunger for creation that Vincent Van Gogh underwent in these parts, yet seeing not a single sunflower at the gare d'Avignon, only platforms, platforms, platforms.

161. the window
seen through the window: a white horse, an evening sky, a freight train, cypress trees. Roman viaducts, modern apartment complex, Esso sign, old Roman mansard roofs, the cathedral of Nîmes, futur-istic cylindrical structures with conical domes.

162. the exchange
at last, a refreshment cart rolling by! 2 or 3 lean sandwiches and Coca Colas, but we pounce on them only to discover that they're just skinny slices of stale ham with no dressing or mustard, nothing, just 2 dry hunks of wilted white bread like pieces of blotting paper; offer-ing Swiss Francs as payment we discover they're not acceptable— God, are we going to lose even these repulsive morsels of non-food? but we're given to understand that *paper* francs are acceptable, not coins; so offering 20 Swiss francs and receiving 31.20 French francs in change, we initiate a discussion in French and English with the other passengers who inform us that the exchange rate on trains is the lowest in the country; thus learning that we have paid about $9, including commission, for 2 miserable tasteless sandwiches and 2 cokes, the result of violating the principle that one had better carry the currency of each country one passes through, especially on a perilous journey such as this, as we have also paid a 20% conversion charge.

163. the sunset
the sun setting after Montpellier with long streaks of red on black smoke from tall chimneys, one silver streak over the red gold, silver smoke from a plane, and as we slowly pass the station at Sète seeing industrial chimneys belching smoke, passing a yacht basin in a har-bor for big ships, all turning into pastel charcoal and the silver of evening.

164. the exquisite youth
at Montpellier—or was it a later station in the darkness?—my senses so captivated that I neglect to write down the name of the stop— where, pressing my face against the glass and peering out wearily, my astonished eye encounters on the opposite platform a large group of

teenage French schoolboys, coming to rest on one in particular, a tall dark gypsy-looking youth of breathtaking beauty who eyes meet mine and shift a moment in embarrassment from my devouring stare, and then hesitantly return until our eyes lock in a brief hypnotic trance, a mutual intrigue hidden from everyone, and I pray silently for another *paraphrane* episode to keep us here longer but the train begins pulling out and I lose sight of him, my fantasies of the sort Cocteau must have had when he first saw Raymond Radiguet.

165. the silly fruit
noticing for the first time the name of the empty plastic yogurt cup (which I had bought prior to departure at Geneva), on the ashtray—Silifruit—silly fruit?!—and gratefully recalling, by free association, that homosexuality is legal in Switzerland from the age of 20 and from the age of 13 in Japan.

166. the scream
stopping before Port Bou, the border town, the announcement that the French police and Spanish Customs officials would board the train and that all passengers are to keep their seats, at which point a woman's highpitched hysterical scream is heard, quite close, as if from the adjoining coach, causing speculation about the reason for this mysterious sound, no satisfactory explanation being given except that of my traveling companion who wryly suggests, "Perhaps it's a body search."

167. the village
at this stop in total darkness outside, our train suspended on a bridge high above the flickering lights below, the comedian informing us that we ought to get out and visit the charming village only a kilometer below the train.

168. the vertigo
playing Twenty Questions and smoking a bummed Marlboro, the train suddenly swimming before me as, leaning back dizzily, I think I'm going to faint—from exhaustion, hunger, smoking.

169. the customs
the customs officers, without examining our luggage, busily stamping our passports and disappearing into the corridor where they begin arguing at length in Spanish with some young worker-type Spaniards, definitely not first-class passengers, who leave the train and are swallowed up in outer darkness as I make for the train platform to reassure myself that my monstrous green valise is indeed still there.

170. the green valise
the green valise that keeps attracting attention because of its enormous bulk and weight, invariably causing strangers to inquire, What have you got in there, gold? to which I invariably reply, No, vitamins.

171. the darkness
the darkness around 9 pm suddenly pierced by a bullring, brilliantly illuminated, then by the Cathedral at Gerona, reminding me that the bulls of Spain, not papal bulls, issue from here.

172. the W.C.
the illuminated W.C. sign starkly outlined in total darkness.

173. the "bevels"
the maître-d', passing through the corridor asking if we desire dinner—we almost jump at him crying in unison, *Si, oui, yes*—who seats us in the dining car after we finally cross the border and, making a sour disapproving face when I say no to wine and yes to mineral water, asking if I want "bevels" and, seeing my uncomprehending stare, repeating, You want bevels? and again, irritated at my incomprehension for he is a busy man, repeating with annoyance, Bevels or no bevels? until I turn for help to my friend who says, I think he's trying to say bubbles, so I say, No bubbles, because I can only dissolve a Swiss Vitamin-C tablet called Alca-C in the non-effervescent mineral water, without "bevels" but the furious maître-d', with an abrupt gesture of dismissal seizes the expensive wine from the table and whisks it away in disgust.

174. the dining car
in the dining car at last satisfying our gnawing hunger while a sinister-looking man with thick eyeglass lenses stares fixedly at me from another table, one eye on me, the other out his window, evoking fantasies of a Fascist spy until I hear the waiter speaking to him in Italian whereupon my fantasy turns him into a gross Fellini monster as I wonder how different democratic Spain will be after my visits to Franco Spain in the '50s and '60s.

175. the train
the train lurching violently ever since we crossed the Spanish border, the whistle hooting incessantly, arousing anxiety about the possible danger of yet another accident after 10 long hours of travel.

176. the agreeable surprise

the agreeable surprise of discovering, on examining the book EUROPE ON $10 A DAY, lent us by the American couple, that hotels and restaurants in Barcelona are about 3 times cheaper than in Switzerland, Germany or Holland, if the guide book is accurate.

177. the disagreeable surprise

the disagreeable surprise of discovering at the end of the line, Barcelona Terminus, only one porter who ignores us for the more substantial middle-class passengers, having to lug all our bags ourselves, hating the monstrous green valise; and on phoning, with the usual difficulties of learning the public phone-booth system in each country, agreeing finally on one of the hotels listed in the guidebook and getting the answer that it is full.

177a. then, under the impatient eyes of others waiting to phone, trying another hotel and succeeding, although the price is much higher than in the book, making our way out of the terminus cumbersomely and finding ourselves in a dark alley with dark cut-throat types hanging around, and then being refused by 2 taxi-drivers for no known reason until, sweating and breathing hard, we lug the luggage to the front of the station where we are again refused by cabdrivers and finally are accepted by a surly uncooperative driver who agrees to take us without helping to put the bags in the cab, which we do ourselves, and then leaning back in the tacky hack around midnight slightly hysterical and furious.

177b. arriving at the hotel on Calle San Fernando only to confront a toothless old desk clerk who vaguely fumbles with the hotel register in great confusion as newly arrived guests mill around and then he lisps that he hasn't a room available but may find one if we pay double what the guidebook says, which we must accept as we no longer have any choice in our wrecked condition.

177c. cursing the inaccurate guidebook and inflation for perpetrating this intolerable hoax on hordes of innocent unsuspecting tourists.

178. the end of the journey

the end of the journey completed, with the usual number of annoyances and agreeable surprises that accompany most long trips and is probably the whole point of travel, helping to relieve the monotony of domestic situations in one's habitual state of boredom with familiar routine.

PREVIOUSLY
unpublished

▼

▼

63rd st. ymca, new york

Through noon's smoke and farewells
my crystal ball rolls in the mud.
Nude on the counterpane
with eyelids half-open I hear
street noises, buzz of a plane.
Boys roar in the gym. A knock
on the door. The Negress with keys
and broom, bucket and gurney
with sheets and pillow cases.
makes beds in the dorm.
Mine will be vacant
where a visitor came.
Now we're on the prowl again.

NY 1942

all
my
life
i've
been
waiting

All my life I've been waiting
for something unusual to happen.
I may yet come into a windfall,
National Endowment of the Hearts.
All my life I've been expecting
a grand finale, an awakening,
love erupting in the streets,
in the bars, in classrooms,
everyone dropping their guard,

their pants, their skirts,
cops weeping tenderly
as they snap off your cuffs,
bankers giving away their money,
politicians telling the truth,
literary critics confessing
that they know nothing
about writing or life.
All my life I've been waiting
for something unusual to happen.

Benidorm, Spain, 1956

all these on xmas day i saw

an eagle in a parking lot under a freeway
brown bird wounded or sick
in downtown desert solitude
flapped to an iron post and clung there

a pale old woman in North Beach
fainting among her shopping bags
eyes rolling till two gentle Chinese ladies
helped her up and to a cab

Bob Kaufman black Rimbaud with lint in his nappy hair
torn shoes and slept-in clothes wandering round and round
surreal master bumming cigarettes with suffering silent look
and a kicking head
why fear tigers when every street corner is a fatal encounter
he said

ca. 1969

american dream

The insatiable desire
of Thomas Wolfe
was hunger for place.

Sherwood Anderson
was lost in pity
for the inarticulate
men and women
hurting each other
in every city.

In each town
many lived
anonymous,
meaningless lives.

Winesburg. Brooklyn.
Omaha.

A whole country
of displaced persons.

New York, 1939

art exhibit

At the desk the old attendant
fills a ledger with our names,
Around us nudes, beaches, trees
are painted in rosy tropical hues.
It's a library show. Visitors vote
for the best. Outdoors the sun is fierce
above poinsettias and palms.
People lounge in deck-chairs
as portable radios squawk
with a jitterbug din.

I gape at a portrait of sand, a whirl
of pastel in a sizzling sky,
an amethyst sea and pink sails on a boat.

I cast my ballot for it in the oaken box.
The old man points to his painting.
"That's mine," he says, proudly. I say
I voted for it. He beams and talks of art
being good for the soul. He teaches
chemistry to boys. "You must be an artist,"
he says. When I say, "No, a poet,"
he names one, famous and inaccessible
and old. They were neighbors, he says.
For years they talked over a fence.
"They all have mansions in Miami now,"
he says wistfully. Having voted
for his canvas *faute de mieux*, I stirred up
his past for a moment. Although young
and unknown, I understood him
better than his old friends did.

Miami, 1941
(revised 28/ix/2002/SF)

as the moon belongs to max ernst

as the moon belongs to Max Ernst
    flowers belong to you

        all flowers
        named & smelled
            precisely

            into words

                become
                        one flower
            eluding words

                    (death
                broke out
            of your senses
        into a new
                        reckoning
                with the sum
                        of memory)

the only healer

     bearing within itself
          yourself
      & my self too

                     from the dark
              ground or from
                  the floor of the
                     sea
its yellow petals stretch
   beyond the eye

               the Chinese were
         continually possessed by it
    & we
    who fail to recognize it
have failed to recognize
             ourselves

                        ca. 1942

asylum

Around and around in moonlight
jaguar and puma and moonmoth
turn and turn. Gently
sumac and elm bear silent
witness as spiders weave
glistening webs on the bars.

                        ca. 1942

at my door

With pockets empty as skulls
   on shores of barren knolls

and wind-whipped cannibal coasts
   where sea cows graze

I saunter by harsh seawater
   beneath the sun's clatter

with the surf in my ear
   and the gull's moan

The years revolve in the twelve
   houses of the sun

where the beach dries
   under the archer's thighs

At night the dogstar howls
   at phosphorescent tides

and the planets veer
   as the world is gulped alive

My mind flaps like a fish
   on the ribbed sand

Tidewaters roar
   at my door

Key West, 1941

at the edge of midnight

at the edge of midnight
holy men bleed in bharat
beads are clicking on strings
and here we are controlling raw tongues
that lick all evidence from the sidewalks
where the cheetah howls
in the glowing chakras of commerce
where Lord Fuzzeye stumbles in his astral office
clawing at stockinged legs of despair
a pair of ducks drowned in the codpiece soup
brewed by mysterious hoodlums in magical dustbins
emerging as one-eyed monsters
drinking comfrey tea at lunch in the gaping apiaries
announcing the opening of a new underground railway
in a world of tampax formulae

HAROLD NORSE & SINCLAIR BEILES
London, Oct. 15, 1967

*written as joint cut-up from mind-images & random glances at newspapers &
books)*

attic of memory

Yellowed heavens, trunk of stars and pasteboard clouds,
Tin angels with leather wings, medallions of Bleeding Hearts,
Hoarse cries of boys in the slant room of summer heat
Musty with smells of underwear, mouldy photos, report cards
(Goldenrod and couchgrass waving in the vacant lot
Where washing flapped and flurried by a cracked brick wall).
Caruso and Mme. Schumann-Heink on scratchy platters
Dardanella plaintive through a raspy lily-horn
Queens of the Night steal through the shadows like musk
Trailing stale whiffs of flaky newsprint, sweetness of lavender,
Stiff rubber bands and tang of old face powder
Motheaten linen, cobwebby pillows, chewed handkerchiefs
Forgotten, address unknown, vanished with close relations
Morgue treasures, catcalls, stings of boyhood
Wisps of voices fading, familiar faces withering

1984

the bad lands, south dakota (summer, 1945)

Submerged Manhattanites
sunk in an alien world
we peered at the waterlogged road
where headlights cast a blurred glow.

Three days and nights the rain poured down,
windshield wipers groaned, the radio
sputtered. When we reached the Bad Lands,
my friend said, "It won't stop for days."

"It will stop," I said prophetically,
"when we leave the car." In dismay
he asked how I knew. It was a gift,
I said, of foretelling.

So we stepped into the murk.
That moment, precisely on cue,
the sun burst out, and the rain
parted like the Red Sea. My friend

gasped, speechless. Between two vast
black walls of water, dazed and alone,
we walked on the infernal plain
where torrential floods of biblical

proportions raced apart, leaving
a shaft of light and spray
and a tunnel vision of the evil land.
We stood dry as a bone between waterfalls.

I filmed warped minarets of twisted
cancerous ochre stone, sculpted
by the stark terrain that dripped
like an ocean bed raised from the sea.

Antic shapes and grave stone faces
of petrified turds, grotesque
as gargoyles in primeval decay,
shimmered with sick beauty.

Silent and tense, my friend took pictures

expecting the waters to converge on us.
I roamed like a tourist in Hell, touching
the yellow wood's fossilized art forms.

Was this Hades for Dakota Indians?
When we reentered the car
the cataracts joined violently
together with a cosmic clash.

Below, we glided like a submarine.
Did it really happen this way
half a century ago—that rare
clairvoyance and miracle?

It happened. I recall it clearly.
The friend and photos are gone.
Only the words, time capsules
of memory, remain.

1995?

the bay

Stretched near Scotch purse we lay
talking until the motors died.
You turned and swore in the grass,
cursing the grandees who killed for gold
at the mission trading posts.
You wanted to slay history's ghosts.
On a eucalyptus branch
a pelican sat. A porpoise nosed
the wave. We watched
hibiscus braid the coral wall,
mingling blood-red with bone-white.
Something you said made me keep still:
"Bitter is love words have to prove."
A plane swooped down, a bayonet
aimed at our hearts. My nerves jammed.
Across the inlet palms shook.
Hunkered down on my haunches
I fondled a cross-barred Venus.
Body language said it all.

Key West, 1942

beat hotel*

In the old Beat Hotel
They're eatin' Naked Lunch
With every psychedelic meal
Sippin' mescaline punch.

Oh, yeah, I wanna room
Where Beatniks used to dwell.
You could always score
At the old Beat Hotel.

A dragon guards the door—
Bluehaired Madame Rachou—
And lets the hip, the cool, the ghoul
And the beautiful pass thru.

Swedish girls with candles blazin'
In their yellow hair
Sing Christmas carols high upon
The snaky winding stair.

Brilliant punks and geniuses
Scramble up our brains,
Cut-up all our words and books,
Collage our joys and pains.

Oh, let's turn back the cuckoo clock,
Let's visit Gay Paree,
Let's find the medieval street
Every girl and boy must see,

The quaint and queer old flaky street
That made Beat history,
Where lies the heart, rue Gît le Coeur,
Long before you and me,

They tore up every floor and made
A first-class posh hotel.
It ain't what it used to be, no more
The old sleazy Beat Hotel

Near the leafy, lovely Boulevard
St. Michel where everyone was cool,

Oh yeah, it's gone with the geniuses.
Farewell old Beat Hotel.

*Paris: ca. 1960

beat hotel, 9 rue gît-le-coeur

. . . appalling, it reeked
of butts (Gauloises and
human) . . . stale wine . . . bohemians
leaning against pocked walls
marked with their scent . . . in grey
rooms . . . Gendarmes eye them,
at the entrance to the
bistro, suspiciously. Smoke-
stained white chenille curtains
drawn to keep out snoops.
Something strange about this place,
they'd mutter, scowling
at tourists and surrealists:
evidemment sales étrangers . . .
disreputable foreigners, hein.
Days of rage in Paris . . . *toujours*
with a kalashnikoff look,
a Molotov cocktail temper,
or an Uzi up your nose.
We're looking for someone, *monsieur,*
who could be you. *Dîtes-donc, alors.*
You don't say. Just keep
your mouth shut, speak
no French, and fade away.

1960

blackout

We sat on the bed talking of Cuba.
Your father's plantation, you said,
rolled to the sea. Señor Figueroa—
fat man with a jaguar face.

Taken with tropical imagery
we heard the sleet on the panes,
ignored the snow and the cold.
You said a Hawaiian kahuna
spilled your blood, staining
sand and coral, crossing
your veins with tribal blood
in sacred brotherhood.
The blackout enclosed us
in the dark, our hands joined,
our lips met in sacred brotherhood.
When the all-clear sounded
lights came on, the maid knocked
at the door, pushed through the halls
with her broom, and we forgot
the frangipani, the loincloths,
and went to a bar and got drunk.

New York 1942

blind

Blind blind blind. I've been blind,
I've been dumb, I've been thick as a tower,
numb as a stone. I've been laying my trip on you.
I don't want to.
The sick sick trip, the insensitive racket,
game of blame, poor me, I'll show you, I'm through.
Sick dread, sick gut, sick rage.
It ends in murdered feelings, it flashes
like a sword or a knife or a kick in the head.
The deadly power of the negative warp,
blind mind we can never know,
insane ego.

1978

buds

A tree
in peach-colored
    lamplight.
The trunk
curves
    upward.
Buds
    point
like
    arrowheads.

ca. 1941

the building

The government building stands at the edge of town.
When dusk falls the windows turn green as pools.

Uniformed guards keep the populace away.
Dogs on leashes sniff at the trees and pee.

In limousines emissaries wear turbans and fezzes.
Portfolios with secret documents contain the future.

At night the building grows more stately and wondrous,
glowing from within like undersea coral reefs.

Nearby bars and grilles shimmer at night
with fluorescent lights reflected in ice.

New York, ca. 1938

california

I dressed and shaved
and went down to the beach
and ran along the shore
nodding to the yogis
contemplating their navels
in the lotus position.
The sun could not rise
without their help.
I returned for lunch
and napped in the afternoon.
When I awoke it was evening.
On the beach the whales were dying,
the sea lions perishing,
the gulls choked with oil.
The air was brown.
There was nothing I could do.
California will sink
into the Pacific
and what is the coastline now
of many a land
will be the bed of the ocean,
said Edgar Cayce.
The people cannot understand.
They cannot draw sane conclusions.
They have been poisoned
by counterfeit nourishment.

They do not see
that they are with the gull
and the sagebrush,
the ocean and the spider,
the sky and the dove.

civilisation

When I read the pages of *Civilisation*
   by Sir Kenneth Clark
      invariably
         I turn

to Federigo di Montefeltro
     Duke of Urbino
     painted by Justus of Ghent.

The embattled Duke sits in full armor,
     his helmet beside him
         on the floor, book in hand

reading
    but prepared to fight
      at a moment's notice
         for poetry
            and humanity.

He founded a kingdom on these.

When his bookseller inquired,
     "What is necessary
         to rule a Kingdom?"

the Duke replied:
    "Essere umano."
      "To be human."

coda for a hairy dance

I like cats licking
   their paws
   kids playing
in marble ruins
cool nites &
sharp stars on
      Greek hills
   youths dancing
with heavy movements
in tavernas
   bawling *bouzouki**
   with ouzo throats
     & resin blood
crackling palms &
villas that peel
   & the sun burning
   my skin coppery
   gold
& words
   rolling
   crashing
     like waves
without end
& without beginning
fantastic yarns in all tongues
cascading visions
   dreams jokes
   passions happenings
     minute after minute
       without end
ebb & flow of a
   fabulous opera
aardvarks hippogryphs gula birds
   gila monsters
     hula dancers
hipsters drifters princes
drinking & smoking
together in bars
     with a yen
   to make one & one
add up to
    if not now WHEN!

the whole arsenal of
　　　　experience
　　　in a surprise
　　package
of images like a
concentrated pill that
hits the central nervous
system

*Greek folk music

1964

conversation by firelight (1944)

We warm ourselves before the fire
and marvel at the colossal death
that is a flicker of history.
The flames go higher.
We stretch before the firelight,
take sides and make predictions.
The flames leap and consume
the logs as we are consumed.

New York, 1944

dead rat on the shore

I saw a dead rat on the shore
in Spain—bloated, gashed, all skin
Children poked it with long sticks
the tide attacked it with sharp shells
the sun struck savagely again and again
casting strange rat-shadows
till a posture of the paws
was like a dancing cancer
and no more ugly than a man
rinsed clean of greed and hate
the rat turned lyrical
in the fierce afternoon
and I left it there

Spain/56

departure

At the railroad yard in Miami we stood
on cross ties and cinders in the mist.
The porter smiled. In the early light
sailors and soldiers departed, steam
valves hissed. At newstands headlines
bannered war. Redcaps collected
footstools, and called "All aboard!"
You boarded and waved from the window
as the train lurched out of Florida
and you blew a farewell kiss.

Miami, 1942

electric shock of orgasm

all forms of love are natural.

Electric shock of orgasm, lightning bolt of ecstasy,
natural force beyond words, flash of flesh beyond belief,
split-second illumination, mystery of creation,
rapturous out-of-body experience through the body,
sexual urge overwhelming reason, again and again
urge for fulfilment, urge for beauty, urge for worship,
urge for body, urge for soul, urge for being,
urge for union with same or opposite sex,
urge to merge, urge to surge, urge to fuse,
urge beyond age, urge beyond rage, urge beyond sage,
urge beyond State, urge beyond hate, urge to procreate,
urge of singular being merging with all being,
electric shock of orgasm illuminating desire.

San Francisco, 8/20-24/1999
Revised Sept. 2/Oct.29/2000

everglades

In avocado groves the jaguar prowls
under the yuccas with drooping bells.
The four-toed grebe lands on lily pads
And mist rises in brackish bayous.
With widespread wings the osprey suns
on broken roots. Cannas flame
like a sea on fire.

Key West ca. 1941

fag-bashing in the afternoon

A shiny blue sedan
behind my car
on a side street

littered
with broken glass
newspapers
homeless
souls. A
struggle   white
arms interlacing   grappling
behind the steering wheel

head

and shoulders protruding
above it   young   muscular
with brutish beauty he leans
down
trunk forward
his
strong arms kneading   churning
two soft   thick arms

entangled
with — some girl   ?

          invisible

head
              between his legs . . .

              Trembling

with voyeur excitement
pretending

            to look for a key
with furtive glances

        watching those
smooth bare arms . . .   ah
passion   I thought   has swept them
   out of their senses
in the heat of the afternoon . . .

          The hidden head
floats   up   beside the youth
   beefy   bleeding   a man ! !

          bolt upright   dazed
          as if in dreamlife
          the bald pate bled . . .

In haste the youth
pulls on a t-shirt
                  attempting

a getaway   !   the old
man trying to
    stop him catches

another blow on his battered
skull   !
             tumbling

          out of the car
          stumbling   emitting
piercing screams
of his whistle

<pre>
                    distress
signals tear
the street to shreds. The
          young man fled.

          Enraged   the old man's
          nose and mouth turn into a snout
          pouting   a small boy's mouth
          twisted with pain
                    a lifetime
          of choked rage

               remembering

(disabled by derision)

     they called him . . . *sissy!*

A stifled scream . . .
Boys don't scream   don't cry.

Old man
blowing his whistle
          at the world

unable to cry   to bear
the bloody mark on his forehead
the world's closed door.
</pre>

                                          2.x.91 SF

farewell allen ginsberg

Wasn't afraid of God or death after his 48th year. —Ginsberg, "Ego Confession"

I know I am deathless . . . Believing I shall come again upon the earth after five-thousand years. —Walt Whitman, Leaves of Grass

A peck providing a morsel of love, a blessing,
always a kiss on the mouth, a gentle greeting,
connecting, networking, always a voice of truth,

now farewell, your last word a cheerful "Toodle-oo!"

Shamanic bard heard round the world,
your electronic voice will haunt us forever.
Two-thousand years ago a poet described us all:
"Nothing exists but atoms and the void," he wrote.
Thus Lucretius survives as you survive, larger than life,
visionary, sage, poet, great ambassador of the universe.

Crowned King of the May in Czechoslovakia,
followed by thousands of youths who kissed you
and pulled your carriage thru the streets of Prague,
you got booted out by the communist secret police
who confiscated your notebooks of dangerous propaganda
for peace and love, for tearing the veil from everyone's eyes,
for exposing truthless beliefs, for exploding popular delusions,
for stirring up youth with flower power and for writing poems
that open the doors of perception and shatter walls of hallucination.

We first met in an empty subway in wartime 1944, New York;
you were a drunken boy, 18, reciting aloud "The Drunken Boat"
by another drunken boy, 19, and you sat across the aisle from me
and I yelled "Rimbaud!" over the roar of the train and you howled,
"You're a poet!" and we both sloshed thru the snow in deserted streets
of Greenwich Village dawn 3 AM to my icy room by the slaughterhouse
and you nervously showed me your poetry and I shyly showed you mine
and that was about all we showed each other, to my everlasting sad
    regret.

A nervous virgin you shyly departed as chaste as you had arrived
and I watched you rise like a meteor and we remained good friends
for more than half a century. Perhaps in another life we'll meet again
and I'll ask, "Haven't we met before?" And you'll say, "You look familiar
Was it five-thousand years ago?" And I'll say, "Sure, let's be friends
    again!"

I will always remember you
on late night New York subways
as a shy virgin in a snowbound trance.
You've taken your last ride underground
and Corso and Kesey wept at your bedside.
Now you're all gone and the world mourns.
Once you said, "You should wanna make love
to everyone in the universe," and you almost did.

Clicking finger cymbals, wearing colored beads and
sitting cross-legged chanting OM in your deep gravel voice
you changed the world. We were mobbed in L.A. you and I
by young people after our reading and we got a great ovation
and on the stage you lifted me up in an ardent brotherly embrace
and pulled the veil from everyone's eyes exposing false delusions,
false beliefs, false accusations, false insinuations, false exaggerations.
O great courage-teacher, you'll haunt us forever in your eternal absence.

San Francisco 7/21/1997; 6/7-14/1999; 25/ix/2002.

first love

I couldn't keep
my eyes off him.
Waking and before
sleeping I gazed
at his gray-blue
eyes that stared
with innocence
at me. I felt sad
for his soft heart
and longed to warn
him of the loss
of friendship and
love. I couldn't
do it. He wouldn't
understand. The
distance was too
great between us.
He was 21, I was
81. Of course it
happened not
once or twice
but again and
again. He lost
everything to
invidious friends.
With longing
I stared at my
young photo
with its gray-blue

eyes, its innocence
buried in a trunk
for 60 years.
Now I know
that it isn't love.
It's a blind date
with one's self.

7/ii/98/SF. Revised 14/iv/2000;5/i/2002/SF

for all we know

"The new always carries with it the sense of violation, of sacrilege. What is dead is sacred. What is new, that is, different, is evil, dangerous, or subversive." — Henry Miller

"Eli, Eli, lama sabachthani? Lord, Lord, why hast thou forsaken me?" — Jesus Christ

"For all we know, the moon is made of green cheese." — Popular saying

For all we know Jesus Christ is alive and well,
    a mystical reality hidden from earth's tunnel vision,
        seen thru an ithyphallic plant, psylocibin, the magic mushroom,
            imagined thru spores bringing great sex thrills and communion
                with His vast immortal soul, unimaginable and more esoteric
                    than the mysterious interconnections of the human brain.

For all we know Jesus Christ can be seen as long ago
    in their holy order the saintly Jewish Essenes saw Him,
        a sage, a young boy, physically Mary's son born in the flesh
            from incomprehensible dimensions sprung from the Lord
                of the Universe, sacred, inexplicable, immortal yet mortal,
                    a dreamer in cosmic seas teaching simple spiritual love,
                        a godlike superhuman Jew nobler than kings and queens,
                        a myth of divine immortality, improbably beyond death.

For all we know Jesus Christ resurrects in the flesh
    when the flame of the flesh erects in ecstasy thru love,
        creating bliss and transporting the soul out of the body
            in momentary orgasmic ascension, split second of wild joy,
                out-of-time-and-space-and-body vast sensation through sex,
                    Christ as kundalini-phallus-yoni, mysterious incredible soul.

For all we know Jesus Christ flows thru our life like a solar power
   to the utmost farthest reaches of the mind and spirit in the cosmos,
      more powerful than hydrogen bombs, His atomic energy permeates
         a manic world of good-and-evil madness, hysteria, hate and love, all
            in depths of body and soul eruption as we come with awesome
            force
              bursting, shimmering iridescent fireworks in a dark night of the
            flesh,
                O magical indelible moment of rapture! O mystery of the holy
            union!
                  For all we know Jesus Christ is a Cosmic Lover in the body of
            us all.
                            SF/1983; 9/23-29; 10/1-4; 9/1999; 10/30/2000

fourteen: a vision

Sleepless one night I gazed from a window
at the stars with awakening teenage wonder
(who am I? where am I going? why?)
then levitated through infinite space
joining vast tides of women and men
nude bodies swirling round and round
soaring in waves of desire, blending
in and out of each other, merging
and separating again and again
writhing into birth, love, death
in a limbo of limbs in waves of desire
women and men and men and men
again and again and women and women
in a limbo of love in a film-noir print
of Purgatory by Dante Alighieri
and Gustave Doré indelibly etched
in my mind when and when and when
many years later I spoke of this
to a famous wise old poet who said
"Only true poets have this vision
at that age only," thanks Robert Graves
again and again I've never ceased
to seek such ecstasy again and again
in beautiful women and beautiful men

für ein neugeborenes

Willkommen in der Menschlichen Rasse
Wir sind alle Schweiner
Hofentlich wirt du besser sein
Aber das ist nicht möglich

which, freely translated, goes:

For A Newborn Baby

Welcome to the human race
We're all a bunch of swine
Hopefully you'll be better
But not bloody likely

the gift of love

Consider the importance now of love,
the darkened room, the body's charm

healing what words have bruised:
the sympathy beneath our feelings.

Consider the importance now of touch
that soothes the ego's rampages,

apostasy of friends turned foes.
We linger in the present moment

away from words that wound and kill
and find the world made new again

as we accept the gift of love,
most dear and most abused.

New York, 1939

the goldfish & the café

I was sitting at the café
with my friend René Fatton
who chewed on a small twig
and grunted
at the passersby
with a ferocious playfulness.
It was Easter it was April it was Paris.
The sun was really shining.
René talked to everybody
crying: *Vive la vie! Vive le monde!*
Egalité! Fraternité! Puberté!
Long live Puberty!
He addressed bums women children dogs.
Then he told the story
with blue-eyed blond-haired wonder—
the story of the goldfish
who lived in the bowl
of the man across the street.
When the man returned from
his Easter vacation
he found the bowl dry
and the goldfish gasping
on the floor.
He fed him fried potatoes
a fine beefsteak
plenty of wine.
And when the goldfish was well
he led him down
the Boulevard St. Michel
on a string.
At the Jardins de Luxembourg
the goldfish felt thirsty
so he stooped over the pool
to drink, but suddenly slipped
fell in & —
drowned!
UGH said René
to the passersby
chewing on his twig—I don't know
what kind of a twig,
maybe alder or birch.
I don't know. It was a twig.

The owner came out & said:
Are you all right? Are you enjoying yourself?
I've never been happier,
smiled René. VIVE-VOUS!
But the owner frowned.
It's all right to be happy, René . . .
but quietly, sir!   quietly!
And the owner's son
came over & said:
Are you sick? Is something wrong?
No, said René. I'M ALIVE!
But the owner's son frowned.
Sounds like a serious illness to me!
and he went off scowling.
Behind the cash register.

Shit! said René. MERDE!
and he broke his twig, saying,
I must go home now
and wash out my ears
with music. . . .

goons in the garden

there are goons in my garden
they wear no shoes & their feet stink
they lounge around on the grass
                    the bluegreen grass
scratching their armpits
    yawning
        stretching
            handling their balls
        in beat up jeans
    swearing
in Elizabethan English

o thou whoreson dog!
i'll impale thee lout anent
    my stiff codpiece!

no walls
the garden stretches
     to pale eternity
  a rusty ancient key
     imprisoned on a cord
        above
           the old oaken bucket
       in this blue ridge dream
& what would happen
       asks a voice
    should the key be free?
         ah then it would fly
            like an arrow
       into the heart of the well
             with a great splash
         releasing golden swallows that
        flock up to the sun

but the goons the goons!
        their big dirty feet
   sticking out of stovepipe jeans
         lazing loafing
             yokelling
shit! i'll kick them out
       give em their walking papers
    cut them from my life

ah but then who'd be left?

don't worry
there'll always be
   goons in the garden

gstaad

The sun makes its brief shy appearance.
Little vapors—where do they come from?—
upward drifting from rockface
and slopes of wild cypress,
cedar and pine,
like cigarette smoke or
big faceless genies.
Geese honk and scratch below
on the vegetable lawn
as mad wet hens
raise a racket
beside the road where cars roll by
and a truck clatters.
A sweet rhythmic tinkle-thunder
as of oriental temple bells
approaches. It's a herd
of 3 stately cows, enormous and brindled,
with giant coppery bells making this music.
They take their time
and traffic has to recognize their majesty,
their right of way:
sacred cows in rain.
And there goes Krishnamurti, umbrella in hand,
blue jeans swinging, mind exploding,
each moment renewed, reborn
in this silverhaired timeless man
walking through rain like light
in the world's gray grief.
I wonder at his presence, watch him
from my chalet window till he vanishes

*

Aureole of sunlight on the mountaintop and
a tiny ant car all creamy, crawling along the greenery
till all the steamy vapors rise and join
to make one disappearing cloud.

*

Not thinking now,
just listening

to movements,
animal, vegetable,
mechanical,
just watching
trees
rubbed with smokemist,
watching things
in themselves
from my window,
clouds, rain, snow,
and a burst of light
illuminating
the valley

*

How long can you look at a snowy Alp?
Trees are blossoming, dandelions smear
their brilliance on green hillsides
where cows munch and bees are busy
and I scratch a young bull's head.
He regards me tenderly, sadly,
he is my only friend.
Perhaps the converse is also true?
Great cows come at a gallop,
they have long sharp horns
that curve beautifully.
They lower their horns at the young bull
who runs away.
Then the biggest cow
snorts a stream of spit
that hits me in the face.

*

1977

the hermitage of arlesheim

A true retreat away from the world
    in silent leafy splendor

    O BEATA SOLITUDINE!
scrawled in black letters on rock

earthen steps strewn with wet
    September leaves

    O SOLA BEATITUDO!
    (scrawled on stone)
    among mossy caverns
       and vast grots

small hut clad in rough bark
near the ROCK OF SOLITUDE
I can't enter the hut
         VERBOTEN!

UP UP to the Hermitage
on twiggy path
to a locked shrine
and sedimentary rock
faint imprint scratched
on the rock wall

3 monkish forms
look abstract
like ancient cave drawings

  VORWORTS! past a barklined cabin
    really a spooky cave
  wreathed with leaves and branches
    recalling long-departed monks
playing with themselves in isolation
  like me with no one beside me
    to comment and giggle
      or shush me
    into awed respect

    bird chirp
  breaking the stillness

Arlesheim's off the tourist track
Ah, here's a gaping hole and stone seat
where some hermit used to sit
on a cave floor full of water
in dark gloom

Did he sit with his feet in cold water?
some new St. Anthony
trying to shake off sexy thoughts?

churchbells toll
in the distance
small birds sing
JUGJUG
a couple hoves
into view   young lad
about 20   eyes brimming
with lust
his girl
equally hot
in his embrace
both stuck
together   both suck
sweet lips in oblivious bliss
then disappear
in forest murmurs

O BEATO DUO!
where hermits struggled
against nature
NO DOGS ALLOWED!
screams a sign in German

another sign informs us

DAS SCHLOSS BIRSECK KANN BESICHTIGT WERDEN
15. MÄRZ/15.OKT.
THE CASTLE CAN BE SEEN BETWEEN
15 MARCH/15 OCT.

cowbells chime dogs bark
and here's pastureland
a farmhouse where
cows graze and dump

                    cowflop
            hens cluck   bitch barks
              like 500 years ago
                   or 5000

        the world's not about to end
        earth still fresh still breathing
        not choked by chemical death
        not crushed by industrial doom
        great feeling of long-lastingness

                   lovers
                   stuck
                 together
                   walk
                   as if
                  keeping
                   each
                   other
                   from
                  falling
                   down
            2 boys in jeans
              speed by
            on a motorbike
             on the road

          straight white line
           cut in sunny sky
          stroke trail of plane
       over 16th century hermitage
          and nearby farmhouse

             lucky to be here
            away from smog
       feeling like Bosch or Burns
          wee sleekit cowerin'
            timorous beastie
      oh what a panic's in thy breastie
             2 young bulls
          lock hornless heads
          under an appletree
                a sign
      half-hidden between boughs:

SCHLOSS REICHENSTEIN

I take the highroad
on this mountain terrain
another sign

NO SHOOTING

then stumble upon
a shooting gallery
hidden among rocks
soldiers in dugout
taking aim
at targets that slide
along rails
how SWISS
like cheese and banks
and chocolate
and watches
and brass bands
the military pops up everywhere
in every mossy nook
and cranny

HELVETIA!

defend your yodelling gold
like Fafner in the Rhine journey!
do Nibelungen guard your treasure?
soldiers shoot
as I pass with my backpack
grimfaced young men
in gray uniforms
Guten Tag! Good day!
they don't respond
They're protecting Swiss chocolate
and Swiss banks
Now at last the castle tower
looms beyond the shooting gallery
and the hermitage at the summit
locked
silent
above
a grandiose panorama

I stand beneath a coat of arms
medieval grandeur
a stranger in a strange land
from another time
will a mastiff leap at my throat?
or a crazed castle keep?
or a Quasimodo creep?
HA! to be shot at from slits in the tower!

should I sneak
thru the underbrush?
thru thick foliage?
I see
Basel below
and no birds sing

1971/Arlesheim, Switzerland
(Revised 12/25/2000, 3/28/2002 SF)

high school

This is a world ambitious for the great,
the perfect body, the discovery
of power and money.

Here the dream of the future, the fantasy
of genius and beauty, fame and luck,
gathers its forces.

The teacher sees the generations pass,
the bright grow dull, the awful happen,
the few succeed.

He judges the unequal struggle
like a harvester reaping his crop,
bumper or barren.

He sees beyond the football field,
the gym, the swimming pool,
the auditorium,

Watching the longings of erotic children,

loveless, hurt and desperate,
    baffled by lack,

And asks the persistent question: "Why are they
    here? Who will protect them from failure
      and suffering?"

The walls with their posters on housing,
    Depression murals, water colors, photos,
      and the hopeful look

Of the young in yearbooks, the literary society,
    debating and glee clubs and art class,
      speak for them:

"Don't ask us; we know nothing; all we know
    is what you teach, we have no answers.
      Ask the principal,

Ask the president, ask the congressman,
    ask the Hollywood star, the judge,
      the movie mogul,

ask the novelist, scientist, sociologist,
    ask the doctor, the psychoanalyst,
      ask the priest, ask God.

Don't ask us. We're the conditioned reflex,
    the imprint of your words, the product,
      the sum of your errors.

We're only on the brink of understanding
    with immature brains and hungry mouths
      and no caresses,

Pride of your old age, cannon-fodder for your wars.
    We're the life you gave, the heart you break.
      We're not the problem."

The unplanned future keeps growing like a fungus
    out of control as we peer with innocence
      at a stranger's world:

One at a subway kiosk selling newspapers

who had meant to become a tycoon; one
    pushing a cart

Who had planned to become an author; one
    in a drunk tank, one in a junkyard,
        one in a madhouse.

They cannot speak, their silence is their death.
    "O must I wander alone, be hurt forever
        by those who belong?

Give me hope, give me joy, give me love.
    I am too young to be spurned
        in boardrooms and offices.

Take me into account while there's still time
    to redeem the failure of nerve,
        the life like a cancer.

Do not abandon me to an uncertain future."
    The world has no answer and we have no voice
        but the cry of rage.

New York, 1938/revised 2/i/2002, SF

hymn to him

1.

He was twelve when he toted a bag
for the mob worth ten grand, bought dope
and girls, drank from the tap and rapped
about juvie and jail. "I got charisma," he said.
A master of Dungeons and Dragons,
card games and tricks, he'd charm the tail
off a dragon. Or man. He can make a man cum
with a kiss. Like his mom he smoked pot
and hustled at twelve. His dads were a blur
of men whose violence came with their dicks.
Bossed and betrayed by adults every day
of his life, kicked, raped and punched, stabbed
and burned, he knew what was felt
on the streets of his project milieu.

2.

He kicks his way through bad dreams,
spending the night bashed and doped.
I watch his heavy-lashed eyes,
the defiant jawline, the parted lips
of a battered child, the shadow of beard.
In exchange for incredible legs
and thighs of a faun and flat ears,
and the hard ass of a statue, I give
shelter and money and head. His body
refreshes my life, a quick dip
in the fountain of youth. Years
leave me empty and wasted until
a boy from the streets, disturbed,
spends the night, giving me freedom
to gaze, touch and kiss, and I cream.

3.

His body's a joy. His face stops men dead.
He is negative, meaning HIV minus.
His life is a drag. Hooking on Polk Street
in adult bookstores, he's used up at twenty.
Hustling pays off in kicks. The rich
and the famous would know. They blow him.
His beauty works like a charm, covers up
everything else. He needs help. This
means blotting it out with his tricks.

4.

Madonna steps into her limo. He sits
next to her. One foot away, he says.
The kids scream. They go wild.
He stays calm, looks like a child.
She touches his face. He breaks out his stash
a foot long on the glass. She snorts it all
in one blast. Forks over two hundred
and fifty. Gives him a kiss. He is stoned.
She floats off to her starstruck world.

5.

One of my dads used to beat me
after raping me. He warned
I'd be dead if I snitched. Another
broke dishes on my head

if he saw food stains after
I washed them. My mom didn't care.
She slapped me to make me a man,
called me sissy, then put me
in placement at nine when they
caught me with another boy.
Boys played with each other
under the blankets at night. I had
them all and learned how to fight.
When I got caught screwing a boy
the guard decked me and sneered:
You fag! I sank my teeth into his leg.
They put me in solitary, said I was nuts,
unpredictable. I was just hurt,
had enough of adults and fought back.

1991

in the museum of modern art
new york

I stood sweating   before   the world
        of exploding   wheat   and
                shuddering   suns
the visceral   churning   paint
        of the mad   Dutchman   who ended
        up   in a tree   with lead
            in his brain   screaming
                        & holy

30 years   after   my vision   of
            heavenly   hell
    in vibrating   yellows   and stormy
            blacks   and thick swollen
            greens   I'd weep   if I could
    but my head   is shot up   with decades
                of painkillers   and
            jackhammers   blast   the wheat

1971

invocation for ira cohen

Ira Cohen, magician,
raconteur, photographer, Jew,
kvetch with bristling black beard,
gold earring, bald head, long hair,
and slinky sorcerer's gown
sweeping thru Amsterdam like a vampire
with silver glitter caste mark
third eye logo
namaste
I know yr *Stauffenberg Cycle*
warning Stay out of Germany!
the swastika swoops at yr magic dome
the world shrinks like yr heart
Achtung!
stay in the Kosmos
stay in Paradiso
stay in Ins and Outs
stay in the red light district
stay in The Golden Hard Cock
stay in Amsterdam
stay
stay
stay
out of Germany!

Ira Cohen, mystic,
visionary, psylocybin poet,
I remember yr first mescaline trip
in the Casbah in Tangier
when you were thin and clean-shaven,
eyeing the mosaics in the hammam
flinging wide the doors of perception
teller of endless tales
in New York monotone city voice
namaste
I know yr *Gnaoua*
warning Stay out of cold logic!
the bald eagle swoops at yr hashish head
the dollar shrinks like yr heart
Achtung!
stay in the center
stay in the love-zone

stay in the nude
stay in the comic strip
stay in the dharma
stay in the smile
stay
stay
stay
out of cold logic!

Ira Cohen, doer,
eater of fame, lover of name,
don't worry it comes without asking
don't chase it, don't sweat it
just let it happen like a *Growing Hand*
forget the Great Society
we make it ourselves, we *are* the impossible dream
we connect when we scream
namaste
I know yr poems to Allen Ginsberg and Bob Dylan
warning Stay out of power!
the crown swoops at yr pate
holiness shrinks like yr heart
Achtung!
stay in the flame
stay in wonder
stay in tenderness
stay in splinters
stay in billiards
stay in identity
stay
stay
stay
out of power!

20.ix.78/Amsterdam

"it must have been so comfy before tv"

It must have been so comfy before TV
and DDT and carbon fumes
when you could eat without being poisoned
and drink without your teeth falling out
it must have been so comfy when the air was real air
and people were real people and evil meant no good
and was it ever like that and did we ever exist
before everything turned into death
or was it always make-believe
my nervous system cannot survive these pollutants
my mind cannot survive lesser evils
I cannot choose between two deaths
my nails are bitten down
my fingers stained with anxiety
my poems are moments snatched from decay
my life is a short story without meaning
and ends with a landlady saying:
Now who will pay the back rent?

jack, how's the void?

For Jack Kerouac

cold mountain water
gushing from pipe
in mossy cattle trough

peaks & valleys
in 3 pm August sun
look immortal

but they'll go like friends
that time and booze caught up with
women & boys & fame & dollars

    —gone!
        they screamed
        of loneliness

    & injustice
    & got older
    talking
        to oblivion

Kerouac you're nothing now
only a name—great one! I
shake your ghosty hand
    in oblivion

Jack, how's the void? we'll meet
there!   big San Remo in the sky!
    nah! we'll never meet
again, estranged
by everything
by time
money
lies

by vanity
by death

flipflops of planetary woe!

                1970/Alps above Gstaad

jesus freaks

I

my old man used to lay on a couch
as I played on the floor
a cigarette dangling from
his hand until
the narks would break in
and rush past me to the toilet
where he was flushing the smack
down the drain.
when he planned armed robbery
his habit was $60. a day
and to steady his nerves
he watched TV, some evangelist
prayin hard

for sinners.
my old man started laughing so much
and screaming, "Hallelujah!" he fell off the couch.
but when the evangelist called everybody
to confess and be saved
he started acting peculiar
like he was gonna crawl right thru the tube.
when the evangelist said, "Put your hand on the TV!
touch it!" he did
and fell down, crying
and rolling and yelling
"I'm saved! I'm saved!"
a little blue light lit up in his head.
and right there he stopped smoking and fixing
and went out to the FourSquare Church
and another miracle, man!
he had this one leg
shorter than the other
from an old car accident.
when the local evangelist said,
"Stretch forth thy leg!" he did
and that leg shot out, it *stretched*
and became equal to the other leg.
you could see where the bone
had lengthened the scar.
everybody prayed
and my old man became a preacher
and a barber
and cuts our hair short.
praise the Lord!
my grandmother was a whore
and my father a junkie.
Brother, come to Christ!

just like old dr. faust

Ah, Señor, I would sell my soul
for a chance to be 20 in Barcelona
on a night like this
student voices under my window
bellowing songs
as they pour into the square
with drunken arrogance

God, if I were 20
I wouldn't waste my time
reading Karl Marx
or learning to be a lawyer
I'd stay drunk and stoned
and fuck the time away
knowing
that in the not too distant future
I'd look from a window at 2 a.m.
beyond the assistance
of Mr. Marx
        or Mr. Freud
or
        Mr. Christ

l.xi.78 / Barcelona

the keys

By Greyhound bus on the Dixie Highway
as we speed past swamps and sawgrass
a drawbridge spanning the estuary
deposits us on shimmering reefs
of opalescent beryl. The wind
weaves in the window as we wind
through narrow lanes, wisps of brine
that tantalize like a dim memory.
As we race down the Keys I recall
Gasparilla and old Mansvelt
in these coves long, long ago
sailing their brigantines—to Torch,
Ramrod and Sugarloaf—swept to lagoons

at Matecumbe, leaning in the wind
—outlaw pirates fleeing hostile Europe
to shelter under palms of paradise.
Calico Jack, Blackbeard, I think of you
on these isles of sun-bleached bones.

Key West, 1941

koko

(A 1985 *Time* Picture of the Year)

The gorilla on her back
in the fetal position
clutches with gargantuan paws
the tiny kitten
to her hairy chest
hugging it almost to death.
But the kitten
has nothing to fear. Brimming
with primate love for the feline
in her gorilla grasp, Koko stares
tenderly as the kitten
stares back on an eyebeam
of mammal communication
signaling trust, though wary,
of her Queen Kong. Only
the furry red head visible,
engulfed entirely, the kitten purrs
if a picture can purr. The
tenderness in both
surpasses understanding.
Kinder and gentler than
homo sapiens, among whom we've seen
more infinitely terrible
specimens, though some
come up to her standards
of decency (most don't), the ape
gives us pause.

31.iii.91/SF

lament for a spanish guitar

The rain tears down your defenses slicing the grin from your mouth.
I rage senselessly because life gets dirty like dishes and I can't accept
that appalling fact. You retreat into the rainbow colors of your guitar.
Sadness of imperfection changes miraculously into melody.
With the folksinger's emotional skill, clutching the cliff of music
you hang from the notes above the pit. I come into your room
wanting to share the sounds that transform our pathos into joy,
my mouth snapping at love. My grin grows back again
My mouth forms words around the music and our feelings rush gently
into the space from which the rain recedes and the light returns.

Barcelona, 1979; San Francisco, 2001

the landlord's daughter
and other tales

I've never been the same since the night I peeked
   from the bay window of my room thru the trees
      over her bedroom where she exposed
         herself one summer evening.

In the parlor I pressed against her as we kissed
   and she said I looked like a movie star
      and whined "Let's do it sitting down!"
        I asked her why but got no answer.

When I pressed harder and twisted her arm
   "Ouch!" she said, "ouch!" and blushed bright red,
      and stammered, "because—because—we're not
        married!" which stunned me and suddenly
      I understood my childhood was over.

           *

          some frightening
          man put his hand
            on my thigh
         when I got up
           he grabbed me
         I said my mom was

in the back row
and I'd tell if he didn't stop
        but he gave me candy
that I wouldn't eat
        I thought it was poison
my mom had warned about
        taking candy from strange
men so I broke away and
        changed my seat
and when I grew up I became
        a strange man

                *

        the sun also rose
    with a clunk in Brooklyn
    I grew like a tree of heaven
in backyards and brownstone stoops
    as Gershwin swept across the city
        with lyric eloquence

    and violence erupted as usual
            to Viennese waltzes
        as Europe got "gobbled up"
            by the "krauts"
    and Adolf did his little pirouette
        under the Arc de Triomphe
    at the flame of the Unknown Soldier
who was going to become much more unknown
    in the Pathé Newsreel Eyes of the World

        my teacher wept in class
    while I groped myself under the desk
    history less interesting than biology
"the tragedy of the dream" not yet on my shoulders
    and the tree of heaven spread over clotheslines
        and pushed through concrete

    Gershwin played such rhapsodies
            of urban blue!
            I hear it now
            blue notes
        in Harlem nite spots
            the Jewish/Negro
            wail

love & hate

Under moonlit marble columns
I saw the twisting female dance
Of a white cat in heat, grimed
And maddened on the stones.
Held off by snarls, swift frenzied claws
The male bided his time; then pounced,
Seized with his teeth her neck.
Spastic with heat, she spat, scratched,
Howled and screeched on the cobbles.
On this street behind the Forum
Pulled by the same animal heat
I, too, love and hate
And like Catullus must admit
I don't know why, and cannot sleep.

Rome 1954

love rinses its hair full of stars

the frozen hotel wears a collar of lips
we follow corpses into a lake
of newspapers and dead flags
flowers scream
images sprout from their sticky leaves
a voice proclaims: I ERASE ALL MEMORY
a nun bleeds in the mirror
a radio scratches the sky with raucous announcements
ice cubes take possession of Vesuvius
chimneys write news items in Persian Rose Smoke
a man comes out of the ground singing

Love rinses its hair full of stars

love-junk

your image keeps probing
with sharp insistence
like a rotten molar's dying nerve

I cannot uproot absence
& sleep is no answer

I'm at the end of empty roads
that stretch for years
(humming a tune) to you
unknown identity
                  who takes shape
to fuck me
          into paranoia
of losing
           you

my body weakens
with terror

knowing

persistent need
that kept us
           (once)
so close

another country
& what is left
of the few familiar
possessions a
handful of old jazz &
francois couperin
        on the old
portable philips
1 lamp
a few unmatched socks
      some fotos

of you & other ex-loves
whom now you have
            joined

                    5

I sit fumbling
in a tiny kitchen
stumbling
over garbage heaps
in cartons
dreaming back to
our best times together
knowing
my blood cannot discharge
what poisons
have gathered there

                    6

sleepless I stare
at a hawk's feather
stuck on the wall
from New Mexico
snow slips over the hill
like a bandage

goofballs turn me on awhile
then I sleep sleep
restless like screaming
but wake too soon in a rush
            of doubt

my yellow eyes fall
on black newsprint
it crawls towards me like insects
on black boots   STOP!
STOP!
            STOP!

                    9

there is only the one
fix? why?
the whole world heaves
like a dream reeling
thru the street & in spite

of lonely nights
there's surely someone
who'll show with the works—strip
down at the right time
w/out too much fuss
& maybe even share this
isolation—fill it
with laughs

10

I throw 3 coins to know
when it will happen
& hang in like an old pro
against the ropes
refusing
to be counted out

Heidelberg, 1966 / *London,* 1967

the madness of the white race

I see you now
a multi-headed mask
cold eyes through white hoods
as once in Alabama I saw you
in the shipyard of Mobile
building Liberty ships
to fight the Nazi terror
a sudden commotion
draws us from sheet metal
into the yard
a mob
goes mad
screaming
with hate
beating a
gray old man
with fists
lead pipes
his black hair torn
his black face bashed
his black blood shed

his black eyes dazed
his black soul crushed
his black life lost
my white face shocked
my white voice mocked
my white soul stunned
my white hope dashed
by the madness
of the white
race

1941, Mobile, Alabama

the madonna of trapani

She wears her jewels, patient,
and a curious triangular smile
whose apex at the bottom of her mouth
is quizzical yet tolerant.

How heavy that gold crown!
rakish, worldly-large
and foreign to such features
more ivory than marble.

And that shiny babe
squirming, almost, in her arms
—can he support such weight of gold?

And those devotions, tireless, of hags
in black, mumbling—waiting for miracles.

The hot church, like a bazaar, hangs cloth
of red and blue, the doors are wide,
the scirocco purls steam out of Africa
over this crowded, orient madonna
who seems, glistening, to sweat.

Believe! believe! the fisher-folk are praying.
The gentle statue echoes: *leave, leave!*

The island, too, is triangular.

Windmills grind sea-salt
where long ago the Turkish sailors hauled
her, among spices, to the Sicilian port.

Believe! the fisher-folk had cried.

And when the Turks would take it back,
they loaded her upon a cart
and gave the oxen head
to draw it seawards—or towards land.
Inland the oxen stomped—so legend goes.

In tobacco shops, on picture cards
she smiles now among movie stars.

The town smells fishy and queer.
Her patience is immense.
You cannot tell
if she is comfortable here.

manlift big 4 rent

(**Technical,** from Gk. *technikós < technë,* belonging to the arts, art, allied
to *techton,* a carpenter. Cf. Skt. *takshan,* a carpenter, from *taksh,* to cut
wood. Allied to **Text,** of a book, an author.—*Skeat*)

In my bedroom over the backyard
fence I hear a loud beeper
from the neighboring yard.
A man on a derrick operates it
with a panel of buttons.
Carpenters hammer and saw
wooden posts, replacing old posts
and stairs for steps they've ripped out.
Two storeys gape like a toothless mouth.
The boss has the look of an Irish poet,
sandy hair mussed, old features
stern, sensitive, a masterbuilder.
Like a feudal guild they possess
dignity. When they nod at me
I nod from my window

over the fence, engrossed
in the lift, its conquest of gravity.
And in the hammering, sawing, drilling
I admire the precision of their art.
Is my work as important as theirs?
Can I earn a weekly wage writing poetry?
Is a poem worth as much as a staircase?
The derrick's 2-foot-high message
in yellow letters with red and black borders
MANLIFT BIG 4 RENT
is poetry. It lifted me too, grateful
for the sounds of distraction
and a finch warbling in the ivy.

SF/27.vi.97; revised 14/iv/2000

me today, you tomorrow

Hodie mihi, cras tibi: motto in the crypt of Santa Maria della Concezione,
on the Via Veneto, Rome

Lately
in a crypt below
a stylish street
I witnessed a monkish practical joke

danse macabre
on ceilings and walls
the Capuchins had made
—grinned at their witty metaphor
while spiders wove
cobwebs in my throat

Lace of fibulas finely spun
chandelier of wrists and fingers
rose of scapulas
copings of thighs!
Here a hooded deathshead monk
peeled skin glove
of hands

flowerbank

of pelvises!   Reclining
  snug on a pillow
  of skulls, some ancient
friar! That pelvic couch was yellow—

O crown and heart of ribs!
You shrunken monks!

    I'm here
and you have gone
to make a lily of Tibias!

miami beach

      Women fat in slacks
lounge in deck chairs on sepia sand.
      At night they partake
      of gruper and pompano
under palms, in coconut suntan oil.
They attend dog races, engrossed
      in whippets
      chasing mechanical hares
      down narrow lanes.
In hotels with potted palms
      and potted husbands
      marimbas pulsate
      to garlanded guitars
      and rhumbas on patios
      never end.
      It's possible
to see rare birds and strange
      fish of opal hues
and nosy porpoises that leap
      into the air.
Fabled flamingoes emerge
      from the Everglades
      on roads lined with fruit
      that produce
      a lush memorial here.

Miami Beach, Jan. 3, 1942

mid-century

In his woolen watch-cap he drew his head further within his mouton collar.

A bus coughed. From the bars neon tubes flickered forlornly with blue and red lights that reflected on dark ice.

The city was deserted. He shuddered and fled past a cafeteria back to his cold, vacant room in a tenement.

New York, ca. 1946

the miracle of san gennaro

Just as the blood
of San Gennaro
liquefies
the throng screams.
in the maddening church
of Naples

on this evening
of the miracle
attended by a mountain
of lights clustered
thicker than oranges
the quartermoon
hangs like another lamp
over Posillipo
and the bay is still
as a pool

one must be careful
near such magic
older than Vesuvius
there on the left
with that h
       y
      p
     o
    t
   e
  n
 u
s
e of stars! the

star-funicular!

behind the lamps
like tangerines
the sybil's cave
is equally still
—whose syllables pour
time like red wine

the blood
has liquefied
today

1958 Naples

missing person

1

They slip away.
They hear a voice
and follow it.

A child, a mate, a parent.
Sometimes they're careless
a pet, a friend and they
leave, irretrievably,
with our feelings.

The work of a lifetime
gone, with no copies.

2

You saw crematoria, corpses, blood;
you saw gas ovens, the bullet, the knife.
The damage is done.

Out the door
one afternoon history disappears
in an amnesiac moment.

You hold an empty bag of words.

Over and over
you replay it
with a happy ending.

3

All night a dog barks: kill it.
Kids in the yard bash trash cans:
strangle them. Blasting radios,
shouting neighbors: shoot them.

You are very tired.

4

It happens to all, said the shaman,
one time or another. We're
reborn each moment, again and again.

A friend said, Listen to music, sleep.
Go out in the air, breathe! said another,
Get laid, said a third. Grief answers,
Get lost! What's gone won't return.

I want to go on a voyage
to the cosmic library
where universal Mind has recorded
every word, written or spoken,
where nothing is lost.

mondo cane

I'm watching a poison sea-urchin
forced down the throat of a giant shark
the islanders are avenging the death of a 9-year-old boy
the shark has devoured
                              then the goose in Strasbourg
                                    the rod-like machine
                                        stuffed down its
                                            throat
to feed it more than it can digest for a week
                    this will expand its liver
                        a disease
                    that provides us
                        with paté de foie gras
                                                the goose's eye
                                                during the process
                                                is something

            I listen to you swear
We're all a bunch of hustlers   & I agree   *Yeah that's true*

watching the poor fish radiated on that atoll in the Pacific
    (their law is the same: the bigger swallows the smaller)
and the turtles who flippered their dying way inland to be pecked at
by birds and scorched by the sun, flippered their fins one final
time in the sand, hallucinating like any human, thinking they had it
        made
                    home, home to the sea

        and the directors of *Mondo Cane* have made their point
and you my friend have made your point   We're all a bunch of bastards
    we have nothing but the poem and that's not much
            it's nothing against earthquake   landslide   tidal wave
                    sunken continents

and the old woman with knobby fingers and nowhere to go has made her
        point
we did a terrible dance together one afternoon, mother
our bellies heaving because life had left us both on the beach
with a headless 12-foot sea lion washed up by the storm
                    its jawbone ripped out
                                        for the ivory

and I find

there is no other point
no
other
point
but toothpaste   bombs   karate
bank accounts and chevrolets
going
down
down
to disoriented
fish

1968

moving toward verona

Moving toward Verona on the summer
road, lined bright with oleander
white and pink, the driver said
to me: "Those two hills, two castles, there
—facing each other—do you know them?"
He (simple tradesman's face) all smiles
was puzzling: only two more ruins
was all I saw as we sped.
So he told me: *Montague and Capulet.*
And courtly music, a slow sarabande,
filled the cabin of the truck.

my body, la bohème, geraniums

    on my sundeck I'm naked
getting my dose of vitamin D
& filthy air of downtown business

    while an operatic tenor
is singing on the roof La Bohème
to cars speeding towards East Bay Bridge

geranium flourish
    with here & there a dry dead broken
limb—grimy dust on leaf & stem—

one is no more than a broken stick putting forth blossoms—

in a Welch's grapejuice jar, leaves
    thrive in the filth & sun!

    say what you will
the aria blooms in traffic & commerce
    like these tough plants

& my own geranium body
    singing with smudges
    & stains of time—

San Francisco 8.x.74

my mother, 87, lives

My mother, 87, lives
in San Diego. She moves
from hotel to hotel
because the room is cold
or the food is bad
or they steal her Social Security
checks or they wait in the hall
to mug her.
She moves back and forth
between 2 hotels
and can't recall which one

she lives in.
"She spills things from her purse
then puts it all back again
forgetting what she looked for.
She don't know your address no more."
The manager tells me this
long distance.
I can do nothing
but send my love.

23.iv.80

naples hospital

out of sight!

hide them!
the incurable

cripple & leper—   get

them away! the
stockyards never stank
so bad

bandages suppurate

on stricken trees
& mad boys pitch
gauze balls
of pus—

            bury
them quick! don't
let 'em stink

to clog the drains of
mercy—

            o San Gennaro*
de' Poveri!
—who

can forget

your horror
once having seen

& smelt you!

Naples 1958

*Oh St. Gennero of the poor!

new orleans

By oleanders and banana leaves
the ancient Negress danced a rigaudon
at the Cabildo. The old lamps glowed
on grillwork balconies and courtyards
as she cried, *Pralines! Pralines!*

In Central Park I saw the moon
above electric billboard ads
and thought of New Orleans.

New Orleans, ca. 1942

a nice young man

We met in a 3rd Avenue bar
around the bend from St. Mark's Place.
The Third Avenue El clattered
over *film noir* streets. Bowery bums
in doorways set themselves on fire
smoking as they dozed. I drank beer
in midsummer heat of New York.
The nice young man wore a seersucker suit,
was soft-eyed and soft-spoken, "in advertising,"
he said, his hand grazing mine as he lit
my cigarette. Later, at my flat, uncertain
and shy in the small dark bedroom
facing a drab brick wall, he asked,
anxiously: "Can the neighbors see us?"

"No," I said.
Awkward and sweating, we stood.
"No," I said. And stared.
Then the fist smashed into my gut.
Doubled over, my own fists clenched, I saw
his face contort as a wet stain appeared
at the bulge in his crotch and he gasped,
"Don't hit me! It's over! That's all, that's all!"
and fled in panic down the stairwell
as I soundlessly screamed in my head.

no se puede vivir sin amar*

How could we know
    that this plaza would hold
a death as fragile
        as the web of a spider

That the puke green walls
    of a cheap hotel
would close like a vise
    on this thing between us?

Chill winter rain
    the flu and *turista*
cut down our choices
    to one wrong move

We'll never hit the Canaries
    Las Palmas or Tenerife
white beaches, coconut palms
    off the coast of Africa

nothing's left
    but the frail web
that each must spin alone
    So long, kid
I'm going home

5.i.79 / barcelona

*You can't live without love

north beach

For Alix Geluardi

in the Coffee Gallery Bob Kaufman sings *Summertime*
shakes my hand asking What do you see when you look at George
      Washington?
I say The American Revolution the big breasts of a hermaphrodite
The White Man is God laughs Bob as he dances drunk
clutching a battered anthology of lonely North Beach poetry
raw from the burning ghats of bars and human wrecks
Salvaged from speed and junk and booze and
one-night stands

the tapedeck plays soap opera music of our tragic script
out of it we make poetry
like sudden life
like the shock of light

the drunken sound from a motley crew
Linda Lovely down Grant Avenue
Eileen in shawls and dresses of colored threads
threads of the beat beauty of peyote
in the flow of pills and weed in Blabbermouth night
I have seen 20 barechested drummers
getting stoned on rooftops says Eileen
chronicler of obsessive visions
Would you wear my eyes? asks Bob

they broke down each other's doors
hocked typewriters and record players
lied, screamed, jumped from windows
died and fell in love
those poets and painters you hung on Marina walls
and visited in prison
in parks waterfronts bars cheap hotels
an ocean of missing persons
departed poets leaving no address
orchestrating distances
in temporary shelters

San Francisco 1973

nude looking at you

for Peter LeBlanc, painter

Goya's famous Maja
looks at you with scorn
and challenge
while the odalisques
of Matisse
and the women
of Modigliani
look elsewhere
or turn their bodies
away

for 2000 years
of Western & oriental
art
there has been no nude
looking at you
with legs open
in welcome
he said.
So for 7 years he kept working
on one drawing
the first nude
looking at you
warmly warmly
openly

but for 7 years
something was wrong
it didn't come true
and then
he gave up
couldn't eat or sleep
he lost 30 pounds
got sick
and wanted to die

at the point
where he lost his will
and weakness took him took him
hallucinating and done for

at that point
when he no longer cared
about anything
he sketched
for the last time
the nude
looking at you

her legs spread wide
her gaping sex
her eyes right on you
almost smiling
as if to say
take me
I'm yours
but don't belong
to any man

in 7 minutes
he sketched it
and 7 years
of uncertainty
were over

the old poet listens

The old poet listens
to Swan Lake
and remembers dancing
when he was lean and powerful.

He gets up, executes a pirouette
precisely, spins
again, grows dizzy,
almost stumbles
but manages somehow
a graceful arabesque.

The mirror and the silence
in his solitary room
do not applaud.

The music, though, continues
tearing at him
like some beautiful, deadly animal
before which he is
defenseless.

He groans, remembering
too much,
and turns it off.

23.vi.80 / Monte Rio

¡olé!

standing like ballet dancers
in white hemp sandals
with long laces black as bulls
the Spanish laborers
move in a *mise en scène* of plaster,
brick and cement.

when angry, instead of swearing
they murmur, "How barbarous!"
with a ducal look.

smiling and languid
among unfinished houses and
hotels they make
by hand, they bear
with patience the foreign
car, the jet, the bomb.

patience
is the name of the dance.
they dance it slow.
a sexy girl
gets a hiss, longdrawn
and dreamy. they
can wait.

among the olive trees
and salamanders skittering

underfoot, they have been waiting
2000 years, left behind
by history,
by politicians,
left to this dusty dance
they must do forever
for a glass of wine,
some bread.

they clap hands,
stamp their feet, shouting

¡olé!

dead
as the dust
under the bull
dragged
from the corrida
by his tail.

1956

on the game in guatemala

You're all whores, thieves and liars.
Okay, I love you
you put on a great performance
in bed, where it counts most.
I really don't mind spending
more than I should
though I'm a poor gringo in the Third World
I understand those crude transparent tales
of a sick aunt you must visit
or a big loan you must pay
But Christ when you steal my money
and go for the watch and neck chain
it's too damn much
and even your handsome face, Alfonso,
begins to take on a ratty look
something sneaks between
your body and mine

and slithers like a salamander
across the ruins
Now I'm aware
of how your feet stink
and hope you'll leave
while I keep a sharp eye on my pants
draped over a chair

orpheus in the underground

Trees and stones don't listen
the rivers are choked with waste
the surf rolls over, dead

The mad judge screams: Orpheus
I sentence you to break your guitar!
Electroshock! Vegetable therapy!

At night when the guards are nodding
Orpheus strikes the bars which sing
a gray wail goes round the sweating beds

Teen-agers riot, armies throw away their arms
printing presses vomit oceans of ink
gargoyles leap shrieking on the backs of priests
saints crumble in their niches masturbating

Dreams break out of locked vaults
Love flies from chairs and sheets of red tape
All living things chant of fulfilled desire

But when day comes the stones are deaf
keys ring and chains clank in the halls
and Orpheus dies insane

once in la linea

once in La Linea across from Gib* I am looking for
a cheap pension or hotel tired hungry broke and this
green jelly trots alongside with lolling tongue
dribbling making friendly signs and I speed up a bit
but there is barnacle bill in beat-up capn's hat
now half a block behind and when I stop the car
he's ready to zoop me into his horrible old life
and I can't shoo him away so he leads me to
this hotel one whiff is enough the whole
joint stinks of lysol or the Spanish
equivalent thereof and again I try
to shake em but the old guy
just manages to look human
in a godforsaken sicken
ing sort of way point
ing to his heart
which I have
been guilty
of weaken
ing by
let
ting
him run
ten blocks
after my car
and I gag when
he grabs my hand
and gums it awful
this melodrama of cun
ning and idiocy gets to
me so I tip him and he looks
with scorn and disbelief at the
five pesetas and I seize the oppor
tunity to gun the car and race right
out of there too fast for him to follow

*Gib: Gibraltar

Spain 1962

palestrina

the nightingales in Palestrina*
     sing
over the easter broom
  here
pierluigi sang
his polyphonic choruses
        to spring

lady & lover
all that
poppied world

the nightbird
  whistles
in the cypress bough

crumbled
the stones of Palestrina
ring to the ass's hoof
the prince of music
   cracks
on his pedestal

     c'hanno perduto
       il ben
     *dell' intelletto***
          in the cypress
& locust leaves

             a skein of olives
winds valley to peak
               where castel san pietro
    rises
on the ruin-plunged city
   over the miles
            of the plain

      mountains weave like clouds
     wrapped in wars
as ancient oxen graze
with peasant or madonna eyes

*Palestrina: Medieval Italian composer, ca. 16th century
**We have lost the value of the intellect (Archaic Italian)

paper moon

He breaks out his stash
from egg crates under the bed.

His fingers tremble.

He remembers the taste,
the smell, the touch
and buries his face
in ersatz allure.

As always the music
begins and he recalls
and starts to hum,
almost breaking
at the centerfold.

He turns the pages
faster, he's burning up.
Every photo's a trap, he's stuck
in a feature, a limb,

a mouth. The song
stabs like the ache
of a sweet tooth, demons
shove wind instruments
up his rear

and he yells, half-crazed,
then hums:

It's only a paper moon. . . .

The music fades as he raves
at the end of the song.

18 March 1991/SF

planes

more in chandelles, execute
a *pas de chat* on a cloud, they
lean with glassy wingtips,
shining eagles in the sun.
then—the dream of Leonardo?—
write their timeless message
in smoke: AEROWAX 29 cents.

New York, ca. 1943

plaza real (barcelona)

1. The Matador

The drunken Don Quixote tramp
removes his threadbare jacket
and challenges the drinking fountain.
Waving his jacket like a matador's cape
he struts to the dangerous drinking fountain.
"Toro, huh, toro!" he taunts proudly
making a few passes, a *veronica,*
and wraps the jacket around his waist
defiantly, then stops in dismay.
The sword! Where's the *sword?*
He staggers and climbs over the fence
and tries to tear off a palm frond
but it's sharp and it cuts his hand
and he bleeds. Proud of the blood
he snorts and turns to face the "bull,"
"sword" in one hand, "cape" in the other.
He glares at drunks asleep on benches
and tourists at café tables on the street
in the cauldron of a Catalonian summer.
Moving in for the kill he tiptoes and plunges
the "sword" frond into the heart of the fountain.
But the frond breaks and he bows disdainfully
to the tourists who burst into loud laughter
with mock *olés* and mock applause.
Spurning the coins they fling at him
he sneers with contempt and struts away.

2. Auto da Fé

A *maricón* is bashed and goes down
spitting blood. Bystanders shout *Olé!*
Old women sell trinkets in the streets
as brass bands march and Inquisitors
in long black gowns wave crucifixes
with bloody wounds as the pained eyes
of Jesus beseech the sky for deliverance
that never comes. But the faithful clutch Him
in a viselike grip He can never escape.
Blood flows from his brow, His heart, His side,
His hands, His feet, and the *maricón* bleeds
as He bleeds and the mothers pray and weep.

*maricón: pejorative for homosexual

3. Garden of Earthly Delights: Hieronymus Bosch
(Prado, Madrid)

Strange figures creep into vast hollows
of fruit where lovers are surprised
by Death in gardens of love-making
with fountains and pavilions
and curiously-wrought forms
of gold, crystal and coral.
A voluptuous nude youth
is a rotting corpse
when turned around.
Another is strung on the neck of a lute,
another in the strings of a harp.
Some are gobbled headfirst
by a bird-headed reptile
with a kettle for its helmet
and excreted into a chamber pot
from which they plunge into a pit.
A nude woman sees her reflection
in a demon's behind. He eats, digests
and excretes the clergy.
Batlike, an insect-toad squats
between the bare breasts of a woman
encircling her with branchlike tentacles.
A man chopped up by a female demon
fries in a skillet; a giant lizard
crawls over the sex of a swooning
woman; insects and rodents

slither through her orifices
and entrails in the red furnace glow
of night ablaze with eerie light.
Composite forms, part human-
animal-bird-plant,
fuse into one monstrous shape
and scuttle around seeking victims.
A pair of wagon-sized ears
advances like an armored tank
with a knife the size of a battering ram
slicing through mounds of human flesh.
Demons devise all manner of torture,
gnawing hearts and souls
exiled by
la sagrada familia
to whom we pray:
Our Father which art
too much for us,
stay there!

4. Guardia Civil

The full moon rises over the rooftops
as children play by fountains and gipsies
dance with flamenco cries. Suddenly
it all changes and we dive into bars
and shops as truckloads of Civil Guards
leap from the vans spraying bullets everywhere.
We emerge with machine guns in our bellies.
"*Señor*, we are tourists sightseeing in the plaza,"
we say but they don't doff their tricorn leather caps
and we don't look into their eyes of death.

5. Postcard

Yankee
sailors swarm in
the smoke
and din of
exhaust fumes.
Bottle
blonde hookers
and dark-skinned boys
push sex
and dope
under

faded facades.
    Now
they are running
and we play
Invisible Tourist
at café tables
as the Guardia Civil
slips toward us like
grim vampires pursuing
    each passport
        like a throat.
            We
are in order and
they tip the brim
of their three-
cornered hats
with icy contempt.

6. The Plaza (Barcelona)

In a bar called Glacier a tenor breaks into Italian opera
under blow-ups of Elvis and Ringo Starr.
In blue jeans and black jackets the macho youths
long to be like them. They dream
in the 18th century plaza
with garbage trucks, rock music and drunks.

Under the glow of Gaudi street lamps
students quaff red wine. On balconies
with wrought-iron lacework, shutters slam shut
in a gust of wind. A brass band blares,
palms sway and clack. Lightning illumines
dark corners, rain smashes like buckshot
then suddenly stops.

A horsedrawn carriage drives by and bagpipes skirl
in the portico where prostitutes peddle their wares.
We watch a cloth bird on stilts and acrobats
and sword-swallowers thrilling the kids.
Music, wine, sex, and a brass band
belts out Bizet (reality's opera set for *Carmen*)
with laments of fierce guitars in *Plaza Real:*
Royal Square, now the people's square,
with flamenco dance
and staccato castanets.

For the traveler life in the plaza shores up
a circus atmosphere.
We will remember street lamps at night
with suspended globes somber at dawn
like a nimbus of haloes.
Like the history of the plaza a shimmer of images
after many years will still remain
with a touch of glamour and deep nostalgia
for the horse-drawn carriages and the skirl
of bagpipes in the portico where teen-age prostitutes
peddle their wares and cloth birds on stilts
are carried and waved as sword-swallowers
and acrobats thrill the crowds with music and wine.
A brass band belts out *Carmen* with fierce guitars
as reality's opera set mingles with love's laments
of jealousy and betrayal in Plaza Real,
real life with flamenco dance and staccato castanets.
For the traveler life in the plaza shores up
a masquerade, a circus atmosphere.
Where do we go from here? We stare
at sights in foreign countries, at odds
with ourselves, alien to rapprochement.
We'll remember the suspended globes
of street lamps somber in the dim dawn.

7. Los Desaparecidos
Have You Had Your Love For Today?
on the T-shirt of a Haitian refugee fleeing
in leaky tubs, running from those who kill those
who cannot defend themselves.
Who can blame these black Christs and bloody Marys?
Even in one-horse islands like the Maldives we see
the tinpot Strong Man search and destroy.
We run away, disappear, pursued
by feelings beyond control, embarking
on perilous journeys to elusive ends
seeking magic formulas to restore love
and finding only more predicaments.
Shall I pursue a search-and-destroy
mission to find myself?
Face an auditor holding tin cans,
play with an E-Meter, mind-machine
leading to memory and anxiety?
Declared a non-person we're ordered to Sea Org

off the coast of Valencia where Our Leader,
denied entry to the UK, charged with fraud,
became a church on a yacht
destroying resistance, causing brain-death.
Miracles are on the menu. The universe speaks
in many tongues we can't understand.
Our dreams reflect it. Bring me to your Leader.
I demand an explanation.

We warm our bodies in a flicker of history
as time transmutes us,
as we burn out
and consume and are consumed,
hungry for flesh and bone.

Barcelona, 1979/San Francisco,
revised 1996/August 19, Nov. 6, 2002

precious stones

"Oh! les pierres précieuses qui se cachaient, —"

On the Rue de la Paix
I smiled at a big diamond.
This hardest of minerals
glowed through the plateglass window
in a warm and friendly way, gave off
secret energies and subtle strength from
deep mines. A dazzling brooch
of inlaid sapphires blinked while
my blazing birthstone in a fabulous
clasp burned red with July.
Are we on the brink of vast mutations?
The dead are alive, they travel
faster than jet planes on the astral plane,
have flown to the moon for centuries,
remain in constant touch with our dreams.
Our dreams are doorways to other bodies.
Even the garbage truck is occult.
We are at the Aquarian Gate where brotherhood begins.
The oracle speaks from the poet's mouth.
His silliest nonsense is serious.

His trance equals the sum of all equations.
He is older than all instruments.
I offer you precious stones:
do not trample them with your mind.

rapists, racists & rats

A rapist holds a knife to the throat
of a woman in a parking lot. She can't cry
out. Now she can't sleep or make love
without terror. She wakes up screaming.

A woman is stabbed in the eyes
with a screwdriver. She can never
identify the man who raped her
and left her bleeding and blind.

I cannot forget the documentary
on waifs and strays huddled in tunnels
in Rio de Janeiro, with rats and cars
gassing them with monoxide. Police
in plainclothes, masked in unmarked vans,
corral them. Sleepy and smiling,
the kids believe it's a game, they're ready
to go for a ride. On a dead-end street
lined up against the wall, still grinning,
unaware of the evil about to befall them,
their frail bodies crumple, soft as a sigh.
I cannot forget those immature faces,
the death by execution, small boys riddled
like dirty rag-dolls by the firing squad.

I cannot forget the tortured monkeys
stretched out on racks with electric wires
in their brains, crucified for dollars,
or live rabbits with lacerated limbs
and hemorrhaging eyes, sacrificed
to lipstick and suntan lotion
for Gillette's Dermal Skin Test.

I cannot forget James Baldwin, his broken

ribs, cracked jaw and split lip, attacked
in a diner for sitting with a white actress
rehearsing his play, *Blues for Mr. Charley.*
When a friend said, "Jimmy, you've got it made,"
he replied, "Oh, no, I'm still black and still queer!"

I cannot forget the old black man beaten
to death in the shipyard where we built
Liberty ships in Mobile, Alabama
to defeat the Nazis we could not defeat
in our own backyard. I cannot forget.

remembering ted berrigan

I get anonymous phone calls.
"Hello, you're one of the giants," he said.
"You have the wrong number," I said.
"Oh, no! Can you send some books, signed?"

Another calls from a university.
"Ann Arbor needs you. Do you like babies?"
"I prefer young adults," I said.
"We only have a baby," he said.
"But we'd love to put you up.
Please come and read for us."

I read with Ted Berrigan once.
He wrote on the flyleaf of *Train Ride,*
"With great affection
& memories of Amsterdam."

I admired the way he bitched his friends,
warmhearted, making shortcomings
funny. "I don't know how I got to be
straight since I never tried to be,"
he said.
"I'm sure it's just like being queer,
only different."

In Amsterdam he lay
in the hotel room wrapped in sheets,

with Dutch cigars & weed.
At my poetry reading we first met,
he greeted me with outspread arms
and said, "Your poem on Frank O'Hara
is the best I've seen on him!"

He didn't leave his room.
Anne said he was ill. When I visited him
he was cheerful. We met once more
at the Grand Piano on Haight Street
where he read & handled a heckler
with grace & skill like a matador
stopping a mad bull.

Everyone loved the way he was cool
until he died, without ego. His style
graced the hardness of reality.
So long, Ted.
We won't meet again.

requiem for st. ronnie kirkland

(1984–1998, martyred by schoolboys)

Teased, punched and kicked,
stoned with rocks since first grade
at age six, he did not choose
to be gay. He knew nothing
of sex, except as kids do.
Nature held sway.

Though girlish in childhood
his family loved him no less.
Boys taunted him, hooted and spat
in his face, yelling sissy and fairy
and sister Mary! They laughed at him,
jeering and sneering all day.

As they got older they goosed him
while rubbing their crotches, muttering,
"Suck this!" and hissing like snakes.

At 14 he put a gun to his head
and ended the torment
before he returned to ninth grade.

The suicide note said, "I hope I can find
the peace in death that I could not find
in life." Was this what Christ taught?
He who was mocked and nailed
to the cross? Now in His name
false "Christians" dish out the same.

1/14/1999/SF

santa cruz

Lounging on beaches by whorled shells
in swirling forms that enhance the sand
like a choreographer's touch
we drink soda pop as a band
plays waltzes, marches, and mazurkas.
Shots resound from the penny arcade.
Swimmers' trunks tight as a fist
grip the fork of thighs and hips
as they dash across the sand
and plunge into surf. I long for them
like a basket case, unable to stand.

ca. 1942

santa fe, new mexico

The Pueblo woman sells rugs and ashtrays,
squats in the shade, peers at the square
where dancers spin, twist and turn.
The fiesta liveliness is catching.
A Mexican voice chants on the bandstand:
Aieeee! *carnavalita, carnavale!*
The sun scorches adobe buildings,
white, orange, cream. I bring home
the memory like a postcard.

Santa Fe, ca. 1943

saving time

We smash butterflies and pass
coal heaps and cheap motels
as our windshield vacuums
the landscape with insects
and small birds and the road
fills with corpses.

Slowing down we glide
into an evening port
where diesel trucks roar
and we sleep.

Around and around in moonlight
jaguar and puma and moonmoth
turn and turn. Gently
sumac and elm bear silent
witness as spiders weave
glistening webs.

Jan. 1941

seven years old in scranton, pennsylvania

I saw it rain on one side of the street.
The sun kept shining on the other side.
One afternoon I watched an eclipse of the sun
and saw the moon and stars gleaming at noon.

On the railroad tracks an old bum stuck his tongue in my mouth.
I gagged and spat and ran home and washed my mouth
again and again with the nozzle of the garden hose
but couldn't wash away the nauseating disgust.

Once I fingered the kinky hair of a black boy
seated in front of me in the second-grade class.
Miss Carpenter quoted *O Captain! My Captain!*
Hearing Walt Whitman the first time I was thrilled.

Every day I smelled the sweet soft coal locomotive smoke

where we lived on the wrong side of the Erie Railroad tracks
In our furnished room I kept playing *Waltz Bluette,*
scratchy and sweet and dreamy on the old phonograph.

My stepfather threw it out the window into the yard.
I never knew why he was cruel and angry and mean.
I wept as I watched the sweet sound of opera bite the dust
with Caruso, Galli Curci, Lily Pons and Madame Schumann-Heinck.

At dusk I saw gaunt coal miners shuffle back home
smudged with soot on weary faces and woebegone eyes
under carbide lamps on charred gray mining caps.
They looked like beaten blackface slaves to me.

A miner once took me far down a deep mine shaft
into hellish tunnels, the bowels of anthracite and slate.
I was scared in the cold darkness and was sent home, safe again.
Aunt Eva kissed me and hung a gold cross on my neck.

Revised 24/26/xi/2001, SF

sicily

1.

I roam the island hitching rides
on copper-colored roads. Donkeys
bray and carts with enormous wheels
and wooden frames, vermilion and blue,
bear painted legends of Roger the Norman
slaying the Saracens. A black jalopy
sputters and sops. Four young locals
ogle my legs, sweaty and bare,
and transport me in a perilous journey
to the 12th century. I'm wedged between
their knees locking mine in a bony vise.
The driver's eyes like stilettos stab mine
through the rear view mirror and never slide
from my face as he laughingly hurtles on.
He keeps turning around to enjoy my fear,
my sweating flesh through mountain passes
and hairpin curves. I bounce like a bag
in the back seat as they boast of Sicilian

bandits and murder at breakneck speed
in their death-defying cradle of myths.

2.

The journey, an endless nightmare, ends
as we rocket through an ancient village
of mud-caked wooden and stucco shacks,
faded red and yellow and burnt umber.
We lurch to a halt on an unpaved street
aby a crumbling house with closed shutters
in the blinding glare of the mid-day heat.
Gaffers and crones and youths appear.
The whole village, it seems, quickly turns out
as unmarried girls, locked up like captives,
peer behind shutters. Everyone gapes.
Ciao, they wave, *ciao*, lost in a dream,
timid and fearful of the Black Hand.

3. *Cefalù*

Giant cacti and banana leaves,
fico d'India and oleander
and bougainvillea flame on the roadside.
Beauty is everywhere, Roman and Greek,
ancient Arabian, Norman and Swabian
around the cathedral for centuries,
on the stark cliffside of Cefalù!
For three-thousand years of plunder and rape
by foreign conquerors with fire and slaughter
—the iron fist of the Norman knights,
the Saracen thrust of the sweeping scythe,
the sign of the crescent, the blade of the cross—
all merged in the blood of the countryside.

4.

Demeter wailed and made the land barren.
The crops died. Now they are bearing
Mary, the Jewish Madonna, clutching her
in their arms, swaying and moving her
and her son back and forth in worship,
kneeling to icons on the church threshold,
entering, withdrawing in church and cavern,
in subterranean rites with shards,
blood and dung scrawled on walls
of castles and caves with ancient names:

Kore, Persephone, Pluto's grotto.
Demeter wailed and made the land barren.

5. *Agrigento*

Agrigento, I want to touch your old world,
I want to feel your classical manner,
and yours too, ancient Siracusa,
the manly grace of the way you hold hands
with each other, the warm embracing touch
of your fingers kand your arms interlaced,
signorino, with tender Arab caresses,
both soft and masculine. It is our bond,
our blood mixture of race, of intimacy.
In the sweltering heat our blood ferments
and desire flows hotly through our veins
with honor and pride bringing us together
in a burning embrace in the sweltering heat.
Arab and Jew, Teuton and Greek,
Norman, Sicilian and Roman all merge
in the melting pot of desire and pride.
Here lie the crossroads of hearts and minds.

6. *Taormina*

Houses the color of sherry and cream,
pistachio and sugar-white stucco walls
in the molten gold of Sicilian sun
flake and decay in hot brilliant light.
Nude boys on cliffs and stone terraces
become ancient myths, young gods with garlands
of flowers and vine leaves in their hair.
They stand or recline under Greek columns,
nude on white terraces with crumbling walls
and a sweeping view of the Ionian sea.
Sun-tanned and languid, freely embracing,
the boys pose for the rich German Baron,
Wilhelm von Gloeden, whose charmed life
in the 19th century was a camera eye
aglow with the living priapic god
in the figure of Pan, of satyrs and fauns,
princes and paupers. All changed in posterity
from farmboy and fisherboy to satyrs and fauns.

7. Monreale

Sweet carob and donkey dung
perfume the afternoon siesta.
Churches shimmer in the heat
of a Palermo afternoon.
Here Norman, Arab and Byzantine
mosaics glitter with purple and gold
in Monreale—a lush terrain
of Hellinic shards, a frieze in a furrow,
an acanthus and pediment,
all under the gaze of a tourist eye
on the road where hills curve and twist
over the valley, the gulf and the bay
with a glitter of silver, an emerald glow.

a sprig of ivy

A sprig of ivy.
shines through rusty wire
dividing the rear of the furniture store
from the rear of my house.

They chopped down the ivy,
dry and crusted with exhaust
        from the thoroughfare
            —exposing the rear
of the furniture store,
        wattled and peeling,
dirty gray tongue in groove,
decayed by time
        and corrosive air.

The thick clustering ivy
that for so long held its place
with a touch of English gentility
is gone. Now the furniture store,
with rows and rows of soulless,
gimcrack, shiny, underclass junk,
protected by plastic dreck,
        exposes a grim gray rear.

Memory stirs: once more
the ancient immigrant (age
        one-hundred-and-one) glides
        in a wheelchair
through ugly furniture
(on channel 9), surveying
her empire. Mrs. B.,
        selfmade millionaire,
in love with tables & chairs,
spins round and round like a debutante
waltzing for the billionaire
White Knight with a tender offer.

The Queen of Furniture will reign forever
over vanities, bureaus, beds, armoires.
She will not rest until she sells
ugly furniture in heaven. The ivy
shudders in the exhausted air.

spring valley elegy

1.

This is the shaky armoire
with half-remembered keepsakes.
This is the clothes brush
of tarnished silver. This
is the glass ball where snowflakes
swirl when you shake it. This
is the unknown doughboy
in a faded photo, one arm around
your shoulder, one hand clasping yours.
He has my ears, my nose, my profile,
some Eric with a von Stroheim look.
"It's only a souvenir from the War,"
you said. No, mother, I'm the souvenir,
the little bastard you couldn't hide
in an old trunk with camphor.

2.

Memories swirl like snowflakes, delicate
in the glass ball where figures skate

on ice. A haunting fragrance pervades
the drawer. Fun mirrors twist me
out of shape in Coney Island. I'm tall
and skinny, short and fat. I grab
my mother's hand. "It's only mirrors,"
she says, and it all disappears—carousel tunes,
boardwalk, childhood, the 1920s, into thin air.

3.

In snowy Central Park, New York,
she sings high coloratura songs
in Russian. Horse-drawn buggies jingle
in the lanes. "Life," she murmurs,
"is sweet." Smiling in cheap furs
her baby face fades away in time.
Now at Spring Valley Nursing Home
in San Diego she wails, "My son
has no moustache! You're not my son!
He disappeared years ago!"
She disappears in a timeless dream.

4.

At the end of the hospital corridor
nurses force mush down her throat.
In a wheelchair against the wall she cries
"*Stop!*" repeatedly. Case-hardened,
they shrug. "Doctor's orders," they say.
Two sandy-haired young attendants
come to move her white enormous bulk
into bed. "What are these crazy nuts doing?"
she moans. The boys are cheerful, sweet.
"Don't worry, honey, we're putting you
to bed." She shoots them a withering look.
"Oh, no, I don't just go to bed with *any* man!"
They laugh and lift her like a bale of hay,
deposit her gently, and leave.

5.

Her fine lank hair in a topknot
glistens blonde and gray.
On her deathbed I snip a wisp
with my Swiss Army knife
and press it in my notebook.
"I didn't recognize you. Didja eat?"

she says, then drifts away again.
"Oh God, where's my son? Didja
know him?" She fiddles with IV tubes
that snake along her arms.
"Mother, I *am* your son!" "My son
is young. You're old. Go away!"

6.

With a tube in her throat leading
into her stomach, a brown woman,
motionless, mute, keeps her face,
grotesque as a gargoyle's, to the wall.
"Here when you get old
nobody cares," says a nurse.
"You go to a hospital or nursing home.
I don't know which is worse.
When I get old I'll go back to the Philippines.
There the whole family and friends
take care of you," says the nurse.
"In America you die like a rat, alone."

7.

At the fleapit San Diego Hotel
for seniors an old janitor appears.
"I'm gonna miss your mother," he says.
"She was one grand ol' lady. Somethin'
special." Silence. "One time I'm dozin'
in the TV lounge when I feel a hand
strokin' my face. She's sittin' beside me.
Oh, Lord, your Mom needed someone
to care for. I can't forget those eyes—
so *blue!*" He fumbles around the desk
for the owner's note: "Fanny's son
will pick up her things." He hands me
an ancient snapshot: Mom in the 1920s—
flapper bob, bangs, mascara, eye-shadow
for those kewpie-doll baby-blue eyes.
Beside her, seated on a faux Corinthian
column of wood in front of a painted ocean
backdrop, age four, I hear *All Alone on the Telephone*
rasping, high-pitched on the gramophone.
The past sweeps through me like a hot wind.
"Haven't you misplaced someone?" it sneers
between murky, stained, cracked walls.

8

A wooden-railed balcony
runs around the second floor
beneath a flaky ceiling (old junk
hotel, reeking of hashish and opium)
overlooking the lobby. I follow Joe
the janitor to the Mini Storage. "Close
this door when you're through."
Mouldy suitcases, soiled kitchenware,
old clothes, torn nylons, panty hose—
rancid debris of a marginal life.
I want to flee but I'm nailed to the spot.

With guilt feelings I sneak into her panties
and look in the mirror. Once, age five,
with her makeup on my face,
in her black pumps I stuck my bare
behind out the window and wiggled it.
Thrilled and important I turned to see
people pointing and laughing at me.

Out of touch, mouth parched with need,
she hoarded old photos, worshiping
loved ones, weeping, praying
that she'd be loved again. Then
she slashed their faces, mutilating
past and present. She kept photos
of her only child, frozen
in memory, forever young.

They strapped her ankles and put
a restraining belt around her chest.
Leaning closer I stroked her hair.
"A woman killed him. She killed my son."
The skin on her hands was cracked
from labor. Lord, let her rest in peace
in your inscrutable eternity.

12.

From nursing home to ashes
strewn from an urn
in mild Pacific waters
where dolphins play and seals
sun themselves on *farallones*
she disappeared in purple seas
and spray of atoms. O wisp of hair!

Revised 28.v.97; 15.i.99;
24.ii.99; 15-18.iii. 18iv.2000. SF

subway john

Meeting in rest rooms
they seek a dream
below the street
where graffiti on walls
inflames desire.
Mouths and thighs
arouse underground hopes.
The rosiest boy
may be their nemesis.
Like beasts of prey,
poised over beauty
they hover with longing.
The bait is joy,
the hook despair.

NY 1942

summer holiday

All afternoon in the stiff grass
writing I lie in the sun, looking
at the Pennsylvania sky, watching
intricate clouds glide by.
Upland, summer trees, some rotten
and bare; rooks flap in the boughs.

From the cowpath a curfew sounds
at nearby camp, over purple mounds.
I make black marks on paper, ignore
large meanings, write about water tanks.

Summer, 1941

a swiss specialist

a swiss specialist
has effected
a miraculous cure
by way of raw foods
but says nothing
about love
or feelings
he cannot repair
this
time-yellowed scrap
of bad news
that haunts my dreams
I have been thru orthodox halls
of hospitals stinking
of men dying
of errors
by clinical madmen
with the best reputations
in white smocks
of ignorance
the unorthodox
too
lack the magic
the inside information
about body
& soul
how many know
anything
of the soul's flame
that consumes the heart
how many have instruments
that measure feeling
what can they say

about love
that haunts me
that reminds me
of something
that is not health
not money
not success
something
that was once
great joy
now
gone

ca. 1966

tangier

Tangier sun and wind
    strike the medina mosque
        blue phallic
arches flanked by skullcaps
barber rugs and green kif
cafés where Ali puffs
dreaming dirhams*

the muezzin traces ALLAH
    thru the moon's
    loudspeaker
over casbah roofs
of Socco Chico**

moneylenders sip mint tea
while gray tourists
whip thru sandalwood
transistors
    tattooed mammas
you-youing
    papoosed
in laundrybags
        peeping
thru djellabas***

the crescent sun plucks rugs
     on lightning terraces
and dries
          ten thousand years
               in a second!

*dirham: coin
**Socco Chico: a marketplace, and a popular tourist atraction
***djellaba: cloak

through jazzrock alleys dada stalked

the gaunt figure of Schwitters haunts the corner of my hotel room
                    zimzim urallalala zam
Hugo Ball looked like an obelisk
                    bifzi bafzi hulalomi
disengaged himself from hate and envy to an Italian village
where he is still remembered
                    holy holy
Tzara picked up the slack and worked the angles
and had a gift for publicity
                    tram tickets
                    a lovely leg
at the Cabaret Voltaire
I wanted to create some kind of sensation
but all I did was nervously clutch my newspaper
and shuffle off feeling silly
                    viola laxato
                    viola zimbrabim
                    viola uli
                    paluji maloo
in your Niederdorf, Zurich,
affluent hippies spruce and clean
cut their way with knifesharp thighs
through jazzrock alleys dada stalked
                    This is how flat the world is
                    The bladder of the swine
                    Vermilion and cinnabar
                    CRU
                    CRU
                    CRU

tough shit

at American Express Athens
as I cashed a travelers check
    a big dog sat on me

I turned to the owner
saying   Would you mind
    telling your dog
        to get off my foot

too bad   she said
tamping out a cigarette
    on her forearm
& smacking a riding crop
        against her boot

I saw the chip on her shoulder
the tense cords in her throat
& went to the next window

     smiling
to the friendly clerk
bowed down in the cashier's cage
I was counting money
when the dog
          bit me
not a real bite
but a nip
        I whirled around
still in control
saying   Your dog bit me!
(in a tone of reasonable
    protest)

tough shit!   she sneered
with towering contempt

    silence fell
at American Express

    so I told her
she was on the wrong end
of the leash

that shut her up
& she twitched viciously out
with nervous tics
                        still sneering

the train

A train in Connecticut
beside coal, rocks, bare trees.

Houses in deep snow.

Passengers move stiffly,
their clothes frozen.

Sailors come and go,
navy blue thighs
full as duffel bags.

Sleepy, they stare
as if their pupils,
absorbed
in clicking rails,
aimed at unreachable
goals.

Night darkens
the window.
A child squalls.

ca. 1941

trans-teutonic express

For Carl Weissner

Castles float
in the German night
where the dollar floats

against the mark
and the train floats
into Mannheim
at midnight in eerie mist.
On the platform I phone
Carl. Pay-phone kaput.
Stuck in the middle
of nowhere I sit
on my luggage.
Ah, Carl floats onto
the deserted platform
and soon we're warm
in a Spanish restaurant,
drinking Fundador
and eating *paella*
under a goat's head
with sunglasses
on the wall. My mind
splits off and floats
out of my body,
drunk in the dawn.
Days later I wave
auf wiedersehen!
Someone is leaning
over my seat. *Bitte,*
haben Sie Feuer?
Amerikaner?
We pass a town
called Günzberg.
Allen Ginsberg
looms everywhere
like Auden's famous line:
"We must love one another or die,"
misquoted by President Johnson
clumsily on TV to millions:
"We must all love each other
or else we must all die."
Auden snuffed it.
"It's a lie!" he said.
Both poets loved only
handsome young men. As for
other men, they'd rather die.

1988?

union square new york

1

bag ladies, frozen & gray
   or beige & charcoal, a race
that fades
      in withered skin

muttering in the square, lips
    ashen with
     unfinished monologies
dumbly shriveling
  in the center of cities
as time closes in—
    who can muster
       help—not more
surely, than a few
    coins to cross the Styx
or street and then
         depart—

2

A brittle desiccated man
hobbles carefully
   past a young
   woman who squats
grinning at pigeons
on the stone steps

   democratic sun
    shine

3

Where do
   Buffalo Bills
  come from? In
flamy
     suits of gold
silk
    and broadbrimmed
Panama
      sporting a cane
& long white hair
with flowing beard

              & moustache
            struts
past the old ladies
    lost in toothless mumbles
        who never notice
          him

                    4
    On motorbikes cops cruise
                past crazies
        oldies eyeing
        punks & junkies, derelicts,
conmen, drunks, mad blacks
        as shoppers stroll
across the street
    to expensive shops
with all manner of things
    for those who are not
    about to die —
        is that old woman
about to die? eyes closed,
    fist held against her mouth,
she's either nodding or
swaying in deep lament
    or just falling
            asleep
in miserable public dotage
        unnoticed

                    5
"Look! a space man! There!"
a man yells, staring upward
over hotels and offices
    above giant billboards
        pointing to the sky.
Nobody looks up. He laughs
uproariously. Plays
    his trick again.
Bystanders shake their heads.

                    6
My mother, in the end,
    might have been one
    of them — insane

       & sick
    nowhere to go
but public ward & nursing home
      on old age pension check
—hard to look at
    she was so vulnerable—

oh, god, revise
     the script, reverse
that martyrdom
& suffering.
         Poverty
       caused it. My throat
        constricts.
I live
   her loss again.

veils of blue kif smoke no more

Brion Gysin let the mice in. We're here to *go!* he cried. I replied, We're here to *come!*

He'd laugh his deep full-throated laugh and make hashish fudge for breakfast at our low-rent Beat Hotel in Paris, 9 rue Gît-le-Coeur, street where the heart lies with its crumbling flakes on old gray facades.

His theme song was: *I'm all washed up! Painter, writer, restaurateur: foutu!*

Listening to him as he lay flat on his back in bed I thought: This man can make you believe anything. But something was missing. He had given up. Yet he enjoyed every moment of failure.

For him failure was only another dramatic monologue.

In Room 25 he dreamed up Cut-ups and invented the Dreamachine.

I introduced Ian Sommerville to Burroughs and Brion. Ian was the missing link, a technical genius, age 19.

The Dreamachine was only a dream until Ian built it and nursed Burroughs off junk. He brought both of them back to life and lost his in an auto accident.

"Let all the poisons that lurk in the mud hatch out!" said the Emperor Claudius in Robert Graves' novel. This was Brion's way of seeing history. Accomplished historian and raconteur, he mingled history with the *Arabian Nights*.

Everything Brion said sounded like a tale from *Scheherazade*. Pan pipes provided a ghostly accompaniment under the surface.

Down in Jajouka in the hills of Morocco, the musicians of Bou Jaloud were never far away. Wherever Brion went—Paris, London, Rome, New York—Morocco went with him. In the ancient rites of Pan, Father of Skins, Goat God, a sixteen-year-old boy chosen each year is the God of Sex in a pagan ceremony from pre-Christian Greece and Rome, kept alive in the hills and deserts of Morocco thru a trance dance. This magic belonged to Brion as the moon belonged to Max Ernst.

Always neat and well-groomed, Brion was most comfortable and happy in a djellabah with a kif-filled sebsi* in his hand. Beneath the djellabah he wore a clean starched shirt and pressed tan chino pants. His sandy grey hair was cut short, military fashion. Tiny purple veins squirming on his pale cheeks and nose came from his frostbitten Alpine Swiss lineage, said Burroughs. Brion was a mix of many North European lines.

*sebsi: pipe

While Brion sang the blues in Room 25, he talked nostalgically of this magical Morocco where later I would spend an enchanted year. All the characters in his Arabian Nights became part of my life—Jane and Paul Bowles, Hamri, Yacoubi, Sherifa and my Mohammed Rifi, a 16-year-old 6-foot Berber from the Rif. Tangier, Fez, Marrakech, and many more towns got lost in kif smoke.

Write it down! Cut it up and write it down! I shouted at Brion. *You started it!*

No! he'd cry. *No! I can't write anymore! I gave up long ago! Rather, it gave me up. Dropped me like a stone. No more! No more! I'm no good as a writer. And who buys my paintings? No! Never! Don't ask me to write!*

It was a familiar ritual. Playing my role, I stimulated the stimulator, simulated the simulator. With green-eyed envy he praised my published writings.

Downstairs in Room 9 on the first floor with my "rotting vegetables"—as he referred to the fresh produce and herbal pharmacopia on my marble-topped dresser—valerian and kif wafted from my room through the dark halls and winding stairs. My first cut-up, *Sniffing Keyholes*, would become my most celebrated piece. Burroughs, the first to see it, praised it enthusiastically. It was the beginning of my cut-up novel, *Beat Hotel*—a weird mishmash of my cut-ups in the hotel. Most of it was stolen with other manuscripts and journals left in the hotel attic in two suitcases when I went to Morocco. Brion had said they'd be safe. *Where are they now?* A few salvaged pages became my slim volume, *Beat Hotel*, minus 200 pages. It was published in US, German and Italian editions.

Finally I wore Brion down. All right, I'll write the history of Cut-ups. But you'll have to edit it. I have no faith in it at all.

A month later he dumped a bulky manuscript on my table in Room 9. It's yours, he said. You made me write it. You're responsible for this. Now show me how good an editor you are. I prided myself on that skill and got out the blue pencil, cut, slashed, revised, suggested and returned it. Now type it up! I said. But who'll publish it? he cried, still harping the minor chord of self-loathing.

Evergreen Review, Grove Press's literary magazine, published my poetry. I had no doubt that they'd welcome Brion. They published Burroughs, Ginsberg and other Beat writers. But Brion was completely unknown. With my note to the editor, Fred Jordan, Brion sent three sections: "Cut-Ups: A Project for Disastrous Success," "Cut-Ups Self-Explained" and "The Pipes of Pan," about the Moroccan Pan ritual. The first two were accepted and published. The third wasn't. I sent it to Ira Cohen in Tangier for the first issue of his magazine, *Gnaoua*, which appeared with my "Sniffing Keyholes" and Burroughs' Cut-Ups from *The Ticket That Exploded*, containing some of my texts folded in—another cut-up technique. At last Brion was launched. I was guilty of doing the job. Characteristically, as he became well-known through collaboration with Burroughs, he never mentioned me. I don't think he ever forgave me for his disastrous success.

NOBODY OWNS WORDS! Brion chanted like a mantra for his Cut-up religion. I nagged him to work on the novel he had abandoned. Again he resisted and again I won. The novel wasn't a cut-up. It was something he talked about for years and hated to finish. If it is published I'll dedicate it to you, said Brion. In London 1967 he came to my flat in St. Mark's Crescent, gave me a copy of the novel, called *The Process*, and said he didn't dedicate it to me. I didn't ask why. I knew why. No good deed goes unpunished.

"Only you ever encouraged me to the point of bullying, Harold. You're responsible for THE PROCESS. It grew out of that time you set me to writing something and I obeyed you. . . . I summon you to stir up a controversy and save me on this writing course you set me on, Harold Norse, when you were sitting down there in Room Nine on your rotting vegetables."

Brion mythologized everything and was famous as an ingrate. He hated his mother and treated her badly. I met her at my Paris reading. She was a professional speech coach. Instantly I saw that his charm and intelligence came from her. He never forgave her for giving him the best education money can buy in the best private schools of England and Canada, where they were from.

I repatriated in 1968 and, many years later, we met again in Amsterdam at the One-World Festival. Brion, Bill Burroughs, Patti Smith and I were on the bill. The audience was huge. We all three had lunch together. I never saw him again.

Brion became famous at last through collaborating with Burroughs, and was awarded the honor of *Chevalier des Arts et des Lettres* in France.

The Dreamachine was bought by the Louvre where it is exhibited.

His ashes were scattered in the Straits of Gibraltar, as he wished, where he would float forever in the odor of kif from the hills of Joujouka.

If you listen carefully you can hear him murmuring . . . *lost in blue kif smoke . . . in veils no more . . . lost in a musical sound like veils of blue kif smoke . . . no more . . . no more . . . lost in ancient magic shaman rituals . . . can you hear me crying no more? no more! oh, the monkey jumps on my back again and again . . . crying . . . never! forever! no more . . . more. . . .*

Revised 1/28-30/, 1998/2/ 14/1999, 4/11/2000
San Francisco

vicious circle

He vowed he would never return again.
This was the end, he was quite certain.

Riding toward the mountains
he looked back at the city
from the window of a bus
passing forsythia and shadblow.
He believed he could live on a hill
practising meditation and abstinence.

Nervously eyeing the passengers
who gazed at the fields that flew by,
he knew as he slumped in his seat,
passing farm houses and barns,
that he would turn back again.

ca. 1941

war poem

On the beach we talk of war
as the sun bleaches the sand.
They say it will be over in a year.
He says it's the fault of the banks.
I say it's the decline of the West.
It's the rise of the East, he says,
We'll be white bones like fossils and shells.
He speaks of infantry, aircraft, tanks.
It could last five years, I say.
He says it's the fault of the Jews.
I say it's irrational fears.
It's the fault of the reds, he says.
I say it's the red, white and blue,
and the fault, my friend, is you.

Miami Beach, ca. 1941/2

the way it was

When I open a drawer
with half-remembered keepsakes
in the shaky bureau
a genie swirls out of a bottle
of suntan oil.
Coney Island hoves into view.
On Surf Avenue
I eat cotton candy
and glazed red jelly apples
on a stick. The concave fun mirror
makes me fat and skinny,
short and tall.

In a faded, yellow snapshot
You are seated beside a doughboy,
his arm around your waist.
You're so wistful and young
I hardly recognize you.
He has my ears, my nose.
When I ask about him you say,
It's only a souvenir
from World War One.
He died for the red, white and blue.

I'm the souvenir, Mother,
the one you couldn't hide
(denial was second-nature to you).

Here is the clothes brush,
tarnished and monogrammed
sterling silver, and here
the snowflakes float
in a paperweight globe
where plastic figures skate
on ice (made in Hong Kong),
frozen like you.

And here's my teenage diary
about the Dad I never saw.
When I mention him you fall
and writhe on the floor.
I'm not supposed to know.

Now I'm crying for your remains,
thimbles, thread, ashes in an urn,
a camphor smell of old clothes.

Mother, I want to talk to you.
But you won't listen.
You never did.

when will we ever learn?

It's a sad place and the winters are lonely. The rain tears down your
defenses, slicing the grin from your teeth. I scream at plastic garbage bags,
senselessly raging because the dishes get dirty like life and I can't accept that
appalling fact. You retreat into the rainbow colors of your guitar and the sad-
ness of imperfection changes miraculously into song. With the folksinger's
emotional skill, clutching the cliff of music, you hang from the notes above
the pit. I come into your bedroom wanting to share the sounds that trans-
form our sickness, my mouth snapping at love. My grin grows back again
as my lips form words around the music and our feelings rush more gently
into the space from which the rain slowly recedes.

when you came to the ultimate poem

In memory of Kenneth Patchen

When you came to the Ultimate Poem
Death wrote its final notice:
Payment due on the 8th. . . .

But what can we do? you wrote

GET READY TO DIE

For sixty years you died
of war, of rage, of grief
in an outpouring of fantasies
of words corrosive with disdain
or nestling gently with tenderness

in the ear infected with lies

How can they send us the checks when we're dead? you asked

They sent you little while you lived
Patchen
those liars
praising art and poetry
in their glass houses
with wall to wall carpeting of bones and dollars
on which with souls of shit
they tread
comfortably

where are those poems
i used to dream?

Where are those poems I used to dream?
whole volumes of epic proportions
all-at-once on a parchment page
memorized in a flash

not dictated but *revealed!*
to my dream eyes like a movie close-up
doubtless the greatest writing
of all time
beside which the Naacal tablets
were pre-stone-age shorthand

I'm convinced!
those poems were from the gods
who play with time
as children play with checkers
Eternity in their hands
a thousand pages per second
of fabulous golden Writ!

waking I realised
that not a word
could be grasped
in this sluggish Form

wise to its poisoned condition

wise to its poisoned condition
the word's washed up step
into the last word in Eternity
thru monster drive-in celluloid dream
machine gun radiation barbed wire tanks
dentifrice hamburger horrors step
into IBM poems dollars where you eat
hasheesh genitals & kiss diamond
wade thru greed & envy as with closed eyes
you contact reflex seas of nouns
punishing shores of adjectives
where blank mind clobbers the ego
& who or what jumps in doppelgänger Absolute Nothing
a dream pounding the waking self with cold sweat
while life coiled in spinal cortex millions of Years
heaves irrational death & Jesus
takes a walk down your street
with his disciples coming
upon decaying dog 2 weeks gone
& disciples turn away in horror
"never seen anything so *awful* Lord"
& Jesus with a smile "my
aint he got beautiful teeth"
as maggoty bowels burst sapphires thru blood clots
& anguished cells of living matter shrink
from hand of infinite annihilation
down lightyears where rose petals dissolve
& Sun extends ultimate penis of Light
to celestial harem of novas satellites planets
in vibrant prisms of colors yet unknown
spurting milky ways of sperm into zodiac cunt
impregnating bulls rams virgins crabs goats scorpions lions twins archers
& what not thru astral jungles of Being
where heaven houses gape starry doors
& host body enters dog snail rat man
& dead worlds vomit virid bubbles thru man's dream of Reason
dead worlds spew sargassos of ovaries
streaming thru caves
while new guinea blacks smear hot cantari
on adolescent cocks swelling leviathan Hard Ons
tumid boys blasting earthquake tidal wave
volcanic ebony orgasms into equators

howling to poles of arctic nights of green
platinum flares modulating to sounds
where icicle becomes oboe
snowflake becomes tremolo
& forms rush thru each other without shame
as shapesounds twine thru spacetime
metamorphine seas!

Written at the Beat Hotel 1960

you, too, are blind

You, too, are blind. You cannot see
the monster you've created isn't me.

You can't see that the monster
is both of us, now mostly you.

This is a double-headed monster
with 2½ personalities in each head

and one of them wishes us dead.
Watch out for him! he's the craziest.

His hatred and malice know no bounds.
He would burn the house down.

Another's the leader, a third the follower.
A fourth wants to be alone to create, to think.

The fifth is a divided lover, warm,
tender, compassionate. I want him back!

Can't we just get rid, once and for all,
of the monster? or at least keep him chained

down in the dungeon of our worst dreams,
out of sight, out of the way?

4th draft
29.iv.78
Monte Rio

the zoo at schönbrunn

what of the poor animals
closed in their orthodox box for the kids
to mock and feed? the
           bear sits on his hairy
                     ass and begs
           and fans one paw
                          for a mint. slaphappy seals
                leap from the pond
           for fish, patient
                              as reverend gentlemen,
with glazed memorial eyes.
                                        Sunday
in Vienna, bandstand and *Wiener Blut*
           the handsome couple
                     doing the waltz
           old sentimental Schmaltz
as if there'd never been a war
                                        or 2.
at this oldest of Europe's zoos
the animals in their dream
                          are haunted
           bone, jaws, fur,
                          eyes of precious stone
           not focussing but looked
                          in repetition's law.
           unutterable melancholy
                and unappeaseable
                     appetite
hurl them round and round
for the long night in their gaze
fills the cage
           with the rank
                odor of
                     necessity.
                     the buzzard on his cliff,
                     the condor, flaming lynx
           stuck
     deep in the mud
                of time.   and the airman
striking
     palace, slum and zoo
                     whirled

in the circle
                of his plane
is bound
        to the animals below
                    in blood.   the
chimpanzee rides his tire
        for laughs and
                upside down pees
        into his mouth. then
            drools it
                out.   the kids,
the parents,
            laugh.

index of first lines